TRANSACTIONS OF THE
AMERICAN PHILOSOPHICAL SOCIETY
HELD AT PHILADELPHIA
FOR PROMOTING USEFUL KNOWLEDGE

VOLUME 69, PART 3 · 1979

The Foundations of English Bankruptcy:
Statutes and Commissions in the Early Modern Period

W. J. JONES
PROFESSOR OF HISTORY, UNIVERSITY OF ALBERTA

THE AMERICAN PHILOSOPHICAL SOCIETY
INDEPENDENCE SQUARE: PHILADELPHIA
July 1979

Library of Congress Catalog
Card Number 78–73169
International Standard Book Number 0–87169–693–2
US ISSN 0065–9746

PREFACE

Bankruptcy has been a hobby of mine for twenty years, a topic looked at casually when time allowed but often interrupted when considered seriously. Across so many years my debts to individuals and institutions have been many. One of the greatest is to the Huntington Library and its staff. Indeed the first version was put together in 1962 when, with the aid of a Huntington grant, I was working on Chancery and Ellesmere. Much is also owed to subsequent assistance from the Canada Council and the Guggenheim Foundation. This is for G.B.J.

ABBREVIATIONS

Adam Smith: Smith, A. S. *The Wealth of Nations,* ed. E. Cannan (New York, 1937).

Additional: Additional manuscripts, British Library, London.

APC: Acts of the Privy Council of England.

Atk.: Atkyns' Reports [26 *English Reports*].

BIHR: Bulletin of the Institute of Historical Research.

Blackstone: Blackstone, W. *Commentaries on the Laws of England,* ed. E. Christian (4 v., London, 1809).

Brown. & Golds.: Brownlow and Goldesborough's Reports [123 *English Reports*].

Bulstrode: Bulstrode's Reports [80 *English Reports*].

Chan. Cases: Cases in Chancery [22 *English Reports*].

Coke, *Fourth Institute:* Coke, E. *The Fourth Part of the Institutes of the Lawes of England* (London, 1669).

Co. Rep.: Coke's Reports [76-77 *English Reports*].

Commons Debates 1621: Commons Debates 1621, ed. W. Notestein, F. H. Relf, and H. Simpson (7 v., New Haven, 1935).

CJ: Journals of the House of Commons.

Cro. Car.: Croke's Reports, temp. Charles I [79 *English Reports*].

Cro. Eliz.: Croke's Reports, temp. Elizabeth I [78 *English Reports*].

Cro. Jac.: Croke's Reports, temp. James I [79 *English Reports*].

CSP Dom.: Calendar of State Papers, Domestic.

CSP For.: Calendar of State Papers, Foreign.

D.K.Rep.: Report[s] of the Deputy Keeper of the Public Records.

Ec.HR: The Economic History Review.

EHR: The English Historical Review.

El.: Bridgewater and Ellesmere manuscripts, Huntington Library.

Eq. Ca. Abr.: Equity Cases Abridged [21-22 *English Reports*].

Goodinge: Goodinge, T. *The Law Against Bankrupts: Or a Treatise Wherein the Statutes Against Bankrupts are Explained* (3rd ed., London, 1713).

Harleian: Harleian manuscripts, British Library, London.

H.M.C. Hatfield: Historical Manuscripts Commission, Manuscripts of the Marquess of Salisbury.

History: History (The Journal of the Historical Association).

Holdsworth: Holdsworth, W. S. *A History of English Law.*

Hutton: Hutton's Reports [123 *English Reports*].

Keble: Keble's Reports [83-84 *English Reports*].

Lansdowne: Lansdowne manuscripts, British Library, London.

LQR: Law Quarterly Review.

L. and P. Henry VIII: Calendar of Letters and Papers, Foreign and Domestic, Henry VIII.

LJ: Journals of the House of Lords.

Ld Ray.: Lord Raymond's Reports [91-92 *English Reports*].

Mod.: Modern Reports [86-88 *English Reports*].

Monro: Monro, C. *Acta Cancellaria* (London, 1847).

Nottingham's Cases: Nottingham's Chancery Cases, ed. D. E. C. Yale, Selden Soc. (2v., 1954, 1961-1962).

Nottingham's "Manual" and *Nottingham's "Prolegomena": Lord Nottingham's "Manual of Chancery Practice" and "Prolegomena of Chancery and Equity,"* ed. D. E. C. Yale (Cambridge, 1965).

Noy: Noy's Reports [74 *English Reports*].

Plucknett: Plucknett, T. F. T. *A Concise History of the Common Law* (5th ed., London, 1956).

P.R.O.: Public Record Office, London:
- C.24: Chancery Town Depositions.
- C.33: Chancery Entry Books of Orders and Decrees.
- C.38: Chancery Reports and Certificates.
- C.39: Chancery Supplementary Reports and Certificates.
- C.67: Chancery Patent Rolls, Supplementary.
- C.193/5: Chancery Miscellaneous, Crown Office Precedent Book.
- Durham 4: Palatinate of Durham, Entry Books of Orders and Decrees.
- E.215: Commission on Fees, James I and Charles I.
- E.333/17: Exchequer First Fruits and Tenths, Miscellaneous Book of Precedents.
- S.P.11: State Papers Domestic, Mary.
- S.P.12: State Papers Domestic, Elizabeth.
- S.P.14: State Papers Domestic, James I.
- S.P.39: Original Warrants for Grants.

Sanders: Sanders, G. W. *Orders of the High Court of Chancery* (London, 1845).

Tothill: Tothill's Chancery Reports [21 *English Reports*].

TRHS: Transactions of the Royal Historical Society.

Yelverton: Yelverton's Reports [80 *English Reports*].

THE FOUNDATIONS OF ENGLISH BANKRUPTCY: STATUTES AND COMMISSIONS IN THE EARLY MODERN PERIOD

W. J. Jones

CONTENTS

I. INTRODUCTION

The English law of bankruptcy is rooted in the assumptions and the legislation of Tudor and early Stuart society. It was then that the essential distinction between bankrupts and other debtors was made. In consequence most debtors, however great their liabilities, could not go bankrupt. During the formative hundred years of this story, debtors were many but bankrupts few. Furthermore, social distinctions may have been reflected even in the fate of those who could have gone bankrupt. Great merchants, although there are some celebrated examples, were an exception. Lesser merchants appear more frequently, but they were not a notable element. The majority of bankrupts were craftsmen, shopkeepers, and small middlemen: bakers and butchers, simple drapers and mercers, buttonsellers, fishmongers, and upholsterers. Between 1592 and 1596, the largest number of known bankruptcy commissions, approximately one-third, was sued out against chapmen.[1]

Before the Restoration, bankruptcies were infrequent. The annual average for the late Elizabethan and Jacobean periods may not have been much above ten, given that more commissions were probably granted in depression years. Between mid-September, 1630, and mid-March, 1631, an official reported transmitting payments for only four commissions issued with respect to persons living in the city of London and its vicinity.[2] In the disturbed years between 1642 and the king's execution in January, 1649, the annual average of enrolled commissions was about twenty-five, the thirty-eight granted in the twelve months from March, 1643, being an exceptional total. In 1652, sixty-eight commissions were awarded, but there were only thirty-one and forty-one in 1653 and 1654 respectively.[3]

It may be that the above figures are underestimates. The details are scattered, and for much of the period commissions were not enrolled. On the other hand, the evidence for 1642–1654 is fairly coherent. During these years, there was a separate series of rolls for bankruptcy commissions. Furthermore, the practices of Chancery clerks do not seem to have been unduly hindered by national events.[4] Nonetheless, it would still be unsafe to assume that all commissions were enrolled, although it is tantalizing to speculate that in this instance civil war might have been the background to greater competence than had been provided by former years of peace. However that may be, it is safe to conclude that bankruptcies, as distinct from failures, were not common, and that their number was in stark contrast to the amount of critical attention devoted to the subject.

In part, this was because the existence of the bankruptcy law had an impact which was much greater than that of its actual operation. It was something to be avoided, and hence the habits of businessmen were influenced. It is clear that many persons, often with the aid of established commercial customs, secured arrangements prior to total disaster, before they committed a technical act of bankruptcy, or even—when the creditors were compelled by mutual self-interest—after these events. If so, much contemporary criticism of the bankruptcy statutes can be modified, although it may not be dismissed. On the other hand, it seems very probable that bankruptcy was commonly avoided as much through calculation as caution. Before 1624, there are grounds for believing that legislation was a failure because the wording of statutes was often inadequate to sustain a claim from creditors that bankruptcy had occurred. This was one reason why con-

[1] The references are in El., scattered between 3043 and 5646.

[2] P.R.O., E.215/2/227.

[3] P.R.O., C.67/76a-85.

[4] For the general problem posed by patent rolls, see R. B. Pugh, "The Patent Rolls of the Interregnum," *BIHR* 23 (1950): pp. 178–181.

temporaries were so critical, and their observations may help to explain the apparent paucity of commissions granted.

Whatever the precise numbers may have been, the incidence of bankruptcy during the period under consideration is insignificant in comparison with the eighteenth century. Indeed the House of Commons, shortly after the Napoleonic Wars, was told that there had been over forty thousand bankruptcies since 1732.[5] Yet there is much to be learned from earlier years, not least because bankruptcy is one of those words which tends to be misused or have multiple meanings. This has bedevilled appreciation of the subject. How often have we heard of bankruptcy with respect to persons who were not, and who could not conceivably have become, bankrupts in law? Our understanding of other circumstances, technicalities, and terms is equally uncertain. The context of explanation is unsatisfactory, inevitably so, and we will only start to have a less than feeble grasp of early modern English society when more of its details have been studied.

Bankruptcy is one detail, a condition often mentioned but rarely understood, a label more likely to be employed with confidence than comprehension. There are dozens of such subjects awaiting exploration. Much has been written about social matters, from prosperity to poverty, without a basic understanding of the bonds, contracts and obligations, or their procedures and significance in law, which provide so much of the data. Bankruptcy as a theme is just one of many. Edward Jenks described it as important but uninteresting. Yet the topic is evocative, for this technicality born of statute was a hinge between law and commerce, a link welded in parliaments which were largely composed of men who dabbled much but belonged properly to neither world. An inquiry into bankruptcy, however limited the subject may seem, provides a poignant illustration of the way in which social distinction and economic fact were meshed with the formulation of law and the methods of its administration. Furthermore, business difficulties and collapses have not received the attention which they deserve.[6] This does not mean that a study of bankruptcy during the early modern period will shed much light upon the fortunes of those who traded. Despite adverse comment from some contemporaries, there is little reason to suppose that commerce was either harmed or helped.

The period between the first bankruptcy statute (1543) and the great civil war, virtually the Tawney Century, has been selected although the evidence is dispersed and nebulous. There is nothing to compare with the later wealth of detail to be found in law reports, treatises, business documents, and the official bankruptcy records of the eighteenth century. Certainly, a proper history of English bankruptcy from the Restoration can and needs to be written on the basis of conventional if complex sources. Before that time, the situation is different and the method has to be different. Some later material has been used, and general excursions attempted, but only in the sense that subsequent situations both reflect upon and were the product of earlier years.

A central feature of early bankruptcy arrangements was the appointment of commissions, a device which was crucial to Tudor notions of administration.

If economic fact and social assumption provided the bone and the flesh of Tudor and early Stuart society, the crown and the Council were the head. Institutions at Westminster, whether always present, like the Exchequer, or occasional, like Parliament, represented major organs of the system. Power, requirement, and responsibility flowed to various arteries: provincial councils, palatine authorities, shires, hundreds, and boroughs. The manor and other little units can be likened to the smaller vessels. Common to this structure was the way in which people were grouped in approved associations. As with guilds and companies, these might be essentially independent although authorized and approved by the state. Then there were commissions, notably those that were a direct creation of the state. A significant few were statutory, but many were institutional in their origin. Some were reasonably permanent, whereas others were temporary.

Recognition has always been accorded to the justices of assize and to some major commissions which were regularly renewed: for example, the High Commission and the provincial councils at Ludlow and York. The celebrated justice of the peace was a commissioner. Less attention has been paid to many short-lived commissions, statutory or otherwise, which operated at every level of English society. These were notable for their variety of membership and function. They might include eminent persons and lawyers, but lesser if nonetheless respectable citizens were of at least equal significance. Commissioners aided the assessment and collection of taxes, the settlement of disputes, and the administration of a multitude of practical problems. They supervised drainage, regulated grain exports, arbitrated disputes, examined witnesses, and surveyed boundaries. In the Elizabethan and early Stuart period, we can be sure that there were dozens, perhaps hundreds, of these and other commissions in existence on any given day. This was part of the reality of government on the grassroots level for a regime which

---

[5] *Suggestions Respecting the Improvement of the Bankrupt Laws* (London, ?1819), f. 2.

[6] See comments made by: R. S. Lopez and I. W. Raymond, *Medieval Trade in the Mediterranean World* (New York, 1955), p. 290, n. 1; V. P. Carossa, "The Waltham Watch Company: A Case History," *Bull. Business Hist. Soc.* (Dec., 1959): pp. 165–187. Some aspects are explored by R. A. Church, "Business History in Britain," *The Jour. European Econ. Hist.* **5** (1976): pp. 209–228.

claimed to exercise a sweeping responsibility although it did not have the sinews of a nation-wide bureaucracy. A sudden cessation of this activity would have endangered the fabric of order and possibly destroyed it. This shadow was apparent in 1640 and 1642.

Temporary commissions, such as those authorized by the early bankruptcy acts and the statutes of sewers, had as many differences and distinctions as were to be found in and between other organs of administration, great or small. Each type of commission was subject to particular instructions according to its task, but there might be broad variations between individual commissions which ostensibly handled similar problems. However, the demand for special skills and specific knowledge was a common factor, not least because the ability of businessmen and lawyers was so diverse. Two outstanding Chancery men, William Lambarde and John Tyndall, had reason on their side when they begged the bench to commission some merchants to help with the analysis of a disputed account concerning figs, since they themselves did "not thoroughly discern of the same."[7] Moreover, there was always need for familiarity with a locality and knowledge of particular persons. The membership of a successful commission was likely to balance many requirements.

Blackstone described the English law of bankruptcy and related Tudor innovations as "capital alterations of our legal polity" which were "highly convenient to that character, which the English now began to re-assume, of a great commercial people." Adam Smith was less assured. Bankruptcy was "perhaps the greatest and most humiliating calamity which can befall an innocent man. The greater part of men, therefore, are sufficiently careful to avoid it. Some, indeed, do not avoid it; as some do not avoid the gallows." These two writers of the eighteenth century, a lawyer and a political economist, nonetheless agreed that bankruptcy had to be considered as a legal circumstance.[8]

A major problem for the historian is that the word *bankruptcy* has been used in two senses. The first is provided by general usage, literary or vernacular, covering people who have become destitute or insolvent, or in which we may, for example, speak of a king or a country as being "on the verge of bankruptcy." The general impression is one of financial calamity. The word is also used to support adverse comment on the intellectual, moral, or political standing of a government, institution, or person—"Bankrupt of life, yet prodigal of ease."[9] This range of meaning can be legitimate for many periods and countries: for Scotland, an authority has noted that "the word by itself has no place at all in the formal language of the law."[10] In England, on the other hand, the terms *bankrupt* and *bankruptcy* have represented a legal concept for over four centuries. This second understanding can be explained by reference to one definition of a bankrupt:

> One who has done some act or suffered some act to be done in consequence of which, under the laws of his country, he is liable to be proceeded against by his creditors for the seizure and distribution among them of his entire property.[11]

The crucial point is that of a man becoming "liable" under "the laws of his country," laws which in England were provided by statute.

One could wish that historians of post-medieval England would avoid using the words *bankrupt* and *bankruptcy* unless the legal meaning is intended. This hope is somewhat futile since contemporaries, including lawyers, used the words to indicate all shades of meaning. In 1571, a member of Parliament—possibly John Popham, a future speaker of the Commons and chief justice of the Queen's Bench—spoke of "treasurers of the Crown, who have in their hands great masses of money, with the which either they themselves or some friends of theirs do purchase lands to their own use, and after become bankrupt." He instanced a debt of £30,000 which had supposedly led to a shortage of money in the Exchequer. Bankruptcy legislation was being prepared at the time, and it is not impossible that he considered such behavior to warrant inclusion. There is insufficient evidence, and a separate act was passed making the property of receivers, tellers, and similar officials liable to payment of their debts.[12]

Statutes which created the law of bankruptcy were mundane attempts to establish new rules within the limited field of debt. They were commonplace and practical measures intended to provide solutions to a selection of immediate problems. These characteristics explain their most obvious defect, a failure to comprehend the complexity of existing law. Later legislation was hardly more successful, and in any case commercial conditions were constantly changing. Debt collection was not the only area where casual reform by statute resulted in fresh intricacies. Statutes poured forth with respect to charities and the criminal law, labor conditions, and imports. Legislation became more detailed as it became more frequent. "Parliament having once taken up a subject was apt to return to it

[7] P.R.O., C.38/3, pt 1, ff. 362b–363, Aldon and Humphrey v. Westwray (24 June, 1600).

[8] Blackstone **4**: p. 430. Adam Smith, p. 325.

[9] Note the examples of usage listed in *The Oxford English Dictionary*.

[10] A. D. Gibb, "Insolvency," *An Introduction to Scottish Legal History*, Stair Soc. **20** (Edinburgh, 1958): p. 222. Prior to 1696, "bankruptcy" and "insolvency" were used as synonymous terms in Scotland. H. Goudy, *A Treatise on the Law of Bankruptcy in Scotland* (Edinburgh, 1914), p. 15.

[11] *Teevan and Smith's Business Law*, by L. Y. Smith, G. C. Robertson, and R. A. Sprecher (St. Paul, 1951), p. 1129.

[12] J. E. Neale, *Elizabeth I and her Parliaments, 1559–1581* (London, 1953), pp. 219, 224.

again and again, piling act upon act, sometimes with confusing results." [13] In the nineteenth century Basil Montagu, an experienced bankruptcy commissioner, remarked that since its inception the bankruptcy law and its administration had been continually fluctuating and a subject of complaint. "As the existing statutes have been found to be insufficient to check existing frauds, or have themselves been productive of injustice; or as new frauds have presented themselves, new statutes have been enacted but the complaints yet continue." [14]

Social conditions may change, procedures and principles of law may develop or be adapted, but bankruptcy proceedings have always had some common objectives and weaknesses. A Stuart commentator on bankruptcy would not, I think, find much alien content in a 1975 report on this subject.[15]

Perhaps we expect too much, but Francis Bacon, for one, did think that the method of drawing up laws in his time was faulty. He was unhappy with the failure of preambles to outline the aims of legislation, and with the obscurity of words in the body of the statute which reflected back on the preamble.[16] The balance and clarity of language within statutes were increasingly important since the early modern period was marked by rapidly changing conditions which transformed authority, enforcement, precedent, procedure, and record. Above all, as Professor Thorne has noted, acts of Parliament had attained a new status by the middle of the sixteenth century. Emphasis would increasingly be placed upon their sanction and not merely upon their contents.[17] Lawyers, legislators, and litigants had an understandable difficulty in coming to terms with novelty. Yet even after according due recognition to these factors, the statutes can seem weak in their construction, expression, and meaning. As with the related areas of debt, imprisonment, and sequestration, it may be surmised that with respect to the evolution of English bankruptcy law generations of men succumbed to that old tendency by which the advantage of experience is squandered.

In a period of just over eighty years, from 1543 to 1624, there were four bankruptcy statutes.[18] There might have been further Stuart legislation but for the failure of Charles I's early parliaments and the troubles of the Long Parliament and Interregnum. Opportunities for statutory amendment were thus destroyed or dissipated. Hence, the task of clarification belonged increasingly to the judges. Faced by specific cases, they had to define the limits of bankruptcy jurisdiction and make adjustments of detail in accordance with the texts of statutes up to and including that of 1624. Whether or not this can be described as subordinate legislation is a moot point.[19] In general Stuart judges, even when faced by novel circumstances, kept close to the statutes. Bankruptcy remained firmly grounded upon legislative provision:

> Bankruptcy is entirely the creation of statute law. There is no such thing as a common law of bankruptcy, although the term is sometimes applied to certain rules of bankruptcy law not to be found specifically enacted in bankruptcy statutes but laid down from time to time by the judges exercising the bankruptcy jurisdiction.[20]

A principle of later bankruptcy proceedings—that "equality is equity"—was always present.[21] Early statutes were intended to secure the property and assets of the bankrupt and distribute them ratably between his creditors. Essential elements were sequestration of assets and the need to impose restraint upon those creditors who might seek full repayment at the expense of others. There was no intention of assisting the bankrupt. The initiative in suing out a commission had to come, at least ostensibly, from creditors. Provision was not made for a petition from the debtor and thus for voluntary bankruptcy. The bankrupt's discharge was introduced in 1705, but even in the twentieth century release from debts has been described as being never more than incidental to the law of bankruptcy.[22]

Early statutes assumed the bankrupt's delinquency. Their tone was condemnatory but this was not always of assistance to creditors, particularly those who under different circumstances might have been willing to grant further time for repayment or make other kinds of concession. Once a bankruptcy commission was sued out, the creditor's freedom of maneuver was circumscribed. Creditors had to swim with the tide or face the possibility of losing all that was due. Furthermore, the tendency to lump bankrupt debtors into a single category was questionable. Bankruptcy was nurtured as a technical and legal notion which only imperfectly fitted the realities of commerce, and yet it only applied to commercial men. Problems of capital,

---

13 Plucknett, p. 325.

14 B. Montagu, *Inquiries Respecting the Courts of Commissioners of Bankrupts and Lord Chancellor's Court* (London, 1825), p. 5.

15 *Bankruptcy,* a report by "Justice," Allan Heyman, Q.C., chairman of committee (London, 1975).

16 *The Works of Francis Bacon,* ed. J. Spedding, R. L. Ellis, and D. D. Heath (Boston, 1857–1874) **9**: pp. 322–324.

17 S. E. Thorne, introd. to *A Discourse upon the Exposicion & Understandinge of Statutes* (San Marino, 1942), pp. 51, 54.

18 34 and 35 Henry VIII c. 4 (1543); 13 Elizabeth I c. 7 (1571); 1 James I c. 15 (1604); 21 James I c. 19 (1624). These four statutes will henceforth be referred to by date and clause. *The Statutes of the Realm* (11 v., London, 1810–1828).

19 Plucknett, p. 335. A belief that such a power was being approached was one factor behind the attempted impeachment of judges in 1641, although bankruptcy was not then a matter of concern.

20 Halsbury's *Laws of England* (London, ed. 1953) **2**: p. 251.

21 W. H. Schrampeter, *Law in its Application to Business* (New York, 1941), p. 883.

22 H. Remington, *A Treatise on the Bankruptcy Laws of the United States* (4th ed., Rochester, 1934) **1**: pp. 1–2.

investment and assets, credit and the availability of cash, were irrelevant. Hence Professor Supple has reason to conclude that for the Tudor-Stuart period bankruptcies are not "as good an index of crises in overseas trade as some historians have imagined." [23] After all, bankruptcy law was created by parliaments controlled by landed men and at a time when the legal profession was dominated by conservative influence and propertarian assumptions. "They continued to try to squeeze the fast multiplying problems and disputes of an adventurous commercial community into the antique legal framework devised for settling the problems of a small class of landowners." [24]

The Privy Council and the court of Chancery provided alleviation in a few cases, but these avenues of discretion, strenuously debated during the reign of James I, were limited by the 1624 statute. There are indications that the situation was again more flexible by the late 1630's. It is possible, but not proven, that during this critical period of Charles I's reign there was some official sympathy with those who might lend the crown money. On the other hand such persons, under normal circumstances, were not those most likely to be treated as bankrupts. Political considerations apart, there was always a sense that some distinction should be made between debtors whose inability was due to misfortune or chance, and those whose circumstances were the consequence of dishonesty, fraud, or reckless behavior. A law which concentrated upon the group rights of creditors was of little help to honest debtors, whereas it might be manipulated by dishonest ones.

With respect to both bankrupts and debtors, argument up to and including modern times has been reminiscent of the sixteenth-century controversy as to whether a line could be drawn between the willful and the unfortunate unemployed. There has been plenty of sympathetic comment, some of it even from the authorities, but bankruptcy as an evasion or as a stepping-stone to greater fortune attracts the public eye. As a lawyer said recently, there can be an impression that the bankrupt drives off in a Cadillac while his creditors trudge home in the snow. "Bankruptcy is when you put your money in your hip pocket and let your creditors take your coat." [25] Thomas Dekker, well before he himself endured over six years' imprisonment for debt (after 1612), made the necessary distinction between the unfortunate and the "politic" bankrupt, by which term he evidently embraced the type of man who managed to evade the bankruptcy statutes. The latter was a "harpy," a "hyena," a "mermaid," a "chameleon," or a "puritan." "It is not the honest bankrupt undone by suretyship, casualties or losses by sea, but a politic bankrupt, a noble-in-the-pound bankrupt, a five-shillings—nay, a ten-groats-in-the-pound bankrupt, a voluntary villain, a devouring locust, a destroying caterpillar, a golden thief." [26]

Debate had little impact, and it is not surprising that the law itself was seen by some as destructive. Were not the statutes as much a cause of bankruptcy as they were a remedy for some particular situations of debt? Doubts about bankruptcy combined easily with general criticism of the legal system aired with some strength after Naseby and Langport. Discontent was also apparent under the later Stuarts, by which time a clear distinction had been drawn between investment and active participation in trade. A real problem continued to be that those to whom the statutes applied, essentially tradesmen and merchants, had played only a minimal part in their construction. The situation was a far cry from the later Benthamite notion of good laws. It is not surprising that great merchants were sometimes critical of the statutes, but those most affected in practice, small tradesmen, had even less opportunity to be heard.

Describing acts of bankruptcy and establishing procedures to secure a ratable division of assets, the statutes created a quasi-jurisdiction. This was quite natural. Legislation in other areas invented or refurbished bodies which had varying degrees of relationship with, and independence from, established courts of law. The history of commissions required to handle charitable uses, marine insurance contracts, sewers, and other problems indicates that in each case a different tale unfolds. In every instance, nonetheless, the current state of law was a major factor. The early bankruptcy statutes created a type of commission which was thrown into the sea of courts and jurisdictions, limitations, procedures, and statutes which already existed. This was to be of the utmost importance not because the common law had all that much to offer but because it had done little to evolve provisions adequate for the circumstances of trade. Procedures for dealing with contract and debt were complex, and the English court system never really came to grips with that most popular of all Tudor and early Stuart devices, the recorded bond. Hence the 1543

[23] B. E. Supple, *Commercial Crisis and Change in England, 1600–1642* (Cambridge, 1959), p. 10. This is so despite the probability that some collapses were not, strictly speaking, bankruptcies. It is also worth noting the point that clothiers seem to have been more exposed in times of slump than were merchants. In more modern times, as the laws changed, there does seem to have been such a relationship. See R. C. O. Matthews, *A Study in Trade-Cycle History: Economic Fluctuations in Great Britain. 1833–1842* (Cambridge, 1954), pp. 16, 19.

[24] M. Birks, *Gentlemen of the Law* (London, 1960), p. 87.

[25] *Colombo's Canadian Quotations* (Edmonton, 1974), pp. 179–180.

[26] T. Dekker, *The Seuen Deadly Sinnes of London* (1606), in *The Non-Dramatic Works of Thomas Dekker*, ed. A. B. Grosart (New York, 1963) **2**: pp. 17, 21; *Lanthorne and Candle-light* (1608), in *Thomas Dekker*, ed. E. D. Pendry (London, 1967), p. 275.

statute was so vague as to be nearly unworkable, and the 1571 statute was so restricted that it unbalanced the English law of bankruptcy for generations. The consequences can be seen in statutory amendments of the seventeenth century and in the limitations and interpretations offered by Westminster judges.

Under Henrician legislation, bankruptcy was handled by specified great officials, one of whom was the lord chancellor. The 1571 statute, in contrast, gave sole authority to the lord chancellor to issue commissions and to determine their composition. For a time there were two systems in existence, but the Henrician form of proceeding withered away. Eventually commissions under the Elizabethan statute, although issued individually, came to be surrounded by a permanent form of organization. The story is typical of that process whereby a remedy is taken up as a matter of government, translated into law, and eventually mechanized. Coke reflected this when he devoted a section of his *Fourth Institute* to "the court of the commissioners upon the statute of bankrupts." [27] This approach invites comparison with a description of nineteenth-century metropolitan bankruptcy commissioners as being "London's main commercial court." [28] It is, therefore, particularly important to be wary of diverse usages of the word *court*. It is true that the seventeenth-century creation of a Register for metropolitan commissions was important with respect to the beginnings of administrative cohesion. However, Elizabethan and Jacobean parliaments did not endow bankruptcy commissions with the attributes of a court. Procedures were crudely outlined, clerical requirements were ignored, and all the statutes were amorphous on the subject of ultimate administrative and legal responsibility.

Nonetheless, bankruptcy commissions did have a distinct identity. Furthermore, as Blackstone pointed out, none of the statutes allowed for appeal from the associated and personal jurisdiction exercised by the lord chancellor.[29] Yet in practice the decision of commissioners that a man was in fact a bankrupt, the prime point of importance for the debtor and his creditors, could be challenged at law. The statutes implied something about this, but not very much, and they appeared to hope that a state of bankruptcy could be assumed provided that it was sworn that a certain type of person had committed a certain type of action. It also came to be understood that the lord chancellor could not refuse a petition for issue of a commission, although Thomas Coventrye, lord keeper from 1625 to 1640, appears to have been ready to exercise discretion in some circumstances. Only in the mid-seventeenth century was the order of possibilities clarified: a debtor who denied bankruptcy could have his denial debated before a court of law, but the commission must first issue.[30]

Bankruptcy commissioners were not judges. Unlike justices of the peace sitting in Quarter Sessions, and distinctly unlike commissioners of sewers, they had only an authority and not a jurisdiction. They had to be wary of exceeding their powers. Experience advised care, and it is probable that sometimes this mitigated the intention of the statutes. There was no alternative, since the performance of bankruptcy commissions also depended on the law as expressed by other statutes or applied by a variety of courts.[31]

In the second half of the seventeenth century, some difficulties were resolved. This was largely due to interpretations offered by Lord Chancellor Nottingham. His work provided a clearer grasp of broad principles and helped to shape Chancery jurisdiction in the years between 1673 and 1682. Many aspects, nonetheless, remained unsatisfactory, not least because classification according to occupation remained a dominant factor. The discharge was introduced in the early eighteenth century, but other legislative experiments were less satisfactory. Complaint ranged from charges of inefficiency to doubts about the probity of those who operated the system. These were to be standard themes discussed well into the Victorian period. In introducing the bankruptcy act for Scotland (1856), the lord advocate remarked that pressure had been put on him to introduce the English law of bankruptcy, "which he had resisted on the ground that our own law, even unreformed, was better and less expensive." [32]

In the twentieth century, bankruptcy laws and procedures have been criticized for reasons which are historically familiar. Why, it has been asked in the United States, was there such a dramatic rise in the number of bankruptcies during the twenty years after 1945? Were not these years generally reflective of prosperity and rising incomes? A team of researchers concluded that the subject received little attention from scholars and the media unless spectacular individuals—business tycoons or film stars—were involved. They also questioned the very basis of bankruptcy arrangements. "Administratively, the bankruptcy system as it is managed through the courts violates most principles of sound organization and management. The system provides inadequate supervision, audit and investigation, leading to opportuni-

[27] Coke, *Fourth Institute*, p. 277.

[28] E. Welbourne, "Bankruptcy Before the Era of Victorian Reform," *The Cambridge Historical Journal* 4 (1932): p. 51.

[29] Blackstone 3: p. 427.

[30] See below, p. 27.

[31] This was still true of the nineteenth century. A warrant issued by a statutory commission might be considered as without authority, and a bankrupt who failed to answer questions "satisfactorily" could be released from prison on *habeas corpus*. A. Rubinstein, *Jurisdiction and Illegality* (Oxford, 1965), p. 111. See, 2 Chan. Cases, 72–73, Perrat v. Ballard (1681).

[32] Gibb, p. 227.

ties for error and fraud. Procedures are slow and archaic; records are incomplete and sloppy."[33] Similar conclusions have been reached, similar comments made, across four hundred years of Anglo-American history.

II. THE FIRST BANKRUPTCY STATUTE

Tudor statutes can be arid documents, but in recent years research has uncovered fascinating stories which help to explain Henry VIII's statute of appeals, the statutes of uses and wills, the "whipping" statute of 1547, the statutes which made up the Elizabethan church settlement, and the celebrated statute of artificers. This work supports Plucknett's suggestion that the apparent dryness of the statute book may be little more than a corollary of ignorance about the historical background. He pondered the contrast between the attitudes of historians and those of contemporaries for whom a statute might have a catastrophic character.

> It has the force of law on "the appointed day"; the day before that, all is void. How it came about is nobody's business; the recommendations (perhaps by an eminent body of commissioners) which initiated it, are irrelevant; the slow fashioning of it in debate and in committee, and the changes it underwent there, are no concern of the lawyers.[1]

In 1543, when the first bankruptcy statute was passed, the government and members of both houses were probably influenced most by the apparent ineptitude of existing rules applying to debt. Their major concern must have been with matters within common law jurisdiction. Maritime and mercantile practice, which in the Middle Ages had spawned a variety of local customs and codes, can have had little relevance to their deliberations. The law merchant, that is, the custom of the merchants, never matched the international strength of canon and civil law. Furthermore, merchant courts in England had not developed to the same degree as in some other places, although the mayors of the staples, usually but not always distinct from the borough mayors, had once enjoyed considerable independence and exercised a nearly exclusive jurisdiction over the persons and goods of merchants trading there.[2] C. T. Carr wrote about "our merchants' independence of the common law," but this does not mean that they could rely unduly upon the law merchant.[3]

Tudor and early Stuart men, whose law was essentially the law of the land, experienced tortuous difficulty in comprehending the technical requirements of commerce, both international and internal. One consequence was that methods of contract, credit, and investment hardly measured up to the requirements of business. Note can be taken, however, of the development of joint-stock companies and thus of a device geared to prospective profits. The bill of lading—in which a ship's master acknowledged receipt of specified goods and undertook to deliver them to a particular consignee—emerged to join the charter-party, a form of mutual contract between master and merchant. The development of the marine insurance contract did something to meet the uncertainties of overseas trade. These and attendant legal arrangements suggest a coming together of Tudor innovation and the "ancient" customs of the merchant community. Nor is it inappropriate to look forward to a gradual "incorporation" of the law merchant within the law of England, a process associated with a great series of judges culminating with Mansfield. However, this has very little to do with the development of English bankruptcy law. Holdsworth, by placing his principal treatment of this topic in a section on the law merchant, obscured discussion of the subject.[4] The bankruptcy statutes, far from having anything to do with the law merchant, were reappraisals of some points which lay within English law as it applied to chattels, debts, land, and sequestration.

It also has to be emphasized that although merchants, those who exported and imported, were embraced by the bankruptcy statutes, the key word was "trader." Middlemen, retailers and wholesalers, often small, made up the mass of businessmen. Their activities were rarely international or even national, and their status was remote from that of those who engaged in high finance. Yet the absence of this distinction is a curious feature of bankruptcy statutes insofar as they grouped together ordinary traders and common shopkeepers, minor manufacturers and great merchants. Indeed the statutes seem to display a blind disregard of the facts and habits of business life. Perhaps this was implicit in existing legal assumptions. "The common law," writes Harding, "was inclined to see commercial life as made up of masters and servants, of classes of person, each with its place and function in the social order, rather than in terms of individual enterprise and contracts."[5]

A mercantile approach towards bankruptcy may have matured in Europe with the collapse of some

[33] David T. Stanley, Marjorie Girth, and others, *Bankruptcy: Problem, Process, Reform* (Washington, D. C., 1971), pp. vii, 1–3.

[1] T. F. T. Plucknett, "Some Proposed Legislation of Henry VIII," *TRHS*, 4th ser. **19** (1936): p. 120.

[2] L. S. Sutherland, "The Law Merchant in England in the Seventeenth and Eighteenth Centuries," *TRHS*, 4th ser. **17** (1934): pp. 149–176. E. E. Rich, "The Mayors of the Staples," *The Cambridge Historical Journal* **4** (1933): pp. 120–142.

[3] C. T. Carr, *Select Charters of Trading Companies (1530–1707)*, Selden Soc. (1913), p. xiv. For a major attempt to sort some of the scanty evidence, see M. M. Postan, *Medieval Trade and Finance* (Cambridge, 1973), pp. 28–91.

[4] Holdsworth **8**: pp. 99–300 (especially pp. 229–245).

[5] A. Harding, *A Social History of English Law* (London, 1966), p. 310.

Italian companies which had been founded in the thirteenth and early fourteenth centuries on the basis of capital derived from interest-bearing loans.[6] Trade, even during the late medieval slump, had been substantial,[7] and at all times it was founded upon an intricate system of financial devices. The medieval period is rightly renowned for its condemnation of usury, but the doctrine of "just price" was flexible. The loaning of money implied a transfer of ownership and there was an obligation for this to be returned. The creditor or seller could justifiably be compensated for any damage, and it was not absurd to construe tardy repayment as a damage.[8] A number of maneuvers, notably those associated with the exchanges, could be employed to ensure a profit. Rates of interest were often quite high. There were, however, restrictions other than those provided by ethics. Although cash transactions must not be underrated, it has been suggested that inelasticity of credit was of major importance. "Medieval capitalism, precocious and adventurous as it was, was sporadic in its incidence. Its progress was hampered by forms of wealth difficult to negotiate. Markets were small, and the spirit which dominated them was local and exclusive." [9]

The great fairs were at the heart of emerging bankruptcy rules. It was presumed that creditors should receive at least part of the sums owing to them as easily and as quickly as possible. A general idea, stemming from Roman law, was that the property of the debtor should be divided equally among the creditors.[10] Under such localized circumstances and procedures, the danger was that emphasis upon the collective equality of creditors would result in disappointed men complaining that the debtor was being treated with undue favor. This discouraged those who might otherwise have drawn a distinction between deliberate and unfortunate debtors, and it aided in the development of fairly stringent rules. In many places, a merchant unable to meet his creditors could be imprisoned and his impounded property sold to satisfy debts. If the amount due was not covered, he might have to endure a further term in prison. He was also liable to expulsion from his guild or other commensurate loss of civic rights. The strict legal possibilities may have been harsher: debtors unable to meet their full obligations could be imprisoned in irons, and a "bankrupt" merchant was apparently beheaded at Barcelona in 1360.[11] Quite naturally, however, the main objective was an effective recovery of debts. This may have been related to the development of rules which encouraged the defaulter to seek resource in flight. Once the act of flight became a customary act of bankruptcy, it was convenient to develop procedures around this circumstance. Some creditors discovered that there were few remedies available when a debtor declined to run away and so had not committed an act of bankruptcy. Fiction sometimes provided the solution, it being supposed that "flight" had occurred.[12]

Flight, fictitious or real, provides a major theme, but it was not the only factor. "Anyone who fails to meet his engagements at the fair settling-days is held for bankrupt," wrote an early fourteenth-century Italian merchant about the Champagne fairs. "He completely loses his credit and cannot show his face." This system for assessing solvency had "the important defect that it acted both too seldom and too late." [13] After all, most creditors were interested either in satisfaction or some kind of composition. Hence, there was the advantage of establishing or presuming an act of flight before the settling day. Behavior which could be construed as an act of bankruptcy opened the way for procedures which gave a particular power to intermediaries. At the fairs of Champagne, it was understood from the twelfth century that a debtor's goods were to be construed as mortgaged to pay his debts. Preference was given to unpaid vendors, and creditors within the fair shared by rate. Creditors outside the fair were excluded from these arrangements, and they could only seek satisfaction from any assets that remained. A majority of creditors, in respect of the money owed and their numbers, could conclude an agreement or composition binding upon the minority. While the discussions went on, the defaulter might even be provided with a safe-conduct and protection against molestation. Provisions such as these, and they were of course marked by local variation, persuaded some people that things were being made too easy for debtors.[14]

---

6 *The Cambridge Economic History of Europe,* ed. M. M. Postan and E. E. Rich (Cambridge, 1952) **2**: p. 319.

7 Although a slump existed, notably in the north and west of Europe, it should not be seen out of context. Medieval trade was significant in comparison with population, and later "trade expansion" had much to do with expanding population. The point is made by J. Bernard in *The Fontana Economic History of Europe: The Middle Ages,* ed. Carlo M. Cipolla (London, 1972), pp. 309–310.

8 Iris Origo, *The Merchant of Prato* (London, 1963), p. 151.

9 Violet Barbour, *Capitalism in Amsterdam in the 17th Century* (Ann Arbor, 1963), p. 11.

10 Holdsworth **8**: p. 229. For a survey of international origins, see L. E. Levinthal, "The Early History of Bankruptcy Law," *University of Pennsylvania Lew Review* **66** (1918): pp. 223–250.

11 Lopez and Raymond, p. 290. R. S. Smith, *The Spanish Guild Merchant: A History of the Consulado* (Durham, N.C., 1940), pp. 25, 27, 58.

12 I. Treiman, "Escaping the Creditor in the Middle Ages," *LQR* **43**: p. 231.

13 R. Ehrenburg, *Capitalism and Finance in the Age of the Renaissance* (London, 1928), p. 318.

14 Lopez and Raymond, pp. 290–302. F. R. Sanborn, *Origins of the Early English Maritime and Commercial Law* (New York, 1930), p. 164. For further examples and the danger of hybrid solutions, see R. de Roover, *Money, Banking and Credit in Mediaeval Bruges* (Cambridge, Mass., 1948), pp. 332–336.

There are inherent pitfalls in assuming too much about "medieval rules" or in essaying generalizations about conditions "on the continent." Although some English developments were doubtless akin to those in Europe, the general impression is that they may have been inadequate for commerce and remarkably unfair to both creditors and debtors. "In all early systems of law," commented Holdsworth, "each creditor is left to pursue his own remedy." The creditor would be inclined to enforce his rights against the property in societies accustomed to organized commerce, credit, and industry. In medieval England, however, the debtor's obligation was of a highly personal nature in that his body could be taken by the creditor.[15] Building on this factor, the Tudors would fashion a statutory law of bankruptcy, a law promulgated by the state as distinct from one which was essentially a convenience to fairs and trading communities.

The statute of 1543 was specifically directed against debtors who fled or who kept to their houses. One theory is that debtors had previously used other means of evasion but that these had gradually been restricted.[16]

A degree of protection had been provided by the doctrine of sanctuary. Insofar as church or monastery was concerned, this had been restricted in the fifteenth century, notably by a papal bull of 1487 directed against dishonest debtors. Events of the 1530's confirmed this trend, but sanctuary remained a significant loophole during and after the Henrician Reformation. It had been most complete in a quarter of Westminster and in liberties such as St. Martin le Grand. An act of 1540 eliminated the old structure in favor of eight "cities of refuge," but many sanctuaries continued although they were questionable in law. Sanctuary as an escape from criminal process was now severely limited, but the testimony and experience of Defoe tell us that it continued to provide protection to debtors.[17]

Another means of escape had been restricted during the fifteenth century. When assets were hidden it had been possible for the creditor to obtain a judgment in an action of debt, and then to secure the imprisonment of the debtor on a *capias ad satisfaciendum* in order to aid execution of the judgment. Debtors had apparently been able to get themselves removed from custody if they could obtain a *corpus cum causa* from Chancery. In that court they could produce indentures and other evidences in defeasance of the original recognizances, so prompting a *scire facias* which required the creditor to appear in Chancery and answer the petition. Until this was done the debtor would be released on a bond, endorsed by a surety, which in default was payable only to the king. According to Treiman, the sureties were often discharged from this liability and so the creditor was left without resource. This device was probably of some use to debtors seeking to escape their obligations, but a statute of 1433 compelled sureties to bind themselves to both the creditors and the king.[18]

The real weakness was not the debtor's ability to evade execution, and sometimes custody, pending execution, but the inadequacy of execution itself. The ability of creditors to seize the assets of a debtor was seriously limited. A sheriff empowered by *fieri facias* could only seize property which he could sell, although from the late thirteenth century half of the debtor's freeholds, under some circumstances, could be taken in execution of a judgment for debt or damages.[19] This was not good enough, and in any case the creditor's position was restricted by defenses which surrounded the debtor. Until the nineteenth century, for example, it was impossible in execution of a judgment to seize choses in action—bills of exchange, checks, banknotes, and bonds. Then there was the relationship between personal immunity and personal property. This often meant that jewelry or clothes which were worn, or any personal property clutched in the hand or carried, might not be capable of seizure.[20] However, the person was not immune, and so imprisonment of the debtor remained fundamental to execution.

Imprisonment tended to be either custodial, as when punishment was the purpose, or coercive, for example when the aim was to enforce collection of debts. Both intentions applied when a person was confined for impeding or disobeying the process or decision of a court.[21]

Imprisonment of crown debtors was an established practice, but the application of such coercion against private debtors has its own story. Acton Burnell (1283) and the statute of merchants (1285) permitted imprisonment under certain conditions, but it was the statute of 1352 which ranked the common creditor with the crown insofar as it allowed imprisonment of the debtor's body until satisfaction had been obtained. "From this statute sprang all the imprisonings for debt, all the debtors' wards, and all the lamentations which they brought in their train." If the Fleet was initially the most famous home of debtors, other

[15] Holdsworth **8**: p. 229.

[16] Treiman, pp. 230–237.

[17] *Ibid.*, pp. 235–236. Plucknett, p. 431. 32 Henry VIII c. 12. Sanctuary was one of the actions mentioned by the Elizabethan statute. 1571, *1. D. Defoe, *An Essay Upon Projects, 1697* (Menston, 1969), pp. 223, 225. See Isobel D. Thornley, "Sanctuary in Medieval London," *Journal of the British Archæological Society,* new ser. **38** (1932–1933): pp. 293–315. I am grateful to Mr. W. Kellaway for this reference.

[18] Holdsworth **8**: p. 231. Treiman, p. 235. 11 Henry VI c. 10.

[19] 13 Edward I c. 18.

[20] G. P. Costigan, Jr., "Those Protective Trusts which are Miscalled 'Spendthrift Trusts' Reexamined," *Legal Essays in Tribute to Orrin Kip McMurray,* ed. M. Radin and A. M. Kidd (Berkeley, 1935), pp. 89–90.

[21] See R. B. Pugh, *Imprisonment in Medieval England* (Cambridge, 1968).

prisons were not far behind. Ludgate was closed for a time in 1419, apparently because too many private debtors preferred to lodge there in preference to meeting their obligations.[22]

Imprisonment for debt, despite its drab and dismal history, has been described as a triumph for the common law.[23] It has also been deplored, and some seventeenth-century men viewed it as being part of the tyranny of the Norman yoke.[24] An inadequate solution for all concerned, the exclusive nature of imprisonment virtually forced the creditor to relinquish other means of obtaining his money.[25] If the plight of debtors was a favorite theme with writers, equal attention was given to the frustrations of creditors who could not lay their hands on money and assets which were being spent to make prison bearable, even enjoyable, and to line the pockets of warders. Alternatively some prisoners had no money, and a man who might have been able to earn some cash to pay his debts was thus incapacitated.[26] The wretched state of prisoners was emphasized by Henry Brinkelow in a blast partly against "that abominable whore of Babylon (Rome I mean)," [27] and partly against many of the ills in English society. This tract, written in or around 1543, was almost contemporary with the first bankruptcy statute and may have been a reaction against it and other social legislation. Brinkelow, once a Grey Friar and now a mercer, inveighed against the practice of shutting up men without trial. He argued that to imprison a man until he died of starvation or disease was murder, and he asserted that prisoners were lodged like hogs and fed like dogs. Tudor prisons could indeed be so appalling as to make Dickensian circumstances appear a rest home. Yet if a prisoner had money—perhaps that ostensibly given him by friends and relatives—he might live in comparative luxury and freedom, provided that he was willing to pay through the nose. If a prisoner desired "to be in commons and to have a bed, he shall pay iiij times more for it than in the dearest inn in England." [28] A rich man could often pay for permission to leave the prison accompanied by a keeper and, although it is not known how far this was allowed in Henry VIII's time, it later became a crying, though doubtless exaggerated, scandal. William Leach, an agitator for law reform during the Interregnum, said that some debtors had traveled all over the country and had even, or so he claimed, gone to the East and West Indies. Some of these supposedly imprisoned debtors had met their creditors "and looked them in the face, and laughed at, and jeered them. . . ." [29]

The prison situation was appreciated by social thinkers who were already discerning a new morality with respect to the poor law, and who perhaps were well in advance of some lawyers with little understanding of Brinkelow's maxim that if a man "offend the law, let him have the law." Yet persistent criticism had only sporadic impact, and in general the unsavory situation continued unabated. Early in the seventeenth century, Dekker penned a description of London, almost a nightmare, conceived as a magic circle drawn by the cries of men, "all penniless, all prisoners."

> Let your eyes walk but over this paper and here survey is drawn. Upon one side of the Thames stand the White Lion, the King's Bench, the Marshalsea, the Clink, the Counter in Southwark; on the other side the Gatehouse, Ludgate, Newgate, Wood St[reet] Counter, Poultry Counter, Finsbury, New Prison, Lob's Pound and the Hole at St. Katherine's. Fourteen Golgothas environing one city! Fourteen charnel houses where men are buried alive! Either this must proceed from much cruelty in the creditor or much deceit in the debtor.

Nothing was done, and the bankruptcy statutes were in fact irrelevant to prison conditions and misuse. The machinery of constraint, as with law reform in general, would have to wait until the nineteenth century, and even then change was slow and miserly.[30]

It is probable that imprisonment for debt and other factors may have made flight appear more attractive in the early Tudor period than it had been previously. This does not mean that it was novel—some English merchants apparently fled abroad in 1414 and doubtless did so at other times—but there had been better ways of evading creditors.[31] Prior to the Henrician statute, flight did not carry that kind of construction which it did at some places on the continent, but it did invite outlawry. This implied forfeiture to the crown, and it was therefore of little benefit to creditors. Certainly, the assumption in 1543 was that too many had found resort in flight. One instance, possibly well known at the time, was the flight in 1535 of Antonio Guidotti. This man, son-in-law of Thomas Cromwell's client, Henry Huttoft, claimed that he was unable to meet bonds entered into on Huttoft's behalf. Guidotti returned, and in 1540 Huttoft begged Cromwell, who had been trying to arrange a settlement, to prevent his

[22] *Ibid.*, pp. 42, 45, 108, 117.

[23] Costigan, p. 106, n. 14.

[24] Margaret James, *Social Problems and Policy During the Puritan Revolution* (London, 1966), p. 327.

[25] Costigan, p. 90.

[26] Prisoners often claimed that they could have paid their debts if allowed another six months. James, p. 329.

[27] Later generations would not need the explanation.

[28] H. Brinkelow, *The Complaynt of Roderyk Mors*, Early English Text Soc. (1874), pp. 27–30. Francis Alford's complaint of 1585 about the imperfections of the legal system noted the plight of prisoners. Lansdowne 44, ff. 2–13. Others commented on the "joyous" life of imprisoned "bankrupts." Lansdowne 99: ff. 185–186.

[29] W. Leach, *Proposals for an Act for the More Speedy Satisfaction of Creditors* (London, 1649), pp. 3–4.

[30] Brinkelow, p. 27. Dekker, *Lanthorne and Candle-light*, pp. 273–274.

[31] Treiman, p. 232.

son-in-law from leaving again until some money and a release on a house in Southampton had been obtained. Guidotti spent some time in the Fleet prison and was temporarily deprived of his rights as a burgess. John Huttoft, Guidotti's brother-in-law, would sit as a member of Parliament for Southampton in the Parliament of 1541–1544 which passed the first bankruptcy statute.[32]

The other assumption in 1543 was that there had been an increasing tendency for debtors to keep to their houses. The pert belief that an Englishman's home is his castle is little more than a popular reference to a legal doctrine of commanding importance. The practical situation was that a debtor—together with such money, property, and valuables that he could gather around him—was virtually inviolate inside his own house. It was almost impossible to break in for the purpose of executing civil process, let alone for seizing assets, although these might not have been paid for. It was noted at the end of Elizabeth's reign that a sheriff, charged with executing a *fieri facias*, could not break through an outside door in order to secure entry, whereas if that door was already open he could force doors within the house and investigate chests in order to seize goods. Indeed if he failed to do this, an action would lie against him.[33] Not many lurking debtors can have left their outer doors unbolted. At times the courts were able to circumvent the situation. Due service of Chancery process in the late years of the sixteenth century could be achieved if the writ was hung on the door. This in itself was an acknowledgment that the server lacked authority to force the door, and that the person sought might be living in a place other than his normal residence. Failure to appear would be contempt of court and the offender might eventually be apprehended. This sort of thing was of little value to creditors, anxious for reimbursement and apprehensive as to what might be going on between the debtor and other creditors.

The 1543 statute, concerned as it was with aspects of insolvency and sequestration, had some antecedents. An early statute of Henry VII against fraudulent alienation tried to limit the availability of sanctuary and other privileged places.[34] A bankruptcy bill reached second reading in the House of Commons during the Reformation Parliament.[35] Perhaps most important was that statute of 1532 which regulated the taking of statutes staple. Staple jurisdiction and independence, already eroded, was now largely taken away, and where it survived remained merely as a forum for recovering small debts. The mercantile community was now almost fully exposed to the normal operations of the common law. Hence, it may be speculated, the traditional evasions of that law had to be adopted, and this may explain the contemporary supposition that flight and keeping to one's house had increased.[36]

The eventual legislation of 1543 grew out of a bill which was carried over from the session which ended in April of the previous year. This "Act Against Such Persons As Do Make Bankrupt" [37] began with a preamble which, in the words of a later authority, might serve a bankruptcy act today: [38]

> Where divers and sundry persons craftily obtaining into their hands great substance of other men's goods do suddenly flee to parts unknown or keep their houses, not minding to pay or restore to any their creditors their debts and duties, but at their own wills and pleasures consume the substance obtained by credit of other men, for their own pleasure and delicate living, against all reason equity and good conscience. . . .[39]

The lord chancellor, the lord treasurer, the lord president,[40] and the lord privy seal, together with other members of the Privy Council and the two chief justices, might order the imprisonment of debtors behaving in the indicated fashion. A distribution was to be arranged, the creditors being reimbursed proportionately according to the amounts owed. Action could only be taken after a written complaint had been made to three of the specified officials, provided that one was the lord chancellor, the lord president, or the lord privy seal. The nature of the estate, property, and effects liable to such action was outlined. Apart from chattels, debts, goods, wares, and other merchandises, the statute applied to annuities, fees, lands, offices, and tenements. The designated authorities—the work would devolve upon commissioners, but this was not stated—were empowered to search, view, rent, appraise, or sell any of these items to the benefit of the creditors.[41] Basil Montagu, writing in the early nine-

[32] G. R. Elton, *Reform and Renewal* (Cambridge, 1973), pp. 116–117. *L. and P. Henry VIII*, viii, no. 878; xii (1), no. 513; xv, no. 385. I am grateful, for these references and other information, to Dr. Mary Robertson of the Huntington Library. C. Platt, *Medieval Southampton: The Port and Trading Community, A. D. 1000–1600* (London, 1973), pp. 242–245. A. A. Ruddock, *Italian Merchants and Shipping in Southampton, 1270–1600* (Southampton, 1951), p. 249.

[33] 1 Brownl. & Golds. **50** (1602).

[34] 3 Henry VII c. 4. *Reeves' History of the English Law*, ed. W. F. Finlason (London, 1869) **3**: p. 290, n. (a).

[35] *L. and P. Henry VIII*, vi, no. 120. Elton, p. 149.

[36] 23 Henry VIII c. 6. Elton, pp. 148–149. Rich, p. 141. London and its merchant community had, and continued to have, a local system for payment of debts, proceedings for debt, seizure of assets—including those locked in warehouses—and compositions. A. Pulling, *A Practical Treatise on the Laws, Customs and Regulations of the City and Port of London* (London, 1842), p. 167 *et seq.*

[37] 34 and 35 Henry VIII c. 4. S. E. Lehmberg, *The Later Parliaments of Henry VIII, 1536–1547* (Cambridge, 1977), pp. 171, 181.

[38] Remington **1**: p. 6.

[39] 1543, *1.

[40] For this position, see G. R. Elton, *The Tudor Constitution* (Cambridge, 1960), pp. 92–93.

[41] 1543, *1.

teenth century, thought that this was contrary to law and justice because it introduced "the forcible and then unknown power of seizing a debtor's property and person by a summary process for the security of his creditors."[42]

A bankrupt could be summoned by proclamation and outlawed if he did not appear within three months "or as soon after as he conveniently may."[43] This allowed for the difficulties of distant traders and presumably gave the absentee, assuming that he heard about the proclamation, time to explain himself in writing and arrange a date for his return. Otherwise, there were few concessions. Bankrupts could be imprisoned. Yet new powers were not provided to deal with traditional defenses of persons who kept to their houses. This may be reflected in an Elizabethan complaint made by some French merchants.

> The English merchant . . . has this privilege, that when he has bought goods and intends to become a bankrupt, he can retire into his house, or even into his shop, provided that the door is closed with a lock or some barrier; and the bailiff cannot touch his goods, nor can anyone disturb him nor demand any account from him, nor arrest him or even talk to him, even though the poor ruined creditors may see the bankrupt in his house, with his wife, his factors and servants, publicly selling their goods in front of their eyes, without being able to attach these goods or any of the debtor's real or personal property.[44]

The 1543 statute tried to prevent creditors from cutting each other's throats. A temporary apportionment by rate was to be enforced and the ability of creditors to take advantage of every available remedy, including private negotiation with the bankrupt, was suspended, not extinguished, for an unspecified time. The bankrupt's liability was not reduced. He was treated as an offender, and hence the statute has been described as "quasi-criminal." His body, lands, and goods were liable to any valid recovery once creditors had received their ratable share of available assets. Creditors, who were not "fully satisfied and paid or otherwise contended," might subsequently seek satisfaction through all the remedies available at law.[45] The situation would revert to that described by Brinkelow as "first come, first served."[46] A bankrupt would then be at the mercy of his creditors despite the apparently bare cupboard of resources available for restitution. The only restriction was that which barred creditors from recovery against assets distributed by virtue of actions taken under authority of the statute.[47]

Some stipulations of the statute dealt with third persons. Anyone suspected of possessing a bankrupt's effects could be summoned and required to make disclosure. The penalty for concealment was a fine, amounting to double the value of the effects concerned, which was to be applied to the benefit of the creditors. A similar penalty was to be levied on creditors who attempted to obtain undue preference from the debtor after the action constituting bankruptcy, or who made approaches outside the procedures allowed by the statute. Collusive recoveries against bankrupts in fraud of creditors were roundly condemned and forbidden.[48]

Insofar as this statute departed, however weakly, from some traditional limitations which had raised a protective fence around debtors and even creditors, there was a need to cover those authorized by it. This was especially so with respect to men who acquired, by purchase or assignment, the goods and lands of the debtor.

> And that every direction order bargain sale and other things done by the said lords authorized as is aforesaid, in writing signed with their hands by authority of this act shall be good and effectual in the law to all intents constructions and purposes against the said offenders their heirs and executors for ever, as though the same order direction bargain and sale had been made by the said offender or offenders at his or their own free will and liberty, by writing indented enrolled in any of the King's courts of record.[49]

Otherwise, apart from general statements, adequate coverage was not really given to those who would execute the provisions of the act. This reflects the failure of the statute to establish much of a procedure beyond the stated requirement of petitioning the lord chancellor and others. Commissioners were not mentioned, and in consequence their position was weaker than it need have been.

The 1543 statute poses a problem for the historian in that the word *bankrupt* was only used in the title.[50] Thereafter mention was made of "divers and sundry persons." In distinct contrast to later statutes, reference was not made to those who lived through buying and selling by way of merchandise. The preamble mentioned "goods" and "houses," but in specifying acts of bankruptcy the statute did not refer to their sale, and it did not mention shops. Assets available to seizure included not only those associated with trade but also landed estates, rights over land, and offices. There is an ambiguity here which is reflected by later commentators.

Cowell indicated that the Henrician statute covered the taking of other men's goods, but he did not, in this context, bring up the subject of merchants and

[42] Montagu, p. 7.
[43] 1543, *5.
[44] Cited Treiman, p. 234.
[45] 1543, *4, 6.
[46] Brinkelow, p. 41.
[47] 1543, *6.
[48] 1543, *2, 3, 4.
[49] 1543, *1.
[50] I am grateful to Mr. H. C. Cobb and Mr. D. Johnson of the House of Lords Record Office for their assistance. In looking at the original statute, I have concluded that both the title and its endorsed form on the reverse side are probably contemporary with the text.

traders.[51] Spence, writing in the nineteenth century, assumed that the Elizabethan statute (1571) "confined" bankruptcy to those who used the trade of merchandise in gross or by retail, language which may indicate that he believed the earlier statute to have been broader in its coverage.[52] Some authorities have accepted that the 1543 act applied only to commercial men,[53] but as Jenks pointed out it "was not, in terms, confined to merchants."[54] Certainly, if read literally, we would have to presume that men other than merchants and traders were included. If so, this legislation reflected a principle which was not to be incorporated into the system of bankruptcy proceedings stemming from 1571 until three tortuous centuries had passed. The Elizabethan statute applied only to those who were merchants or exercised the trade of merchandise, or sought their living through buying and selling. Hence Blackstone's description of a bankrupt as "a trader, who secretes himself, or does certain other acts, tending to defraud his creditors."[55]

The 1543 statute poses some problems. The evidence of subsequent commissions is scattered and nebulous. One possibility is that the word *bankrupt*, although only mentioned in the statute's title, was already understood to have a particular meaning. Prior to 1543, bankruptcy may have acquired a specific association with trade. However, the term would continue to be used in a pejorative sense as in Edward Hall's mid-Tudor description of Warbeck's forces: "some bankrupts, some false English sanctuary men, some thieves, robbers and vagabonds. . . ."[56] Other legislative proposals of the Henrician period may indicate a differentiation according to occupation and status.[57] It was suggested in 1535 that "merchants shall employ their goods continually in traffic and not in purchasing lands." Four years later, there was a notion that merchants might be prevented from buying lands above a certain value. This kind of thinking was also current in 1559, when Elizabeth's first Parliament met. One idea was that merchants should not be allowed to purchase more than £50 *per annum* of inheritance, whereas aldermen and sheriffs of London might buy up to the value of £200 *per annum* because they approached the degree of knighthood.[58]

[51] T. Cowell, *The Interpreter* (1637), *sub tit.* "Bankrupts."

[52] G. Spence, *The Equitable Jurisdiction of the Court of Chancery* (Philadelphia, 1846, 1850) 1: p. 198. However his use of the word *confined* seems to represent a confusion in the relationship between the two statutes.

[53] Teevan and Smith, p. 253.

[54] E. Jenks, *A Short History of English Law* (London, 1949), p. 383.

[55] Blackstone 2: p. 284.

[56] *Hall's Chronicle*, ed. of 1548 (London, 1809), p. 472.

[57] See also W. S. Holdsworth, "The Development of the Law Merchant and its Courts," *Select Essays in Anglo-American Legal History* (Boston, 1907) 1: p. 327, n.1.

[58] *L. and P. Henry VIII*, ix, no. 725; xiv (1), no. 655. *H.M.C. Hatfield* 1: p. 163. Acknowledgment is due to L. Stone, "The Political Programme of Thomas Cromwell," *BIHR* 24 (1951): pp. 1–18. Stone's general argument was countered by G. R. Elton, "Parliamentary Drafts, 1529–40," *BIHR* 25 (1952): pp. 117–132. More recently, see Elton's *Reform and Renewal*.

The Henrician statute is also noteworthy in that it did not make an overt distinction between aliens and nationals. Presumably aliens could be both bankrupts and creditors, but this was not stated. Foreign merchants claimed exemption and they were not directly embraced by the 1571 statute. This was resented by English merchants who were themselves subject to bankruptcy laws in the Low Countries and elsewhere.[59]

The 1543 statute was riddled with inadequacies and uncertainties. The Privy Council, whose members had been mentioned, helped at times and occasionally intervened on behalf of creditors.[60] A more cogent possibility was that the lord chancellor might develop a jurisdiction in Chancery similar to that which in Elizabethan times he seemed to be assuming over marine insurance. It was natural to utilize Chancery powers since the lord chancellor was a leading official named in the statute, and since commissions were appointed under the Great Seal. It may be that through such assistance the 1543 statute, despite its weaknesses, did provide some sort of basis for operations against bankrupts.[61]

The Henrician statute was not abrogated by that of 1571. Cowell was quite right to begin his summary of bankruptcy law with a comment on the act of 1543.[62] The point is often confused. Holdsworth, for example, remarked that the first statute had been "replaced" by the Elizabethan one.[63] Coke's employment of loose language—he remarked that the 1543 statute was "altered" by later legislation—may have helped in the creation of a false impression.[64] Miscon-

[59] P.R.O., S.P.12/146, no. 125 (? *circa* 1580), "Touching the Right that Strangers have to Partake of Bankrupt Goods with English Creditors." The text of this document, which centers upon the Low Countries, may explain some of the difficulties which faced those who framed the 1571 act: "At the making of the said law by common report the strangers then resident in London being dealt with in that behalf utterly refused to be subject to any such law. . . ."

[60] *APC* 1552–1554, pp. 116, 250; 1554–1556, p. 344.

[61] W. J. Jones, "Elizabethan Marine Insurance: The Judicial Undergrowth," *Business History* 2 (1960): pp. 53 *et seq.* See below, p. 41. An example of Lord Chancellor Heath trying to help out in difficult circumstances is in P.R.O., S.P.11/11, no. 11 (1557).

[62] Cowell, *sub tit.* "Bankrupts."

[63] Holdsworth 8: p. 237.

[64] Coke, *Fourth Institute*, p. 277. One editorial comment on Coke's *Reports* inaccurately asserts that the 1571 statute "wholly superseded" that of 1543. 2 Co.Rep., 25a, n. (B), 76 *English Reports*. The notion that the first statute was "altered," itself misleading, survived to be repeated in later works. See M. Bacon, *A New Abridgement of the Law*, rev. B. Wilson and J. Bouvier (Philadelphia, 1852) 1: p. 628. Spence's use of the word "confined" (see above, n. 52) suggests that he too misinterpreted the force of the 1571 statute. Scott rightly observed that an act was passed to "amend" the ex-

ception was probably aided by the fact that after 1571 little use seems to have been made of the earlier statute. Since the 1624 act applied the Elizabethan system equally to both aliens and nationals, it could be imagined that Henrician legislation had expired. It was not mentioned. Yet a later seventeenth-century commentator, Billinghurst, reported that though in his time the Henrician statute was "out of use" he did not "find it actually repealed," and he thought it not "altogether superfluous to take note of it." [65]

Theory apart, there is practical evidence that the Henrician statute was occasionally used after 1571. In February, 1595, a commission was granted by Lord Keeper Puckering and Chief Justice Popham with respect to the bankruptcy of two partners—Thomas Crumpe, a vintner, and William Worsoppe, a mercer, both of London—who were said to owe at least £1,300. Their creditors were seven English merchants and six merchant strangers. The 1543 statute, it was noted, "provided as well for strangers as for Englishmen to recover their just debts and duties to them due and owing in such cases as are therein expressed." [66] Later, cheek by jowl with an example of a petition and commission under the statutes of 1571 and 1604, the clerk of the crown in Chancery copied into his precedent book for the years 1603–1608 an example of a commission granted according to the Henrician statute. The petition from two merchant strangers had been made to Lord Chancellor Ellesmere, the chancellor of the Duchy of Lancaster, and the chief justice of the Common Pleas with respect to the bankruptcy of Zacharie le Pie of Chichester.[67] Likewise, in the early years of James I, there was the complicated affair of Matthew de Renzi, merchant stranger of Bishopgate, who was made a bankrupt despite his claim to have a prior protection. Large sums and rival groups of creditors, national and international, were involved. He fled to Ireland, claiming to be honest and ascribing his difficulties to others who had gone broke.[68]

There is reason to doubt if the Henrician statute was very effective, and commissions must have been infrequent after 1571. It was poorly worded and few could hope for a successful conclusion. Nonetheless, it had provided a novel means of proceeding, and some of its provisions were suggestive of later practice. It embraced the principle that absconding or defecting debtors should be punished, and it initiated a range of procedures which included the power to summon and examine third parties suspected of concealing property. Above all, it established the notion that creditors shared a community of interests. Since it was axiomatic that all should be reimbursed on an equal basis, the bankrupt's property was to be seized by a common agent and thereafter there was to be a distribution *pro rata* of the proceeds. Holdsworth's conclusion that it was essentially an attempt to prevent frauds on creditors is still valid.[69] This theme was fundamental to future legislation. "These statutes of bankruptcy are favorably to be construed for the creditors, being made for the suppression of fraud." [70]

III. ELIZABETHAN AND EARLY STUART STATUTES AND COMMISSIONS

Some assumptions of the Henrician statute were included in the 1571 act. Coupled with new ideas and Jacobean amendment, the principles and procedures for bankruptcy then established satisfied few. Garret de Malynes, commenting on the provisions of 1571 and 1604, thought that there were grounds for praise but that really dishonest men could "prevent the means of suing for the same." The intention of the statutes could be broken "as easily as a spider's web." [1] This was also the opinion of Dekker. The problem was in part one of detail, and some improvement was made in 1624. Even so, hindsight tells us that most leading principles of later bankruptcy law, with the exception of the discharge and voluntary bankruptcy, had already been introduced.

There were economic and financial worries in 1571, but legislation probably stemmed primarily from disquiet about existing procedures. Other factors merely worked to give this disquiet a hearing. Bankruptcy bills had been introduced and made some progress in 1563, the year of the great apprenticeship statute, and in 1566, when Elizabeth had made a hasty termination of the session.[2] Nonetheless, a re-examination of the bankruptcy laws was always most likely in periods of commercial anxiety. In 1571, as Parliament met, some prophesied that all trades connected with buying and selling were in danger of rapid decay. A list of bankrupts—nineteen of the forty mentioned concerned London—emphasized the number of industrialists, merchants, and tradesmen who had lost

---

isting law relating to bankrupts, but he was silent on both the nature of the law and the nature of the amendment. W. R. Scott, *The Constitution and Finance of English, Scottish, and Irish Joint-Stock Companies to 1720* (Cambridge, 1912) **1**: p. 53. Even the P.R.O. *Guide* perpetuates error by stating that the statute of 1543 was "repealed" by that of 1571. *Guide to the Contents of the Public Record Office* (London, 1963) **1**: p. 166. However, not all recent descriptions are inaccurate. Halsbury (**2**: p. 251) merely notes that the 1543 statute was "followed" by subsequent legislation.

[65] G. Billinghurst, *All the Statutes now in Force and Use Concerning Bankrupts* (London, 1695), p. 105.

[66] El. 5525.

[67] P.R.O., C.193/5, no. 80. Professor M. Pulman kindly checked this reference for me.

[68] *H.M.C. Hatfield,* **17**: pp. 593–594; **18**: pp. 10, 24, 239, 323; **19**: pp. 69, 76; **24**: pp. 53, 55.

[69] Holdsworth **1**: p. 470.

[70] Goodinge, p. 34.

[1] G. de Malynes, *Lex Mercatoria* (London, 1686), p. 157.

[2] *CJ* **1**: pp. 68–69, 70, 72, 74–75, 79–80.

their credit. The abuses and deceits of "bankrupts" were described as intolerable. The existing machinery of law was seen as weak, and there was a demand that Parliament must act.[3]

This sense of urgency cannot be separated from other concerns. Legislation against fraudulent conveyances, certainly a related matter, was approved.[4] The bill against defaulting tellers was passed.[5] During a famous debate about usury and in other discussions, members of Parliament talked about the evils of bankruptcy, debt, luxurious living, overspending, and usury. There was little satisfaction with a 1563 statute which had attempted to limit the availability of credit for the purchase of imported apparel and goods.[6] The new usury statute may have been crucial. Except for the period, 1545–1552, the taking of interest had been forbidden, and it has been suggested that this may have restricted the use of borrowed capital in the wool trade. If a more permissive approach was now to be allowed, it may well have been supposed that this would encourage borrowing and therefore necessitate a more stringent control of mercantile and trading debts.[7] Indeed many of these bills can be regarded as constituting a packet of proposed legislation.

In 1571 the bankruptcy bill, along with that against fraudulent collectors and receivers, was among the first to be considered by the upper house. It was sent down, engrossed on parchment, with a message recommending expedition. This was on May 16. The House of Commons concluded that in view of the consideration given to the matter by the Lords, there was no need on their part for either engrossment or the striking of a committee. The first reading was received on 17 May, the second on the twenty first, and the third three days later.[8]

[3] Lansdowne 13, ff. 54–55. The largest claim, against a bankrupt of unspecified occupation from Buckinghamshire, was for £6,000. Scott 1: p. 53. Neale, *Parliaments, 1559–1581*, p. 219. For failures in London during the 1560's, particularly that of Sir Thomas Lodge, see G. D. Ramsey, *The City of London in International Politics at the Accession of Elizabeth Tudor* (Manchester, 1975), pp. 57–59, 239.

[4] 13 Elizabeth I c. 5.

[5] See above, p. 7.

[6] Traders were supposed to insist upon payment in cash unless the customer had £3,000 *per annum*. 5 Elizabeth I c. 6. In 1559, it had been proposed that bankruptcy be made a felony. *H.M.C. Hatfield* 1: p. 164.

[7] 13 Elizabeth I c. 8. P. J. Bowden, *The Wool Trade in Tudor and Stuart England* (London, 1962), p. 100. A bill for usury was proposed in 1604 and one against pawnbrokers passed (1 James I c. 21); bills for both bankruptcy and usury were considered in 1621. The act for usury, passed in 1624 (21 James I c. 17), also tightened up controls on the activities of brokers and scriveners. In this respect, note the title of the 1624 bankruptcy statute. *CJ* 1: p. 204. *Commons Debates 1621* 7: pp. 209–210.

[8] *LJ* 1: pp. 670, 672, 685, 687. *CJ* 1: pp. 90–91, 92. S. D'Ewes, *A Compleat Journal of the Votes, Speeches and Debates . . . Throughout the Whole Reign of Queen Elizabeth* (1693), pp. 184, 186.

Intimations of prosperity, encouraged by the revival of Anglo-Flemish trade in April, 1573, marked the decade, but in 1581 there was an attempt to clarify some difficulties in the bankruptcy law which had come to light. A bill brought from the Lords survived its second reading in the Commons before being "dashed" upon the question.[9] The advantageous trend petered out in the 1580's, formal war with Spain broke out, and the mid-1590's were exceptionally bad: harvests failed, the real value of wages fell dramatically, and the textile industry all but foundered. In 1601, Parliament considered a bill against "cozening bankrupts and lewd apprentices and factors." This was notable because of its harsh tone and because it associated together three different categories of malefactors. It was proposed that bankrupts should be treated as embezzlers unless there was positive evidence that financial difficulty resulted from bad debts or losses at sea. A first reading was obtained on 14 December, but the bill did not proceed. Dissolution was imminent, as the House of Commons had been warned on 10 December by the queen. Urged by Elizabeth to speed up business, the members of Parliament were more concerned with other matters, in particular a bill against the transportation of ordnance which government spokesmen seemed determined to obstruct.[10]

When the first Parliament of James I met in 1604, it was possible to be optimistic. The worst moments of the 1590's had passed, and the war was over. On the other hand plague had made its mark, and there was the usual worry about that perennially ailing mainstay of the economy, the cloth trade. An act intended to eradicate some imperfections in the bankruptcy system was passed, but this legislation was not as harsh as that proposed in 1601.[11] In 1610 the subject came up again. Some members of Parliament accused Salisbury, the lord treasurer, of having damaged trade through his extension of impositions and suggested that he was therefore responsible for a number of bankruptcies. Salisbury was probably justified in dismissing this as speculation. In any case, this argument was only incidental to the great debates then under way.[12] A bankruptcy bill was introduced in 1614, but there could be no progress in this brief "Addled Parliament."[13] Subsequently, problems which had not been perceived when the 1604 act was passed attracted attention as the general trade prosperity of James's first decade, itself unspectacular,

[9] *CJ* 1: pp. 133–134. If the document noted above (Chap. II n. 59) can indeed be assigned to 1580, then it is possible that there had been some intention of meeting complaints about foreigners.

[10] P.R.O., S.P.12/283, nos 22, 23. J. E. Neale, *Elizabeth I and her Parliaments, 1584–1601* (London, 1957), pp. 421, 423.

[11] *CJ* 1: p. 236.

[12] *Proceedings in Parliament 1610*, ed. Elizabeth Read Foster (New Haven, 1966) 1: p. 131; 2: pp. 334, 403.

[13] *CJ* 1: p. 481.

expired with the Cockayne fiasco and the disintegration of peace in Europe. The whole period from the accession of James I to the Restoration "was not marked by conspicuous growth: on the contrary, it was a time of painful economic readjustment in a darkening European context." [14]

"I had rather be a plowman than a merchant," said a member of Parliament in 1621. All sorts of explanations were offered, but while many discussed the relationship between crumbling English cloth exports and the economic and monetary consequences of wars in Europe, few could agree on the exact causal connection.[15] Many remedies were suggested, and one of these—not unrelated to the attack upon Bacon's performance as lord chancellor—was a reshaping of the 1571 and 1604 bankruptcy statutes. Commercial crises intensified what many had said for years: the existing bankruptcy law was ineffective because the statutes were full of gaping loopholes. In other ways a lead had already been given in Scotland, where an act of the lords of Council and Session against unlawful dispositions and alienations of bankrupts, made in July, 1620, was ratified in 1621.[16] In England a bankruptcy bill, which provided for corporal punishment under certain circumstances, was introduced by Sir Francis Crane, a member of Parliament for Penryn. An extreme suggestion was that some bankrupts should be whipped to death. Sir Edward Coke felt that bankrupts might deserve this fate, but he did not like "laws written in blood." Wentworth and others expressed the real nature of current anger: many clothiers had failed and it was supposed that this was often due to the deceitful bankruptcy of their financial associates. It was said that clothiers were demanding a new act. Considerable progress was made, but nothing was achieved since this Parliament collapsed amid disagreement with the king on other matters.[17]

The depression continued. In 1622 it was reported from Suffolk that manufacturers had suffered great losses, in part because of bankruptcies.[18] By 1624, however, the political climate had altered. Prince Charles and Buckingham were in pursuit of diplomatic revenge and native popularity; as Cranfield fell a new bankruptcy statute was born. It was modeled upon the design of 1621, but excluded bloodthirsty suggestions. Even the proposal, put forward again, that bankruptcy should be made a felony was left out. It was, nonetheless, the most stringent bankruptcy statute which had yet been produced. In other respects this Parliament, hostile to monopolies, sought a greater freedom—in terms of economic activity—for the landowner, the farmer, and even those who wished to participate in the cloth trade. This had little to do with the circumstances of tradesmen and most merchants. They might in some respects be allowed a greater freedom of enterprise and maneuver—the 1604 session of Parliament had also been marked by a campaign against certain company regulations—but this could entail a stricter set of regulations to satisfy a society of landed producers and investors.[19] Furthermore, there was still a backlash against the memory of Bacon's innovations and past interventions by the Privy Council.[20] An attempt to tighten the bankruptcy laws was not out of touch with the economic ethos of 1624.

Henceforth, and for a few decades, the initiative in providing refinement passed from Parliament to the judiciary. The latter could do no more than interpret complex problems as they arose. Political circumstances precluded legislation. This applies to all aspects of debt. In August, 1641, the House of Commons rejected a bill intended to aid creditors and relieve debtors unable to meet their obligations. The proposal concerned a field of contention much broader than bankruptcy, and there was little time in which to consider such matters.[21]

It would be several decades before the existing bankruptcy statutes were revised. In the meantime, there were a multitude of judicial and occasionally executive explanations, interpretations, and modifications. Sometimes this was because of specific and immediate doubts brought to the notice of the courts by litigants. At other times general and social circumstances called for an evaluation, as when, in the early years of the Interregnum, commissioners of bankruptcy found that a debtor's estate had been sequestered because he had borne arms against Parliament. If the cause of sequestration had happened after the action of bankruptcy they might, with reasonable hope of success, beg that the sequestration be discharged. Alternatively, and this was most likely if the order of events was reversed, the commissioners might request a composition for the sequestered estate, perhaps paying the composi-

[14] C. Wilson, *England's Apprenticeship, 1603–1763* (London, 1965), p. xi.

[15] Supple, pp. 54, 58. It has been argued that contemporaries who hesitated to put the war high on their list of causes for the depression may not have been far wrong. J. G. Gould, "The Trade Depression of the Early 1620's," *Ec.HR*, 2nd ser. 7 (1954): pp. 81–90.

[16] *The Acts of Parliaments of Scotland* **4**: pp. 615–616. G. Mackenzie, *Observations on the 18 Act 23 Parliament, King James VI* (Edinburgh, 1675).

[17] *CJ* **1**: pp. 532, 537, 551, 575, 626, 632. *Commons Debates 1621* **2**: pp. 162, 211, 267; **5**: pp. 176, 266, n. 1, 457, 505; **6**: p. 182. M. Prestwich, *Cranfield: Politics and Profits under the Early Stuarts* (Oxford, 1966), pp. 304–305.

[18] Supple, pp. 52 *et seq.* E. M. Leonard, *The Early History of English Poor Relief* (Cambridge, 1900), p. 148.

[19] *CJ* **1**: pp. 684, 694, 751, 779, 782. *Commons Debates 1621* **3**: p. 296. Wilson, p. 54. In any case, although one clause referred to "bodies politic or corporate," the monopolies statute excluded London, corporate towns, corporations, and fellowships. Carr, p. lxxii.

[20] See below, pp. 40, 45–48.

[21] *CJ* **2**: p. 277.

tion fine. The property could then be disposed of to the benefit of the creditors.[22] These were exceptional times, but the value of composition had been stressed and this might be of service in the future.

BANKRUPTS

Under the statutes of 1571 and 1604 English subjects, born or denizen, could commit an act of bankruptcy.[23] Aliens, a significant minority in the business community, were ignored but not directly excluded. Hence Englishmen feared, as a member of Parliament put it in 1621, "that strangers may transport themselves and [their] estates beyond [the] seas." [24] Aliens were specifically brought into the system both as bankrupts and creditors in 1624.[25] This statute also included scriveners, as had been propsed in 1621.[26] These men were important because like brokers—familiar in the world of finance but not mentioned in the statute—they engaged in incipient forms of banking. They traded in money, and their failure or dishonesty could have widespread repercussions. Here again bankruptcy legislation must be related to that concerning usury: the 1624 usury act noted scriveners and prescribed imprisonment for those who took more than the proper rate of interest.[27] There is evidence that scriveners had previously been declared bankrupt, but this had clearly been open to question.[28] Similar exigencies doubtless explain an order of 1645 that those responsible for rendering accounts were to be treated as bankrupts if they were in prison or absent for one month.[29]

The statutes were progressively explanatory. Initially it was stated that persons using the trade of merchandise—by bargaining, exchange and selling—were covered, as were those who sought their trade or living by buying and selling.[30] However, the introductory statements of 1604 and 1624, unlike that of 1571, did not specify merchants as such. This raised a question of law upon the construction of the statutes themselves, and this is one area in which it is more than ordinarily impossible to draw a general rule from particular cases. The point, for example, has been made that using an act of merchandise is common to every man. Every person buys and very often he sells as well, though this is less frequent. The implication of the statutes was that those covered must sell as well as buy as a means of living. Distinctions were difficult to determine, and we should not expect consistency. By and large, however, there were two developments. Over several decades, the application of these statutes was slowly limited to men and women who can be described as merchants and traders, and it was gradually assumed that they did not apply to landed persons. Second, by close interpretation of the words, specific means of living were indicated as being covered by the statutes. Even so, it was possible for one baker to be within the statutes whereas another was outside.[31]

One of the fascinations of bankruptcy is the way in which it compelled judges and lawyers to grope towards their own definitions of some social distinctions. In particular, there was the problem of determining what a gentleman was, the more so as it tended to be assumed that such a being could not really live by buying and selling. The statutes had said nothing about gentlemen. Certainly there was plenty of contemporary advice. A gentleman, it was said, should be taken for a gentleman or spend his money like a gentleman. He was "one who can live idly and without manual labor, and will bear the port, charge and countenance of a gentleman." [32] At times the debate, or rather the series of debates, could seem remote from reality. Was it possible to be a gentleman in one sense and yet to live by buying and selling? At first sight it would seem that in many cases the answer could only be positive. Furthermore, successful men who had risen in trade, or their sons, bought their way into land and later into landed society. Nor was it uncommon for younger sons to seek careers in trade, although subsequently they might revert to the habits and manner of country gentlemen.[33] The perennial problem of younger sons was related to primogeniture, a practice which was not legally required with respect to the devise of lands. John Earle wrote about the misfortune of younger sons of gentlemen denied the means to maintain that status but expected to live up to their birth. Withdrawal to the Low Countries or marriage to a rich widow often represented the last

[22] *Cal. Committee for Compounding Cases: Domestic, 1643–1660* pt 2: pp. 1019, 1099; pt 3: pp. 2351-2352; pt 4: p. 2501.

[23] 1571, *1; 1604, *1.

[24] *Commons Debates 1621* **5**: p. 176; **7**: pp. 104–108. By 1611, it had been decided that aliens could be made bankrupt, although they could not be petitioners. Hence an action of words lay. In any case, the allegation was damaging and there was, of course, the Henrician statute. Bulstrode, 134–135, Tirlot v. Morris; Yelverton, 198.

[25] 1624, *2.

[26] 1624, *2. *Commons Debates 1621* **7**: p. 105.

[27] 21 James I c. 17, *2.

[28] In 1596 a commission issued with respect to John Deane, scrivener of Holborn, who had gone broke for over £4,000. El. 5370. Scriveners were unique in that they were specifically mentioned in the 1624 statute. Hence, Nottingham would insist that a bankrupt scrivener should be named as such and not simply be described as a tradesman who lived by buying and selling. *Nottingham's Cases* **1**: p. 314.

[29] *Acts and Ordinances of the Interregnum, 1642–60* **1**: p. 720.

[30] 1571, *1; 1604, *1; 1624, *1, 2.

[31] See the analysis in *Petersdorff's Abridgement* (New York, 1829) **3**: pp. 315-320. There is a separate and very different story concerning interpretation of "exercising a trade" with respect to the Elizabethan statute of artificers (1563). However, in some cases this statute was used to determine whether a man was a trader and thus within the bankruptcy laws.

[32] Cited Wilson, p. 112.

[33] *Ibid.*, p. 10.

refuge. Some drifted into trade. This, as Edward Chamberlayne noted, could be managed without apprenticeship, but it seems that a number were in fact apprenticed to merchants.[34]

The difficulties implicit in the situation began to trouble the courts in the latter part of James I's reign. In 1620, the Chancery was confronted by a man who had been born a gentleman but made his living through buying and selling iron and similar transactions. A Chancery master, advising that the bankruptcy statutes seemed to apply, admitted that he had doubts "because it is a new case, and wanteth precedents, and concerneth a gentleman of good family, bred in another course." [35] There were many who occupied a gray area, such as the Cheshire person who described himself in 1640 as "a gentleman by birth and a linen draper by trade." [36] However, the judges were not directly concerned with social assumption and they were not asked to define the nature of a gentleman. Their task was to determine if a person gained his living by buying and selling and whether his transactions were comprehended within the meaning of the bankruptcy statutes. Thus a farmer, gentleman or otherwise, bought and sold, but he sold more than he bought in the way of business, and he was, anyhow, working his own estate. It followed that he was not embraced by the statutes. A number of distinctly commercial means of livelihood were likewise held to be excluded.[37]

Early adventurers into Virginia or Greenland, in contrast to Muscovy merchants, were not within the statutes. It was held that although they exchanged "trifles" with "the savages" their main concern was with plantation and discovery.[38] An important distinction was that eventually made between investment and active participation in commerce. Guidelines in this respect were not easily established and they did not exist before 1640. The critical case was that of Sir John Wolstenholme, a stockholder in the East India Company and formerly a prominent figure in the city of London, who was alleged to have gone bankrupt in or around June, 1646, to the tune of over £2,000. A bankruptcy commission was issued in July, 1650, and its membership was reconstituted in May, 1652. This was maintained in 1653 even though Wolstenholme had lands worth £3,000 *per annum* and it could not be established that he obtained "the greatest part of his living by buying and selling." All this was considered as being overshadowed by his work as an active member of the East India Company and its managing committee. After years of hesitation, the impact of this decision could have been cataclysmic: not least because some law reformers had castigated the inefficiency of laws which did not apply to debtors of all classes. Instead, the Restoration confirmed trends which are perhaps discernible during the Protectorate. The "Act Declaratory Concerning Bankrupts" of 1662 confronted the fact that persons "not bred up to trade" became members of public companies. In respect of their stock, members of the East India Company, the Guinea Company, and the "Royal Fishing Trade" were specifically excluded from liability under the bankruptcy statutes. The Wolstenholme decision was declared contrary to law and voided.[39] The supposition that members of a chartered company might not be declared bankrupt in respect of their stock was from the beginning extended by statute to shareholders of the Bank of England.[40]

In 1661, the reissued charter of the Levant Company had accorded a distinct position to contributors of capital and directors who might have little other connection with practical trading activities. It was stated that members of the company must be freemen of the city unless they lived within twenty miles of London and were "noblemen and gentlemen of quality who never were apprentices to, nor bred in, nor have applied themselves to any course of trade as their calling." [41] Such a stipulation, so important to the history of company development, reflects upon the financial involvement of aristocrats, gentlemen, lawyers, and other classes or professions in England's commercial expansion. It also reflects the long-existing gulf between great merchants and craftsmen or retailers. On the other side of the coin, it was decided by the second half of the seventeenth century that a chartered company could not be held liable in respect of the bankruptcy of one of its members. This was often stated as an important justification when a charter was being solicited; otherwise "the stock will be liable to the particular and private debts of the sev-

[34] J. Earle, *Microcosmography* (London, ed. of 1897), pp. 22–24. E. Chamberlayne, *Angliæ Notitia or the Present State of England* (2nd ed., London, 1669), pp. 444–445. Joan Thirsk, "Younger Sons in the Seventeenth Century," *History* **54** (Oct., 1969): pp. 358–377.

[35] Monro, p. 286.

[36] Wilson, p. 14. Of course, many general matters concerning status and honor were determined in the court of chivalry.

[37] Hutton, pp. 46, 49–50; 3 Mod., 328–331, Newton v. Trigg (1685).

[38] J. Stone, *The Reading upon the Statute of the Thirteenth of Elizabeth, Chapter 7, Touching Bankrupts* (London, 1656), p. 42.

[39] P.R.O., C.67/81, no. 11; C.67/83, no. 70. 14 Charles II c. 24. For some details on the Wolstenholme family, see T. K. Rabb, *Enterprise and Empire: Merchant and Gentry Investment in the Expansion of England, 1575–1630* (Cambridge, Mass., 1967), pp. 173–174. At this time, the Guinea and East India Companies were unique in their fiscal structure. Elsewhere each individual traded on his own account and thus, it was pointed out, could go bankrupt even if a gentleman. 2 Keble, 487, Cotton v. Daintry (1669). The Royal Fishing Company was incorporated in 1664.

[40] 8 and 9 William III c. 20, *47.

[41] Carr, p. xli, n. 9. The immediate purpose of this provision was to protect London by forcing merchants to take up freedom of the city. A. C. Wood, *A History of the Levant Company* (Oxford, 1935), p. 95.

eral partners and subject to be torn to pieces upon the bankruptcy of any of them."[42] In all this the judges played a part; across the seventeenth century their rulings assume considerable significance. However, cases that have been reported often center as much upon usage of the word *bankrupt* as upon the statutes.

Holdsworth warned that one of the most inadequate types of case law is to be found in that growing around the interpretation of words,[43] but judges over a long period do appear to have done their best by adhering to a narrow kind of logic. Many cases required them to decide whether a person could become a bankrupt. Most of these, although contrivance may be suspected, were not ostensible challenges to bankruptcy commissions which had been sued out. The question was whether use of the word *bankrupt* and other language constituted scandalous words. The phrase "knavish bankrupt" was often cited, and in the reign of James I it was ruled that "bankrupt knave" could be construed as two substantives and therefore might be scandalous and actionable. In most cases, it was necessary to decide if the person claiming to have been slandered was capable of becoming a bankrupt under the statutes. If he was, the words were heinous, damaging and scandalous. Malynes summed up the position: "so that to call a decayed gentleman a bankrupt (although he have had dealing in the world) beareth no action at the common law, unless he were a merchant or shopkeeper, etc."[44]

Before the end of the sixteenth century, it had been decided that it was actionable to call a shoemaker a bankrupt because he obtained his living through buying and selling.[45] This was clarified in the reign of Charles I when it was argued that a shoemaker lived by his credit as much as by his labor. As a corollary, it was stressed that those who lived only by manual labor—for instance, husbandmen and laborers—could not be brought within the statutes.[46] Similar reasoning was applied to other men and their crafts. In the reign of James I, for example, it was decided that a dyer was a trader within the meaning of the statutes.[47] The plaintiff in one action for words argued that he bargained and sold lead, but the defendant said there was no proof that this was the plaintiff's trade or that it constituted his means of living. In any case, he was styled as a gentleman. Nonetheless, it was decided that an action lay, and an Elizabethan decision was cited to the effect that a tanner could have such an action.[48] Soon after it was made clear that all points had to be established. Buying and selling were not enough. It had also to be shown that this activity constituted both the trade and the livelihood of the complaining party.[49] Inevitably this approach allowed of many variations. In the middle of the seventeenth century, it was understood that the statutes applied to innkeepers,[50] but it was later decided that these should be excluded. An innkeeper who put an unreasonable price on the goods which he sold to travelers would be committing an offense which came within the jurisdiction of the justices of the peace. Although he bought things, he did not sell them in such a fashion as to become a trader. Furthermore, unlike a dyer or a shoemaker, he did not work with other men's goods in the normal sense. He did not buy and sell by way of contract, but for a price made his lodging, comfort, and provisions available to travelers.[51] In 1697 these principles were again confirmed, and it was repeated that farmers were not traders within the meaning of the acts. Soon after an old principle was underlined when it was predictably ruled that an infant could not be made a bankrupt because his debts were voidable: "no man can be a bankrupt for debts which he is not obliged to pay."[52] In this case the judges had taken a direct look at a bankruptcy problem, but in most situations their intervention, as it affected interpretation of the bankruptcy statutes, was subsidiary to the principal issue in dispute.[53]

---

[42] Carr, pp. xvii–xviii, ci–cii. In the nineteenth century, members were still liable for the debts of their company, but a careful distinction was made between the individual and the company. Bankruptcy of the company was not to be construed as the bankruptcy of any member. For this and later developments of the nineteenth century, including the position of shareholders and the role of Chancery, see C. A. Cooke, *Corporation, Trust and Company* (Manchester, 1951), pp. 139–140, 146–151, 161–163, 172.

[43] Holdsworth **5**: pp. 206–207.

[44] Cro. Jac., 345, Selby v. Carrier (*ca.* 1614). D. Mellinkoff, *The Language of the Law* (Boston, 1963), p. 175. Malynes, *Lex Mercatoria*, p. 157.

[45] Cro. Eliz., 268, Stanley v. Osbaston (*ca.* 1592).

[46] Cro. Car., 31, Crumpe v. Barne (1626). Goodinge, p. 12.

[47] Cro. Jac., 585, Squire v. Johns (1620). A dyer had previously had a bankruptcy commission awarded against him. El. 3543.

[48] Hutton, 46, Allen v. Swift (1621). There was question in another case whether indeed a tanner could have an action for the words, "thou art a bankrupt knave." 1 Brownl. & Golds., 16, York v. Cecil (1616). In 1652, a bankruptcy commission was issued with respect to a tanner of Derby. P.R.O., C.67/83, no. 29.

[49] Hutton, 49–50, Hawkins v. Cutts (1622). Occupations cannot be put into neat categories. One favorite example of the times was provided by bakers. Generally these were within the statutes, but a person could be known as a baker and largely work as a baker and yet be excluded because the trading element was not strong enough or because the work was actually subsidiary to the means of livelihood, as in the case of a servant in a large establishment.

[50] Stone, *Reading*, p. 43. P.R.O., C.67/81, no. 31 is a commission with respect to the bankruptcy of an "innholder" of Essex.

[51] 3 Mod., 328–331, Newton v. Trigg (1685). See Cro. Car., 549–551, Crisp v. Pratt (1635).

[52] 1 Ld Ray., 286–287, Meggot v. Mills (1697); 443, Rex v. Cole (1699–1700).

[53] There were a host of these decisions which grew in number from the Restoration. A summary is to be found in 2 Co. Rep., 25a, n. (B), 76 *English Reports*. A survey was provided by Goodinge, pp. 166–175.

Women appear as bankrupts, occasionally as partners but more commonly as widows who had assumed a shop or trade. Furthermore, a commercially active wife might have a distinct position under the custom of London: a majority of Common Pleas judges did not accept the proposition that she was construed by law to be the servant of her husband. For by the custom it was possible for her to be a *feme sole merchant*: "the *feme* trades by herself in one trade, with which her husband doth not meddle, and buys and sells in that trade." [54]

ACTS OF BANKRUPTCY

A person could only become a bankrupt if he behaved in a fashion specified by the statutes, and if his creditors opted to follow a procedure allowed by this legislation. It was always, if reluctantly, recognized that men might be unfortunate—bad debts and losses at sea were favorite examples—but this had nothing to do with it. The nature and size of the debt, unless it was small, was irrelevant. Bankruptcy followed from a particular kind of action committed by a definable man in a stipulated situation. The occupation of the debtor and the act of bankruptcy were equally important. Thus in the middle of the seventeenth century, bankruptcy commissions usually specified that the debtor employed himself in merchandise by way of bargaining and exchanging, and that he had gone bankrupt with the intent of defrauding and hindering the petitioning creditors.[55] Intent was always important. The debtor might commit one of the stipulated actions and yet claim that it was fortuitous.

According to the 1571 statute, a person could be declared bankrupt if he left the country, otherwise absented himself, kept to his house, sought sanctuary, was arrested for debt "or other thing not grown or due for money delivered wares sold or any other just or lawful cause or good consideration or purposes," was outlawed, or departed from his house with the intention of defrauding creditors. Clearly these conditions were often in need of interpretation, and they probably provided the principal basis for early disputes at law. The charge that a debtor kept to his house, for example, had to be proved by consistent behavior. Unless the intent was to commit bankruptcy or to defraud creditors, one who retreated behind his doors to evade certain types of process but subsequently went out was not a bankrupt. Likewise, a number of cases determined that a trader might be consistently unavailable at his house, but he had not committed an act of bankruptcy if he continued to appear and be seen in such central trading places as the Exchange.[56]

[54] Cro. Car., 68–69, Langham v. Bewett (1627).

[55] For example, P.R.O., C.67/77, no. 2. The bankrupt was a fishmonger of London.

[56] 1571, *1. Cro. Eliz., 13 (1582). In 1613, a newly chosen chamberlain of Bristol was dismissed. This man, "being indebted and behind hand by losses at sea, was fain to keep house at St. James's Fair following for debt." *Merchants and Merchandise in Seventeenth-Century Bristol*, ed. P. McGrath, Bristol Rec. Soc. (1955), p. 173.

That the descriptions given in 1571 were insufficient to embrace the variety of situations which might arise was tacitly acknowledged by the 1604 statute. The list of circumstances then given, together with verbal modifications, may provide a clue as to some of the difficulties which had occurred.[57]

In 1604, there was a greater concentration upon fraudulent behavior. The phrase "yield him or herself to prison" was employed in both statutes, but it was now clear that conniving at one's own arrest or procuring the attachment and sequestration of one's goods were actions constituting bankruptcy. Imprisonment for six months on account of debt was to be construed as revealing that kind of dishonesty which justified bankruptcy proceedings. Equally important was the simple statement that a fraudulent grant or conveyance of lands, tenements, goods, and chattels constituted an act of bankruptcy. The 1571 statute had only specified punishment for those who fraudulently acquired the debtor's assets before or after the act of bankruptcy.[58]

If we are to believe Dekker and Malynes, granted that the former talked about bankrupts in a loose fashion, the statutes so far had failed abysmally. Dekker made strident comments on the futility of legislation passed in 1543, 1571, and 1604. He was incensed at the way in which the broad and high-sounding preamble to the Henrician act, which in its wording should have eliminated the scope for scoundrels, seemed to count for nothing. This time considering the wiles of the crafty rather than the calamity of the unfortunate, he described how "politic bankrupts" manipulated both the bankruptcy laws and imprisonment for debt itself. A "man-eater" could defeat descriptions of an act of bankruptcy by locking himself in his house and yet making judicious appearances. He would barricade his lair with double locks, triple doors, invincible bolts, and pieces of timber, yet emerge to sell "the goods of his neighbor before his face without blushes." As for imprisonment, that had become a form of refuge.

> Strong and cunning nets were spread by those Parliaments to catch these foxes. Yet how many of them have been since, and at this hour are, earthed in the King's Bench, the Fleet and that abused sanctuary of Ludgate! Here they play at bowls, lie in fair chambers within the Rule, fare like Dives, laugh at Lazarus, can walk up and down many times by *habeas corpus* and jeer their creditors. There they lie barricadoed within King Lud's bulwark against gun-shot; there they strut up and down the prison like magnificos in Venice on the Rialto, brave in their clothes, spruce in ruffs, with gold-wrought night-caps on their heads. They feed deliciously, plenteously, voluptuously,

[57] 1571, *1; 1604, *1.

[58] 1571, *1, 6; 1604, *1.

have excellent wines to drink, handsome wives to lie with when they please, who come in not like the wives of prisoners but of the best and wealthiest citizens. These men command the stone walls, not the walls them.

Dekker was colorful, but unlike some other critics of prison life he commented directly on the bankruptcy statutes. His tirade illustrates the swell of public anger and the feeling that hitherto statutory description of acts of bankruptcy was so inept that proceedings could not even be begun in many cases. This was the lengthy background to the second Jacobean statute, that of the king's last Parliament. Something would be done along the desired lines, and this would be the basis for bankruptcy proceedings until the end of the century. The revisions as first sight seem tepid and unsatisfactory, as doubtless they were, but the presumed increase in the number of bankruptcy commissions sued out by and after the Restoration may indicate that some sinew had been added to the rules.[59]

In 1624, previous descriptions of acts of bankruptcy were repeated and extended. In particular, the statute mentioned procurement of protections and attempts to get creditors to accept compositions whereby they either took less than was due or conceded further time for payment. These provisions were blows against the Privy Council and some courts, especially Chancery, but it was still quite proper for debtors to arrange meetings with creditors prior to debts becoming due in order to solicit licenses for further time or other arrangements. This would not be an act of bankruptcy since neither fraud nor the intent to defraud was present.[60] Other circumstances included failure to pay, or an attempt to compound for, a debt of £100 or more six months after it was due, or arrest for such a debt. An act of bankruptcy had also occurred if nothing was received within six months of a writ to recover debt being sued out with proper notice, or if the debtor stayed in prison for two months on this or any other action for debt. A person arrested for debt—again this was to be £100 or more—who escaped or obtained some sort of bail was to be adjudged a bankrupt, the state of bankruptcy beginning from the time of the original arrest. Thus was it hoped to bar much of the in-and-out usage of prison as a sanctuary to evade bankruptcy which Dekker had deplored.[61]

[59] Dekker, *Sinnes of London*, pp. 23–24; *Lanthorne and Candle-light*, pp. 275–276. Other writers were equally critical. In 1618, Geoffrey Mynshul described prisons as "your bankrupt's banqueting house" where debtors made themselves "galley-slaves only to wear golden fetters." D. Veall, *The Popular Movement for Law Reform, 1640–1660* (Oxford, 1970), p. 14.

[60] 1624, *2. Goodinge, p. 28. This was an affirmation of common business practice, if properly conducted.

[61] 1624, *2.

INITIAL PROCEDURE

The lord chancellor alone was authorized to issue commissions of bankruptcy under the Great Seal and to appoint "such wise and honest discreet persons as to him shall seem good." He would do this on receiving a complaint or petition in writing.[62] The practice developed, certainly during the Stuart period, that this must be accompanied by an affidavit that debts were owed—from 1624 the specific sum of £100 or more had to be mentioned—and that an act of bankruptcy had been committed.[63] The petitioning creditors would suggest the names of possible commissioners in a separate document, and these would be listed by the clerk of the commissions for the benefit of the lord chancellor. After names had been deleted or added, the petition and docket were returned to the clerk who then engrossed a commission on parchment for the seal. In the seventeenth century, petitioning creditors were required to enter bonds as to the veracity of their claim that the debtor was a bankrupt. This, although not automatic, was probably also done in the Elizabethan period.[64]

In selecting and adding names, lord chancellors prior to the 1630's probably tried to avoid using the same people on too many occasions. There was also the danger, as Nottingham later pointed out, of "worthy" men being named, perhaps to give credit to the commission, and yet not attending the proceedings.[65] During Puckering's lord keepership in the 1590's, most commissions seem to have numbered seven persons with a quorum of four, but some numbered nine with a quorum of five. Some smaller commissions were appointed but this was unusual, and indeed Puckering seems to have increased the membership of many suggested commissions from five to seven. The commission, as it finally appeared, often contained a number of people, for instance members of the debtor's own company, who might be expected to deal fairly with him.[66] However, the prime purpose was to employ men who were familiar with the debtor, his holdings, worth and trade. One commission was altered because the men appointed lived rather far away from the bankrupt.[67] All the creditors of Christopher Gaunt, a chapman of King's Lynn, were members of London companies, but the commission was made up of five men from King's Lynn, including the recorder, together with Nicholas Hare

[62] 1571, *2. The occasional complaint was made to the queen and forwarded to the lord chancellor. *CSP Dom.* 1581–1590, p. 271.

[63] Goodinge, p. 2.

[64] P.R.O., E.333/17. When demanded, the minimum sum was usually £200, and this became standard from 1619. Sanders 1, i: p. 122. Nottingham once demanded £500. *Nottingham's 'Manual'*, p. 163.

[65] Sanders 1, i: p. 122. *Nottingham's 'Manual'*, pp. 163–164.

[66] El. 4092, 4093, 4271, 4279, 4395.

[67] El. 5392.

of Stoebarden, Norfolk, and a solitary London merchant.[68] In another case, three merchant tailors were included in the commission although all the creditors followed that trade.[69] Aldermen, businessmen, and gentlemen made up the bulk of commissioners appointed in the 1590's. On occasion, a scrivener was appointed.[70] Legal talent included local recorders, serjeants-at-law, and persons such as William Aubrey, Julius Caesar, and Henry Hobart.[71] William Mill, clerk of the Star Chamber, was appointed to one commission, and Mr. Justic Clench was selected when Thomas Dedham of Ipswich went broke.[72] Francis Bacon, as lord chancellor in 1619, directed that someone learned in the law must always be included, and there is evidence to suggest that this became more or less the rule.[73]

At least up to the 1630's, there does not seem to have been much departure from late Elizabethan practice. A typical commission might include three barristers and four "attorneys" (the use of this word did not carry the usual connotation, and the men so described were gentlemen or merchants).[74] However, by the outbreak of the civil war, and probably before, commissions tended to be smaller, numbering five or even three, and lawyers were less noticeable. This was apparently because a slate of regular or professional commissioners had emerged, those who would be condemned by Leach as "monopolizing commissioners and officers, or so pretended. . . ."[75] Between 1642 and 1654, the events of war and Interregnum making little difference to the pattern, some names come up repeatedly: John, George, and William Norbury, members of a Chancery clerical family; Anthony Boys, George Cotton, and John Penrice. In other words, the situation was that which a few decades earlier may have been deemed undesirable.[76] It was usual to specify one of these men as a member of the quorum although others might also be named to the commission. This is most apparent with respect to bankruptcies in London and its environs. On occasion, the commission included one of the regulars but indicated that he was to be a sleeping partner. John Penrice mostly appeared on London commissions, but in the case of a Bristol mercer he was placed second on the commission to John Wentworth, Esq., who was to do the actual work. The implication is that the regular panel had a financial interest in the work of bankruptcy commissions. It must be supposed that the emergence of these men is closely related to the growth of an administrative organization surrounding the issue and documentation of commissions.[77]

Once the commissioners had been appointed, the next task was to find the bankrupt. Since his nonavailability—usually he was described as being "late" of London or some other place—was often the occasion for proceedings, this might be no more than a formality. In these circumstances, the 1571 statute required the commissioners to ensure that a proclamation was made in the appropriate market place on five market days. Nonappearance placed the bankrupt outside royal protection, and his helpers and concealers were to be fined and imprisoned.[78] Under the 1604 statute lawful warning was to be left in writing on three occasions at the place where the bankrupt, his wife and family had normally lived or lodged during the previous year. After failure to appear, the commissioners were to send a precept to the relevant local officials—for instance, the bailiffs of Southwark—requiring them to make proclamation on five market days. If the bankrupt still did not come in, he could be arrested by warrant of the commissioners wherever he was found, "in place privileged or not."[79] This phrase was ambiguous. Election to the House of Commons as a device to frustrate creditors was not unknown. Bacon, replying to the speaker's request for privileges in 1621, said that freedom from arrest was granted but the king trusted that the House would be "moderate in granting their protections." It was "a great abuse to justice, a distaste to his Majesty, a scandal to themselves, and a wrong to their creditors, for them to countenance bankrupts, and by that means to free dishonest men from the arrest of such as were truly damnified by their bad dealing."[80] Whatever members of Parliament may have thought about the lord chancellor's own leniency towards some debtors, they were still worried about evasions of the bankruptcy statutes. It was proposed that those who failed to appear—a neglect described as worse than burglary or highway robbery—should be treated as felons and face a possible death penalty. A

[68] El. 3558.

[69] El. 3998.

[70] El. 3429.

[71] El. 4072, 4395, 4871, 5370.

[72] El. 3991, 4279.

[73] Sanders 1, i: p. 122. Malynes confirms the extensive use of lawyers. *Lex Mercatoria*, p. 158. However, Bacon's order may indicate that the legal element had been declining or questioned. See also *Nottingham's 'Manual'*, p. 163.

[74] P.R.O., E.333/17.

[75] Leach, *Proposals for an Act*, p. 17.

[76] P.R.O., C.67/76a-85.

[77] P.R.O., C.67/83, no. 25 (1652).

[78] 1571, *8.

[79] 1604, *4. W. West, *The Second Part of Symboleography* (London, 1618), sect., 154–159.

[80] Bacon was probably using the word *bankrupt* in its popular sense. The problem posed by debtor members of Parliament, who were for a time able to evade their creditors, was an old one. Little had been done to improve the situation by the eighteenth century. L. B. Namier, *The Structure of Politics at the Accession of George III* (London, 1957), pp. 55, n. 1, 59–61. Namier may have used the word *bankrupt* where *debtor* would be more appropriate. For the position of peers, as later explained, see 1 Atk., 201, *ex parte* Meymot (1747); 4 George III c. 33.

variety of such proposals, made in both 1621 and 1624, found no place in the legislation of the latter year.[81]

It is probable that nearly all bankrupts, appearing of their own volition or apprehended, were imprisoned. If, however, a bankrupt's behavior was reasonable, he could subsequently be licensed to move about freely in order to assist in the settlement of his affairs and debts. Before this freedom could normally be granted, the first task of the commissioners was to examine creditors and other witnesses in order to establish the facts: whether the debtor's living and trade brought him within the statutes, the nature of the alleged act of bankruptcy, and the structure of his debts and obligations. If sufficient facts were proven, the commissioners would declare the debtor to be a bankrupt. The debtor, however, might deny that he had committed any such act, challenge the petitioners' version of his debts, or argue that he was not a trader within the meaning of the bankruptcy legislation. At least with respect to the latter point, it seems that in the early Stuart period he might file a *caveat* against grant of the commission or petition the lord chancellor to suspend an awarded commission by *supersedeas* until the point was decided. Nottingham recalled having seen a note that a commission had once been granted solely to determine whether the debtor was a bankrupt, but he concluded that such limited commissions were improper. In the 1640's, it seems to have been decided that the commission ought to be granted and doubts or questions tried upon the commission. This was in accordance with the implications of some rather indirectly worded clauses of the 1604 and 1624 statutes. It clearly was intended that the commissioners were to prove the debtor's status and make a declaration of bankruptcy. On the other hand, it seems that by the end of the seventeenth century they tended in their wording and pronouncements to be increasingly cautious. Rather than risking actions against themselves, despite the ground rules for such established in 1604, it may even be that they welcomed initiative from interested parties which left the fact of bankruptcy to trial at law. This could be achieved in many ways, possibly after distribution had commenced. Thus Goodinge noted, for example, that any execution on a judgment that debt was due could be stopped by alleging that a commission of bankruptcy had been issued against the successful plaintiff. Having chosen this course, the assignee of the commission had to take out a special *scire facias* or bring an action of detinue on the judgment to try whether or not the man was a bankrupt.[82]

[81] P.R.O., S.P.14/160, no. 74.

[82] Goodinge, pp. 48, 62, 106. Noy, 140, Edward's Case (n.d.). Monro, p. 286. *Nottingham's 'Manual'*, pp. 161–164. 1604, *11; 1624, *13.

CLERKS AND OFFICIALS

The lord chancellor was authorized to issue bankruptcy commissions but none of the statutes indicated who was to do the clerical work. It was probably assumed that the task could be delegated. After 1571 the work was done by Jasper Fisher, one of the Chancery six clerks. Fisher died insolvent after building a house in London equipped with "gardens of pleasure, bowling-alleys and the like," which became known as "Fisher's Folly."[83] Later in Elizabeth's reign, responsibility was assumed by Thomas Powle. This decrepit but influential official held several positions in the court of Chancery including those of a six clerk and clerk of the crown. On his death, the job was granted by Lord Keeper Egerton to Bartrobe Lukin, but early in the reign of James I this was challenged by the new clerk of the crown, George Coppin.[84]

Coppin claimed that the clerk of the crown in Chancery, as a minister of the court of Parliament, was vested with the right to make all commissions created by statute. Lord Keeper Nicholas Bacon, said Coppin, would not have allowed Jasper Fisher to do this work if he had been aware of the rights and responsibilities of the clerk of the crown. He dismissed as a fabrication Lukin's argument that Lord Chancellor Hatton (1587–1591) had given this responsibility to one of his followers. In fact the real difficulty was posed by Powle's career. He had continued as nominal clerk of the crown although he had conveyed responsibility to a deputy, a surrender so complete that the *House of Commons Journal* sometimes refers to that deputy as "clerk of the crown." Bankruptcy commissions, however, had been engrossed in Powle's six clerk's office and this seemed to suggest that the work was considered to be distinct.[85] It is difficult not to feel some sympathy for the tenor of Coppin's arguments, but events since the 1571 statute were against him. Egerton's inquiry into Chancery fees, ordered in 1598, treated the clerk who made out bankruptcy commissions as a distinct official. This independence was to be maintained, although the position was again at times associated with the clerk of the crown.[86]

The dispute may help to explain the failure to enroll bankruptcy commissions noted by William Lambarde in 1596. Other commissions were also not being enrolled, but bankruptcy commissions were not included by name in the 1599 Chancery order listing commissions which should henceforth be enrolled.

[83] Monro, p. 343.

[84] El. 2955, 2956.

[85] El. 2954–2957, 2999. W. J. Jones, *The Elizabethan Court of Chancery* (Oxford, 1967), pp. 130–134.

[86] *Parliamentary Accounts and Papers*, 1830–1831, viii (1), p. 25. H. C. Maxwell-Lyte, *Historical Notes on the Use of the Great Seal of England* (London, 1926), pp. 272, 280–281.

Uncertainty over responsibility and fees may have been a factor.[87]

Administrators involved in the issue of bankruptcy commissions were subjected to close scrutiny by commissioners authorized to inquire into fees during the 1620's and the 1630's. According to the 1598 inquiry into Chancery fees, the cost of obtaining a bankruptcy commission was in part rated upon the valuation of those goods for which the debtor had gone broke. There was a minimum charge of two shillings, and additional fees included two shillings for the seal and two shillings and four pence for enrollment. These costs were justified by Lukin on the grounds that preparation of commissions involved labor out of all proportion to the paucity of their number.[88] Lukin was probably responsible for establishing a fee of £4 13s. 4d. for making the bill, preparing the docket of the commission for engrossment, and securing the seal. However, James I granted an office to John Latch and Humphrey Bradbourne. The work was done by their deputy, Matthew Colborne, who had a position in a six clerk's office and was also deputy for the office of writing patents of denization. He probably took over the clerical work involved in the issue of bankruptcy commissions, and he was accused in the early 1630's of allowing the basic fee to rise to £5 10s. 0d.[89]

Another position, that of examiner and register of commissions of bankruptcy, created in 1618, was granted to Edward Hawkins with reversion to Christopher Colby and further reversion to the son of Hawkins. The senior Hawkins worked through a deputy, and the office was established in Ivy Lane, St. Paul's. This creation by letters patent was criticized, not least because of the uncertainty surrounding fees and gratuities. Yet the office can probably be regarded as more helpful than malign. King James said that he was advised by Bacon and other experts, and it was said that there had been confusion in the keeping of bankruptcy documents and proceedings, with resulting difficulties for persons who were "aggrieved." [90] This was a typical apologia for the creation of a new office, and the list of advisers mentioned calls to mind the referees attacked in the 1621 Parliament. In this instance, however, there seems to have been some justification. It is doubtful if the clerk who issued bankruptcy commissions had been able to handle subsequent challenges or the need of persons to whom goods had been assigned to establish their titles.

The new office was responsible for most of the necessary paper and procedural work for commissions executed within the city of London and its suburbs. This included proclamations and warrants of appearance, apprehension, and summons; the drawing and writing of interrogatories and the taking of depositions; the drawing and engrossing of indentures of assignment and schedules, provision of copies, and much other work. This list of responsibilities gives some indication of practical matters outside the scope of statute. Clerks were appointed, and by 1638 the office had passed to John Booker, who, like his predecessors, worked through a deputy, John Bolles. The need for commissions to be made public as soon as possible, so that creditors would receive notice, had been put forward as an argument for the creation of this register. In practice the effective deputy was expected to attend meetings of commissioners, and he became an expert and adviser on procedures.[91] Despite objections, this office was described as very "commodious" to the public by one who wanted similar arrangements to be made for the rest of England. Charles I granted a patent in March, 1639, for the creation of an office to deal with bankruptcy commissions executed outside the metropolitan area, but this was revoked in the following month.[92] Despite contortions of policy, a beginning had nonetheless been made toward a division between the London area and the rest of the country which was to be a feature of bankruptcy proceedings in the eighteenth century. Perhaps this distinction received an impetus during the Republic, when commissioners for imprisoned debtors in the metropolitan area were required to act as though they were commissioners of bankruptcy. If so, it also means that an attempt was being made to breach the wall between bankrupts and other debtors. It was stated that those imprisoned for debt

[87] P. L. Ward, "William Lambarde's Collections on Chancery," *Harvard Library Bulletin* (1953) **7**: p. 281 and n. 40. Sanders **1**, i: pp. 80–82.

[88] *Parliamentary Papers*, p. 25. Sanders **1**, i: p. 141. El. 2957.

[89] *CSP Dom.* 1619–1623, p. 12. P.R.O., E.215/1/2/23; E.215/2/224, 225, 226. In August, 1632, the office for executing the laws and statutes against bankrupts was renewed to John Latch and Thomas Jennys. *D.K.Rep.* **48**, App.: p. 462.

[90] P.R.O., E.215/3/235. During James I's reign, various proposals dealing with bankruptcy matters were put forward by projectors. *Commons Debates 1621* **7**: 469 n.1.

[91] *CSP Dom.* 1611–1618, pp. 539, 567. P.R.O., E.215/1/2/22; E.215/2/227; E.215/2/229, nos. 1, 2; E.215/3/232–235. It was established that this official was a sworn officer of Chancery, constantly attendant on the court, and thus possessing all the privileges due to that position. This meant, among other things, that he was privileged to sue and be sued in Chancery insofar as the court had jurisdiction. Sanders 1, i: p. 141. Publication of commissions was sometimes delayed, and so creditors did not receive immediate notice. *Nottingham's 'Manual'*, p. 164.

[92] *CSP Dom.* 1640–1641, p. 356. W. H. Price, *The English Patents of Monopoly* (Cambridge, Mass., 1913), pp. 171, 174. *Privy Council Registers* 1637–1645 (London, 1967–1968) **5**: p. 209; **10**: p. 438. Complaints in the reign of Charles II led to the appointment of an inspector who was also given responsibility for keeping commissions, depositions, and proceedings. The places "adjacent" to London and Westminster expanded to comprise Middlesex, Essex, Hertfordshire, Surrey, Sussex, Buckinghamshire, Berkshire, and Kent. Sanders 1, i: pp. 354–355.

would become bankrupts unless they settled their accounts by 1 April, 1654.[93]

GENERAL POWERS OF THE COMMISSIONERS

Bankruptcy commissions were expected to obtain restitution for the creditors. The only concession made to the bankrupt was his right to receive an account, information about the disposal of his lands and goods, and delivery of anything which remained after the creditors had been satisfied.[94]

The 1571 statute empowered commissioners to apprehend the bankrupt's person and to dispose of his property to the benefit of the creditors.[95] This involved the seizure, valuation, and sale of chattels, effects, goods, lands, and movables, including cash and debts. Unless directly transferred to creditors, everything was to be sold for their benefit. One or two of the creditors would be appointed as overseers for this valuation, sale, and distribution.[96]

The most obvious difficulty was occasioned by one of the specified acts of bankruptcy: when a debtor locked himself in his house. The statutes of 1571 and 1604 gave inadequate guidance as to how the bankrupt and his property were to be seized. To open the door of a house implied the use of force, but this was not sanctioned. Hence the complaints of Dekker and that provision of the 1624 statute which empowered commissioners to break open the doors of houses and shops.[97]

The 1571 statute was weak in other ways. The commissioners were authorized to examine various persons,[98] but nothing was said as to the examination of the bankrupt himself. It seems that "secret" and "subtle" bankrupts refused to be examined. This anomaly was tackled in 1604. Bankrupts, refusing examination on interrogatories as to the whereabouts of their possessions, were henceforth to be imprisoned until they submitted. Perjury, to the value of £10 or more to the damage of the creditors, could bring the offender to the pillory. Here he was to stand for two hours with one ear nailed and then cut off.[99] This punishment was confirmed in 1624 and extended to bankrupts who were convicted of conveying or concealing property worth £20. Indictment was to be at the assizes or general sessions in the place where the debtor had become bankrupt.[100]

It took decades before commissions were given an effective authority for interrogation. The bankrupt himself might be acquiescent or apprehended, but under the rules of 1571 and 1604 little could be done about his wife, even though she might have concealed cash, jewelry, plate, and other property. It was ruled that examination of a bankrupt's wife to prove bankruptcy certainly was contrary to law. As a corollary it was noted that a wife, unlike a son, was not bound to "reveal" her husband's treason. However, the 1624 statute allowed her to be examined for discovery of assets.[101]

Other persons had always been liable to sworn examination about the bankrupt's effects, conducted in any style convenient to the commissioners. This implied that *viva voce* examination was acceptable, but written interrogatories and depositions were probably favored. Anyone who refused to be examined, who declined to disclose effects in his possession, or who fraudulently obtained effects, was liable to a penalty double the value of the goods. In 1571, however, guidelines were not given as to how examination might be compelled or a double penalty collected.[102]

Parliament in 1604 tried to remove difficulties which had restricted operation of the Elizabethan statute. Persons suspected of having a bankrupt's property were to be submitted to sworn examination on interrogatories. Recalcitrants could be arrested and imprisoned, without bail or mainprise, until they complied. Those suspected of perjury were to be prosecuted under the 1563 perjury statute. On the other hand, some consideration was shown: witnesses were to receive their costs and charges.[103] The ability of commissioners to examine was again strengthened in 1624.[104]

The powers of bankruptcy commissioners were terminated by the death of the sovereign, but late in the Restoration period it was decided that a new commission could work from the point where the previous one had expired.[105] This problem was not abnormal. Bankruptcy commissions were also faced by less regal forms of extinction. The 1604 statute permitted continuation of proceedings despite the death of the bankrupt.[106] It was later explained that the commission was nonetheless extinguished unless it had started work before the bankrupt died.[107]

There were other statutory weaknesses. Eliza-

---

[93] *Acts and Ordinances of the Interregnum* 2: pp. 753–754, 763.

[94] 1571, *4. 1604, *10.

[95] 1571, *2.

[96] West, sect., 154–159.

[97] 1624, *7. See above, pp. 24–25.

[98] 1571, *5, 6. See below.

[99] 1604, *4. Although not stated, conviction could possibly be under the perjury statute of 1563 which was mentioned in connection with the perjury of witnesses and others. 1604, *6.

[100] 1624, *6.

[101] 1624, *5. 1 Brownl. & Golds., 47 (1612). *Commons Debates 1621* 3: p. 296.

[102] 1571, *5. 1624, *8. Witnesses not involved as creditors could be examined. E.333/17.

[103] 1604, *5, 6.

[104] 1624, *8.

[105] 1 Eq. Ca. Abr., 52 (1687). Only altered by 5 George II c. 30, *45.

[106] 1604, *12. This presumably was from the date when the commission made a declaration of bankruptcy.

[107] *Nottingham's Cases* 1: p. 315. 1 Eq. Ca. Abr., 52 (1687).

bethan and early Stuart bankruptcy commissions, certainly before 1624, worked under some very severe handicaps.

CREDITORS

In most situations of debt there was bound to be suspicion among creditors, the fear being that some would come to terms with the debtor or with the administrators of an estate. One case, although not a matter of bankruptcy, illustrates the reality of this danger.

Magdalene Stoakes was the widow and executrix of a man who had left goods worth £5,000. This was supposedly sufficient to cover the testator's debts and legacies, but he had stood surety for several people. These combined with the widow to obtain judgments "by consent" at common law "of all the forfeiture[s] of the said bonds suffered (for the most part) by herself to incur, and for some others of which there was composition made in the life of the said testator, and for some after his death." In consequence "there were none of the creditors paid, but such only as the defendant, Stoakes, favored . . . whereas the complainant [in Chancery] with divers others were left unsatisfied of their due and lawful debts growing by like bonds and specialities." The executrix, indeed, had pleaded against an action of debt that she had insufficient assets to satisfy the debts claimed by those creditors who had not already made an agreement with her. Issue was reached, but before judgment a bill was exhibited in Chancery. The reason for this switch in tactics and courts was apparent. As William Lambarde put it, "the said recoveries will not be adjudged fraudulent at the common law, because the same were had upon just forfeitures in the eyes of that law" even though they had been "procured by combination and practice to the defeating of the testator's other due debts." The executrix had made "easy compositions with the creditors, that were parties to the fraud, which nevertheless will be taken for no fraud at the common law." Chancery, concluded Lambarde, could well be occupied "in examining these practices, the rather because many nowadays grow bold to commit the same, and such like, upon assurance that by the common law they are not to be touched therefore." [108]

Lambarde's report has been mentioned here because he clearly thought that a problem existed, and because in the search for solutions he was helping to inaugurate an approach which two decades later would have shattering consequences for Francis Bacon.[109] In the meantime, bankruptcy statutes were based upon the proposition that individual creditors should not benefit or receive back debts at the expense of other creditors. Coke, looking at the situation with a particular eye to the 1571 statute, pointed out that the intention was to

> relieve the creditors of the bankrupt equally, and that there should be an equal and ratable proportion observed in the distribution of the bankrupt's goods amongst the creditors, having regard to the quantity of their several debts; so that one should not prevent the other, but all should be in *æquali jure*.[110]

The commissioners were indeed authorized to make a proportionate division among the creditors.[111] However, they were plagued by creditors who, although they had joined in the commission, claimed priority on the ground of legal decisions and recorded bonds—valid forms of judgment—on which execution had not been sued out. Only in 1624, after the major crisis of 1616,[112] was statutory guidance provided. This took the form of a restatement that creditors joining in the commission must comply with the essential principle of equal division. This rule was to cover all judgments and bonds—including those of sureties—execution of which had not been sued out before the debtor committed his act of bankruptcy.[113]

A single creditor or group of creditors could petition for a commission. The first two statutes gave little guidance in these circumstances, but a convention de-

---

[108] P.R.O., C.39/24, Muschamp v. Stoakes (1598). The statutes against fraudulent conveyances might also help. Henry VII's statute (see above, p. 15) had voided fraudulent alienations by the debtor, but it needed subsequent legislation—notably the combined effort of the two 1571 statutes—to build some few fences against alienation for the benefit of others, notably favored creditors. Reeves **3**: p. 291 n.(a). Hudson noted that "where a man being indebted to many will deliver his goods to the satisfying of one expecting relief from him, and so the rest are wholly unsatisfied, this delivery (although there were a just debt)" constituted a fraudulent deed within the meaning of 13 Elizabeth I c. 5. W. Hudson, "A Treatise on the Court of Star Chamber," *Collectanea Juridica*, ed. F. Hargrave 2 (London, 1792): p. 97. See below for problems of composition and conformity, pp. 45–48.

[109] See below, pp. 45–48.

[110] 2 Co. Rep., 25b.

[111] There was always concern that the bankrupt might get his friends to petition for a commission. These pseudo-creditors might, as Nottingham feared, "huddle up" the execution of a commission and so defeat the interests of other creditors. He proposed that petitioners should be required to provide an affidavit that they would prosecute the commission truly and *bonâ fide*, and affirm that they did not have any secret arrangements with the bankrupt. *Nottingham's 'Manual'*, p. 163.

[112] See below, p. 45.

[113] 1624, *8. Nottingham modified this position when he ruled that a plaintiff on a judgment could have an equity which outranked the equity of other creditors. This arose from a case in which a creditor had failed to join in a commission because he relied on a judgment and execution. The sum owed to him exceeded the total owing to other creditors, but the judgment was only acknowledged after the act of bankruptcy had been committed. Although the commission was closed, Nottingham secured an agreement whereby the single creditor could join in it, pay his share of the expenses, and yet keep what was already in his hands *pro ratâ* towards his own satisfaction. *Nottingham's Cases* **2**: pp. 491–492.

veloped, confirmed in 1624, that those who exhibited a petition must be owed debts totaling at least £100.[114] In many cases, however, this sum was too trifling to have significance. At other times, the £100 claimed may either have been a fiction or may have included the total value of penalties as well as the actual capital debt. This was rather hard, as Nottingham took pains to stress, since a penalty was normally double the value of the debt.[115]

The 1571 statute did not deny the right of creditors to join in the commission after it had been sued out, but it failed to indicate how and when they could become associated. In 1604, however, it was enacted that creditors might join in the commission, thus sharing its costs and expenses, up to four months after it had been sued out. Thereafter the commissioners could start sharing out the proceeds.[116] In practice, it became understood that distribution might begin after four months. When this was not possible, commissioners would promise to give further time and provide notice.[117] At the very least, it had been ensured that commissioners devoted at least a third of a year to the consideration of their task, but much of this time must in any case have been spent in initial procedures and inquiries.[118] The statutes did not take direct notice of creditors who made no attempt to join in or who declined to do so. It is possible that those who remained outside cherished hopes of working through other means, perhaps the good offices provided by the Privy Council, and they may have tried to prevent a state of bankruptcy being declared. The 1624 statute, with the longest list yet of actions constituting bankruptcy, struck a blow at these creditors, and also at the crumbling authority of the Privy Council in matters of debt.[119]

Creditors regained their freedom of action when the commission was wound up. The bankrupt was not discharged from any remaining liability, and creditors could proceed individually against him at law and use any means of recovery available. This may have encouraged bankrupts to do their best to prolong the life of commissions. Some lasted for many years, and there were grounds for this in the 1571 reference to creditors who were not fully satified or "otherwise contended." [120] It is of course evident that some commissioners, possibly encouraged by higher authority, tried to get creditors to give further time for the remaining sums or even to express satisfaction, but such experimentation must in no way be confused with the notion of a discharge.[121]

PROBLEMS OF PROPERTY

The 1571 statute made the acts of commissioners valid against the bankrupt, his wife, heirs, assignees, and all persons who might claim by, from, or under him. It also covered lords of the manor from whom copyhold or customary lands were held. A protection was thus given to the disposal of property by the commissioners. This was clear enough. It was rather less easy to be certain as to the assets which could be disposed of, and this was especially so when these had been previously conveyed.[122]

It is possible that some inadequacies of the Elizabethan statute may have been due to hasty drafting and insufficient reflection by the House of Commons.[123] Apparently as an afterthought, an exception was annexed as a schedule to the original bill. This stated that a *bona fide* conveyance of lands or tenements made before the action of bankrupty was not to be questioned.[124] The 1604 statute tried to close loopholes.[125] All conveyances made before the action of bankruptcy were to be void, unless it could be shown that they had been made for good consideration and value, for example as part of a marriage contract. The onus of proof was in effect switched to the bankrupt and to those to whom he had conveyed.[126] A time limit was not provided, but the judges would warn creditors not to fasten upon deeds made long previous to an act of bankruptcy.[127] A period of five years may have become the yardstick.[128]

At this point, acts of bankruptcy and powers of recovery over property became fused. It was a chicken-

114 1624, *2. P.R.O., E.333/17.

115 *Nottingham's Cases* 2: pp. 570–571.

116 1604, *2.

117 Some commissions, after giving this promise, were accused of making a sudden distribution among a few creditors. Nottingham required commissioners to execute at a specified time and place, all of which was to be announced at least fourteen days before distribution. *Nottingham's 'Manual'*, p. 163.

118 The four months could expire before some creditors were aware of what was going on (*ibid.*, p. 164), but it was supposedly adequate for sending notice even to those who lived in remote parts. Hutton, 37–38, Ruggles Case. There was nothing to prevent creditors from joining after the four months and initial distribution, but this was only with respect to any residue and cannot often have been advantageous. 2 Chan. Cases, 153–154, Harding v. Marsh (1683).

119 See below, p. 40.

120 1571, *9.

121 See below, p. 49.

122 1571, *2, 3. If the commissioners sold copyhold or customary lands, the purchasers had to satisfy the lord of his entry fine before admittance. Lands and chattels held by the bankrupt as feoffee to charitable uses were not his assets. For these and other problems, see G. Jones, *History of the Law of Charity, 1532–1827* (Cambridge, 1969), pp. 95–96. Money and goods, taken from a debtor on an extent a few days before issue of a bankruptcy commission, was not subject to distribution. Cro. Car., 149–150, Audley v. Halsey (1629).

123 See above, p. 19.

124 1571, *11.

125 This approach seems to have replaced the abortive attempt in 1601 to fashion a new and harsher approach towards bankrupts. See above, p. 19.

126 1604, *3.

127 Hutton, 42–43, Cartwright v. Underhill (1617).

128 See below, at n. 131.

and-egg situation insofar as the 1604 statute implied that an act of bankruptcy occurred if a grant or conveyance could be deemed as in fraud of creditors.[129] Basil Montagu argued that these words had a technical meaning in that they were confined to deeds, that is, instruments under hand and seal. Thus if a debtor executed a deed by which he conveyed one-twentieth of his property with the intention of favoring one of his creditors, he committed an act of bankruptcy, and this was what the statute intended. However, if he delivered all or part of his property by means other than deed, or executed a warrant of attorney by which the property might be taken, he did not commit an act of bankruptcy even if he was deliberately favoring one of the creditors. This, claimed Montagu, was "an apparent deviation from the original intention of the legislature." [130]

The 1624 statute was stringent, although from the viewpoint of commissioners and some creditors it may have been considered as faintly liberal. It established that purchases made for good and valuable consideration could not be impeached if five years passed between the act of bankruptcy and the petition to prove the man a bankrupt.[131] Was this an invitation? The statute also declared that goods in the actual possession of the bankrupt, by consent of the real proprietors, were liable to be distributed towards payment of the debts. It was argued, in explanation, that many persons, aware that they were going to become bankrupts, conveyed goods to other men on good consideration, although they kept them "and are reputed the owners thereof, and dispose the same as their own." [132] The commissioners were also empowered to sell lands, including those entailed, and action of this kind was to be valid against the heirs.[133] Commissioners might make a disposal of mortgaged estates which could be redeemed by the bankrupt.[134]

The situation with respect to assets acquired after the act of bankruptcy was clearer. Any lands or effects which came into the hands of the bankrupt, notably by reversion or inheritance, could be distributed by the commissioners during the life of the commission. The point should have been obvious, but even this item received a somewhat indirect wording in the 1571 statute, and it followed after that clause which allowed subsequent freedom of action to creditors.[135]

Bad debts were often the explanation for insolvency. The commissioners were supposed to collect debts owing to the bankrupt, and to distribute the proceeds among the creditors.[136] However, the 1571 statute gave little guidance as to what should be done when the bankrupt's debtor did not pay. There was no suggestion as to how the penalty on a bond could be executed. Power of assignment or transfer was not given to the commissioners. Yet in most instances it cannot have been desirable to give the bankrupt himself a free hand in recovering debts, and he was not supposed to have the money to pay lawyers and clerks. In 1604, the commissioners were authorized to assign bonds, debts, deeds, and recognizances so that their assignees, usually the bankrupt's creditors, could proceed in their own names.[137] The bankrupt's debtors were to be given due notice of the new state of affairs, and until this was done there was no bar against the bankrupt himself being repaid.[138] Creditors might use legal proceedings to enforce payment of debts, but money thus recovered, costs being deducted, was to be distributed.[139]

Measures such as those described above did little more than scratch the surface of accumulated legal rights and rules. In the reign of Charles II, some of the difficulties were summed up by Nottingham. When money was recovered by a Chancery decree, execution was not to be stayed even though the plaintiff was declared a bankrupt between decree and execution. On the other hand, money recovered by a Chancery decree for a man who was already declared to be a bankrupt could be assigned by the commissioners. The assignees were to have the benefit of recovery, and they could establish their right by exhibiting a bill in Chancery against the bankrupt and his debtor. This, Nottingham pointed out, was quite different from the situation at law where money recovered by a bankrupt could not be assigned before or after execution.[140]

A simple conclusion with respect to powers over

[129] 1604, *1.

[130] B. Montagu, *Some Observations upon the Bill for the Improvement of the Bankrupt Laws* (London, 1822), p. 8.

[131] 1624, *13.

[132] 1624, *10. However, it may be that, as Lord Hardwicke later asserted, this provision was not acted upon until 1736. Jenks, p. 277, n. 1.

[133] 1624, *11. The power to bar estates tail was a striking feature, and it apparently anticipated the plan adopted by the fines and recoveries act of 1833. Holdsworth **8**: p. 239, n. 5.

[134] 1624, *12. This was an uncertain authority both in terms of immediate law and the unresolved development of the equity of redemption. 1 Eq. Ca. Abr., 53. R. W. Turner, *The Equity of Redemption* (Cambridge, 1931), pp. 28, 55, 71–72, 82.

[135] 1571, *9, 10.

[136] 1571, *5.

[137] 1604, *8.

[138] 1604, *9. Nottingham, however, ruled that a voluntary payment to a bankrupt had to be paid again to the assignees of the commission. *Nottingham's Cases* **1**: p. 277. He admitted that no one could feel safe in paying a debt to a bankrupt or in receiving a debt from someone he knew to be a bankrupt. *Ibid.* **1**: p. 348. For a case where a creditor petitioned in Chancery for protection because he knew of a secret act of bankruptcy by his debtor, see *Nottingham's 'Prolegomena'*, p. 350. For the vexed question of damages recovered on a judgment clearly before the act of bankruptcy, see Cro. Car., 166, Benson v. Flower (1629).

[139] 1604, *7.

[140] *Nottingham's 'Manual'*, pp. 162–163.

property is that all these statutes were inadequate. The measures of 1604 and 1624 illustrated rather than solved problems which had been set in 1571. One more example may be given. The *quominus* fiction was based upon the fact or pretense that a creditor was indebted to the sovereign. In consequence, proceedings in the Exchequer were allowed. It would seem that commissioners were sometimes frustrated by creditors who secured an independent extent on this basis. In 1624, therefore, commissioners were empowered to inquire into the facts, and if fraud was present they were to convey or sell the debts or goods to the benefit of all the creditors. In theory this was a significant development, but in practice its utility may be doubted. The loopholes in statutory explanation were still there. What did the words *fraudulent* and *reputed* mean? How could an equity of redemption be utilized? These questions and others could only be decided by the courts.[141]

Problems of property, along with the determination of persons embraced by the statutes, represented areas in which there was great need for interpretation. Was there any significance, for example, in the fact that the Elizabethan act specifically mentioned copyholds whereas the two Jacobean ones did not? Quite properly, the judges decided that nothing need be read into this. In any case, it is apparent that the intention in 1604 and 1624 was to expand and not to repeal. However, as it was observed, the statutes "ought to be expounded liberally, and shall be construed accordingly, to make as strong provision as they may against the bankrupt." [142]

THE STATUS OF BANKRUPTCY COMMISSIONERS

Bankruptcy commissioners were sometimes accused of peculation, and their actions were occasionally said to be illegal and without authority.

Commissioners were most often critized for not attending meetings. The task, however, involved considerable expenditure of time: one commission held eighteen meetings between 22 November, 1622 and 1 October, 1623. Officials claimed to sit for hours, from 7:00 A.M until noon, or from 2 until 8:00 P.M, sometimes having to disperse for lack of a quorum.[143] Commissioners expected to be reimbursed for their personal expenses, but this was not mentioned in the statutes. It was, in consequence, easy to suggest that they had used the commission for their own gain, and the implication was reinforced in Charles I's reign once professional commissioners began to dominate.[144] Commissioners, it was said, "swallowed up as much of the poor bankrupt or pretended bankrupt his estate, by often and unnecessary sitting about the same. . . ." [145] Yet statutory guidance was not given.[146] The way was therefore open for proceedings in a variety of courts. Early in the reign of James I, Chancery gave relief to a "concealer" from whom too much had been taken "upon indirect dealing by commissioners." [147] In 1607 a group of commissioners, two of whom were possibly from Gray's Inn, were accused in Star Chamber of taking too much. The sums involved were small: two commissioners were said to have taken £5 and a third £12 in respect of riding charges and their pains. Coke said that judges, who got their fee from the crown, could not take other fees save in certain specified cases,[148] but these men were only commissioners. They were unsworn persons put in trust, and therefore they might take such fees as would reimburse them for their expenses.[149] He recognized, however, that it was difficult to draw lines of distinction, and said that "he was sorry they had taken anything." The court concurred with the tenor of Coke's remarks, and it was held that justifiable remuneration was proper. Lord Chancellor Ellesmere, however, disagreed with some of Coke's sentiments. Indeed he wished that the commissioners had taken more—"for with a lawyer *cessans lucrum damnum est*"—and he suggested that failure to receive adequate reimbursement for expenses would damage the competent execution of commissions.[150] The court fined some other persons who, claiming warrant from the commissioners of bankruptcy, had caused a riot by

---

141 1624, *9. There was uncertainty as to whether an act of bankruptcy committed in Ireland made a man bankrupt in England. *Nottingham's Cases* 2: p. 744. For this, and also whether those born in the Isle of Man could be bankrupts, see Goodinge, p. 34.

142 1571, *2. Cro. Car., 550, Crisp v. Pratt (1635). For copyholders, see also Cro. Car., 568–570, Parker v. Bleeke (1638). Goodinge, p. 97.

143 P.R.O., E215/3/232, 233, 234.

144 See above, p. 26.

145 Leach, *Proposals for an Act*, p. 17.

146 Nottingham acknowledged that commissioners should be reimbursed and that a case which involved frauds, concealments, and law-suits could legitimately create expenses which might erode the bankrupt's estate. However, he threw some light on improper practices when he said that expenses should not be allowed for meetings in taverns and for entertaining the commissioners. *Nottingham's 'Manual'*, pp. 164–165.

147 Tothill, 62, Wood v. Hayes (1606–1607).

148 For example, special assizes or error in London.

149 Coke was careful to point out that they must not contract a bargain beforehand for a reward or fee. An elaborate oath for commissioners of sewers was written into their controlling Statute (23 Henry VIII c. 5, *2) but bankruptcy commissioners were apparently only sworn from 1719, an oath being included in the 1732 statute. Holdsworth 1: p. 471. 5 George II c. 30, *43. Despite some evidence, I am not sure that there was anything to prevent the lord chancellor on his own authority from requiring bankruptcy commissioners to be sworn. In 1676, considering complaints of a creditor, Nottingham was at first unwilling to hear the case "because the commissioners were on their oaths, and if they did wrong were liable to an action at law . . . ." *Nottingham's Cases* 1: p. 313.

150 J. Hawarde, *Les Reportes del Cases in Camera Stellata*, ed. W. P. Baildon (London, 1894), pp. 342–343.

going with guns and other weapons to arrest the bankrupt during divine service on the sabbath.[151]

On 12 February, 1587, a group of creditors petitioned the lord chancellor after the alleged bankruptcy of John Cook. A commission was issued on 17 February. The sum claimed by the petitioning creditors was £271 1s. 0d. Four days later, the bankrupt conveyed goods worth £24 to Robert Tibnam, who was owed £64. Tibnam did not join in the commission, and his factor, Thomas Mills, refused to have anything to do with its proceedings. The commissioners, therefore, sold the assets to the other creditors, who subsequently brought an action. The question at issue was whether the sale by the commissioners was good despite the bankrupt's delivery of the same goods to Tibnam. Chief Justice Wray and his colleagues decided that the conveyance was valid. In explanation, it was said that the 1571 statute had been intended to secure an equal distribution among creditors, and that the bankrupt could not give preference to a single creditor at the expense of others. In any case, the bankrupt could not dispose of property after the award of a commission.

> It would be unequal and unconscionable, and a great defect in the law, if after that he hath utterly discredited himself by becoming a bankrupt, the law should credit him to make distribution of his goods to whom he pleased, being a bankrupt man, and of no credit . . . . And the court resolved that the proviso concerning gifts and grants *bona fide*, makes no gift or grant good, which the bankrupt makes after he become bankrupt, but excludes them out of the penalty inflicted by the same proviso.

A creditor declining to join in the commission had forfeited his freedom of action until that commission had been wound up. The commission of bankruptcy itself was described as "matter of record" of which everyone must take notice.

> This act gives benefit to those who will inquire and come in as creditors, and not to those, who either out of obstinacy refuse, or through carelessness neglect, to come before the commissioners, and pray the benefit of the said statute; for *vigilantibus et non dormientibus jura subveniunt*, for otherwise a debt might be concealed, or a creditor might absent himself, and so avoid all the proceedings of the commissioners by force of the said act. And every creditor may take notice of the commission, being matter of record, as is aforesaid, and so no inconvenience can happen to any creditor who will be vigilant; but great inconvenience will follow and the whole effect of the act be overthrown, if other construction should be made.[152]

Wray and his fellow judges had rejected the claims of a creditor who had tried to seek restitution outside the operations of a bankruptcy commission. There would be other cases and the commissioners, who worked by virtue of the 1571 and subsequent statutes, were not always to find their position so clearly maintained before the courts.

Seventeenth-century bankruptcy commissions have been described as the outstanding example of a judicial body, not possessing the attributes of a court of record, the decisions of which could be examined through collateral proceedings in the courts.[153] The commission had a statutory basis and the fact of its issue was supposedly a matter of record. The commissioners, however, did not constitute a court of record. At the beginning of the eighteenth century, Holt inferred that bankruptcy commissioners "had only an authority and not a jurisdiction."[154] Unlike commissions of sewers and justices of the peace, bankruptcy commissions were not apparently subject to writs of *certiorari*.[155] Indeed, insofar as this writ was used to transfer the record, with respect to bankruptcy commissions there was little to transfer. Even if the notion of "record"—which has its own meaning—is debased to that of documentation, there was only the original petition made to the chancellor and the possibility of some depositions and proceedings which could not in any case be read in Westminster Hall.[156] Even with the slow development of *certiorari* "to quash" after 1635, Miss Henderson has found no case before 1760 in which a *certiorari* actually was issued to a body which was clearly not a court of record.[157] The truth of the matter is that commissioners of bankruptcy were not judges, and they were appointed only in respect of the immediate case. At the most they were temporary and unsworn commissioners in whom was reposed a fiduciary trust. The point is clear from Coke.[158]

Certiorari was not applicable, but actions of tort lay to hand.[159] Commissioners could not expect protection if their decisions or acts were declared wrong in law. The 1604 statute tried to tackle the problem: if an action of trespass or any other suit was brought against the commissioners they were, by citing the authority of the two statutes, to plead the general issue and thus stand upon their statutory authority. If

[151] *Ibid.*, p. 343. Process could be served in church but an arrest could not be made.

[152] 2 Co. Rep. 25–26, The Case of Bankrupts (1589).

[153] Rubinstein, p. 60. Only in the nineteenth century was the so-called *Marshalsea* rule extended to bankruptcy commissions.

[154] Edith G. Henderson, *Foundations of English Administrative Law* (Cambridge, Mass., 1963), p. 114.

[155] *Ibid.*, pp. 28, 112.

[156] *Nottingham's Cases* 2: pp. 570–571.

[157] Henderson, p. 116.

[158] See above, p. 33.

[159] Rubinstein, p. 56. In 1666, it was pointed out that if the commissioners of bankruptcy decided contrary to law then the aggrieved party had his remedy by action. 2 Keble, 82, Bell v. Partridge. Holt, who could otherwise be misleading (see Henderson, p. 112), pointed out that "commissioners of bankrupts may commit a man for refusing to be examined concerning the estate of the bankrupt; but they are not judges; and their proceedings are traversable because their power of imprisonment is only *quousque*, etc." 1 Ld Ray., 467, De Groenvelt v. Burwell (1697).

the defendants, that is the commissioners, were upheld they were to receive costs.[160]

The actions of commissioners were constantly liable to challenge. In *Bonham's Case* it was said that the decision of commissioners that a man was a bankrupt could be traversed in an action of false imprisonment.[161] Hence, it is understandable that extreme caution in not overstepping the limits of authority became the rule. This was because collateral proceedings before the courts provided a form of supervision. Another form of supervision could be found in the general powers of the Privy Council, and in the indeterminate position of the lord chancellor, who alone had authority to issue a bankruptcy commission.

IV. PRIVY COUNCIL AND CHANCERY

Legislation provided narrow, and at times ambiguous, descriptions of persons liable to become bankrupt together with an outline of actions which constituted bankruptcy. Some people evaded bankruptcy because they did not behave in a specified fashion. Others were beyond the scope of bankruptcy procedures, whatever they did. Furthermore, the statutes required an initiative from creditors. These often saw no value in a state of bankruptcy being declared, possibly because they were willing to allow further time or even a composition. Hence all sorts of men were debtors, but only a tiny fraction could be bankrupts. It was along this sometimes fragile border between debt and bankruptcy that the Privy Council and the court of Chancery occasionally played a role of significance.

THE PRIVY COUNCIL AND DEBTORS

The situation of a debtor, dishonest or otherwise, was often fairly helpless unless he could persuade some agency to intervene on his behalf. The Privy Council naturally tried to aid enforcement of debt payments, but it also attempted to discourage or ameliorate imprisonment. One method was to secure an extension of time. This was particularly important since legal proceedings had the habit of escalating until the drain on the debtor's credit, which could also extend through to his sureties, reached disastrous proportions. A second method was to support or provide arbitration procedures after which, if the assets were not enough, a composition might be obtained.[1]

The absurdity of procedures in relation to debt was understood by many, but it was very difficult to find alternatives. In 1604, a bill to relieve prisoners in execution was turned down by the House of Commons. Only limited help could be expected from the statute of that year concerning small debts (those under forty shillings) and the relief of poor debtors in London.[2]

The Elizabethan Privy Council set up a series of commissions which were authorized to deal with the creditors of imprisoned debtors. One commission, specifically concerned with the King's Bench prison, was appointed in 1576 and was active for thirteen years. The commissioners were required to sit regularly, and a measure of their performance can be seen in the issue of commissions to handle the affairs of debtors in other prisons. The King's Bench commission was reorganized in 1589 and given authority to imprison for disobedience.[3]

The commissioners, notably those concerned with the King's Bench prison and the Fleet, were supposed to deal with creditors in the hope of securing a composition. However, their legal position was open to question, and they were sometimes sued in Common Pleas by virtue of informations on the statutes of *praemunire*. The Privy Council, in September, 1589, required the two chief justices, who had been made commissioners, to give advice when difficulties arose. It was also ordered that some commissioners should be ready to sit at least two days a week.[4]

Despite conundrums of jurisdiction, the late Elizabethan Council was ambitious in its attempts to help incarcerated debtors. In 1592, letters to the commissioners referred to complaints made by prisoners and noted some of the recognized problems. It was pointed out that many died in prison and that the creditors lost their money. Monthly meetings were to be held to hear "hard" cases, and creditors who would not come to heel were to be dealt with severely. The Privy Council appreciated the reluctance of commissioners to "constrain" creditors—it was admitted that their powers were insufficient—and advised that in cases of obstinacy the sitting commissioners should call upon "such other persons of quality and calling" as were named in the commission. In these and other circumstances, advice was to be sought from the two chief justices.[5] The shroud of legality was too doubtful, difficulties continued, and the mechanism was apparently abandoned for a time in the reign of James I. There were, of course, individual interventions, and commissions were set up for the King's Bench

[160] 1604, *11.

[161] 8 Co. Rep., 121a.

[1] J. P. Dawson, "The Privy Council and Private Law in the Tudor and Stuart Periods," *Michigan Law Review* **48** (1950) : pp. 411–413. Vincent Ponko, Jr., "The Privy Council and the Spirit of Elizabethan Economic Management," *Trans. Amer. Philos. Soc.* **58**, 4 (1968) : pp. 53–54.

[2] *CJ* 1 : p. 290. In 1604 and 1606, statutes were passed which attempted to improve the situation for both creditors and debtors in London with respect to debts under forty shillings. 1 James I c. 14; 3 James I c. 15.

[3] Dawson, "Privy Council," pp. 415–416.

[4] *APC* 1581–1582, p. 175; 1587–1588, p. 99; 1589–1590, p. 109.

[5] *APC* 1591–1592, pp. 384–386.

prison and the Fleet in 1618.[6] Malynes thought that the commissioners had done a good job, and in 1622 he advocated their revival.[7] The 1624 statute crippled such approaches, but only if the debtor was capable of being a bankrupt. With respect to other debtors, the Council would make further attempts. In 1630, a commission empowered the archbishop of Canterbury, the bishop of London, the lord mayor of London, and others to compound with the creditors of prisoners when the debt was less than £200. Prisoners soon claimed that nothing was achieved. The problem was nationwide: the palatine Chancery at Durham issued commissions in 1638 and 1640 because of the numbers of imprisoned small debtors without means of repayment. "Most of the creditors are very unmerciful so as the poor prisoners are like to die and end their days there." [8]

It was only natural that intervention in favor of imprisoned debtors should raise difficulties. When possible, it was much easier for the Council to act at an earlier stage, and some debtors were not slow to seek help. Certainly the Council always appeared ready to influence creditors who stood out against a suggested composition—either in terms of time or in other ways—especially when it seemed that the debtor would meet his obligations if allowed liberty.[9] It might appoint a commission to treat with the creditors and to report back if any refused to cooperate. In this eventuality, the point was made that further action could be taken for the debtor's relief in equity and conscience.[10] Creditors, it must be remembered, would wish to be spared the cost and delay of litigation and debtors had many possibilities open to them. However, the cases that catch the eye tend to be those which center upon reluctant creditors.

On one occasion, the Council commissioned the lord mayor, sheriffs, and aldermen of London to meet with a set of creditors, "especially such as will be most rigorous." Their task, after suitable inquiries, was to secure time for the debtor to recover his own goods which were scattered in the houses of other persons. In the meantime, at least until discussions with the creditors had been completed, the sheriffs and the secondaries of both compters were to see that no arrest, action, or attachment was made against the debtor.[11] The Council would even authorize a commission of merchants to inquire specifically into the claims, reimbursement, and attitudes of creditors.[12] Thus in 1614, it helped a clothier of Cranbrooke who had, according to his own statement, given too much credit to people who subsequently went bankrupt, and who was now ready to accept almost any settlement, preferably a composition, if only he could get time to repair his estate. The creditors of a bankrupt were often on the verge of that state themselves.[13]

Malynes gave strong approval to the system whereby licenses from merchants, a traditional procedure, were given to debtors so that they could continue in business and thus enhance the possibility of a speedy settlement.[14] Creditors who had been soothed by Privy Council intervention might well provide their debtor with a license. Otherwise the Council could solicit or order some such grant. There were also letters of protection granted by the sovereign, commonly through the lord chancellor. These were normally issued to persons who had to go abroad or were engaged in government business, and therefore unable to attend to their personal affairs.[15]

Various forms of license and protection were always available. They were either a fact with which the Privy Council had to deal or an allowance sponsored by it. With or without an original petition from the creditors, the Council might endeavor to ensure through commissioners that a commercial debtor was allowed to "pass with free liberty" in order to recover debts, and it would protect him from writs, arrests, and executions.[16] In the reign of James I an important grocer, Andrew Palmer, delivered all his effects to his creditors and undertook to pay all his debts over further time in return for "a letter of license under their hands." This expired before everything had been repaid, but the Privy Council came to Palmer's help after he had been thrown into Canterbury prison by three creditors, and again when subsequently he was in the King's Bench prison.[17] In the 1570's, the Council supported a debtor who had obtained a letter of protection and who promised that the principal would be repaid with ten per cent profit if he and his surety were left alone. This seemed to be an

---

[6] Dawson, "Privy Council," p. 416.

[7] Malynes, *Lex Mercatoria*, p. 157. William Leach also advocated a system of commissions, albeit of a different nature, for the mutual relief of creditors and poor prisoners. *Proposals for an Act for Speedy Settling at Large all Prisoners, both for Damages and Debt* (London, 1649).

[8] *D.K.Rep.* App., Privy Seals, Signet Bills, etc., 1625–1632, p. 173. P.R.O., Durham 4/1, pp. 572, 573. *CSP Dom.* 1629–1631, p. 370. For debates and proposals during the Commonwealth as to imprisoned debtors, see Veall, pp. 142–151.

[9] *APC* 1613–1614, pp. 102–103, 169–170, 472, 522–523. See *CSP Dom.* 1633–1634, pp. 307–308; 1637, p. 239.

[10] *APC* 1590, p. 98.

[11] *APC* 1581–1582, pp. 112–113.

[12] *APC* 1577–1578, p. 71. The debtor was listed as being a bankrupt.

[13] *APC* 1613–1614, p. 472. In 1576, the Council aided a creditor serving in Ireland whose debtors refused to come to a composition. *APC* 1575–1577, pp. 212–213. For some difficulties of a merchant moneylender in securing repayment from great clients, see A. H. Dodd, "Mr. Myddelton, the Merchant of Tower Street," *Elizabethan Government and Society*, ed. S. T. Bindoff, J. Hurstfield, C. Williams (London, 1961), p. 262.

[14] Malynes, *Lex Mercatoria*, p. 157.

[15] Jones, *Chancery*, pp. 204–206.

[16] *APC* 1587–1588, pp. 16–17.

[17] *APC* 1616–1617, pp. 120–121, 190.

instance where a man with essentially good credit had been placed under impossible pressure. Commissioners, in this case men of such high standing as the lord mayor and the master of the rolls, were required to achieve such an accord, but it was stipulated that the letter of protection must be surrendered.[18] The Elizabethan Council also seems to have endorsed, at least tacitly, the position of foreign merchants who preferred traditional ways. When an Italian was unable to meet his debts, the Council wrote to the master of the rolls and the solicitor general in support of the merchant's request for a year's freedom from arrest and molestation by his creditors. This was to be "upon some reasonable order by them or other indifferent person to be made between them." [19]

Examples could be multiplied, although one must be careful not to exaggerate the extent of Privy Council activity. Affairs of debt noted in the register are few. There is, however, one exceptional story which spans the central period of Elizabeth's reign. This concerns a merchant who does not appear to have gone bankrupt. His plight, and his ability to manipulate Privy Council support, does much to illustrate the approach of that body towards debtors from the mercantile community.

WILLIAM NUTSHAWE

The story of William Nutshawe, merchant of Southampton, was set against a background provided by broad considerations of foreign policy and England's varying relations with France. In general, English merchants enjoyed favorable conditions under the Treaty of Blois, arranged by Charles IX in 1572 and confirmed by Henry III in 1575. The effect of this was disrupted but not entirely destroyed by the later civil wars. On the grounds of breach in continuity, however, Henry IV would not recognize the treaty.[20]

In Nutshawe's case, diplomatic circumstances encouraged the Privy Council to provide support because his troubles did not stem from dishonesty. On the other hand, there must have been some question as to how far his misfortune resulted from rash behavior. The Council seems to have given him the benefit of the doubt, but the venture which drew him into trouble was something of a gamble.

This saga began in the late 1560's when a consignment of wheat sent to La Rochelle was captured by the French royal forces. Nutshawe had bills for his consignment and expected repayment, but the official French position, while it would fluctuate, was that the cargo was good prize since it had been intended for the king's enemies. This was the substance of one judgment eventually delivered by the French Council.[21]

By October, 1573, when Lord Treasurer Burghley and other ministers were preoccupied with marriage negotiations, the English representative in Paris, Dr. Valentine Dale, was pursuing the matter. Some months later, he reported that there was a reasonable hope of the claim being settled. Dale was confident. He sent Nutshawe, who had come over in attendance of his suit, home "with good and evident testimony of his rights and of the diligence of them both." It was, nonetheless, confessed that the attitude of the French government left much to be desired. A warrant for repayment had been granted to Nutshawe, but it "was directed to such men as either say they have no money, or that they have nothing to do with the matter, or dwell as far as Marseilles and in the Island of Rhé, and such other places as are more than dangerous to come by." The death of Charles IX threatened to blight even this devious progress, but Dale's dispatches continued to be optimistic. He reported that restitution for wrongs done to English merchants had been ordered and that satisfaction for Nutshawe figured prominently in this command. It was a forlorn expectation. The argument dragged on, and it assumed enough significance to appear first among the items on Lord North's "Private Memorial" when he arrived in Paris on a special embassy. North, a Leicester supporter, was not inclined to aid pacific arrangements between the two countries. At any rate Dale, who was Burghley's man, was ready to drop the matter. Nonetheless, it was kept alive by occasional intimations of a settlement.[22]

Meanwhile, Nutshawe's creditors at home were impatient. On 12 July, 1575, the Privy Council requested them to forbear for six months so that he could again visit France in order to prosecute his suit. Two days later, his favorable standing with the Council was emphasized when the commissioners in restraint of grain for Dorset were ordered to permit him to buy and export two hundred quarters, "if the same may be conveniently spared without enhancing the prices of the markets." [23] Not long after, following assurances from Henry III and his ambassador in London, de la Mothe Fénélon, the Privy Council again required Nutshawe's creditors to forbear for six months, "by which time he may be either paid in France, or her Majesty upon denial of justice is to take other order for him and other her subjects in like suit." [24]

---

[18] *APC* 1571–1575, p. 128.

[19] *APC* 1577–1578, p. 403.

[20] Beatrice Reynolds, "Elizabethan Traders in Normandy," *Jour. Mod. Hist.* 9 (1937) pp. 289–303. See generally R. B. Wernham, *Before the Armada* (London, 1966) and C. Read, *Lord Burghley and Queen Elizabeth* (New York, 1960).

[21] *CSP For.* 1585–1586, p. 245.

[22] *CSP For.* 1572–1574, pp. 433, 467, 471, 507, 533, 563, 570–571.

[23] *APC* 1575–1577, pp. 5–6.

[24] *APC* 1575–1577, pp. 78–79.

Promises rather than outright failure were the product of the next two years. Dale grew tired of the rigmarole whereby he was balked by protestations of settlement, which he had to accept with as good grace as he could muster. "These doings," he wrote to Burghley, "will make a man *Didymus* in all things." After a particularly irritating passage—as humorous as it was absurd—he remarked, "God help them that have to do in this court." Nutshawe had actually been given warrants for repayment, but no day was specified. The French treasurer would not be drawn into naming a time for satisfaction, but he tried to extract an absolute acquittance from Nutshawe. This move was roundly dismissed by Dale as a trick, and he subsequently reported that the warrants were anyhow on money owing to the French crown. They were directed to the treasurer of the Espargne, but this official maintained that they could only be paid out of a debt due to the king at Angers. Messengers were sent but, or so it was asserted, they were attacked and robbed, and one of their companions slain. In any case, the debtors of the French crown refused to pay up. This, Dale was told, was because "they cannot enjoy the bargain for the which they should pay their money, by reason of a former bargain made by the King unto another." Yet Nutshawe could only be paid through this source. Described as wearied, discouraged, and burdened with debt, he left Paris.[25]

In July, 1576, the Privy Council was again asking Nutshawe's creditors to forbear. Dale reported in August, however, that the money was at last available. The treasurer of the Espargne wanted an acquittance, but Dale insisted that this could be given in England to the French ambassador or to a man whose goods were stayed at Nutshawe's suit. Nothing happened, but this hint from the French authorities may have been prompted by Nutshawe's search for other forms of remuneration. He obtained an order from the court of Admiralty for stay of certain sums in the hands of London merchants, "appertaining by way of assurance to some merchants of Paris." [26] Nutshawe, together with a ship and goods, was arrested in April, 1578, on complaint that the vessel was a French one taken by him in an act of piracy two years previously. He replied that the ship had been in his possession for ten years, and in a counter accusation stated that he himself had been the victim of French pirates.[27] The Privy Council again protected him on 24 August, 1578. This time he was awarded an eight-month barrier against molestation of his person, goods, and sureties.[28] It transpired that he had appropriated a ship of Marshal de Biron. This may have been a castaway. There were other French complaints, some of which were probably unjustified, but the Privy Council ordered the captain of the Isle of Wight to impound one of Nutshawe's ships, "The Barque of Boulogne." [29] Yet on 28 June, 1579, the Council required his creditors to forbear for another ten months, and in justification they cited his great losses, the arrest of his goods in France, and his deprivations at sea.[30]

The Privy Council was willing to go to remarkable lengths to protect Nutshawe and to improve his position. In May, 1580, he was given a license to export three hundred quarters of grain from Norfolk. Councillors must have been aware that their attitude was exceptional. Two months earlier, in stipulating another three-months forbearance, the language of the Council was less direct and more apologetic than on previous occasions. Instead of issuing a command, it was indicated that the Council would "take in good part" the creditors adopting an attitude of restraint.[31]

The affair dragged on during the 1580's. French intransigence was matched by Nutshawe's ability to take reprisal against French goods in England. It was asserted that his exploits on the seas had led to the seizure of property worth over forty thousand crowns in less than four months, "and some of the poor people have died of despair." It is surprising, therefore, to find that Mauvissière, French ambassador in England from 1575 to 1585, transmitted over £880 early in 1585. In fact the ambassador, by his own account, had acted prematurely and without proper authority. He was sharply reminded by his superiors that the grain in dispute had been consigned to La Rochelle in contravention of the commands and interests of the king of France. The French government, possibly in reaction to Nutshawe's recent activities but also because of the changed mood in Paris, was no longer willing to talk about repayment. It had reverted to the position that nothing was due. Mauvissière professed to have acted on the request of Henry III that he do his best to maintain good relations with Queen Elizabeth and her subjects. For this error in interpretation he was called before the French Council, where, as he sadly told Walsingham, he tried to show that Nutshawe had been paid by the king's order: "which they would not believe." Mauvissière must have regretted his "simplicity urged on by a desire to do good." [32] The French ambassador may have made a mistake, but perhaps unwittingly he relieved the Privy Council from further responsibility. At any rate Nutshawe's wife, in an appeal to the Coun-

[25] *CSP For.* 1575–1577, pp. 88, 125, 154, 173–174, 178, 203, 213, 237, 238, 252, 278–279, 316.

[26] *APC* 1575–1577, pp. 154, 174. *CSP For.* 1575–1577, p. 365.

[27] *CSP For.* 1577–1578, p. 634; 1579–1580, p. 14.

[28] *APC* 1577–1578, p. 315.

[29] *APC* 1578–1580, pp. 36, 99, 105, 259. The ship was eventually bargained for by a gentleman follower of the Duke of Anjou.

[30] *APC* 1578–1580, p. 171.

[31] *APC* 1578–1580, pp. 427–428; 1580–1581, p. 7.

[32] *CSP For.* 1584–1585, p. 547; 1585–1586, p. 245.

cil, subsequently deplored the severity of her husband's creditors.[33]

For the better part of two decades, the Privy Council had protected Nutshawe. His initial circumstances were not greatly different from those of other debtors who were actually declared to be bankrupt. During this period, however, he had not apparently committed an act recognized by the bankruptcy statutes, or at least one which allowed the effective operation of bankruptcy commissioners. Had he been careless about obtaining official sanction for his journeys abroad, or if he had stayed too long in his house (possibly due to illness) the way might have been open for bankruptcy proceedings, assuming that this was desired by a sufficient number of creditors. This exceptional story is important because it illustrates the fine line which separated bankruptcy from general situations of debt or insolvency.

THE PRIVY COUNCIL AND BANKRUPTS

The Privy Council occasionally intervened in the conduct of bankruptcy proceedings. Warning letters were sent to some commissioners who were suspected of being laggards,[34] and the lord chancellor was notified when it was reported that nothing was being done.[35] Once, in 1619, it was doubted if there were grounds for a commission of bankruptcy which had been issued. Debts due had been paid, other debts were not yet due, and the debtor had not absented himself. Hence the Council appointed its own commission with instructions to mediate outstanding difficulties and report obstinate creditors.[36] A somewhat similar situation occurred in the reign of Elizabeth after a bankruptcy commission had been sued out by some foreign merchants, presumably under the 1543 statute. The commissioners and creditors had then agreed to give further time, since the debtor appeared to be capable of meeting his obligations. Bonds were entered for this curious composition, but the debtor subsequently claimed to have acted under duress.[37] On another occasion, the Council was asked to consider a man who had conveyed his possessions to his son-in-law, and then "shifted himself out of the way, and become voluntarily in quality of a bankrupt," leaving his sureties to carry the burden.[38]

Most interventions by the Privy Council can be described as incidental. When Anthony Tuck, a merchant of Rouen, went broke in that town, the Council ordered the lord mayor of London to arrange his arrest and to have him kept in the house of some honest merchant. His goods in England were impounded towards the satisfaction of his English creditors, but London authorities directed the surplus to be used in meeting a debt of £65 owed to a French creditor.[39] Late in 1591, during a vacancy in the lord chancellorship, there was hesitation over a petition for a bankruptcy commission; the Council asked the lord mayor and the wardens of the haberdashers "to take order" with the debtor for satisfaction of what was owing or else certify "whether you shall find him to be bankrupt." [40]

The Council sometimes tried to obtain forbearance by arguing that delay might be more beneficial to all concerned than a partitition of available assets. In 1619, it acted over the head of a bankruptcy commission, but on this occasion the problem was one of public concern. Many clothiers, few of whom were noticeably wealthy, obtained wool from the farmer on a credit basis, paying for it when the cloths had been disposed of by the merchant. If the merchant's credit collapsed, the repercussions would spread back to shatter both clothier and farmer. This had happened in the particular case. The bankrupt merchant, who owed £20,000 to eighty clothiers in Essex and Suffolk, had conveyed his property to others. Unemployment was feared, and the Council had reason to suppose that its own commission, which included the master of the rolls and Sir Edward Coke, might be preferable to proceedings under the bankrupty statutes.[41]

The good offices of the Council were sometimes solicited by creditors outside the commission. The rule of rate and rate alike, to the exclusion of those outside, was sometimes improper or unfair. In January, 1582, shortly after Philip II had taken over Portugal, it was ordered that the ambassador of the late king of Portugal, who was owed £100 by a bankrupt, was to be paid in full, since he had come to England as representative of a living king "and is not as yet but to be esteemed as a public person." [42] In another case, the bankruptcy commission had made a distribution, the two bankrupts had died, and the petitioner who was owed £100 could not get aything, although £80 was left. The actual decision was left to the lord keeper, but the Council suggested that any surplus

[33] P.R.O., S.P.12/235, no. 91. He is described as "late" of Southampton.

[34] *APC* 1580–1581, pp. 341–342.

[35] *APC* 1629–1630, pp. 391–393.

[36] *APC* 1619–1621, p. 32.

[37] *APC* 1586–1587, pp. 95–96.

[38] *APC* 1586–1587, pp. 78–79.

[39] *APC* 1571–1575, pp. 301, 375. This was well within the power of the city authorities if the creditors were citizens of London, but in this instance evidently some or all did not have this status. It may be noted that in the early seventeenth century Chancery assisted foreign creditors when an Englishman, resident abroad, transferred his property and person to England. Tothill, 68–69, Monro, pp. 167–169, Seve v. Colly (1610–1612).

[40] *APC* 1591–1592, p. 130.

[41] *APC* 1619–1621, pp. 79–80. J. E. Pilgrim, "The Cloth Industry in Essex and Suffolk, 1558–1640," unpub. London M.A. thesis (1938), p. 165.

[42] *APC* 1581–1582, pp. 310–311.

might as well be paid to this man.[43] A more interesting case concerned the sale of kerseys worth £40 to a merchant just prior to his bankruptcy. The vendors wanted the kerseys returned, since their retention by the commissioners would enforce sharing in bankruptcy proceedings, with the distinct possibility that only a percentage would be recovered. Although the rules prevented special consideration after the issue of a bankruptcy commission, the Council wrote to the Earl of Pembroke, asking him to deal in equity and conscience in the matter.[44]

Not too much should be made of the scattered handful of bankruptcy situations tackled by the Privy Council. Even so, its position and freedom of initiative were severely damaged by the 1624 statute. This struck against those who by petition or bill tried to get their creditors to accept less than was due or to secure a longer day of repayment than was allowed in the original agreement.[45] The Council's former interest in prisoners had for the time been shattered, and its general position with respect to debtors had been undermined. Seeking a protection could henceforth be construed as an act of bankruptcy if the statutes applied. However, the possibility of Council intervention in bankruptcy proceedings was not totally destroyed. It continued to be involved with debtors, possibly on a reduced scale, and occasionally it acted on petitions complaining about the handling of bankruptcy matters.[46]

After 1624, nonetheless, approaches by a debtor to the Council could result in his being declared a bankrupt, if his occupation was embraced by the relevant statutes. In theory, a minority of creditors could petition for a bankruptcy commission if the majority, using the good offices of the Council, were willing to agree to extra time or even accept a composition for the total sum due. However, there were still circumstances in which the Council might act. In one case, it was supposed that those owing money to a debtor had withheld payment for fear that they might "be forced to pay over again upon a commission of bankrupts." This was in 1637, and the Council did "not hold it reasonable that the commissions of bankrupts should be used to uphold and strengthen the willfulness of a few against the general and charitable consent of the greatest number of creditors." Lord Keeper Coventrye agreed with this sentiment, and he promised to ensure that a commission was not issued at the behest of creditors who had refused a composition. The Council was going against the tide of parliamentary sentiment expressed in 1621, but it was by no means clear that Coventrye had the power to refuse a commission. Nottingham later decided that this option did not exist.[47] In the late 1630's however, it looks as though the Council was being more assertive and trying to escape from a situation in which its role had been circumscribed. The possibilities cannot be assessed because the immediate future lay with Long Parliament, Civil Wars, and Interregnum.

THE LORD CHANCELLOR AND THE COURT OF CHANCERY

The courts of law and their records obviously provide a fuller background to the affairs of men who might become bankrupt than is true of the occasional activity of the Privy Council. Most important was the position of the lord chancellor and the court of Chancery.

The jurisdiction of the court of Chancery cannot be defined in terms of economic or social convenience. It handled litigation of commercial or industrial content on grounds which were far removed from any claim to supervise the business and trading community. The historian searching for evidence of international mercantile transactions should turn first to the records of the High Court of Admiralty. Nonetheless, Chancery records are rich in information about contracts, credit methods, and the debts of merchants and tradesmen. Particular note may be taken of the bill of exchange which Chancery, apparently to a lesser degree than the Admiralty, was prepared to recognize as a valid contract. By this means, a man who owed money could empower a creditor abroad to recover from a debtor who was also abroad. It was common to assign bills of exchange, and so they served as "a 'traveller's cheque' as much as a way of paying debts." [48] The bill of exchange was not fully negotiable, but Chancery acknowledged its validity just as it recognized most technicalities surrounding situations of debt and contract. This meant that it often had to find out the relevant customs and practices of merchants or discover the proper form and conditions of such an instrument.[49] Chancery would play some part in bringing about a common form for bills of exchange and hasten their recognition at common law.[50] Bankruptcy, in contrast, was a statutory creation surrounded by complications both novel and traditional. As in the general area of debt, the Chan-

[43] *APC* 1577–1578, p. 15.

[44] *APC* 1577–1578, pp. 37, 66.

[45] 1624, *2.

[46] *Privy Council Registers* 1637–1645, **2**: p. 410; **3**: pp. 36–37.

[47] *CSP Dom.* 1636–1637, p. 351. See below, p. 49.

[48] Harding, pp. 318–319.

[49] One case resulted in an order for repayment of a debt of £72 lent by bill of exchange for dealings in broadcloths and kerseys. P.R.O., C.33/81, ff. 21v–22, Pinsowld v. Puliston (1590). It appears that a person who accepted a bill of exchange was not liable to pay on it unless he was challenged within three days after the sum was due. P.R.O., C.24/100, Whit v. Lenarte (1571).

[50] Most generalizations are open to question until more records have been studied. Chancery probably had an advan-

cery bench would discover that attempts to arrange compositions or encourage restraint (both being normal mercantile practices) would, in the reign of James I, raise a tide of opposition which could not be resisted.

The court of Chancery, which embraced both an equitable and a common law jurisdiction, was very much the court of the lord chancellor. It is often necessary, therefore, to draw a distinction between the jurisdiction of the lord chancellor and that of his court, because he exercised powers, sometimes bestowed by statute, which related to his position as a great officer of state rather than to his status as the judge of Chancery. Examples can be seen in affairs of marine insurance, charitable uses, and his traditional role as protector of infants and lunatics. Sometimes these powers expired. Others endured, and since it was only natural for the chancellor to utilize the facilities and process of Chancery his particular responsibility might merge with the general jurisdiction of the court. We are thus dealing with a distinction which was sometimes tenuous and temporary. The lord chancellor, for example, had authority to issue a *ne exeat regnum* to prevent an individual from going abroad, but motions to obtain or quash this writ could result in debate before the Chancery bench. The matter was so important (it was used against "great bankrupts, in whose estate many subjects are interested") that rules concerning the issue of this process were included in the general orders of the court.[51]

Nonetheless, distinctions between chancellor and Chancery were valid. The early bankruptcy statutes gave certain powers and responsibilities to the lord chancellor without reference to the court of Chancery. Faced by a fairly chaotic conflict of facts, interpretations, and jurisdictional doubts, Nottingham in the later seventeenth century produced an interpretation of the situation as it had developed since 1571. He illustrated that the state of affairs was seriously at fault, and then implemented as far as possible his own proposals for improving the authority of the lord chancellor.[52]

Although the lord chancellor was only one among several dignitaries mentioned by the Henrician statute, he was the most obvious official to be included in a petition. In practice, this meant that the clerical services of Chancery would be called upon. In the early years of Elizabeth's reign, Lord Keeper Bacon sometimes appointed a commission orally from the Chancery bench. The details were entered into the books kept by the register of the court. Once this was done, it was logical to utilize Chancery process against recalcitrants, whether these were bankrupts, creditors, or commissioners. Indeed instructions were sometimes given that commissioners should refer to the court if difficulties occurred.[53] This possibility was particularly valuable to creditors seeking protection from subsequent suits aimed at recovering a bankrupt's effects. A Chancery injunction was awarded against the administrator of a bankrupt who had commenced action at law for recovery of the goods distributed by the commission.[54]

While there do not seem to have been many cases, a Chancery jurisdiction over bankruptcy, as defined by the 1543 statute, was apparently developing prior to 1571. This may be why the 1571 statute gave sole authority for the issue of commissions to the lord chancellor. However, this Elizabethan legislation was sufficiently precise to make the development of a regular Chancery jurisdiction well-nigh impossible, while being too imprecise to allow of any adequate alternative. Even so, Chancery was still the most obvious court to be used as an ancillary to bankruptcy proceedings: it could compel a sworn taking of accounts,[55] and it could probably enforce discovery against a bankrupt and others.[56] Decades later, Nottingham said that the particular value of Chancery proceedings was that all the parties could be brought before the court.[57] However, these and other powers did not imply an automatic or special relationship. Chancery was used in this way to aid proceedings before all kinds of courts and tribunals, lay and ecclesiastical, civil and criminal, royal and manorial.

The general nature of Chancery's jurisdiction was

---

tage because of its ability to make a simple order for payment. Courts following a common law procedure were more circumscribed, but something could be done to achieve the same end through *assumpsit*, and in 1666 acceptance was obtained of an action on the case upon the custom of merchants. Harding, p. 319. For the employment of bills of exchange with respect to inland transactions in the mid-seventeeth century, and resulting common law complexities, see J. K. Horsefield, *British Monetary Experiments, 1650–1710* (London, 1960), pp. xii–xiii. For bills of exchange in general and other matters, see J. Milnes Holden, *The History of Negotiable Instruments in English Law* (London, 1955).

51 Sanders 1, i: pp. 120–121. Jones, *Chancery*, p. 204.

52 Nottingham's major reflections are in the *'Manual'*, pp. 161–165. See below, pp. 40–41. Some subsequent developments can be seen from 1 Eq. Ca. Abr., 52–56.

53 P.R.O., C.33/27, ff. 105, 262v., 270v., Frenche *et alii*, *quer*., Frycand v. Calverly, and Spinola v. Mere (1562); C.33/29, f. 340, Berde *et alii*, *quer*. (1564).

54 P.R.O., C.33/31, f. 90v., Austen v. Bawe (1565).

55 In October, 1614, Ellesmere indicated that Chancery's ability to examine accounts on oath was severely limited unless covin and fraud were suspected. Sanders 1, i: p. 86.

56 See *Nottingham's Cases* 1: pp. cxvii, 221. One defendant, a scrivener, demurred. He argued that the information was privileged and that the confidence reposed in him should be respected as would be that between a lawyer and his client. Nottingham, however, said that a scrivener, far from being a "civil confessor as a lawyer is," was "a person suspected in law as apt to make unlawful concealments." *Ibid.* 2: pp. 498–499. For discovery against a creditor, see *ibid.* 2: pp. 554–555.

57 *Nottingham's 'Manual'*, pp. 162–163.

sufficient to ensure that the court sometimes played a supervisory role. Granted that someone exhibited a bill of complaint, the court could oversee the proceedings of commissioners in selling the goods and lands of bankrupts, and it could try to ensure that all the creditors benefited equally.[58] One group of commissioners, having impounded the assets, was dubious whether an act of bankruptcy had in fact occurred. Debts were nonetheless owed, and Chancery in effect influenced the commission towards making a composition.[59] This court had no claim of jurisdiction over title to real property, but it could be of assistance in sorting out tricky questions surrounding the ownership of personal property when, for example, the rights of third parties were involved. In the middle of Elizabeth's reign, Nicholas Stockbridge bought goods at Antwerp from Danyell Rantflesh and promised to deliver kerseys in repayment on the next arrival of ships from London. Stockbridge paid the customs at London. The goods were then handed over to Thomas Speart, who almost immediately went bankrupt. Chancery decided that some items belonged to Stockbridge, and that they ought not to be handed over to Speart's creditors. The interesting factor is the procedure adopted. Petitioned by Rantflesh and others, the court had referred the matter to the bankruptcy commissioners. The latter, in reporting the proper course to take, acted more in accordance with authority given by Chancery than that provided by their commission.[60] The point has been seen before. It was wrong to force a man into being a creditor when his goods could be returned. Otherwise, intending bankrupts could manipulate the situation, and there was always the possibility of securing a composition or more favorable arrangements under the continuing cloak of a bankruptcy commission. Thomas Speart, for example, had previously been bankrupt and was probably a shrewd operator. His former creditors, some "poor" clothiers in the north of England, had discovered that his assets hardly covered one-third of his debts.[61]

A late Elizabethan case underlines the kind of problem posed by those who deliberately courted bankruptcy. John de Boys, a merchant stranger, handed over some brass to an English creditor, Coolye. This was partly to satisfy the debt and partly in return for cloth. He undertook to pay for all cloth received above the value of the brass. De Boys was making similar arrangements with other creditors, and so Coolye delivered only enough cloth to cover the value of the brass. De Boys, however, was "playing bankrupt." He made a "colorable" deed of gift to some other merchants, and these claimed that Coolye should fulfill his bargain and deliver all the cloth. This would have compelled him to become a joint creditor and only receive a rate for what he was owed. He, therefore, initiated proceedings in Chancery. The recommendation of a master was that the contract should be voided, since Coolye would otherwise be stampeded into the position of becoming a creditor after the declaration of bankruptcy.[62]

Depositions in another late Elizabethan case illustrate the information which may be culled from Chancery proceedings. Robert Nicholson, a London merchant, went bankrupt and was imprisoned. The exact circumstances of this confinement are not clear. However, he had consigned much of his estate to a single creditor, and the Chancery suit apparently represented an attempt by other creditors to overturn a *fait accompli* against which the bankruptcy commission, armed only with the authority provided in 1571, was nearly powerless. Witnesses examined in Chancery revealed that Nicholson's house in the Poultry had contained plate and household stuff worth £200, twenty-two packs of flax worth £400, and other commodities including buckram, wool, and Hampshire kerseys. Corn, cattle, and household items were at another house in Bramley, Surrey. Nicholson also had valuable interests overseas. His factor in Elburg, a London vintner, said that Nicholson "when he brake" had property worth twelve thousand florins (£2,400) in money, bills, and goods: alum, gilt leather, iron, amber, flax, hemp, canvas, linen cloth, and other fabrics. Most of this had been assigned to the principal creditor in a transaction which required the factor to work for the new owner, in return for which "his salary and pains should be satisfied to his contentment." The debtor was subtle. He had committed his supposed act of bankruptcy on 12 February, 1600, but official news of this would have taken some time to reach Elburg. In the meantime, the factor had been ordered to supervise a transference of assets to the principal creditor and his agents. This conveyance was made on 4 April. One of the conditions was that goods bought for Nicholson, whether before or after this date, should also be conveyed. This Chancery case, therefore, seems to involve the position of an individual creditor and the status of after-acquired property, consideration of which was com-

[58] P.R.O., C.33/81, f. 71: C.38/83, f. 22v. The lord chancellor could stand on both sides of the divide. In the reign of Elizabeth, Bromley authorized a commission to settle the debts of Anthony Marley, partner in an ironfounding enterprise at Merthyr, who was in danger of going bankrupt. In fact he seems to have done so, and Bromley's successor, Hatton, was involved in attempts to enforce settlement of the bankruptcy commission's arrangements. J. W. Gough, *The Rise of the Entrepreneur* (London, 1969), p. 83.

[59] P.R.O., C.33/103, f. 35, Bird v. Gamersall (1602). The case is possibly related to the one noted below, n. 63.

[60] P.R.O., C.38/1, Rantflesh v. Barneham (1582).

[61] *CSP Dom.* 1547–1580, p. 569.

[62] P.R.O., C.38/2, Coolye v. Victor (1597).

plicated by the fact that the goods in question were purchased abroad.[63]

Sloppy work by commissioners could also involve Chancery and other courts. This was most likely when insufficient attention was paid to the fact that a commission had to work not in a vacuum but amid a host of legal rights. *Allen's Case,* which lasted for over a decade and helped to raise fundamental questions as to Chancery jurisdiction, is a classic example.[64]

The story began with a merchant and former sheriff of York who went bankrupt in 1603 on being outlawed for debt. The bankruptcy commission sold his lands, said to be worth £2,400, to Allen and another creditor for £400. This was because the property was saddled with encumbrances made before the bankrupt had become indebted to any of the petitioners who had solicited the commission. However, it was stipulated that if this property was resold for a greater sum within three years, the profit was to be shared among all the creditors. Subsequently, in 1606, the commissioners arranged a composition for all the debts to be paid at the rate of ten shillings in the pound. This agreement was coupled with a bargain and sale of the lands to two other creditors at their real value. These two, one of whom had not initially joined in the bankruptcy proceedings, undertook to pay off the debts and encumbrances. Allen and his friend rejected this arrangement. They claimed that the encumbrances, essentially the debts due to others, were fraudulent, and they initiated proceedings in Chancery. It was quite proper to sue in Chancery if there was a doubt about the encumbrances, and it must also be said that the commissioners had rather complicated the situation. The two other creditors joined with the bankrupt in a cross bill calling for performance of the composition arranged by the commissioners and conveyance of the land. The resulting decree was in favor of Allen and his associate. They were to keep the lands, paying the remaining £30 due on a mortgage, and other encumbrances including a statute for £2,000 were discharged. Proceedings of execution upon a remaining statute of £1,500 were subsequently stayed. All this had taken some time, but the basic point was that within the three years originally specified the bankruptcy commissioners had found purchasers willing to pay the real value of the lands and to assume responsibility for payment of debts under the composition. Allen and his friend, if they intended to keep the lands as allowed by Chancery, should therefore have paid over the difference. This they declined to do.

There were many complications and characters involved at this stage, not least Allen's seizure of beasts belonging to the bankrupt's father and resulting actions in the King's Bench. The positions of the commissioners and Chancery were reconcilable, but both were concentrating upon different aspects of the dispute. The bankrupt and his wife, who had been turned out by force of a Chancery commission in support of Allen, died of the plague in London during July, 1610, leaving seven children, one of whom was "sucking at nurse." The lord chancellor thus received an extra responsibility by virtue of the special care for children reposed in him. "The pitiful cries of the father and mother (dying as is aforesaid) and of the poor orphans do call to God for relief and moved the heart of the lord chancellor." The case was reopened on behalf of the children, and Francis Moore, who had been on the Commons committee in 1604, was assigned as their counsel. John Tyndall, the Chancery master who was repeatedly involved in this matter, eventually produced a report which was the basis of a new Chancery decree. Allen and his friend were to receive their costs, but the proportional agreement reached by the bankruptcy commissioners was incorporated in the decree. Allen could keep the lands and pay over the additional value, or part with the lands and share with other creditors and the children in the profits. He refused to make the required election, and so late in 1613 another decree was issued. This, while still considerate towards Allen and his associate, was more favorable towards the children and other creditors. Allen was still to receive his costs, and debts due to him were to be paid at a rate decided by Tyndall, which some called generous. However, the lands were to be reconveyed to the benefit of all the creditors according to the composition, and it was calculated that this would leave £600 for the children. The Chancery bench and the bankruptcy commissioners were now in line with their priorities.

Allen was committed when he refused to perform the above decree. He subsequently produced two "judgments" in the Common Pleas for the entire debt owing to him which had been entered *after* the bankruptcy commission had been sued out and which had not, of course, been executed. It would be argued that he had not dwelt upon these in the course of the Chancery proceedings, or even mentioned them in his original bill and subsequent pleadings. He went on to claim that his freehold was being called in question by Chancery, and that this was contrary to Magna

[63] P.R.O., C.24/292, no. 12, Bird v. Carrell.

[64] There is a wealth of manuscript sources, including El. 5935–5936; Additional 11,596, f. 118 *et seq.*; Harleian 4265, p. 78 *et seq.* I have not had the time to trace through the most obvious and major source, the Chancery records. For this and related cases, see: J. P. Dawson, "Coke and Ellesmere Disinterred: The Attack on the Chancery in 1616," *Illinois Law Review* **36** (1941): pp. 127–152; J. H. Baker, "The Common Lawyers and the Chancery: 1616," *The Irish Jurist* **4** (1969): pp. 368–392; L. A. Knafla, *Law and Politics in Jacobean England* (Cambridge, 1977), pp. 155–181. This case, as perhaps the most important in the history of English bankruptcy, received more attention than any other from Goodinge, pp. 156–163.

Carta. Yet he had been one of those responsible for suing out the bankruptcy commission, and he had initiated proceedings in Chancery. Abusing the procedures of both commission and court, he was interpreted as trying to defraud his fellow creditors and the bankrupt's children in a fashion which was described as barbarous, covetous, and unconscionable.

The central point was that once bankruptcy had been declared, whatever the complications, Allen could not seek execution on judgments. The latter were suspended until distribution of the available assets had been completed. Thereafter they could be used against anything left over, but this avenue, particularly with respect to the children, was blocked by Chancery.

Allen's Case is renowned. It helped to lure an enthusiastic Coke into trouble, and it played a part in the jurisdictional disputes of 1615 and 1616. The questions raised by this case were similar to those found in others, notably with respect to arguments over Chancery activity after judgment at law. There were other cases and other men. Most of the issues then contested so fiercely, and Allen's subsequent activities, lie outside the scope of this study, as do many events in which Bacon, Coke, and Ellesmere were involved. The case is singular because it contained a number of specific elements which were clear by 1613. Up to a point, Chancery could claim priority of suit on the basis of Allen's own bill of complaint, but this was of minor import. Most crucial was the degree to which the lord chancellor was acting on the basis of responsibilities which were not intrinsic to the court of Chancery. These included his duty to protect the interests of orphaned infants. Hence Tyndall in his deliberations was required to keep an eye on anything which could be done for their relief. Even more significant, however much the situation may have been confused by commissioners and their composition, was the bankruptcy matter. The activities of bankruptcy commissioners might be challenged and found wanting at law, but they were vested firmly in statute. Hence it had already been recognized that a debt assigned by such a commission became "a debt transferred by Parliament." [65] Allen was trying to upset the dispositions of bankruptcy commissioners. When he tried to secure execution on judgments made after the action which constituted bankruptcy, he was trying to evade the intention of statute. Eventually the lord chancellor, as the statutory authority who had granted the commission, acted to preserve the intent of bankruptcy legislation.

It has been seen that in circumstances of both bankruptcy and debt there was considerable anxiety lest one or more creditors, possibly through arrangements with the debtor, might secure repayment at the expense of other creditors. It seems probable that Allen had been preparing the ground in such a direction. Late in Elizabeth's reign, William Lambarde had suggested that Chancery should become more involved in stopping this kind of thing. He also thought that existing legal procedures and conventions were inadequate. In a case involving the goods and debts of an intestate, one party was owed £50 but Lambarde wondered if the court really intended that this should be paid if other creditors received nothing in consequence. His own view was that there ought to be a system for proportional satisfaction, "being the fittest means (in so weak an estate of the deceased) to make conscionable satisfaction of such as he died indebted." [66] In other words, the problem could arise even without collusion. It was particularly acute when, as in the above case, the debtor had died and his remaining resources were insufficient. In circumstances far less extreme than these, many people advocated composition either in terms of further time or of reducing and perhaps sharing the total sum. Yet to do this, and follow Lambarde's suggestion that Chancery should arrange proportional or considerate settlements, would only be possible if dissenting creditors were restrained from exacting their legitimate rights.

One of the difficulties implicit in this situation was that recorded obligations—recognizances, statutes staple, statutes merchant—had the same quality as judgments handed down in open court. Indeed they were judgments which the "debtor" acknowledged in advance. They were obligations of record, conditional or future judgments, and hence in later language statutes merchant were often known as "pocket judgments." Naturally there were many variants, notably with respect to the giving or confessing of acknowledgment and subsequent procedure ranging from execution to action of debt upon the obligation. Even so, there was a distinction of both common sense and technicality between such forms and final judgments handed down in open court. Coke described the practical difference:

> Although both are records, yet the judgment in the King's court upon judicial and ordinary proceeding is more notorious and conspicuous, and of more high and eminent degree than a statute or recognizance taken in private, and by consent of the parties, and therefore preferred in judgment of law before a recognizance or statute. . . .[67]

Recorded and enrolled bonds of this nature were the most important contract mechanisms of the Tudor and early Stuart period. Sometimes, they repre-

[65] Cro. Jac., 105, The Case of Bradshaw (1605).

[66] See above, p. 30. P.R.O., C.38/4, Gybson v. Lownde (1600).

[67] 4 Co. Rep., 60*a*. See generally W. J. Jones, "An Introduction to Petty Bag Proceedings in the Reign of Elizabeth I," *California Law Review* **51** (1963): pp. 882–905.

sented real debts or the sureties for debts, but they also covered a wide range of undertakings from business matters to hunting expeditions. Attempts to block execution provided much business to English bill courts, whether established at Westminster or in the provinces and palatines.[68]

The irony in the situation is that there are indications that Lord Chancellor Ellesmere had been laying down ground rules, in effect restrictions, to govern the kind of relief allowed by Chancery. Long before 1615, he had complained about the number of persons in execution upon judgment for debt or damages who were allowed freedom from prison on the surety of a relative, or temporarily released from custody by *habeas corpus*. This, he stated, encouraged them to take no care to meet their debts.[69] As far as his own court was concerned, he could be more positive. In October, 1614, it was ordered that injunctions were not to issue to stay proceedings after judgment, verdict, and issue unless Chancery had priority of suit and proceedings there had been effectively pursued. Bills of complaint to stay payment of debts due on recorded bonds (or, for that matter, conditions broken on leases and mortgages) were not to be considered if there was evidence of willful default or gross negligence.[70] A number of litigants, including Allen —that he was fraudulent should not cloud the issue— helped to produce a crisis.

The confrontation on grounds of jurisdiction which exploded in 1615 and 1616, and to which the names of Coke and Ellesmere are attached, was at least partly occasioned by political circumstances. Genuine legal matters were raised, but it was not simply a conflict between these two judges. Moreover, issues presented were not always those for which either had prepared himself. They may even have thought alike on some of the points which attracted attention. However, the question of jurisdiction had been raised, and it could not be avoided. One result was an affirmation of Chancery jurisdiction, drafted by Bacon and inspired by Ellesmere: that plaintiffs had a right "to be relieved according to equity and conscience after judgments in the courts of common law in cases where the judges of the common law could not relieve them."[71]

After the rumpus of 1616, the nature of Chancery powers was ostensibly unchanged. Yet its ability to intervene after judgment at law had been upheld and defined.[72] On this basis, Francis Bacon tried to build a systematic policy for the relief of debtors.

Bankruptcy was a means whereby the creditors shared available assets. During the life of the commission the bankrupt could, if allowed, earn money toward payment of his remaining debts. The notion of composition was always present and possible but was not mentioned by the statutes, and there was no discharge. This was deplored by an Elizabethan commentator: "For as the execution of the statute taketh from the bankrupt all that he hath to the utter overthrow of him and his family and the creditors commonly not half paid, so good compositions bringeth in time full payment to the creditors and preservation to the poor men." It has already been seen that compositions on a ratable basis were encouraged by such late Elizabethan lawyers as Lambarde, and there are occasional instances in which creditors seem to have been required to compound. The Privy Council might forward such an arrangement. The real possibility, however, was that a regular relationship might be established between composition, bankruptcy commissions, and the court of Chancery. In a disordered fashion, these elements became conjoined in *Allen's Case*, but the notion was older. In the mid-1590's, one debtor agreed with creditors on a composition for repayment at the rate of two-thirds in the pound, but dissenting creditors had him arrested and forced him to enter a statute for payment of the full debts owing to them. The other creditors, therefore, took out a bankruptcy commission which seized the assets; their rivals proceeded with execution and took out an extent upon the statute. A bill was exhibited in Chancery and an injunction issued to stop the execution.[73]

There was nothing new about conformity and composition. Various compositions and methods of conformity were commonly arranged in the city of London, usually by license but sometimes in collaboration with commissioners of bankruptcy. More generally the procedure of bill of conformity, it was said, had originally developed in the court of Requests before this avenue was blocked by prohibitions. It was then adopted in Chancery by Ellesmere who was "very wary in granting" such petitions, doing so only "in case of extremity." However, a significant aspect of Bacon's control of the Chancery bench in the brief period, 1617–1621, was the way in which he tried to associate the impulse towards composition with conformity among creditors, and also tried to make this burgeoning system apply to situations of bankruptcy. The resulting situation was deemed deplorable by many. "Of late much lenity has been used to all

[68] There were other means, such as *audita querela*, which might be of help in combating or delaying a creditor who sued out execution upon a recorded obligation, but most of these methods had little relevance to the particular circumstances being considered here.

[69] El. 2623. Knafla, p. 276.

[70] Sanders 1, i: pp. 86–87.

[71] *Ibid.* 1, i: p. 90.

[72] Decades later, Nottingham referred to the "exploded opinion" that to sue in Chancery after judgment was a *praemunire*. *Nottingham's Cases* 2: p. 870.

[73] P.R.O., S.P.12/146, no. 125. I. Treiman, "Majority Control in Compositions: Its Historical Origins and Development," *Virginia Law Review* 24 (1938): p. 519.

debtors, so that many [creditors], after four or five years suit and charges in this court, were glad to go away with their principal without costs or damages."[74]

Any attempt to arrange a composition, even if it was just with the standard intention of providing further time, meant that influence had to be used against creditors who wished to secure an immediate and full recovery of what was owing. The situation was eased when a commission had been sued out under the bankruptcy statutes. This was because the creditors' ability had been suspended by legislation. Even so, there was always the possibility of difficulty occasioned by creditors who chose not to join or who flouted agreements. Allen illustrates the point: he had asked for and joined with the commission, but he had not found its arrangements to his liking. If his position had been maintained, the system of bankruptcy proceedings would have been undermined.

In 1620, one case concerned a debtor and his creditors who had agreed on payment through installments spread over a period of years. However, a single creditor persuaded the debtor to enter a statute merchant as additional security which would give him a legal advantage if the debtor defaulted. Consequently, the other creditors sued out a bankruptcy commission. In any case, the first installment was not paid on time and the statute merchant was put into execution. The greater part of the estate was extended. Turning to Chancery, the other creditors obtained an order that the extent was to be stayed, the statute merchant was to be surrendered, and the bankruptcy commission was to proceed without hindrance.[75] It is not entirely clear whether the recent agreement was abrogated. This may have been so because the debtor should not have made a commitment to one man which threatened the interests of other creditors. However, it is possible that the bankruptcy commission was expected to confirm the agreement. It was, after all, a year which witnessed the climax of Bacon's policy of conformity.

Building on the long-established sense that some situations were unfair, Bacon tried to create a coherent system. Success would have meant the establishment of a new segment of procedure and jurisdiction; indeed it was a complaint of critics in 1621 that this had already happened. The idea was that majority groups of creditors, representing at least two-thirds of the sum due, would petition in Chancery to compel the other creditors into joining a ratable composition or provision for further time. These bills of conformity might have been impossible had not Chancery's powers after judgment at law been so unequivocally explained in 1616.

The case of *Tiffin v. Hart*, 1618–1619, concerned an insolvent who died leaving a debt of over £9,800, most of which was secured by bonds. His sons offered to surrender both his and their estates, valued at £5,500, if the creditors would accept a proportionate settlement in full discharge. Few were willing, but after a petition to the king, who set up a committee, the creditors were divided on this offer: fifty-five accepted, but twenty-five (who were owed less than twenty-five per cent of the total) refused and commenced action at law. The sons and the majority group of creditors countered with a bill in Chancery and secured an injunction for stay of the proceedings at law. After a second petition to the king, which was referred to the lord chancellor, it was subsequently held that the dissenting creditors were to be bound by the agreement of the majority. The only exception was that those who had advanced money held in trust for infants, or free of interest, were to be repaid in full by specified installments.[76]

Creditors who refused composition might be "unreasonable,"[77] but often some had lent money on terms more generous and less profitable to themselves than was the case with those who were willing to accept a composition. Such people were irritated by Bacon's policy of enforcing conformity and enraged by his apparent readiness to imprison dissenters.

One debtor had been allowed further time by the majority of his creditors, but their bill of conformity was rejected when they failed to rebut a defense motion for dismissal. Probably this was a procedural error. In consequence, the king was petitioned. He referred the matter to the bishop of London and three others who were described as "a commission in the nature of a commission of bankruptcy." They concluded that none of the creditors could receive satisfaction unless further time was given. The matter came back into Chancery where it was decided that the debtor was to be given four years in which to

---

[74] Tothill, 47, Mildmay v. Wentworth (1613). *APC* 1590, p. 98. *Common Debates 1621* **5**: p. 39; **6**: pp. 63–64. T. Powel, *The Mysterie of Lending and Borrowing* (London, 1623), pp. 11, 18, 51. Turner, *Equity of Redemption*, p. 31.

[75] J. Ritchie, *Reports of Cases Decided by Francis Bacon, 1617–21* (London, 1932) pp. 165–166, Overman v. Wright (1620). See the Elizabethan case above, at n. 73.

[76] *Ibid.*, pp. 161–164.

[77] *Ibid.*, p. 165, Ryder v. Turner (1617). One who benefited was Sir Henry Finch, serjeant-at-law, who had served as a referee in *Tiffin v. Hart.* He became insolvent, but although his only means of repayment was through his profession, the creditors had brought actions on the bonds against him and his sons. *Ibid.*, pp. 166–167, Finch v. Hicks (1620). In 1621, this case was instanced by Coke and Cranfield as an appalling example. Prestwich, pp. 299–300. Some years later his son, John Finch, the future chief justice and lord keeper, who had agreed to pay what was owing, received a protection for one year from arrest for debt. P.R.O., S.P.39/14, no. 66.

meet his obligations, and in the meantime actions at law, including those against his sureties, were stayed.[78]

Whatever its "nature," the commission appointed in the above case cannot be regarded as a commission of bankruptcy. The affair, however, seems to fit in with a procedural device which was being developed. Most plaintiffs maintained their suits in Chancery, but the court did not really want to imprison defendants who resisted composition. A formula might be constructed in those instances where the debtor could be declared a bankrupt. The majority creditors, in association with the debtor, would submit a bill of conformity in Chancery, subsequently petitioning the lord chancellor for a bankruptcy commission. This would be granted, but the petitioners would be asked to secure a binding and final composition. Since the majority creditors were already agreed, this would not cause difficulty. Minority creditors, those who opposed composition, could either come to heel and join or remain aloof and risk recovering nothing. The settlement arranged by the bankruptcy commission, which by itself had no authority to make a final composition, would be confirmed by the Chancery, which had prior jurisdiction because of the bill of conformity. Those clauses of the bankruptcy statutes which made it possible for creditors to take their own legal initiatives, once the commission had done its work, would thus be negated.[79]

A clever procedure had been developed to support the notion that a bankruptcy commission, where feasible, should try to secure a composition. This was just a little segment of the policy of conformity sustained by Bacon from 1617. He himself had known what it was like to live under almost unbearable stress as a debtor. Furthermore, his brief period as lord keeper and then as lord chancellor, 1617–1621,[80] coincided with a shattering depression. Business failures were widespread, landed men were suffering, workers were unemployed, and creditors were rarely in a worse position to insist upon complete and individual satisfaction. In trying to produce a procedure to meet situations which many had previously considered absurd, Bacon had the advantage that Chancery's position had recently been clarified. But his approach was not liked. The former warden of the Fleet claimed that Chancery had become more lavish in granting writs of *habeas corpus* to aid debtors. On the other hand, he opined that although hardly any creditors were actually restrained because of bills of conformity, the very possibility aroused anger and apprehension: "Creditors were in dread of those bills and were against those bills for fear they might be imprisoned and checked in their prosecution of debtors. . . ."[81] Hostility was expressed by people who had immediate reason to feel that they had been wronged, and by those who believed that all bills of conformity gave unjustifiable encouragement to willful debtors. In these years of slump, some claimed that bills of conformity invited foreigners to withdraw their capital and interests from England.[82] It was easy to portray the predicament of minority creditors as a denial of justice. They could lose money or even end up in prison merely for trying to obtain their due on the basis of contracts, judgments, and obligations which had been entered into freely.

It is the above contradiction which makes arguments of 1620–1621 more poignant than those of 1615–1616. On the previous occasion, the debate had been largely fortuitous. Now it was a genuine clash, enhanced but not created by the slump, between a reasoned expectation of legal forms and a conscious attempt to limit the effect of these forms. In the summer of 1620, James I was petitioned by Londoners to do something about bills of conformity.[83] In October, Bacon issued orders which refined and limited the conditions under which they might be considered: "that no compulsory order be granted to enforce creditors to conform themselves and agree unto any rate or composition at the suit or petition of the debtor or insolvent himself but only at the suit of the creditors in imitation and according to the equity of the statute of bankrupts." Petitioning creditors now had to represent three-quarters of the sum due. There were other limitations, and in any case Chancery would only proceed with great caution. Bacon, however, was still clinging to his fundamental principle: it was possible to link the social justification for composition in matters of debt with the restricted but explicit notions of bankruptcy.[84]

This was only one of the issues which Bacon had to face in 1621. Had this been all, he might have been able to ride out the storm and even justify bills of conformity on grounds of social need. Only it was not all. Bacon was implicated in the onslaught upon the referees, the Chancery was under general attack because of its complexity and cost, and Buckingham was not prepared to risk himself to save the lord chancellor. Bacon was charged with taking gratuities. Chancery was accused of damaging commerce. A member of Parliament voiced the idea that although a predecessor had helped to create the problem, the consequences "will proceed from Chancellor to Chancery."[85] Bacon was under fire from too many directions. On 31 March, a royal proclamation provided

[78] Ritchie, pp. 191–192, Brooke v. Goode (1619).
[79] *Ibid.*, p. 193, Bourne v. Ironmonger (1619).
[80] Bacon received the higher title on 4 January, 1618.

[81] A. Harris. *The Œconomy of the Fleete*, ed. A. Jessup, Camden Soc., new ser. 25 (1879), pp. 107–109.
[82] *Commons Debates 1621* 7: p. 581.
[83] *Ibid.* 4: p. 67.
[84] Sanders 1, i: pp. 129–131.
[85] *CJ* 1: p. 573.

that bills of conformity were to be dismissed unless all the creditors had consented, and new bills were not to be received. On 18 April, this was implemented by a Chancery order. The possibility of using Chancery or any other court (others were covered by the proclamation) to arrange a composition was not totally erased. Henceforth, however, petitioning creditors would have to represent three-quarters of the sum owing, acceptance would have to be achieved without compulsion, and the debtor was not to be a petitioner.[86]

In 1624, the critics completed their victory. Under the new bankruptcy statue, a person who sought a composition for further time was liable to become a bankrupt, assuming that his trade or means of livelihood made this possible, unless he made his approach in good time and with the utmost propriety. Otherwise a debtor could, by the very attempt at negotiation with creditors, be construed as having committed an act of bankruptcy. In these circumstances, a minority of creditors might petition for a commission of bankruptcy, and as yet no one had said that the lord chancellor could refuse such a request. Thus subsequently it is possible to find victims, such as an unfortunate feltmaker, once employing dozens but now fallen on bad times, who was imprisoned for debt. Fifteen of his creditors agreed to give him respite for four years, but the remaining two refused and obtained a bankruptcy commission.[87]

NOTTINGHAM

In the 1630's, Lord Keeper Coventrye and the Privy Council tried to probe the situation, but they could not produce any concrete reappraisals. Interpretation of the statutory system belonged increasingly to the judges, and this was so whether under monarchy or republic. It was apparent that some tricky questions had been posed, but these did not receive positive answers. It cannot be said that they were even accorded serious analysis.

First and foremost, there was the old conundrum of the lord chancellor's authority. Under the Henrician statute, it is clear that jurisdiction in all ways was directly in the hands of those who had power to act, and the lord chancellor was always the most prominent of these and probably the effective agent in practice. If he chose to appoint commissioners to do the job, this was out of necessity and convenience. The Elizabethan statute, however, specifically mentioned the appointment of commissioners. During the hundred years after 1571, the lord chancellor seems on occasion to have made or unmade commissions and tried to ensure that these did not abuse their position. On the other hand, it does not appear that he reviewed their decisions.[88] No one was absolutely sure if the chancellor could refuse a request for a commission, and certainly there was no clear idea as to the extent of his authority once a commission had issued. But if the authority of the chancellor was in any way vague, it followed that the authority of the commissioners was equally amorphous. The situation was abominably obscure, and Holdsworth had natural difficulties in trying to explain the structure of authority created by the 1571 act. This "gave to the chancellor power to appoint, by commission under the Great Seal, certain persons to exercise the powers of the chancellor over the person and property of the bankrupt. The act gave no jurisdiction in bankruptcy to the court of Chancery. It gave the chancellor no control over the commissioners." The chancellor might seem to be no more than the statutory, administrative means through which a satisfactory commission could be appointed. Could it then be said that the commissioners were exercising his power? This, of course, was the kind of point which Coke tried to explain to James I when it was a matter of debating judicial independence, but it is unlikely that such sophistication was applied to the comparatively miniscule circumstance of bankruptcy commissioners.[89]

In practice, most chancellors were uncertain about their authority and were cautious in their actions, but hardly anyone thought that a commission of bankruptcy had a judicial status distinct from the power of the chancellor. In the reign of Charles II, Nottingham cut through the tangle by deciding that the grant of a commission of bankruptcy was analogous to the grant of a commission of sewers. He then proceeded to demolish this conclusion as undesirable.[90]

---

[86] Sanders 1, i: pp. 132–134. Lansdowne 569, f. 26. Despite these restrictions, it was claimed that debtors still found means to restrain their creditors. *Commons Debates 1621* **7**: pp. 581–582.

[87] Treiman, "Majority Control," p. 521.

[88] *Nottingham's Cases* **1**: p. cxv. In a case already noted, the lord chancellor suspended the proceedings of a commission by ordering issue of a *supersedeas*. A *procedendo*, permitting continuation, was later awarded. Monro, p. 286.

[89] Holdsworth **1**: p. 470. Holdsworth presumed that in the seventeenth century commissioners who were in legal difficulty "applied" to the common law courts. The degree to which this was true is uncertain, but in any case action by the chancellor or proceedings in Chancery were not excluded. Most of the legal difficulties experienced resulted in the commissioners appearing as defendants and pleading the authority of their commission in actions with respect to which the chancellor could be of little help.

[90] *Nottingham's 'Manual'*, p. 161. The impact of Nottingham's work can be seen in Blackstone's conclusion (**3**: p. 427) that the lord chancellor had a summary jurisdiction "in many matters consequential or previous to the commissions. . . ." Holdsworth (**1**: p. 471), describing the eighteenth-century situation, went a little too far: "Original jurisdiction was exercised by commissioners. Their appointment was in the absolute control of the lord chancellor; but when appointed he had no control over them." According to

Nottingham began by acknowledging that there was complete uncertainty as to whether the lord chancellor had discretion to grant or refuse a commission. He accepted that the power to grant, based upon the 1571 statute, might be interpreted as implying that there must be a right of denial. He was also aware that several *caveats*, against granting commissions until the arguments of the parties had been heard, were entered during Coventrye's lord keepership. However, his conclusion, aided by a decision of 1647–1648, was that the application represented a petition of right. This could not be refused and the commissions were granted *de jure*. In addition, and despite varying precedents, he concluded that the lord chancellor could not grant a limited or qualified commission.[91]

Nottingham would have made a good historian. On the evidence of the past, he was capable of reaching an interpretation which was repugnant to him. He then commented unfavorably on the situation:

> This makes the commissioners of bankruptcy very untractable and hard to be regulated, because they think they have authority by act of Parliament and though they execute it never so extravagantly, yet they need fear no control but that of an action against them at law.

He suggested that the lord chancellor should have the power to "supersede" a commission "if they proceed indiscreetly." Though what had been done could not be undone, a new commission of "wiser men" could handle the remaining business.[92]

Nottingham was most concerned with those situations when the indiscretion and ill-doings of the commissioners had become apparent. Even so, action should only be taken after due consideration and examination. If the bankrupt and all the creditors were satisfied that the commissioners were behaving improperly, a petition for a *supersedeas* should be allowed. If the petition was not unanimous, however, extreme care was needed for fear of collusion. In this circumstance, suggested Nottingham, the commissioners should be asked how far they had proceeded. Only if the four-month period, before which distribution could not begin, was not completed, or nearly so, should a *supersedeas* issue.[93]

Nottingham's analysis and the procedure proposed opened the way for a new jurisdiction. He was cautious, and he was reluctant to grant appeals from statutory jurisdictions. He seems to have believed that the speed of remedy offered usually outweighed most grievances. He did hear a complaint that the commissioners had not allowed proof of a debt, but he was doubtful, since the commissioners were liable to an action at law. The precedent, he feared, might result in the execution of all bankruptcy commissions being inspected.[94] There can be little doubt that Nottingham intended supervision to be exercised with restraint, but the culmination of his work was the development in Chancery of an appellate bankruptcy jurisdiction.

AFTER NOTTINGHAM

From the end of the seventeenth century, the lord chancellor's interest in the affairs of bankrupts and bankruptcy commissions was gradually extended. There was also a renewal of statutory activity, and legislation in the reign of Anne really indicates the start of a new chapter. Most notable was a statute late in her reign which voided existing descriptions of a bankrupt.[95] One novelty was the bankrupt's certificate of discharge, which could be allowed by the lord chancellor or any two judges to whom he referred the matter.[96] By another statute, the commissioners were required to assign the bankrupt's effects to persons picked by the creditors. These assignees, construed in law as trustees, were subject to the chancellor's equitable jurisdiction, and proceedings by English bill could be commenced against them in the normal fashion.[97] In 1732, they were declared to be officials of the Great Seal. Then and subsequently, their duties were clarified: collection of the bankrupt's effects, payment of dividends, and presentation to the commissioners of proper accounts for receipts and expenditures. Under certain circumstances the chancellor, if petitioned by creditors, could dismiss the assignees or suspend the commission.[98]

The chancellor's control over bankruptcy proceedings had been recognized by statute. In practice, he would continue to work through his court, and Chancery's involvement with bankruptcy matters apparently increased radically from the 1730's. It has been suggested that this was encouraged, at least in part, by an awareness of the large fees which thereby accrued

Montagu, the issue of commissions and all questions arising were the original jurisdiction of the lord chancellor. However, execution of commissions was given to commissioners who were assistant judges provided by Parliament for the lord chancellor. Whether the lord chancellor had a direct jurisdiction was uncertain, but Montagu thought that this was probably so since he could make an order on a petition just as he could make a decree in Chancery. B. Montagu, *Inquiries*.

[91] *Nottingham's 'Manual'*, pp. 161–162. The word "may" was construed as "must": the lord chancellor "must" grant a commission. 1 Eq. Ca. Abr., 52.

[92] *Nottingham's 'Manual'*, p. 162.

[93] *Ibid.*, p. 164.

[94] *Nottingham's Cases* **1**: pp. cxiii–cxvi, 313.

[95] 10 Anne c. 25.

[96] 4 and 5 Anne c. 4. Holdsworth (**1**: p. 470), on the authority of C. P. Cooper, concluded that the chancellor usually referred this matter to the judges, until Hardwicke's time (1737–1757).

[97] 6 Anne c. 22.

[98] Holdsworth **1**: p. 470. 5 George II c. 30.

to the chancellor.[99] In 1831, as part of a general move towards reorganization of the court of Chancery, some attempt was made to improve the situation. Jurisdiction in bankruptcy was transferred from the lord chancellor to a chief judge in bankruptcy, who was to be assisted by three judges and six commissioners. The line of appeal was to a court of review and then to the lord chancellor,[100] but in 1847 this court of review was abolished and its jurisdiction given to a vice-chancellor.[101]

The flaw in Nottingham's inheritance should have been apparent to later chancellors and to legislators, at least from the reign of Anne. The chancellor's ability to exercise his powers and initiative weakened under the monolithic slowness of eighteenth and early nineteenth-century Chancery proceedings. Bankruptcy questions were just one more burden, and Montagu noted that in the early nineteenth century Chancery business was constantly interrupted by such matters.[102] It would, however, be false to pinpoint a single area of jurisdicion. The problems of Chancery were far greater than that. This was a tribunal which was clearly overworked and which had never struggled free from the complex machinery of pleading and proof bestowed upon it by Elizabethan chancellors. That this endowment was vital to its position is a standard contradiction of modern administrative development. In these conditions, adequate control over the bankruptcy commissioners, who exercised original jurisdiction, was not in fact possible. This partly explains why bankruptcy commissioners acquired a scandalous reputation because of their charges, their apparent ability to become principal beneficiaries from the estates of bankrupts, and their capacity to evade statutes aimed at limiting reprehensible habits.[103] Equally disturbing was the widespread evasion of bankruptcy proceedings by debtors.[104] Lists of commissioners of bankruptcy existed in London, and though there were not at first similar lists for the rest of the country, the situation seems to have been equally appalling. Eradication of this state of affairs became a major concern of nineteenth-century legal reformers. In 1869, the London court of bankruptcy was established, and the situation was again transformed by the Judicature Act of 1873. The county commissioners were replaced by local bankruptcy courts, and these were eventually superseded by the county courts.[105]

Debtors in seventeenth-century Massachusetts, as in England, had no procedure approaching the modern discharge of bankruptcy, and they were probably even more helpless than those in the mother country with respect to their ability to secure a composition.[106] After the revolution, the bankruptcy laws of the United States continued to be an offspring of Tudor and Stuart ideas. However, article I, section 8, of the constitution, ratified in June, 1788, contained a commitment to establish uniform laws with respect to bankruptcies. An act of 1800, repealed after three years, applied only to traders, but legislation of 1841, also repealed shortly, and the important act of 1867 applied to persons other than traders and merchants.[107] By this time, the United Kingdom Parliament had also moved in the same direction.

Early eighteenth-century legislation in England reveals some changes in attitudes. The very idea of a discharge, although itself a source of abuse, must have done something to solve the old problem of further liability on which so many attempts at composition had foundered. Statute even permitted an allowance for maintenance to be made to a bankrupt who surrendered promptly.[108] There may well have been some sympathy, but if so, it was checked by the somewhat severe provisions of the 1732 statute, passed during a period when considerable additions were being made to the list of capital offenses.[109] Thereafter, a string of statutes tackled a variety of problems: wages, estates tail, arrears of rent, and so on.[110] In 1847, a court for the relief of insolvent debtors was set up. This was designed to assist insolvents who were not merchants or traders

[99] Holdsworth 1: p. 471. For a comment on Mansfield and the activities of the King's Bench in hearing references from the chancellors or actions brought by receivers, see Harding, p. 317.

[100] 1 and 2 William IV c. 56.

[101] Holdsworth 1: p. 443. 10 and 11 Victoria c. 102, *2. The statute of 6 George IV c. 16 had repealed existing bankruptcy legislation and consolidated the bankruptcy laws.

[102] Montagu, *Inquiries*.

[103] The 1705 statute inhibited allowance for "eating and drinking" by the commissioners and others at meetings of creditors. 4 and 5 Anne c. 4, *21.

[104] J. H. T. Hughes, *Fluctuations in Trade, Industry and Finance: A Study of British Economic Development, 1850–1860* (Oxford, 1960), p. 33.

[105] Holdsworth 1: pp. 444, 471–473.

[106] However, other rules concerning debtors "were far in advance of contemporary English practice." G. L. Haskins, *Law and Authority in Early Massachusetts* (New York, 1960), pp. 215–220, 286.

[107] Teevan and Smith, p. 953. For a brief account of events, see C. Warren, *Bankruptcy in United States History* (Cambridge, Mass., 1935). In the last quarter of the nineteenth century, some felt that there was a disturbing swing in favor of creditors. The case for voluntary bankruptcy was argued in the House of Representatives by a lawyer who felt that this trend should be restrained. F. G. Newlands, *Bankruptcy, its Cause and Remedy* (Washington, 1896).

[108] 4 and 5 Anne c. 4, *8.

[109] See Jenks, pp. 384–388. The establishment of the death penalty for non-surrender and concealment occasioned few prosecutions and, in a period of almost ninety years, only about four executions. The overall trend towards severity must not be exaggerated. A statute of 1774, describing many bankrupts and debtors as well-meaning but unfortunate, asserted that such "have always been deemed the proper objects of public compassion." 14 George III c. 77.

[110] Jenks, pp. 384–385.

and who could not be made bankrupt. The idea was that they could escape imprisonment for debt by surrendering their property.[111] The device indicates the degree to which bankruptcy had gradually come to be seen as having distinct advantages for the debtor. The surprising thing is that, once the discharge had been introduced, it should have taken so long for bankruptcy principles to be extended beyond those who lived through buying and selling, and even after 1847 variations were still played on the ancient theme of occupational distinction. The comprehensive statute of 1849, while introducing several new rules, made little breach in the durability of this particular legacy.[112] Only in 1861 was the distinction between traders and non-traders abolished.[113] Married women were still excluded, and a statute of 1869 confined its "voluntary settlement" clause to traders.[114]

By the mid-nineteenth century the game laws, another species of regulation, had undergone revision. They have been described as "a privilege conferred by a ruling class on itself merely as a perquisite of ruling"; change occurred when "the rule of the landed of which those laws were the symbol" weakened.[115] Whereas the game laws had excluded most classes of men from hunting, the bankruptcy laws had confined one category within a particular set of rules affecting the payment of debts. There were, of course, major differences between the two positions. But if it can be argued that the game laws, whatever their economic value, symbolized a social privilege, the bankruptcy laws came to represent certain privileges, notably the discharge, which could be of advantage to other classes of men.

English bankruptcy had its inception in four Tudor and early Stuart statutes. The law then created was penal in character, and there is no need to quarrel with contemporaries who conceived that the statutes were made against certain categories of debtor. The idea of helping bankrupts was not present. It must be asked how far these attitudes were a product of the contemporary social structure and its assumptions.

V. GENTLEMEN, LAWYERS, MERCHANTS, AND TRADESMEN

A clear expansion of England's economy only occurred in the second half of the seventeenth century. Earlier, despite an initial and spurious prosperity for the first decade of James's reign, there was often little confidence and much gloom. The 1624 bankruptcy statute was framed in this atmosphere, and yet it would have to do service in the more halcyon days of the Restoration. Furthermore, the commissioners were hampered by restraints and inadequacies, bearable and even understandable prior to the 1650's, which demanded revision.

The central conundrum, although founded on unavoidable statute law, can only be described in social terms: everything had come to depend upon the assumption that it was feasible to make a differential analysis of men according to their occupations, sources of income, and modes of life. The statutes themselves provided labels, but they did little in the way of providing definitions. In consequence, the commissioners sometimes occupied a no-man's-land between the label and the task of determining what it meant. However, the situation can be stated crudely: if a person could be construed as living by buying and selling, and if he committed an act which had been specified by the bankruptcy statutes, then his prospects were governed by procedures which did not apply to others. A peculiar department had been created within the varied laws and rules of debt. It was a legal distinction, but it was also a social one.

Any bankrupt is and was a person unable to back his formerly assumed credit with cash. Accountancy books and manuals have been cited as evidence for the development of credit organization in late Tudor England, but it would be difficult to assert that techniques of banking and credit were seen by contemporaries as adequate.[1] On the other hand, merchants were practical: they only relied upon such credit facilities as were available. Cash was still the favored basis for commercial transactions. Professor Supple has stressed the mobility of mercantile assets and capital in the early Stuart period, and he has illustrated the degree to which hard money was used. This was particularly so in the market for white cloth: merchants generally had to conclude immediate transactions for the purchase of cloth coming up to London.[2] Nonetheless, there were serious limitations. The general rate of interest and profit was probably too low with respect to the long-term average rate of return on trading capital.[3] Merchants, whether creditors or debtors, not uncommonly failed to secure loans, translate assets into cash, or take up money by bills of exchange.

---

111 10 and 11 Victoria c. 102, *4.

112 12 and 13 Victoria c. 106.

113 24 and 25 Victoria c. 134. This statute abolished the court for the relief of insolvent debtors. The companies act of 1862 coalesced the concepts of joint-stock and incorporation. The principle was reached that a company could go into liquidation but could not be made bankrupt. Cooke, pp. 18, 172.

114 Jenks, p. 386.

115 J. H. Hexter, *Reappraisals in History* (New York, 1963), p. 17.

---

1 R. D. Richards, *The Early History of Banking* (London, 1929), pp. 20–21.

2 Supple, pp. 10, 40, 173. It has been suggested that small graziers, lacking capital, purchased sheep on credit and paid after the wool had been sold. Large graziers, capable of extending credit to middlemen and manufacturers, might be in a different situation. Bowden, pp. 13–14.

3 R. Grassby, "The Rate of Profit in Seventeenth-Century England," *EHR* **84** (1969): pp. 732–733.

Whatever the relationship between cash and credit may have been, living on credit was habitual. Failure to meet obligations, no less than evasion of paying debts, was certainly not confined to merchants and traders. It may be that the landed gentleman, whose flow of income could be irregular, was particularly compelled to rely upon his credit. Those who depended upon lands and tenements might distrust existing banking arrangements, such as they were, and choose to store surplus capital as bullion and plate. At the same time, however, they were exploiting the rules of conveyancing and exploring the subtleties of mortgage and redemption. Furthermore, many of those who borrowed had good credit, and the fact of their borrowing should not be construed as financial difficulty.

Although merchants probably made a greater use of cash than has sometimes been appreciated, it may be that contemporary and landed observers, the parliamentary types, overestimated the extent to which this ability prevailed among *all types* of traders, including those who had to trust the credit of their customers. Likewise, the prosperity of the business community seems to have been magnified in the eyes of others, and this without much appreciation either of distinctions of wealth, and thus of opportunities for profit within that community, or of the much vaguer but nonetheless real distinctions of rank between the various styles of trading. The bankruptcy statutes seem to have been based upon the assumption that traders pressed to repay debts should be able to find cash, possibly by selling assets, or be able to provide some suitable alternative. If this was not so, a bankruptcy commission might take over and do the job for them. The implication was that excuses or requests for extra time were likely to be dishonest or futile. There was no provision for the retailer, who bought and sold on credit because he lacked an alternative, or for the merchant who had allowed the bulk of his assets to be tied up, let us suppose safely, in another country. If a ship came home after the appointment of a commission, guidelines had not been provided to govern or encourage termination of the proceedings.

It might be argued that these strictures miss the point. The number of bankruptcy commissions was small in comparison with litigation for recovery of debts or goods. There must be a supposition that in most instances genuine failure had occurred and that bankrupts had lost their credit reputations in the eyes of men of their own kind. It was mostly businessmen who sued out commissions. The trouble was that once an initiative was taken, other creditors had little alternative. Bankruptcy was intimately concerned with the dissolution of a man's credit, a point different from his potential ability or inability to repay all his debts. Delay on the part of hesitant creditors was pointless, and if protracted might result in their exclusion from a share in the fruits of the proceedings. Once the claim of bankruptcy was raised, the only sensible approach was that of "follow the leader."

Whatever advice was given, it was Parliament and not the business community which framed these statutes. Hence bankruptcy law during its first two centuries was welded between two conflicting points of view. The assumptions and attitudes of landed men were sometimes best expressed by lawyers, and mercantile doubt or dissent found expression in the writings of contemporary economic disputants. These different points of view are reflected in the works of Coke and Malynes. At this elevated level, however, little attention was paid to ordinary shopkeepers and traders—the butchers, bakers, and chandlers—although these comprised the overwhelming majority of those who went bankrupt.

Coke's writings are of great importance and even his defects, often as disturbing as they are discernible, cannot detract from the brilliance of the whole or from the particular genius of this tempestuous character. He was proud of never casting "his penny into the water,"[4] and he sometimes had harsh things to say about merchants. This does not mean that he was obtuse, and he probably thought more about economic problems than many other lawyers. The catalog of his library contains fifteen "books of trade," including Wheeler's *Treatise of Commerce.* Other works touched agriculture: these were mostly in Italian, although Tusser was there.[5] Coke, who participated in several cases of commercial interest, was an intelligent and well-read person whose ideas and assumptions may be taken as reasonably representative of the considered mood which lay behind statutes and even government policy. Among privy councillors he alone supported Cockayn's project and with the king completed a trio which promoted that disastrous and probably fraudulent undertaking. The point is not that the bulk of advice was against the project, or that he subsequently turned against it, but that the chief justice was acting as a commercial adviser. Yet his attitude towards the bankruptcy laws, coming as it did from a well-furred elder of the legal profession, may help us to understand why it was that so many merchants wanted to have as little as possible to do with lawyers, their ways, and their logic.

Writing about bankruptcy in the fourth volume of his *Institutes,* composed in the late 1620's, Coke moved dangerously close to that deadly flaw of insularity which could discolor expositions of English law and institutions. "We have fetched as well the name as the wickedness of bankrupts from foreign

[4] Cited, L. Stone, *The Crisis of the Aristocracy, 1558–1641* (Oxford, 1965), p. 377.

[5] *A Catalogue of the Library of Sir Edward Coke,* ed. W. O. Hassall (New Haven, 1950), pp. 80–81, 83, 85.

nations." Granted that this predicament was a matter of statutory creation, he was justified insofar as he conceived that it could not have existed prior to the first bankruptcy statute. Yet he managed to blend this truism into an impression that similar behavior—"bankruptcy" as a socially recognizable circumstance—had also been unknown in England. Apart from a medieval statute which was concerned with Lombards,[6] he took the absence of legislation before 1543 as evidence that Englishmen had behaved with propriety. "In former times as the name of bankrupt, so was the offense itself (as hath been said) a stranger to an Englishman, who of all other nations was freest of bankruptcy."[7]

Coke in this chapter did not consider the possibility that later medieval society had developed procedures inadequate for many peculiarities of debt. It should also be remembered that England, despite certain important branches of commerce, had not been a trading center comparable to Northern Italy, the Low Countries, or Barcelona, where countless mercantile themes and interests could intermingle. He did, however, appreciate that responsibility for subsequent developments could not be placed solely on the shoulders of corrupting continental influences. Those at home had gone astray. Hence Coke, perhaps making an overly literal interpretation of the preamble to the Henrician statute, declared that it had been necessary because English merchants had wallowed in extravagance, "costly building, costly diet, and costly apparel," which had caused them to waste their wealth and neglect their trade.[8]

The charge of extravagance could be laid with equal ease against other ranks in society, notably the highest, but this suspicion about merchants was a common attitude of the time. At the end of the seventeenth century, Sir Richard Cock reflected the same kind of thinking, although he thought that the bankruptcy laws encouraged rather than deterred such appalling behavior. Merchants and traders, he said, were addicted to an expensive and vain style of living. When losses occurred, bankruptcy enabled them "to cheat their creditors, and to give of[f] trading to the ruin of their own and other families and the great damage of the public."[9]

Bankrupts were considered by some as worse than highway robbers and more damaging than foreign enemies.[10] Before the civil wars, John Stone gave a reading on the 1571 statute which associated an increase in the number of merchants with the enhancement of their "cunning and crafty dealings." He had little doubt but that the bankruptcy statutes were justifiably made "against" merchants.[11] Stone acquired a great reputation as a bankruptcy expert which survived into the following century. Thomas Goodinge and E. Green brought his observations up to date and added their own comments, but both applauded and confirmed a principal argument of the reading. They believed that as merchants grew more numerous their behavior deteriorated, and that this decline was initially accelerated because it had been easier for merchants to recover debts from others than it was to recover debts from merchants.[12]

Stone's reading, apart from its brief social comment, is of symbolic importance because the substance of his lecture was concerned with statutory interpretation, judicial precedent, and book law. His concentration upon pre-Elizabethan rules, sometimes utilized in hypothetical cases, illustrates both an apparent weakness of the bankruptcy statutes (he himself was only concerned with that of 1571) and the problems of a legal generation which was seeking to discover precedents from previous ages at a time when the notion of precedent, as understood by men of his own day, was still undergoing birth pangs. This work has hardly the slightest appreciation of commercial issues, the complexities of credit, or fluctuations in the terms of trade. In a duller vein, the approach was to be repeated by Billinghurst's list of statutes and cases concerning bankrupts. This was a practical handbook of legal rules: the atmosphere of the courts is predominant; the odor of the countinghouse is not so much irrelevant as it is ignored.[13]

Among mercantile commentators few paid so much attention to bankruptcy as did Garret de Malynes. He was a practical man of affairs, and something of a rogue, who had known both success and failure. At times he was respected as an expert, but his life had embraced curious paths of litigation. As a debtor, he seems to have been a pretty scurrilous character who plagued his creditors with lawsuits, one who could turn prison into a place of good living and a base for further stratagems. As such he may be considered as one of those who provided ammunition to critics of business behavior. Yet some of his reflections on economic affairs were marked by an interest in the applicability of theoretical propositions. In the early 1620's his advice was sought, and if not sought it was proffered, when problems of trade, the coinage, and the exchanges perplexed government and Parliament. He was particularly concerned with tight credit and

---

6 Treiman, "Escaping the Creditor," p. 232. The word *Lombard* was applied to most North Italian merchants, including Venetians, but it was also used generally for moneylenders and pawnbrokers.

7 Coke, *Fourth Institute*, p. 277.

8 *Ibid.*

9 Cited in *Seventeenth-Century Economic Documents*, ed. Joan Thirsk and J. P. Cooper (Oxford, 1972), p. 104.

10 Lansdowne 99, f. 185.

11 Stone, *Reading*, p. 3.

12 Goodinge, preface. E. Green, *The Spirit of the Bankrupt Laws* (London, 1767), preface.

13 Billinghurst also noted statutes concerned with fraudulent conveyances.

believed that England's difficulties resulted from an undervaluation of her currency, which prompted the export of specie and dramatically affected the foreign exchanges. In order to discuss all this he had to embrace a number of immediate and limited issues, including those posed by bankrupts and debtors. He was perverse, but he remains of interest.[14]

Malynes mused on the extent to which business implied a morality at odds with the ancient and equally traditional concepts of a non-commercial society. General understandings of honesty and dishonesty might be irrelevant to affairs of trade. It was apparent that unthinking behavior on the part of potential debtors and unreasonable pressure from precipitate creditors could lead to trouble. Malynes pointed out the significance of these elements (which Coke ignored), but he argued that the possibility of drifting into a near-bankrupt state arose not so much from the acts of men, however much these might tilt the balance towards disaster, as from the intrinsic nature of the merchant's estate. A single loss at a time when all one's money was laid out could throw an unbearable strain upon the merchant's credit, however sound it might appear to be on paper. Accordingly, he warned merchants to keep a reserve for emergencies and to avoid the temptation of sinking all their credit into financial and trading ventures on the seas and abroad: "he who is furthest from his goods is nearest to his loss." [15] Assets might well outweigh liabilities; even so, the problem was to secure a desirable liquidity for immediate needs. Failed merchants might have survived, "but that being out of their monies, and their monies out of the kingdom, maketh them to go out of their credits." [16] Distant though the wealth might be, the commercial man was tied to it not as master but as slave. The least rumor was enough to galvanize creditors. Malynes, who loved proverbs and homilies, recalled the ape tied to a clog who thought he kept it though it kept him.[17]

Certainly there were many commercial disasters, and it has to be remembered that laws and procedures concerning debt, irrespective of the bankruptcy statutes, were also capable of destroying a merchant whose credit should have been good. It has been suggested that for the seventeenth century as a whole the rate of business failure was high. The long-term rate of return on trading capital was low. In particular, much capital invested before the Civil War in discovery, colonies, and the development of heavy industry "sank without trace." [18]

Merchants had to exist amid circumstances which rarely promised consistent good fortune. "A man might make one hundred per cent profit, followed by one hundred per cent loss, in the same business within a year." [19] The ablest merchant could be shattered by bad luck, and many were more deficient than able in their accounting methods and business techniques. In any case, the only real guarantee against disaster was to keep disproportionately large sums in safe reserve. This meant that the return of profit would be small, but in building up capital, careful saving was more important than quick earnings.[20] Malynes would have agreed. As it was, too many did not have such reserves or, possibly through no fault of their own, found that too much money had been committed unfortunately. "Though interest at the statutory rate was charged for forbearance, large sums were lost or tied up in doubtful and desperate debts and unpaid bills; often men with limited capital could not wait for good market conditions and were forced to sell at a loss." [21]

Survival in this climate was not an easy matter. Concentration upon secure trades, albeit accepting a low return, might seem to have been the sensible policy. Perhaps all trades were insecure, and the element of risk may have been greater than the average returns received by the poorer merchants.[22] Furthermore, some people entangled themselves in situations which were hopeless by any standard. A classic Elizabethan example is provided by Michael Lok, whose association with Frobisher in the Cathay Company became a mining speculation carried on with a "reckless improvidence . . . well-nigh incredible to modern minds." In fairness to Coke, Stone, and others, it was also incredible to some contemporaries. Lok, who had committed his entire fortune and credit, was destroyed by his associates and called to account by all the creditors. He was incarcerated in a debtor's prison, and even Frobisher assailed him. "Undoubtedly he was to blame, but for folly and not fraud." [23]

A marine or other disaster could occasion widespread failures as overextended merchants struggled to meet obligations which would not otherwise have worried them, and which might not have been cata-

[14] Supple, p. 174. L. Stone, *An Elizabethan: Sir Horatio Palavacino* (Oxford, 1956), pp. 225–228.

[15] Malynes, *Lex Mercatoria*, p. 156.

[16] G. de Malynes, *The Maintenance of Free Trade* (London, 1622), p. 123.

[17] Malynes, *Lex Mercatoria*, p. 156.

[18] Grassby, "The Rate of Profit," p. 732. R. Grassby, "The Personal Wealth of the Business Community in Seventeenth-Century England," *Ec.HR*, 2nd ser. (1970) **22**: p. 223. An outstanding example is provided by the spectacular failure of the Courteens, which drained and shattered the wealth of their relative by marriage, John, first earl of Bridgewater, the son of Lord Chancellor Ellesmere.

[19] Grassby, "The Rate of Profit," p. 738.

[20] *Ibid.*

[21] *Ibid.*, p. 737.

[22] *Ibid.*, p. 733.

[23] J. A. Williamson, *The Age of Drake* (London, 1960), pp. 153–165. See Carole Shammas, "The 'Invisible Merchant' and Property Rights," *Business History* **17** (1975): pp. 95–108.

strophic if they had been given further time.[24] From this point of view, it was difficult to accept the realities of the situation as created by statute. Merchants could appreciate that failure was a misfortune for both creditors and debtors, but some suspected that the specification of behavior which constituted an act of bankruptcy had very little to do with mercantile practice. It was an artificial creation of legislation cast into the deep seas of preexisting law, the product of a social system which strove to establish clear-cut rules towards stability. Furthermore, the lawyers, legislators, and judges who had assumed the responsibility for defining bankruptcy were inclined to think in terms of fraudulent behavior. While not discounting underhand dealings and the regular element of risk in business, the merchant still had to accept that the status of being a bankrupt was determined by an arbitrary legal rule. It was not unlike driving on the wrong side of the road. This was really the point made by Malynes. The laws were there. If they were not enforced there would be chaos, and merchants who failed to make their dispositions with an eye to these laws were foolish.

The establishment of a set of rules which were theoretical, rather than hewed out of the needs and experience of commerce, made it possible to suppose that the only determining factor was chance. If Malynes was not really hostile to the bankruptcy statutes, he nonetheless noted their divorce from trading practice. Others used similar conclusions to buttress their dislike of the law as it stood, or to fuel arguments about advantages which change might bring for the economy and thus for the nation.

Honesty and dishonesty, despite lawyers who harped on fraud, had indeed ceased to count when chance and circumstance brought some within one sphere of technicality whereas it allowed or compelled others to stay outside. Many merchants and even some great clothiers could withstand the strain put upon them in times of general commercial difficulty,[25] but this was not always what mattered. Theoretically a merchant or trader, who was quite capable of keeping his head above water, might do something which would put him within the scope of the statutes and so encourage his creditors to petition for a commission. This rarely happened to the great ones, but the possibility was annoying. Bankruptcy had little to do with financial inability—although this might fairly be deduced from behavior—because it was anchored to a list of actions mentioned in legislation, actions which often needed interpretation. As Professor Harper has written of the navigation acts: "the work of Parliament was done, but the acts on the statute books were not the law applied at the waterside." [26]

Merchants were disgruntled. Acid comments were made in the Restoration period when economic optimism encouraged inquiries into the means whereby England's prosperity could be developed. Capital for investment might come from surplus agricultural production, re-exports, or foreign trade. There seemed some reason to query devices which strained credit.[27] Whether or not any particular year seemed good or bad, questions were naturally raised. The Lords committee on the decay of rents and trade was told in 1669 that the statutes of artificers and bankrupts were prejudicial to trade. In 1674, Sir Richard Haines painted a gloomy picture: "a general poverty seems to have invaded the whole nation, leases being continually thrown up in the country, and tradesmen daily breaking in the City." Not so long after, it was asked why traders "were never so poor or broke so fast (thought never so fine) as now." [28]

It is difficult to measure such things, but there seems very little reason to believe that bankruptcy laws actually damaged trade. Their greatest impact was on the habits of traders. The divergence between commercial and legal priorities should not be exaggerated or used to draw stark conclusions in the wrong direction. As a nineteenth-century observer remarked, there was bound to be a relationship if only because social problems were tackled in the courts and by legislation, but this was not a one-way relationship. In the end, legal rules had to be accommodated to social habits. Perhaps, as Welbourne has concluded for the Hanoverian period, it was the machinery of administration rather than the bankruptcy law itself which justified disquiet. Whatever may be said of lawyers and the stupidity and delays of law, "perhaps the pathology of the business world deserves a little closer attention than it has received from students of risk." [29]

Malynes had concentrated upon merchants trading overseas. Even so his adversary, Misselden, felt that they were underestimated, not to say besmirched, by Malynes, whose knowledge, logic, and personal career offended him. He "is not of us." Readers were warned against those who came in sheep's clothing,

[24] See N. S. B. Gras, *Business and Capitalism* (New York, 1939), p. 161.

[25] Supple, p. 11.

[26] L. A. Harper, *The English Navigation Laws* (New York, 1939), p. 63.

[27] See K. G. Davies, "Joint-Stock Investment in the Later Seventeenth Century," *Essays in Economic History*, ed. E. M. Carus-Wilson 2 (London, 1962): p. 275.

[28] *Seventeenth-Century Economic Documents*, pp. 70, 88. (Sir William Petyt), "*Britania Languens* or A Discourse of Trade" (1680), *Early English Tracts on Commerce*, ed. J. R. McCulloch. (Cambridge, 1952), p. 455. It has been suggested that tradesmen extended credit because they had little choice. Stone, *Aristocracy*, p. 515. Bankruptcy laws can, perhaps, be viewed in part as an undeserved penalty of this compulsion.

[29] *Suggestions* (?1819), f. 2. Welbourne, pp. 51, 62.

though Malynes was "so easy a combatant, that a man may give him any advantage of the weapon." It was, in truth, a debate marked by animosity. "I marvel who made Malynes a law-maker for merchants, if he be so ignorant of their profession! . . . The profession of a merchant is more noble than to be so disabled and disgraced by such a fellow as Malynes is." [30]

Misselden was not concerned with bankruptcy as such, but like many contemporaries he was appalled by the nature and prolixity of legal proceedings. He contrasted deficient (lack of money, for example) with efficient causes of the decay of trade. Among the latter, usury and unnecessary suits in law occupied a high place. The situation would be vastly improved if only "men bestowed half that study and cost in trade, which nowadays is spent in temerous and rash suits of law. . . ." He harshly criticized the development of fictions and their attendant personnel—those wretched fellows, John Doe and Richard Roe, and those dubious sureties, John Cheape and Richard Side.[31] The total picture was depressing. "A great number of his Majesty's good and loving subjects are vexed, imprisoned, impoverished, and overthrown. And while the litigants strive together, another taketh away the fish . . . and the men's time and means being spent in law which should be employed in trade. . . ." Again and again the point was hammered home: "no kingdom hath better laws; no kingdom so full fraught with tedious, needless, endless suits of law." He suggested that some practices in restraint of litigation employed at Lyons, Rouen, and Toulouse might be adapted with benefit to English conditions. There was, however, a gleam of hope: "suits of law do seem immortal, time doth increase them and length of time would not determine them, if the wisdom of those great fathers of the law did not put an end to the malice of litigants, as is now worthily observed in Chancery, to his honor and memory that hath so happily begun the same." [32] He added the suggestion that ordinary courts could be relieved by having mercantile cases diverted to authorized experts. Parliament could do something to improve the situation, and he instanced with approval the system of marine insurance founded by statute in 1601.[33]

In deploring the legal position, Misselden reproved merchants who seemed incapable of avoiding litigation. The commercial man might think that his class wished to avoid unnecessary dealings with the alien breed of lawyers, but this was little more than part of a tendency to keep close to their own mercantile society. It was merchants and traders themselves who chose to use, or not to use, the rules provided by the legal system. They were the sponsors of litigation. Anyone who has made a study of the legal records will appreciate the force of Professor Willan's remark that "merchants defended their rights, or alleged rights, to personal property with the same tenacity as Elizabethan landowners defended their titles, or alleged titles, to real property." [34] Whatever the pressures imposed upon them, merchants and traders were likely to be the creditors who decided to petition for a commission of bankruptcy.

In a situation recalling the pot that termed the kettle black, standard complaints against the law and the legal profession were intensified. Lawyers and procedures, it was later asserted, combined to produce inappropriate, long-winded, and costly requirements which were damaging to trade.[35] It was particularly resented that the harm done to others should be rewarded with material success, something that was probably overestimated. Early in the reign of Charles I, a bank was proposed to finance war expenditures and otherwise make loans at five per cent. It was to be funded in part by an annual levy on attorneys, clerks, and lawyers since these, it was argued, were seldom or never taxed in respect of military service or required to serve in person. Instead they lived "safe and secure" while attending their "benefits and profits." [36]

It was for their easy condemnation of lawyers and gentlemen that Thomas Mun chided his fellow merchants. He had written a paper at the behest of the East India Company and thus of the elite in overseas commerce and their landed associates and investors. This tract, which was praised by Misselden,[37] was expanded into a larger work. Even if lawyers were covetous, Mun argued, there could be little ill effect without the perverse nature of litigants. Merchants chose to go to law, and doubtless some lost their money through the exercise of this choice. The legal profession, which he described as "noble," was a necessity even if the actual cases, delays and charges could be represented as destructive of individuals and their estates. He could not see that this had any real impact on the economic position of the country. Furthermore, he was inclined to reject most of the criticism directed against the nobility, the gentry, and

[30] E. Misselden, *The Circle of Commerce* (London, 1623), preface and pp. 17–19, 111. Malynes was swift to counterattack against Misselden's arguments and "uncivil speeches." *The Center of the Circle of Commerce* (London, 1623).

[31] These developments were often obstructive, but in other areas fictions were ways in which courts tried to innovate and keep in touch with changing demands.

[32] This seems to refer to Bacon, but the wording is ambiguous.

[33] E. Misselden, *Free Trade, or the Meanes to Make Trade Florish* (London, 1622), pp. 29, 32, 33–34, 119, 120, 122–123.

[34] T. S. Willan, *Studies in Elizabethan Foreign Trade* (Manchester, 1959), p. 131.

[35] (Petyt), *"Britania Languens,"* pp. 368, 378–379.

[36] Richards, pp. 94–95.

[37] Misselden, *Circle of Commerce.*

others because of their presumed overspending on buildings, fine clothes, and other luxuries.[38]

Although comment can at times be found, it is only with Defoe, who was personally involved, that there emerges a major critic of the bankruptcy laws who was more concerned with tradesmen than with international merchants. Like Dekker, who was also very much aware of the distinction, Defoe could be extravagant and imaginative in his descriptions and conclusions, but one can only agree with his opinion, published in 1697, that the current situation was absurd. The 1624 statute might well have been justified by circumstances at the time, but decades had passed and conditions were now vastly different. Society and law, business and legal procedures, had changed. Debtors had once again developed too many means of frustrating or evading the statutes. Others, who could not escape, were trapped. These were treated with an insane cruelty which did not benefit the creditor save to satisfy his malice.[39]

Defoe, who had his own axes to grind, succeeded across thirty years in castigating all elements involved in bankruptcy. According to him, the law was generally good, but in this instance it was hopeless. Commissions were incompetent, consuming money that might otherwise have been used for payment of debts. Any sensible creditor would arrange a composition according to the understood practices of the business community; those that opted for statutory procedures were stupid or vile. Traders were worthy, but too many drifted into disaster through luxurious living, enjoyable pastimes, early marriages, and inept business methods, particularly in the giving and taking of credit. Some bankrupts were unfortunates, but it was Defoe's opinion that most of them deserved to be called knaves and dishonest men. Yet whatever might be thought of bankrupts, nothing could justify the statutes which Defoe described as barbarous. "It leaves the debtor no way to show himself honest . . . for it makes him perfectly uncapable of any thing but *starving.*" This ghastly legislation, which flouted the commercial instinct to secure compositions, "for ever shuts up all doors to the debtor's recovery; as if breaking were a crime so capital, that he ought to be cast out of human society, and exposed to extremeties worse than death." [40]

Adam Smith, not very concerned with the inadequate shackles of legal rules, wrote comments not unlike those of Malynes. Failure (and possibly bankruptcy) was implicit in the very nature of trade: it occurred most frequently in hazardous trades. In this respect, Smith's writings reflect an air of resignation as to the facts of life.[41] A greater change of emphasis is to be seen in the writings of a lawyer. Blackstone, who was as ready to condemn extravagant living as Coke had been, classified bankruptcy as the eighth way in English law whereby lands and tenements might be forfeited.[42] It might even be seen as a commendable assistance to commerce. This appraisal might be different from that of Coke, but Blackstone too could be confident in the virtues of his law; and it must be remembered that statutory amendments of the eighteenth century had introduced a variety of changes, notably the discharge, which had considerable significance.[43]

Blackstone admired English law, but many popular voices conceived bankruptcy as a fraud. Oliver Goldsmith had previously expressed current doubts about commercial wealth.[44] Bankruptcy, wrote a pamphleteer, "is now considered an infallible method for one in tattered circumstances to make himself whole again. It is called the emetic of an undone man." A picture of deceit was painted. "One auspicious morning" a man, at the height of his financial reputation, puts his most valuable effects into a casket and steals away. Those who have loaned him money panic and offer a two-thirds composition, but receive no answer. "The creditors meet; they come, they go; they torment themselves." Eventually they "whisper" that they are willing to *lose* two-thirds. Everything is arranged, and the bankrupt reappears with some thousands in specie. "Will not a man who takes such prudential steps but once in his life be able to make a figure ever after?" [45]

Popular opinion would never take kindly to the bankrupt. The shades of uncertainty were expressed in an American book review, written in 1834.

> But it is sometimes said that most debtors, who do not pay their debts, are in some degree guilty, and merit punishment. This seems to us not quite true. Some debtors, we admit, are mere swindlers and sharpers. Others have become involved by daring speculations. Some are the victims of extravagance. Others fail from

[38] L. Muchmore, "A Note on Thomas Mun's 'England's Treasure by Forraign Trade'," *Ec.HR*, 2nd ser. 23 (1970) : pp. 498–503. T. Mun, *England's Treasure by Forraign Trade*, ed. of 1664 (Oxford, 1959), pp. 59–60.

[39] Defoe, *Essay Upon Projects*, pp. 195–196.

[40] *Ibid.*, pp. 191, 194. D. Defoe, *The Complete English Tradesman* 1 (London, 1726) : pp. 95–96 *et passim*. See also D. Defoe, *Remarks on the Bill to Prevent Frauds Committed by Bankrupts* (London, 1706).

[41] Adam Smith, pp. 111, 325.

[42] The other seven were: by crimes and misdemeanors; by alienation contrary to law; by non-presentation, when the forfeiture was deemed to be a lapse; by simony; by non-performance of conditions; by waste; by breach of copyhold customs. Blackstone 2: pp. 267, 284.

[43] Blackstone, who was certainly eager to applaud restraints upon mercantile excess, could refer, somewhat in the manner of Smith, to the bankrupt as an "unfortunate person," but the adjective was more redolent of meaning than it sometimes is today. *Ibid.* 2: p. 284.

[44] Wilson, p. 12. See also M. M. Goldsmith, "Mandeville and the Spirit of Capitalism," *The Journal of British Studies* 17 (1977) : pp. 63–81.

[45] *The Bankrupt: A Modern Character* (n.d.).

want of skill and judgment in conducting their business. We find in the conduct of debtors every moral shade, from gross fraud to the slightest negligence and entire innocence. The high degrees of fraud are comparatively rare. Slighter degrees of misconduct are more common. But judged by the current rules of mercantile honesty, we believe the majority of insolvent debtors upright and honorable.[46]

The anonymous writer was rather smug, but the points considered could have been applied to the Elizabethan and early Stuart period. Notions of property might shift, but they did not differ to a very great degree when it came to an interpretation of individual action. Elizabethans believed in land, and nineteenth-century Bostonians believed in wealth. The man who failed to live up to these assumptions, whether by accident or design, had offended against society.

English law, by the very nature of its medieval legacy, distinguished to some extent between commercial wealth and landed property. It reflected the attitudes of those who stayed in one place and in one social position. It had difficulty in adapting to a social mobility which was natural. The land was the life of the law and, wrote Plucknett, "the separation of commerce from the normal occupation of the nation was further emphasized by the fact that the merchants had their own organization and their own law." Only as late as 1690 did the law embrace the possibility that one who was not a merchant might be party to a bill of exchange.[47] This does not mean that landed men were not vitally interested in commerce. Agriculture, the source of income or employment for most people, was "itself increasingly marked by the application of capital, enterprise, novel methods, and the quest for markets. The dynamic of the time was commercial." [48] Furthermore, non-merchant participation along the lines of investment was increasingly important. Merchants, for their part, became landowners, and the two groups intermarried. One has only to look at the career of Cranfield or the disastrous association of the Earl of Bridgewater with the Courteens. Professor Stone's study of Palaviacino provides "an almost perfect textbook case of this transformation of merchant into landowner. . . ." [49] English social life was fluid. It was possible to move from one level to another. That hybrid, the merchant-landowning-gentleman, however, is hardly visible. While landed families fueled business ranks, and others managed to obscure their mercantile origins, there was always something which distinguished the merchant from the rest of society. "What was peculiar to the merchant was the form in which his wealth was held and the use which he made of his assets." [50]

Apart from the clarification provided by the act of 1662, there was no legislation for seven decades after 1624. Throughout this time, social distinctions were hardened and perpetuated. The point was doubtless appreciated by Defoe.[51] There were two basic assumptions enshrined in the statutes of 1571, 1604, and 1624. In the first place, it was supposed that merchants and traders, that is, international merchants, great financiers, shopkeepers, and craftsmen, could be lumped together in a single category. Secondly, it was assumed that in this context all traders, merchants and retailers, could be separated rationally from landed gentlemen. If the latter notion caused some trouble, as it was also to do in the eighteenth century, it was the first supposition which was most strikingly out of touch with the conventions of the business world.

Economic historians have long recognized that English conditions separated the merchant, in the sense of being an exporter or importer, from the trader.[52] Malynes, Misselden, and Mun wrote from the viewpoint of their own kind. This is understandable, and people associated with that circle were possibly more literate and sophisticated than the average run of retailers, but it means that we cannot take them as representing the views of traders and shopkeepers. There was a gulf between the two groups. Indeed the distinction between foreign trade and retail trading or shopkeeping was long established in many organizations before it was reflected, for example, in the 1605 charter of the Levant Company and the 1611 charter of the French merchants. Just as the Inns of Court strengthened their barriers against attorneys, so the great merchants wished to have little to do with tradesmen and others on whom they looked down. For a member of one of these companies to be a retailer, remarked Heckscher, was as much a crime as "offenses and the practices of evil demeanor." [53]

Distinctions within the business community were complex and not easy for some contemporaries to grasp. Generally, it was conventional to rely on three main categories: merchants (overseas traders);

---

[46] From *American Jurist* 11 (1834) : cited Costigan, p. 107, n. 15.

[47] Plucknett, pp. 65–66.

[48] Wilson, p. x.

[49] Stone, *Palaviacino*, p. 268.

[50] R. Grassby, "English Merchant Capitalism in the late Seventeenth Century. The Composition of Business Fortunes," *Past and Present* 46 (Feb. 1970) : pp. 87–88.

[51] See above, p. 57.

[52] Sutherland, p. 156.

[53] E. F. Heckscher, *Mercantilism*, rev. ed. E. F. Söderlund, 1 (London, 1955) : pp. 378–379. Shopkeepers and retailers were excluded from the Spanish Company. Pauline Croft, *The Spanish Company*, London Rec. Soc. (London, 1973), p. xxxv. For the fifteenth-century position, including gradations of prejudice towards retail trade among the gentry, see Sylvia L. Thrupp, *The Merchant Class of Medieval London* (Chicago, 1948), chap. 6, "Trade and Gentility."

tradesmen (skilled craftsmen); and retailers (those who sold the goods of others).[54] Defoe, however, said that *tradesman* meant different things in different parts of the British Isles, but that in England generally it meant wholesalers or retailers "who do not actually work upon, make, or manufacture the goods they sell." He would not apply the word *tradesman* to those who engaged in handicrafts and manufactures. He was, however, talking about two groups who occupied the middle ground: below them he placed workmen, laborers, and servants; above he placed merchants and explained that in England this word involved foreign commerce.[55]

In lumping together all who made their living through merchandise and trade, the bankruptcy statutes glossed over vast social distinctions which were very real. In the same breath, the statutes also created a legal fence between the upper echelons of commerce and landed gentlemen. This too was not always in accordance with the facts of either society or the law in general. Edward Chamberlayne pointed out that merchants trading abroad had a reputation which far exceeded that of chapmen or others who lived by buying and selling. These latter were a "baser sort of people" whereas "to become a merchant of foreign commerce, without serving any apprenticeship, hath been allowed no disparagement to a gentleman born, especially to a younger brother." [56] Indeed, he wrote, "in cases and causes, the law of England hath conceived a better opinion of the yeomanry that occupy lands, than of tradesmen, artificers or laborers." [57]

Contemporaries were by no means entirely clear about their own society and its distinctions. Historians of our own day, not to mention those of the past, have engaged in rewarding studies of social evolution, class, and occupational distinction. Clear guidelines, however, cannot be drawn. Statutes must be appreciated in terms of the social assumptions at the time of their enactment. With respect to subsequent interpretation before the courts, similar considerations must be kept constantly in mind. There can be no subject which more demands an awareness of such themes, even though conclusions are impossible, than bankruptcy. We may not be able to describe how men in Parliament thought, but at least the question can be asked and kept to the fore. If we are right in supposing that the statutes fluffed the realities of contemporary social distinction, may it not be supposed that a clue can be found in the composition of Parliament?

In the eighteenth century the discharge was introduced; in the next some significant changes were made in the classification of those who could become bankrupt. It was a slow process, but it is one matched by the growing importance in politics and society of merchants, financiers, and industrialists. Their presence was evident in the House of Commons, it was not absent from the House of Lords, and increasingly they gained the ear of government. This was not true of those Tudor and Jacobean parliaments which engineered and passed the initial banruptcy statutes.

The Henrician statute, whatever its imperfections of language, was passed at a time when fifteenth-century rules governing the qualifications of a member of Parliament were still accorded some respect. The decisive period, that between 1571 and 1624, represents those years in which gentlemen flooded the House of Commons through their ability to secure election in the boroughs. During the parliaments of Elizabeth, James I, and Charles I, men of business were a distinct minority in the House of Commons. One analysis suggests that there were only forty-two commercial men ("merchants") among the 464 members of Parliament who sat in 1614.[58] It is not impossible that delusions about maritime warfare and its profits may have been engendered by the small number of merchants who actually sat in the House of Commons.[59] It is, of course, true that London financiers might on occasion exercise a dramatic authority. This was most apparent early in 1641 when money had to be raised to satisfy the Scots and calm a disorderly rabble of defeated English soldiers. Situations such as this were rare, and an analysis of the Commons which met in November, 1640, indicates the dominant strength of landed interests.[60]

[54] Grassby, "Personal Wealth," pp. 222–223.

[55] Defoe, *Complete Tradesman* 1: pp. 1–3. There was no real definition of a trader at law; or rather there were different strands of development for the interpretation of different statutes.

[56] Chamberlayne, *State of England*, pp. 444–445. He was pointing out that by law a ward within age could bring an action for disparagement against his guardian for offering marriage with a tradesman or chapman. There are examples of men engaged in mundane occupations being able to bear the style of gentleman. Wilson, p. 14. This may give force to a conclusion that for the purposes of the House of Commons during the early Long Parliament "a merchant was probably anyone who so regarded himself." D. Brunton and D. H. Pennington, *Members of the Long Parliament* (London, 1954), p. 53. Chap. 4 of this book is valuable. I do not, however, think that the impression of an almost casual approach towards social distinctions should be taken very far. The House of Commons was a community in itself, that was its secret, but it was not English society.

[57] Chamberlayne, p. 442.

[58] T. L. Moir, *The Addled Parliament of 1614* (Oxford, 1958), p. 57.

[59] J. P. Kenyon, *The Stuart Constitution* (Cambridge, 1966), p. 29.

[60] A breakdown of the occupations and family status of members called to the Long Parliament suggests that there were fifty-five merchants and tradesmen out of a total of 547. Of the "tradesmen"—this classification ignores a very necessary distinction—two were elder sons of "knights and gentlemen," four were younger sons, three were sons of "new gentry," one was the son of a churchman, and another was the son of a

If men of commerce were a weak force in Elizabethan and early Stuart parliaments, retailers and craftsmen counted for nothing. The attitude of authority has been delicately described by Professor Wilson.

> Whether "government" meant Privy Council under the monarchy or the Council of State in Commonwealth times, it listened to merchant petitions, sometimes accepting, sometimes rejecting. It was rarely dictated to, even though the early Stuarts often stooped to folly. On the rare occasions when Government gave in to the clamor of the City—as it did over the second Dutch War—it was persuaded less by the merchants themselves than by a court clique who thought they could further their own interests by an alliance with the City.[61]

Since the essence of policy was paternal, there was care for trade but not for traders. It has been observed that "a bankrupt merchant left the state unmoved, but a ship rotting by the quayside was a matter for concern."[62] The emphasis on landed property increased. By a statute of 1711, impressive landed qualifications were expected of members of Parliament.[63] It became necessary to be a freeholder, even to be a juryman: "full citizenship, in fact, was open only to the property holder,"[64] and for "property," read "land." Professor Wilson's conclusions carry an unmistakable ring of truth.

> The suspicion of business wealth as a social solvent and a certain lingering nostalgia for an ordered, traditional society was to die hard. . . . Few successful businessmen passed immediately into the charmed circle of government, and the few who did—like Cranfield—had to face powerful opposition from the older incumbents of office who regarded them as upstarts. Adam Smith's picture of seventeenth-century governments as puppets of a cunning clique of merchants was a long way wide of the mark.[65]

Although there were to be many significant developments affecting commerce in the seventeenth century, landed producers were more successful than merchants in attaining a revaluation of legal rules and limitations. Business wealth was small in comparison with "the capital assets of the Crown, the Church, and the landed interest." The merchants, it has been observed, "were outnumbered, divided, and socially disoriented," and "trade could hardly have been a wide channel of social and economic advancement."[66] Certainly, they lacked effective political power, and they could have had little influence on the framing of the early bankruptcy statutes. Retailers and shopkeepers were even less influential, and their voices were not heard in Parliament. For all the participation of commercial members of Parliament—those for London, Newcastle, and York were specifically mentioned in 1604—Commons committees working on bankruptcy bills represent the usual dominance of landed gentry and lawyers.[67]

If we turn to the eighteenth century and the Regency period, gentlemen and peers who felt insulted when called upon to meet a tradesman's bill are a recognizable element. A shopkeeper who adopted similar standards would meet with short shrift, even though he might have run into difficulty through allowing credit to his gentry customers. These were common attitudes which Hanoverians had inherited. A statute of 1610 placed considerable onus on tradesmen by discharging all debts claimed from customers after twelve months if based upon shop books or accounts. Quite rightly intended to prevent double payments, it pointed out that buyers could not be expected to keep receipts for so long a period. Instead, before expiry of the allowed time, the shopkeeper was told that he ought to obtain bills or obligations acknowledging the sum due or commence action at law. This requirement, it was stressed with rare regard for these particular distinctions, did not apply to the commercial transactions of "merchant and merchant, merchant and tradesman, or between tradesman and tradesman." According to a treatise subtitled "The Tickling Torture" the courtier neither could nor wanted to pay, the country gentleman preferred that his sureties should pay, and the "citizen" was pleased to pay according to some rate which might amount to no more than five shillings in the pound.[68]

We have heard about the difficulties of the aristocracy, for whom the Elizabethan and early Stuart period has been represented as involving a crisis of confidence, and about the misfortunes of at least one section of the gentry. Aristocracy and gentry may represent little more than devious footnotes of social classification, but the agonies and ambitions, legal or economic, of social mobility represent real and compelling themes. We are aware of contemporary fears of vagabondage and thus of a hunger march of peasants driven off the land. These fears were exaggerated, but there was at one time a flow of population,

lawyer. Twenty-seven came from trading families, three were sons of yeomen, and one was the son of a mariner. The social origins of the remainder could not be determined. Gentlemen (333) comprised the largest group. There were seventy-four "lawyers," twenty-seven royal officials, and twenty-two courtiers. Mary F. Keeler, *The Long Parliament 1640–1641. A Biographical Study of its Members*, Mem. Amer. Philos. Soc. **36** (Philadelphia, 1954): pp. 21, n. 108, 23 (Table 5).

[61] Wilson, pp. 12–13.

[62] R. W. K. Hinton, "The Mercantile System in the Time of Thomas Mun," *Ec.HR*, 2nd ser. **8** (1955): p. 279.

[63] 9 Anne c. 5.

[64] Wilson, p. 9.

[65] *Ibid.*, pp. 12–13. See also C. Wilson, "Government Policy and Private Interest in Modern English History," *Historical Studies*, ed. T. W. Moody **6** (London, 1968): pp. 85–99.

[66] Grassby, "English Merchant Capitalism," p. 87; "The Rate of Profit," p. 733.

[67] *CJ* 1: pp. 208–209, 228, 552.

[68] 7 James I c. 10. Powel, *The Mysterie of Lending and Borrowing*, pp. 13, 18.

not least from decaying towns, towards London. It is reasonable to note the growing dominance of the metropolis, and the erratic fortunes of other ports. Clerks and officials in the institutions of Westminster felt threatened by patentees, subordinates, and public criticism. It would seem that many sections of the community were afflicted, but what are we to make of tradesmen and merchants?

Some merchants and traders were rich, and others were poor; some fell and others rose. These fluctuations in society were irrelevant. The bankruptcy statutes had ensured that a man who lived through merchandise was possibly circumscribed by a law which did not cover those who relied upon estates, cash crops, and investment.

While clear definition of social groupings is both difficult and dangerous, Sir Lewis Namier recognized the necessity of distinctions as it affected the membership of the House of Commons. "Merchants in the eighteenth century meant businessmen, and the term was as wide as trade is even now; bankers and manufacturers were included. But I do not include among the merchants country gentlemen who owned mines or even iron works but clearly did not belong to the business community . . . ."[69] For an earlier period, that after 1688, Professor Plumb has referred to a confirmation of the authority of certain men of property "whose tap-root was in land but whose side-roots reached out to commerce, industry, and finance."[70] The description is valuable. For while the bankruptcy statutes implied an existing social distinction, drew the lines of that distinction yet more firmly, and helped to maintain it, it still does not follow that the distinction was a practical one. Law is often seen as a reflection of society, and this is true of the early bankruptcy statutes and the decisions made upon them in the early seventeenth century. Nonetheless the law-makers, both legislators and judges, while they did their best to handle immediate problems, rather dodged the questions posed by those "side-roots." The law of bankruptcy was not particularly suited to the problems of merchants, as distinguished from the shopkeepers and small manufacturers such as bakers and shoemakers.

John Wheeler, writing late in Elizabeth's reign, protested against those who

> scorn to be called merchants. Whereas indeed merchandise, which is used by way of proper vocation, being rightly considered of, is not to be despised, or accounted base by men of judgement, but to the contrary . . . the estate is honorable, and may be exercised not only of those of the third estate (as we term them) but also by the nobles, and chiefest men of this realm with commendable profit, and without any derogation to their nobilities, high degrees and conditions. . . .[71]

But it was not to be. "Distrust of the self-made man of money, and an instinctive belief in government by traditional means and a traditional ruling class was strong in the seventeenth century."[72] Not without reason did Jenks describe the Tudor and Stuart bankruptcy statutes as representing "pitiless severity . . . towards the unfortunate merchant."[73] This is a distortion only in its concentration upon the word *merchant* rather than upon shopkeepers and tradesmen. The power of commerce would grow, but this cannot easily be equated with the social or political status accorded to merchants and traders.

Professor Plumb has argued that after 1688 the "middle class" thrived socially and economically, but not politically. The phrase "middle class" is of dubious value for this period and, in any case, it has broader connotations than *trader* or similar terms. However, his exposition of this argument is to the point. "The power of the land and of commerce fused to create a paradise for gentlemen, for the aristocracy of birth; it thus became much easier for England to adopt an imperial authority . . . rather than to adjust its institutions and its social system to the needs of an industrial society."[74] Even in the late nineteenth century, there could still be a feeling that the man who was "in trade" was "not quite, quite." Bagehot gave his impression of this attitude. "The order of nobility is of great use, too, not only in what it creates but in what it prevents. It prevents the rule of wealth—the religion of gold. This is the obvious and natural idol of the Anglo-Saxon. He is always trying to make money; he reckons everything in coin; he bows down before a great heap, and gallops as he passes a little heap."[75]

Tudor and early Stuart bankruptcy statutes had been framed by men who assumed social distinctions which were not so very diverse from Victorian attitudes. Yet the nature of debt and credit is practical: it is a matter of what men do and not of how they appear to others; even though this always plays a part in any decision to extend credit.

[69] Namier, p. 49, n. 1.

[70] J. H. Plumb, *The Growth of Political Stability in England, 1675–1725* (London, 1967), p. 69.

[71] J. Wheeler, *A Treatise of Commerce* (1601), ed. G. B. Hotchkiss (New York, 1931), p. 7. Note the discussion provided by Stone, *Aristocracy*, pp. 335 *et seq.*

[72] Wilson, p. 12.

[73] Jenks, p. 383.

[74] Plumb, p. 187.

[75] W. Bagehot, *The English Constitution* (1933), p. 80, cited Wilson, p. 12.

INDEX

www.ingramcontent.com/pod-product-compliance
Lightning Source LLC
LaVergne TN
LVHW081937200926
848484LV00009B/2447

* 9 7 8 1 4 2 2 3 7 4 9 5 5 *

Parenting Styles and Practices

Edited by María Cristina Richaud, Jael Vargas Rubilar and Viviana Noemí Lemos

Published in London, United Kingdom

Parenting Styles and Practices
http://dx.doi.org/10.5772/intechopen.1003373
Edited by María Cristina Richaud, Jael Vargas Rubilar and Viviana Noemí Lemos

Contributors
Carmela Carotenuto, Channel Lowery, Duncan Borg Ellul, Israel Kibirige, Israel Masiko Kafeero, Jael Vargas-Rubilar, Jesmond Friggieri, Jessica M. Coleman, Joan M. Blakey, Labibah M. Buraik, Marco Giordano, Marilena Di Lollo, María Cristina Richaud, Nuzhat Sultana, Ramona Rolle-Berg, Renée Rolle-Whatley, Suzanne C. Purdy, Viviana Noemí Lemos

First published in London, United Kingdom, 2025 by IntechOpen
IntechOpen is the global imprint of INTECHOPEN LIMITED, registered in England and Wales, registration number: 11086078, 167-169 Great Portland Street, London, W1W 5PF, United Kingdom

For EU product safety concerns: IN TECH d.o.o., Prolaz Marije Krucifikse Kozulić 3, 51000 Rijeka, Croatia, info@intechopen.com or visit our website at intechopen.com.

British Library Cataloguing-in-Publication Data
A catalogue record for this book is available from the British Library

Parenting Styles and Practices
Edited by María Cristina Richaud, Jael Vargas Rubilar and Viviana Noemí Lemos
p. cm.

This title is part of the Education and Human Development Book Series, Volume 32
Topic: Human Development
Series Editor: Katherine Meltzoff
Topic Editor: Tal Dotan Ben-Soussan

Print ISBN 978-1-83769-425-9
Online ISBN 978-1-83769-424-2
eBook (PDF) ISBN 978-1-83769-426-6
ISSN 2755-9513

IntechOpen Book Series

Education and Human Development

Volume 32

Aims and Scope of the Series

Education and Human Development is an interdisciplinary research area that aims to shed light on topics related to both learning and development. This Series is intended for researchers, practitioners, and students who are interested in understanding more about these fields and their applications.

Meet the Series Editor

Katherine Meltzoff received her BA in Psychology from Trinity College, in Connecticut, USA and her Ph.D. in Experimental Psychology from the University of California, San Diego. She completed her postdoctoral work at the Yale Child Study Center with Dr. James McPartland. Dr. Meltzoff' doctoral dissertation explored neural correlates of reward anticipation to social versus nonsocial stimuli in children with and without autism spectrum disorders (ASD). She has been a faculty member at the University of California, Riverside in the School of Education since 2016. Her research focuses on translational studies to explore the reward system in ASD, as well as how anxiety contributes to social challenges in ASD. She also investigates how behavioral interventions affect neural activity, behavior, and school performance in children with ASD. She is also involved in the diagnosis of children with ASD and is a licensed clinical psychologist in California. She is the Assistant Director of the SEARCH Center at UCR and is a faculty member in the Graduate Program in Neuroscience.

Meet the Volume Editors

María Cristina Richaud has a Ph.D. in Psychology from the University of Buenos Aires in Argentina. She led the Interdisciplinary Center for Research in Mathematical and Experimental Psychology (CIIPME), which operates under Argentina's National Council of Scientific and Technical Research (CONICET). She has also attained the rank of Superior Researcher at CONICET. Dr. Richaud currently works at the Institute of Family Sciences of the Universidad Austral and is a scientific advisor to the Universidad Adventista del Plata, both in Argentina. Dr Richaud's primary scholarly interest is in social cognitive variables in children and adolescents, parenting, and the study of problems of children at risk for poverty. She has received different awards for her distinguished work, such as the 2013 APA Award for Distinguished Contributions to the International Advancement of Psychology.

Jael Vargas-Rubilar holds a Ph.D. in Psychology from the Pontifical Catholic University of Argentina. She is currently an Adjunct Researcher at the National Scientific and Technical Research Council (CONICET) at the Interdisciplinary Center for Research in Health and Behavioral Sciences (CIICSAC), Adventist University of the Plata (UAP), Argentina. She is a postgraduate professor in the course on Interdisciplinary Intervention in the Family Context of the Master's program in Interventions for Vulnerable Populations at Austral University in Argentina. Dr. Vargas-Rubilar has conducted and published various studies on parenting and its relationship with the socioemotional and cognitive development of children and adolescents. Additionally, she has designed and implemented intervention programs to strengthen positive parenting in socially vulnerable contexts.

Viviana Lemos has a Ph.D. in Psychology from the National University of San Luis in Argentina. She is a Researcher at the National Council for Scientific and Technical Research (CONICET) in the Principal Researcher category. She currently directs the Interdisciplinary Center for Research in Health and Behavioral Sciences (CIICSAC) of the Universidad Adventista del Plata (UAP). She has done fruitful work in the training of human resources and has published more than a hundred scientific publications linked to her lines of research focused on the study, evaluation, and promotion of various socio-emotional resources in children and adolescents.

Contents

Preface

Parenting is an evolving and deeply complex human endeavor that influences not only individual children but also the fabric of society at large. Across cultures and historical periods, how parents nurture, guide, and educate their children has been shaped by a confluence of social norms, psychological theories, and economic realities. Researchers and practitioners alike continue to explore the intricate dynamics of parenting styles, their impact on child development, and the role of education and social support in optimizing parenting practices.

This book aims to contribute to the academic discourse by examining the multidimensional aspects of parenting from both theoretical and practical perspectives. The chapters included in this volume delve into the evolution of parenting approaches, their psychological underpinnings, and their implications for children's growth and development. Each chapter critically analyses parenting frameworks, their effectiveness, and their intersection with broader societal structures.

The first chapter, *The Evolution of Parenting: Styles or Principles?* sets the stage by tracing the historical and philosophical trajectories of parenting styles. It questions whether parenting should be understood through rigid classifications or as a fluid set of principles adapted to changing circumstances. This foundational discussion paves the way for *Parenting Styles and Practices: Facing the Parenting Storm*, which explores contemporary challenges in parenting and the pressures that parents face in an era of rapid social change.

Moving beyond conventional frameworks, *Reverent Parenting: The Veiled Ontology of Self-Awakening* introduces a nuanced perspective that ties parenting to self-awareness and personal growth, emphasizing the interconnectedness between parent and child. This theme is further explored in *Parenting Styles and Competencies: Their Influence on Children's Development*, which examines how different parenting approaches shape cognitive, emotional, and social competencies in children.

Recognizing the critical role of communication in development, *Supporting Children's Communication Development through Parental Education* highlights the importance of equipping parents with knowledge and strategies to foster their children's linguistic and social skills. This chapter underscores the significance of parental education as a cornerstone for child development.

Expanding the scope of parenting discussions, *Self-Help Among Foster Parents in Italy: Analysis of the Phenomenon and Implications for Social Services and Researchers* presents an empirical study on foster parenting. It sheds light on the self-help mechanisms foster parents employ and the implications for social service interventions and policy development.

Lastly, *Choosing Schools: The Trade-Offs Parents of Black Students Must Navigate* addresses the complexities of school choice among Black families. It explores the intersection of race, education, and parenting, providing critical insights into how parents navigate systemic barriers in pursuing quality education for their children and how they have to navigate between securing quality education and ensuring their children's overall health and well-being.

This book is intended for researchers, educators, policymakers, and practitioners who seek a deeper understanding of parenting dynamics. It offers a blend of theoretical perspectives and empirical findings that contribute to the broader discourse on parenting and child development. This volume aims to enrich research and inform evidence-based practices that support families and children in diverse contexts by examining parenting through historical, psychological, social, and educational lenses.

We hope this book serves as both an intellectual stimulus and a practical resource for those dedicated to understanding and improving the landscape of parenting and child development.

María Cristina Richaud, Jael Vargas-Rubilar and Viviana Noemí Lemos
National Scientific and Technical Research Council (CONICET),
Interdisciplinary Center for Health and Behavior Sciences Research (CIICSAC),
Adventist University of the Plata,
Libertador San Martín, Argentina

Chapter 1

The Evolution of Parenting: Styles or Principles?

Jesmond Friggieri and Duncan Borg Ellul

Abstract

Parenting is often viewed as a natural process, with many parents replicating their upbringing. However, as societies evolve rapidly, it has become clear that parenting is more complex. Over recent decades, various approaches, such as positive parenting, have emerged to support parents in improving their methods. While these models offer strategies, they often need to catch up in adapting to the diverse and fast-changing contexts of modern life. The "one-size-fits-all" approach has become obsolete in education and parenting. This chapter introduces a new, transversal, and systemic approach to parenting based on core principles rather than rigid strategies. By understanding and applying these principles, parents can confidently choose the right strategy for their children, tailored to specific behaviours, cultural contexts, and developmental stages. The proposed approach emphasises that successful parenting must be flexible, context-driven, and grounded in a principled decision-making process. We will explore how these foundational principles enhance parenting, ensuring adaptability and effectiveness across diverse situations and cultures.

Keywords: parenting styles, principles, child development, consistency, leadership

1. Introduction

Parenting has become an increasingly challenging endeavour. In today's fast-changing world, many parents struggle to feel confident in effectively raising their children for the future [1, 2]. With rapid societal shifts, the rise of social media, and the dominance of subjectivity over objectivity in a postmodern society, parents are often left wondering, "Is there one most effective parenting style?" "And if there is not, how should parents raise their children?"

The concept of a single, stereotypical parenting style no longer reflects the diversity of modern families. Today, families are so varied that it is difficult to confine parenting approaches to just one model. Parenting has changed significantly over the decades, from rigid, authoritarian models to more adaptable, principle-based approaches. The following timeline illustrates critical milestones in the evolution of parenting styles, showing the gradual shift toward flexibility and positive parenting (**Figure 1**).

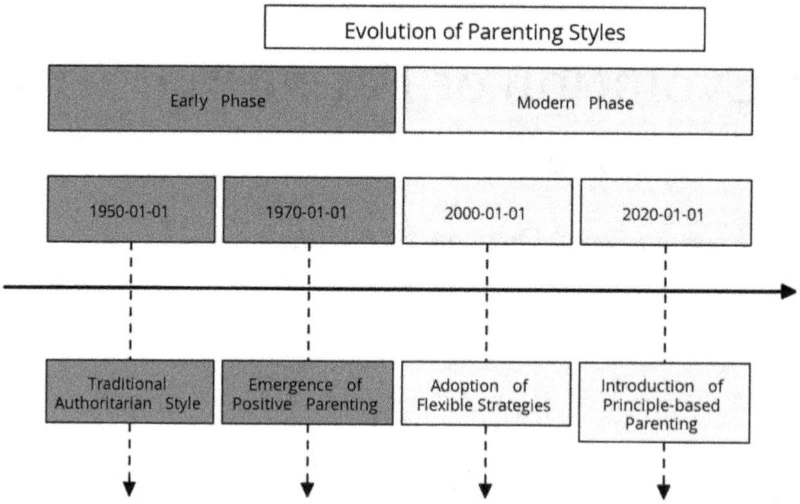

Figure 1.
Evolution of parenting styles.

Today, most parents find themselves in the role because they deliberately choose to have children or because circumstances unfold unexpectedly [3]. In either case, parenting often is not something meticulously planned out in advance. Instead, the immediate focus for many parents, especially those with their first child, is on the tangible aspects of raising a child. They think about physical growth, education, and other measurable milestones. However, for first-time parents, the experience can feel overwhelming, and the instinct to protect often takes precedence over broader considerations about the child's development. This instinct to protect is powerful, yet it can sometimes be misunderstood. Rather than allowing their child to explore and learn from the world, many parents, especially new ones, become overly cautious, shielding their children from minor risks [3]. While this protective impulse comes from a place of love and care, it can limit the child's ability to develop independence and resilience. Understanding when and how to balance protection with freedom is one of the most challenging aspects of parenting.

The way parents learn how to protect and care for their children is deeply rooted in their upbringing. Most parents model their parenting style after their parents, consciously or subconsciously following the same patterns. For some, this means repeating the methods they were raised with, mainly if they had positive experiences. For others, especially those who endured trauma or hardship, the focus becomes breaking that cycle, striving to do the opposite of what their parents did. In either case, the lessons learnt from childhood significantly shape how parents raise their children.

Today, one of the most widely promoted approaches is positive parenting. This method emphasises encouragement, empathy, and mutual respect rather than punishment or control [4]. However, while it offers a compassionate framework, positive parenting can often feel artificial or difficult to implement in real-life situations [1]. The strategies are typically designed for specific contexts and require careful adaptation to suit a variety of family dynamics. Not all parents find it easy to adjust the approach to their unique circumstances, but the adaptability of these strategies empowers parents to see what works best for their family. Successfully applying positive parenting requires critical thinking, self-awareness, and a broad understanding of child development [5, 6], which may feel overwhelming for many parents. We propose a parenting approach based on core principles rather than specific strategies. Strategies, after all, should emanate from solid guiding principles. Once parents have established a straightforward principle, such as empathy, respect, or balance, they can more easily adopt the right strategies for their unique family context. Instead of viewing strategies as cause-and-effect responses to immediate problems, they should be seen as part of a holistic approach that considers the needs and dynamics of the entire family. A well-chosen strategy should address the present situation and positively impact the child's long-term development and the family's overall well-being. This long-term perspective can reassure parents that their efforts contribute to their child's future.

Principles guide our mindset and keep us focused on long-term goals. In parenting, principles are essential for maintaining consistency and purpose, guiding us toward thoughtful decisions rather than reactive responses. The Principles for Parenting Styles we propose are grounded in the Systemic Theory of Family Therapy. This theory suggests that children exist within a more extensive system; the family and any strategy parents choose must consider the impact on the individual child and the entire family dynamic [7]. Decisions made in the present must reflect both past experiences and future implications. A strategy that benefits the child now might have ripple effects throughout the family, influencing siblings, partners, and the overall emotional climate.

Considering this approach, we will briefly explain systems theory, the foundation for the four principles that should guide parenting styles. These principles provide a framework from which all effective strategies should emerge, helping parents critically evaluate their decisions. By grounding their choices in these four core principles, parents can avoid making decisions in isolation and instead consider the broader, systemic impact on the entire family. This ensures that parenting decisions are not made in a vacuum but are part of a holistic approach that considers the well-being of all family members, in the both present and long terms [8].

2. Systemic perspective of the family therapy

While systems theory can be complex, especially when adapting it to specific therapeutic strategies, its basic principles are straightforward. No matter the form a family takes—whether traditional, single-parent, blended, or otherwise—a family is always a system [9]. A system, whether a family, an organisation, or even an object, is defined by the interactions between its parts [10]. In a family, this means each member affects the whole system, and in turn, the family influences each member [11]. Understanding this dynamic helps parents recognise that any action taken within the family will ripple out and affect all members, in the both present and over time. The systems theory can be synthesised into six key concepts, namely, (i) circularity, (ii) connectedness, (iii) feedback loop, (iv) homeostasis, (v) hermeneutics, and (vi) cyberntics.

2.1 Circularity vs. linearity

In traditional psychological approaches, signs and symptoms of mental health difficulties were often viewed as the result of a specific cause, following a linear cause-and-effect model. This perspective persists in some approaches today [12].

However, systems theory introduced a revolutionary shift in understanding certain behaviours, suggesting they are not merely the result of one specific cause but are shaped by the entire system in which the individual lives [10]. Children, like adults, do not exist in isolation; the complex interactions within their families influence them [13].

The systems theory developed by Mara Selvini Palazzoli suggests that while specific mental health issues, such as schizophrenia, may have biological origins, the way these issues develop and whether the individual improves or not is significantly affected by the family system [14]. Palazzoli and the Milan approach to family therapy worked with patients diagnosed with schizophrenia, an illness typically considered congenital. Yet their work demonstrated that the system around the patient, how family members respond to the disease, their beliefs about it, and how they interact can change the patient's behaviour. In turn, changes in the patient's behaviour influence the behaviours and emotional responses of parents and siblings, creating a dynamic feedback loop within the family. Therefore, parenting decisions should be made holistically, ensuring that strategies consider the well-being of all family members and the overall family dynamics [12, 13]. In family therapy, the shift from viewing the individual as a separate entity to understanding them as part of a more extensive system has led to remarkable improvements in treatment outcomes [12]. When both the individual and the family system are addressed, positive changes occur not only in the person with mental health challenges but also in the family that surrounds them. A key concept in systems theory is circularity, which refers to the idea that changes in one part of the system affect the entire system. The metaphor of a cobweb below can illustrate this aspect (**Figure 2**).

Each family member is like a thread connected to the whole web in this metaphor. When one member moves emotionally or behaviourally, the entire cobweb shifts in response. This interconnectedness shows that any change in one individual inevitably impacts the rest of the system. This leads to the second key concept, which builds on this idea of mutual influence within the family system.

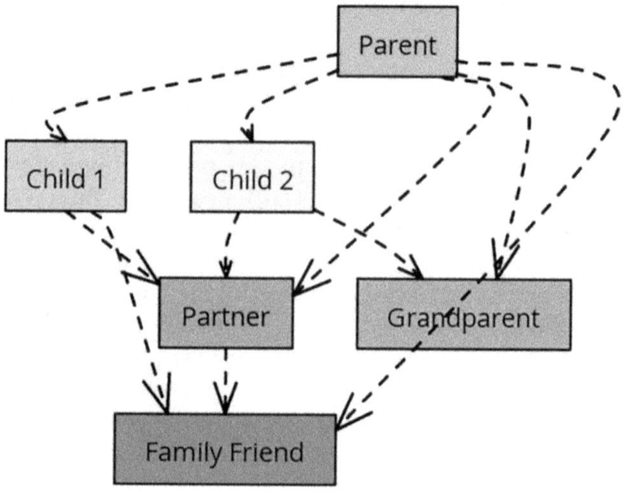

Figure 2.
Family cobweb: Thread connections.

2.2 Connectedness

In a family system, no individual, whether parent, child, or significant other, acts in isolation. Every action is a reaction to the movements of the other members within the system [9]. Connectedness, in this context, refers to emotional closeness and how family members might be disconnected from each other [15]. Disconnection, whether emotional or communicative, can be as impactful as connection [10].

The importance of connectedness to human development is well-established in the attachment theories of Bowlby, Ainsworth, and Howarth [16]. These theories demonstrate that the bonds between parents and children are built over time, and these bonds form the basis for how family members react to and make decisions with one another [17]. This connectedness within the family system either strengthens or deteriorates over time, depending on the feedback loops created by decisions and interactions [18]. Importantly, this process is not linear. Instead, it is circular and multi-directional, and every action, whether big or small, sends ripples through the entire system [19–22]. Just as a positive interaction can consolidate the bonds within the family, a negative one can weaken them [23]. The ongoing feedback from one family member to another plays a critical role in determining whether the family grows more connected or drifts apart over time.

2.3 Feedback loop

The feedback loop is crucial in developing proper connectivity between family members, and the quality of feedback can significantly affect the functionality or dysfunctionality of the entire system [24]. The diagram below illustrates the continuous feedback loop in family dynamics, showing how actions and reactions among family members create an ongoing cycle that impacts the system's overall health and connectivity (**Figure 3**).

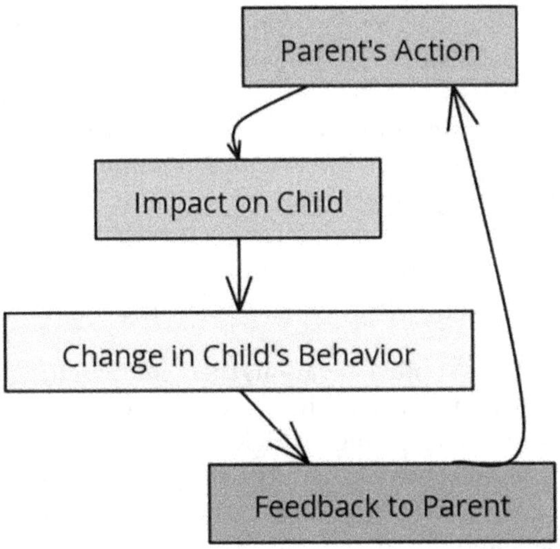

Figure 3.
Feedback loop in family dynamics.

Family members may become disconnected from the system without consistent feedback, leading to temporary dysfunction. However, since families consist of human beings [25], and human beings possess a remarkable capacity for adaptability [26], members of the system will naturally attempt to rebalance. This rebalancing can only occur through continuous feedback [27], where members become aware of how their actions affect themselves and the entire family system.

Feedback can alter the harmony and functionality of the system at any given moment [28]. For this reason, self-awareness and reflective skills are essential for each family member to recognise how their behaviour impacts the whole. Maintaining this awareness allows the family system to remain functional and balanced [29]. This brings us to the following concept: homeostasis, which refers to the system's ability to maintain internal stability despite external changes.

2.4 Homeostasis

Members within a family system naturally work toward achieving functionality in pursuit of stability, continuity, and consistency. Each member, whether parent, child, or significant other, performs specific roles contributing to the system's functionality or dysfunctionality. Many of these interactions are driven by automatic, learnt behaviours, often happening beneath the surface. However, every action within the system impacts others, whether the individuals involved are fully aware [30].

Systems theory brings awareness to these underlying processes and focuses on how relationships contribute to the homeostasis of the family unit [23, 31]. Beyond maintaining functionality, systems theory helps family members understand how their relationships can improve by reflecting on the feedback exchanged between them. This reflection encourages family members to become more conscious of how their actions affect the overall system, strengthening relationships and enhancing functionality [19, 32].

Everyone, whether parent or child, brings their unique story, experiences, and emotional baggage to the family, and reactions can be interpreted differently [33]. This is where the feedback loop becomes essential for clarification. Family members must acknowledge and accept each person's narratives, considering factors such as age, context, and personal history [22, 34], which influence how behaviours are interpreted.

Furthermore, family systems often rely on therapeutic interventions to address dysfunctions and enhance positive interactions. Techniques such as reflecting teams and family therapy supervision are instrumental in creating space for multiple perspectives and improving family members' understanding [22]. Different approaches to therapy, such as third-order critical family therapy [23], also contribute to rethinking traditional models of psychopathology and enhancing family dynamics.

Systems theory has been applied in various therapeutic settings, including treating addictions [30] and developing insights into how individuals' personal histories affect their health behaviours [19]. Targeting biological aspects, such as signalling pathways for disease treatment, can also parallel family therapy's focus on systemic interaction by understanding how changes within one part of the system influence others [33, 35]. Such an understanding can be transformative for addressing diseases and dysfunctional family interactions that have far-reaching consequences on members' well-being. This brings us to the fifth key concept: hermeneutics, or the interpretation of meaning within relationships.

2.5 Hermeneutics: The narrative stance

Though rooted in systems theory, this concept introduces a new dimension to understanding family dynamics: it is not just the impact of one family member's behaviour on another but also how that behaviour is interpreted. How family members interpret reactions, consciously and unconsciously, can make all the difference. Significantly, this interpretation is influenced by the subjective perspectives of individuals, including children, and is shaped by a mix of experiences, thoughts, and emotions [36].

As we grow, our brain builds narratives based on pre-existing beliefs shaped by past experiences and the feedback we have received [23]. Adults, for example, often interpret others' actions through the lens of these core beliefs, which may determine how they respond or provide feedback in return. Though we may hold various beliefs about many things, at the core of human relationships are one or two fundamental beliefs that drive our interactions, beliefs shaped by early experiences and critical relationships.

For children, this process is different. Their belief systems are still developing and heavily influenced by the feedback they receive from adults, especially their parents. By the time children reach late childhood, their belief systems are generally well-formed, and these systems influence how they interpret others' behaviour. A child's belief system can be rigid or flexible, depending on the variety of responses and experiences they have had with adults [36].

As children enter adolescence, they experiment with seeking independence from their parents' feedback, often leading to conflicts. Adolescents begin to challenge the belief systems developed in childhood, and through new experiences, they either reinforce or reshape these beliefs. However, research shows [23, 36] that childhood experiences have a lasting impact on the belief system, even into adulthood.

A third scenario that applies to both adults and children is the experience of trauma. Traumatic events caused by others or uncontrollable natural forces can profoundly alter or reinforce a person's belief system. Trauma often leads to significant shifts in behaviour as the individual tries to integrate or reconcile the event with their existing beliefs [23]. This brings us to a critical question: "Can we change our belief systems if they contribute to dysfunction either at the individual or family level?" This question leads us to the final concept of systems theory.

2.6 First-order, second-order, and third-order cybernetics

Family therapy initially focused on behaviour modification, known as first-order cybernetics. However, while this approach provided short-term relief, deeper belief systems often undermined lasting change, leading to a shift toward second-order cybernetics. This second approach emphasised reshaping individual beliefs within the family, influenced by cognitive behavioural therapy, which led to more sustainable outcomes. Eventually, therapists recognised the need to balance changes in both belief systems and behaviour, giving rise to third-order cybernetics [26, 37]. The following diagram illustrates the fundamental concepts of systems theory, including feedback loops, circularity, and the evolution of cybernetics in family therapy (**Figure 4**).

This evolution consolidates five core concepts of systems theory: (i) circularity, (ii) feedback, (iii) connectivity, (iv) balance, and (v) interpretation (hermeneutics) [28, 38, 39]. Long-term change is facilitated when families understand the circular nature of their interactions, reflect on feedback, and enhance their connections

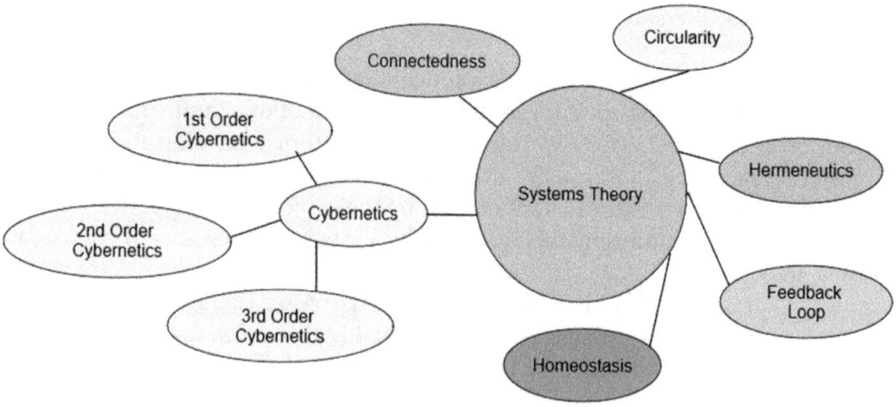

Figure 4.
Critical concepts of systems theory.

while maintaining systemic balance. Effective therapeutic interventions help families transition from conflicting narratives to a shared understanding. When consistent beliefs and behaviours are lacking, family members may distance themselves or split from the system.

3. The achievements of systems theory

One of the critical achievements of family systems theory is its holistic perspective on family dynamics. The theory recognises that one individual does not cause family problems but emerges from how family members interact [40]. Instead of fixing symptoms of unbalanced relationships, the theory emphasises improving relationships, enabling the family to work together to address problems. This approach removes the need to place blame on any one person and instead encourages family members to recognise how each of them contributes to the difficulty [41].

In therapy, families are led to explore new ways of interacting, with an increased awareness of their belief systems and how these influence the current situation. As a result, family members learn to navigate conflicts with greater empathy and understanding, helping the family to function more harmoniously [42]. Family systems theory offers both horizontal and vertical perspectives on family interactions. The horizontal perspective focuses on how family members interact, emphasising the importance of their interrelationships [43]. The vertical perspective refers to external forces, such as societal expectations, economic pressures, or natural events, that impact the family, even though the family may have no control over them [44]. Finally, systems theory also accounts for the intrapersonal processes of everyone within the family, recognising that personal experiences and internal emotions influence relationships within the family system [45].

Further, David Campbell extended family systems theory to the field of organisational theory, drawing parallels between how families and organisations operate. Just like a family, an organisation comprises individuals whose relationships and dynamics affect the overall direction and productivity of the system [46]. This shift introduced a breakthrough in management and leadership theory, highlighting the importance of relational dynamics in organisational success [47]. For example, when management fails to consider the well-being of its employees, it creates a disconnect that affects employee satisfaction. Over time, this dissatisfaction can negatively impact the entire organisation, as unaddressed problems "fire back" on management through reduced productivity, higher turnover, or disengagement [48]. [49] suggest that, by applying systems theory to organisations, leaders can better understand how their teams' internal dynamics influence the company's larger goals and work proactively to create a balanced and functional organisational environment.

Just as systems theory helps organisational leaders understand and influence the interactions within their teams, it can also guide parents in fostering a healthy and adaptive family environment. David Campbell's extension of family systems theory to the field of organisational theory illustrates that the dynamics of families and organisations share key similarities: both are systems composed of individuals whose relationships impact the system's overall functioning and success [46]. When parents, like organisational leaders, fail to consider family members, emotional and psychological well-being, it can create disconnects that affect family cohesion, much like how employee dissatisfaction can negatively impact an organisation [48].

These forces are found in the interactions between family members and the feedback loops that shape behaviours and beliefs over time [50]. The key to overcoming family challenges does not lie in attempting to solve the isolated issue itself but rather in focusing on the relationships and interactions that contribute to the overall functionality of the family [51]. Parents can bring about meaningful, lasting change by looking beyond symptoms and examining the processes that bind the family system [52].

Families can navigate even the most difficult challenges with resilience and adaptability when they strengthen their relationships and develop a deeper understanding of how each member contributes to the family system. This perspective shifts the focus from merely managing problems to fostering the dynamics that encourage a well-functioning, supportive, and adaptive family environment [53].

Following this in-depth exploration of systems theory, defining the four basic principles of parenting styles is essential. Central to systems theory is the emphasis on relationships, processes, and accepting change as a natural response to the dynamic nature of family life [54]. When addressing family issues, such as illness, substance abuse, betrayal, or severe conflict, focusing solely on the content of the problem risks overlooking the underlying relational forces that allow the problem to persist or dissolve [55].

4. The four principles of parenting

Focusing on relationships allows parents to step away from relying solely on strategies and instead view strategies as tools to be used as needed in various circumstances. When parents prioritise relationships over strategies, they create a preventive framework that helps them approach difficult situations with a long-term perspective. This shift enables parents to build a solid relational foundation with their children, ensuring strategies are applied thoughtfully rather than reactively. The four principles of parenting styles are grounded in research on strategies for managing different family challenges [56–65].

These principles emerge from the common patterns found across various situations, whether marital betrayal, substance abuse, physical illness of a family member, violence, or disability. The key question we must ask is: "What do these situations have in common from a relationship perspective?"

The answer lies in one central theme: the loss of attachment. All these difficulties involve, in some way, a disruption of the bond between family members [65]. The parents' most important role is to build a robust and healthy attachment with their children. A secure attachment fosters the development of children into resilient, critical, positive, and responsible adults [61, 63]. The four principles we propose are designed to guide parents in creating and maintaining this vital attachment, which is the foundation of their child's long-term emotional, social, and intellectual development.

The pie chart below illustrates an evenly balanced approach to parenting, emphasising the equal importance of leadership, consistency, responsibility, and resilience. Each of these principles occupies 25% of the distribution, suggesting that effective parenting relies on maintaining balance among these aspects. Leadership and consistency provide guidance and stability, while responsibility and resilience encourage growth and adaptability. The equal division underscores that no one principle should dominate; a holistic approach where all these elements are nurtured equally may lead to more effective parenting outcomes (**Figure 5**).

4.1 Principle 1: Parental leadership

Leadership is typically associated with management and organisations; however, we can also view the family as a small organisation. "If David Campbell applied the systems theory of family therapy to organisations, why not apply management and leadership concepts to families as well?" While families may be small units, they require similar forms of leadership and organisation to ensure functionality and harmony [66]. In the past, when families often consisted of many children, parents had to be highly organised. They managed everything from infrastructure and finances to coordinate activities, roles that are strikingly like the responsibilities of leaders within larger organisations. Today, while families tend to be smaller, the same principles of organisation, management, and leadership still apply [67]. Whether a family is large

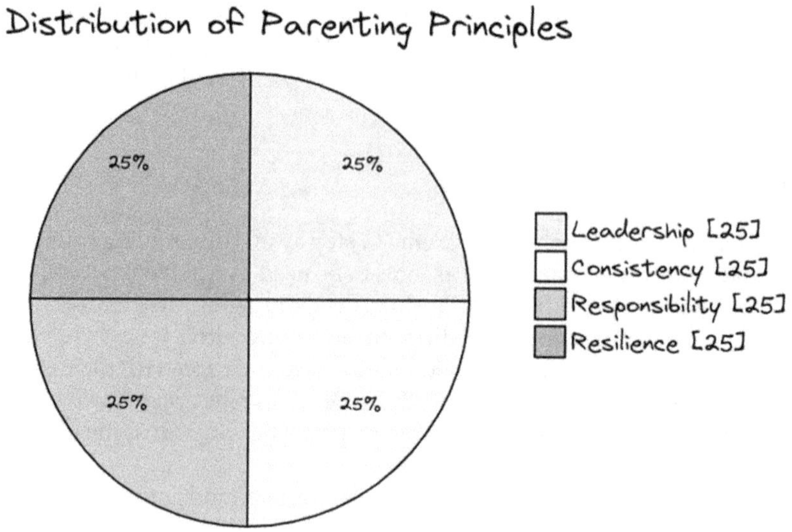

Figure 5.
Principles of parenting overview.

or small, parents serve as leaders, guiding the family toward shared goals, resolving conflicts, and ensuring everyone works harmoniously together [68]. By adopting a leadership mindset, parents can bring structure, clarity, and vision to their family life, helping to foster a sense of purpose and unity within the family system.

In today's world, where gender equity has become a crucial focus and financial demands require both parents to work, families operate more like small organisations. Tasks are increasingly shared between partners, and there is a growing need for structure and clear communication to balance responsibilities at work and home [33, 54, 69]. Whether consciously or unconsciously, the family functions similarly to an organisation [70–72]. Like in a business, roles must be clearly defined, leadership shared, and resources managed effectively. Like managers, parents must collaborate, delegate tasks, and meet the family's emotional and practical needs.

The analogical similarities between families and organisations are apparent: both involve leadership, resource management, collaboration, and problem-solving. In families, as in organisations, success depends on how well these dynamics are managed and how equitably tasks and decisions are shared between all members. Parents are, by nature, the managers and leaders of the small organisation we call a family. Just as business partners conceive and build a company through their shared vision, parents make their family through their relationship with children resulting from this foundation.

This dynamic is like a family business where two siblings start a company with a unified goal. In this case, the parents are the two partners who must establish a shared vision and mission before raising children, ensuring they are aligned in their approach to parenting. Like any successful business, the vision and mission give the family direction. Parents must ask themselves, "What do we want for our family?" "What values and principles will guide us in raising our children?" A shared sense of purpose creates consistency in decision-making and helps the family function smoothly, even in challenging times. Like a business that thrives on a clear, shared objective, a family needs that same sense of unity. By consolidating their relationship around a shared vision, parents can foster a stable, nurturing environment for their children, setting the foundation for their family's growth and success.

Before conceiving children, parents should first consciously conceive their vision and mission as a couple. This involves asking themselves critical questions: "Why are we together?" "What will keep us together in the long term?" "How will we support each other through life's challenges?" It is essential to align on these core issues before stepping into the role of parents. If they choose to have children, parents must also reflect on: "What do we want for our children?" "What values and principles do we want to instil in them?" "How can we work together as partners to support their growth and well-being?" These discussions help ensure that parents approach family life with clarity and unity.

Perhaps the most critical question they could ask is, "Will we be partners because of our children or the strength of our relationship?" Parents must build an independent relationship, not one held together solely by parenting responsibilities. By consciously addressing these questions, parents can create a strong foundation for their family based on a shared vision, mutual support, and love beyond the roles of being a mother or father.

Unfolding a relationship's unconscious and subconscious dynamics is no easy task, and living 24 hours daily presents constant challenges [68]. However, if parents genuinely want the best for themselves and, by extension, for their children, this complex and often uncomfortable work is essential. Organisational leaders must engage with their team's more profound emotional and psychological dynamics, and parents must do the same within their family unit.

Parents need to develop leadership and managerial skills to create a solid vision for their relationship and their children's growth [70]. Once parents have established a clear vision and mission for their partnership, the next question becomes, "What is their vision and mission for their children?" "Does this mean parents should determine their children's career path or life choices?" Not at all. Parents' vision and mission for their children should focus on developing a healthy, well-rounded personality, not dictating their future. This means nurturing their children's emotional, intellectual, and social well-being and fostering independence, resilience, and self-awareness [69, 66]. Parents' roles are to guide and support their children as they grow, helping them develop into confident and capable individuals, not to predetermine their futures [71]. For this to happen, parents must first explore and unfold their subconscious and unconscious beliefs about parenting, relationships, and leadership. Parents can approach their role with greater clarity and intentionality by understanding their deeply held assumptions. When parents are aligned on a vision for their relationship, this naturally leads to a clearer vision for how they will support the development of their children's character and well-being [67, 68]. For example, a couple might realise that both are deeply career oriented. While they love each other, their professional ambitions are the primary focus of their lives. "Is there anything inherently wrong with this?" Not at all. This can work beautifully if they can balance their lives and support each other in pursuing their careers while maintaining a strong partnership. However, if they decide to have children, they must carefully consider how children will fit into this equation. Children require attention, affection, and quality time [33, 54], which may conflict with the couple's existing vision for their personal and professional lives [73].

The question then becomes, "How will they lead and manage their children when both are career-driven?" This challenge is not impossible to overcome but requires conscious and intentional decision-making. The couple must consider how to balance their own needs with the needs of their children [70]. This may involve drastic decisions in some cases, such as one partner temporarily stepping back from their career to provide more time and care for the children. These decisions must be made collaboratively, ensuring that both partners are on the same page and that the children benefit from a stable and loving environment. This example leads us to the following critical principle of parenting: Consistency. When parents are both career-oriented, they must work together to provide a consistent and reliable environment for their children. Consistency helps children feel secure, even when life is busy or demanding [68]. Whether it is ensuring regular family time or maintaining consistent routines, it is essential that children feel they are a priority, even in a high-achieving household.

4.2 Principle 2: Consistency and boundaries

Consistency is crucial in organisations and families because it provides stability, clear expectations, and security. The proverb "The boat that has two captains sinks" highlights the potential chaos and confusion that can arise when leadership is divided or inconsistent. This raises an important question: "Is it possible to have two leaders or managers within the same organisation, or in this case, the same family?" The answer is yes, but it requires a strong foundation of collaboration and teamwork to ensure that the family moves in one unified direction, aligned with the vision and mission the parents have established [74]. Having two leaders is not always easy. Children may receive mixed signals without consistency, and the family can quickly become disjointed.

Consistency means that parents must present a unified front, ensuring that their decisions and actions align, creating a stable environment for their children. Consistency helps ensure the family functions smoothly, with each member knowing what to expect and how to contribute [75, 76]. At the same time, collaboration between the parents is essential. In any family or organisation, it is natural for one partner to take the lead in certain areas, while the other leads in others. This leadership division can be effective if both partners communicate clearly and support each other's decisions. For instance, one parent might take charge of finances, while the other focuses on emotional caregiving. The key is ensuring that these leadership roles complement one another and that the overall direction of the family remains cohesive. Parents can maintain consistent leadership by working together, discussing challenges openly, and balancing responsibilities while ensuring their family moves forward with unity and purpose.

Parents must work together to lead their relationship and family in the right direction. Decisions must be made together, with both partners involved in the process. However, in cases where one partner does not fully agree with a decision, it is essential that they are still back their partner in front of the children. Children are more affected by inconsistent messages and confusion between parents than by occasional decision-making mistakes [77]. Inconsistency can create a sense of instability and uncertainty for children. For example, if one parent enforces a rule while the other contradicts it, children may struggle to understand boundaries, leading to confusion or behavioural issues. It is not the mistake in judgement that causes harm; instead, it is the mixed signals that create stress and unpredictability in a child's world.

When parents disagree, they must resolve the issue privately, away from the children. This allows them to present a united front, showing they are on the same page despite initial differences. This consistency in communication is vital to providing a sense of security for children, who thrive on predictability and clear boundaries [78]. By supporting each other, even when there are momentary disagreements, parents can maintain the stability their children need, creating an environment where the focus remains on the well-being and growth of the family.

As part of our human nature, we naturally seek shortcuts and easier ways of getting what we want. This also applies to children, who often unconsciously or subconsciously learn to identify the "easy parent" over time. They quickly determine which parent is more likely to say "yes" to specific requests and which one might be stricter or more likely to say "no." In many families, children choose the parent they speak to base on the desired outcome [74]. So, it is essential that the message given to the children be consistent and that they are given the same direction. Boundaries in such a case are imperative, as the children need to keep one point of reference for their direction, and this should be both parents working together and giving the same message. This dynamic is not limited to parents. Children may also turn to other significant adults, such as grandparents, aunts, or even teachers, to seek approval or a more favourable answer. While it is natural for children to form close bonds with these figures, the messages they receive must be consistent with the messages from their parents. If children receive conflicting guidance from different adults, it can create confusion and undermine the boundaries parents are trying to set [75]. It is also crucial for parents to communicate with other significant adults in their child's life. Whether it is grandparents or other relatives, parents need to ensure that everyone involved is on the same page. This can be done by having open discussions about family rules, values, and expectations so that the child receives a consistent message from all adults [78]. This dynamic becomes more complex in situations involving single parents, marital discord, or when third parties, such as grandparents or other close relatives, play a significant role in a child's life. However, while these circumstances present challenges, parents can still develop and maintain a shared vision for their children even if they are not living together. Achieving this may require more effort but is far from impossible [76].

One of the most critical elements of maintaining consistency in these situations is the ability of parents to separate their issues from their children's needs. When parents are experiencing marital discord or are no longer together, it is essential to create clear boundaries between their conflicts and how they parent their children. This allows children to continue receiving consistent guidance and support, even if the relationship between the parents is strained [77]. Collaboration and communication are key for single parents or those in co-parenting situations. Parents need to work together to create a co-parenting plan that outlines shared values, expectations, and rules for the children, ensuring that both homes provide the same messages. Regular communication about the children's needs and challenges will help maintain consistency, even if the parents live apart [74]. The same applies when third parties, such as grandparents or other close relatives, are involved. Children often form strong attachments to these individuals, and parents must establish clear boundaries and communicate openly with them to ensure that everyone is on the same page. Discussions about family rules and values help prevent conflicting messages from reaching the children, allowing for a more cohesive upbringing [75, 76]. While these situations are undoubtedly more complex, parents can still provide a unified front and consistent messaging by focusing on their shared vision for their children's well-being.

For example, a couple with two children, a 9-year-old boy and a 6-year-old girl, work due to financial constraints. The maternal grandparents pick the children up after school and stay with them until 6 pm, when one of the parents picks them up. During this time, the grandparents help the children with their homework, and the children have dinner with the parents once they are home. The father often works late and arrives around 8 pm. As a result, the mother typically makes most of the day-to-day decisions. However, the father does not always agree with her choices, and they argue about what should have been done. Adding to the complexity, some decisions are made by the grandparents. When the children want something they know their father would disagree with, such as sweets, fast food, screen time, or video games, they often ask the grandparents, who are more lenient. The father sometimes comes home to find his son still doing homework with the mother, leading to frustration and tension.

The mother struggles to set boundaries with her mother (the children's grandmother), who frequently gratifies her grandson's requests. The arguments between the parents often revolve around the grandmother's leniency and the fact that their son can get his way. The focus of the discussion, however, should not be the mother-in-law but rather how the parents can manage and lead their children effectively and give them a consistent message. This might require the parents to have a difficult conversation with the grandparents, explaining their boundaries and expectations for their children's upbringing. Of course, this would not be easy, as habits are difficult to change, especially when extended family is involved. However, the parents must work as a team, backing up each other's decisions and presenting a united front. Sometimes, it may even require one parent to work reduced hours or spend more time at home to ensure the children receive the attention and guidance they need. But before any external changes can be made, the parents must align their messages and lead and manage the family "boat" together, steering in the same direction. Without consistency, any changes made will be ineffective [75]. Since the children are 6 and 9 years old, it is also essential to involve them in the solution. This leads us to the following important principle: responsibility and choice. At this age, children can understand boundaries and take responsibility for their own actions. Parents can teach their children the value of making responsible choices by involving them in setting rules and making decisions. This helps the children develop independence and reinforces the parents' authority by making the children part of the decision-making process.

4.3 Principle 3: Responsibility and choice

"Can children genuinely bear the weight of responsibility for their actions?" "Are they capable of making informed choices?" Many parents might instinctively answer "no" to these questions, but this belief is primarily a misconception. Children possess a surprising degree of awareness. They are often fully conscious of when to charm their parents or avoid certain behaviours to prevent disappointment. While some of this behaviour may initially be shaped by conditioning, as children grow, particularly beyond the age of six, as noted in Piaget's theory of child development, their decision-making increasingly stems from logical reasoning [79]. At this stage, they begin to take greater ownership of their actions, understanding the consequences and making choices based on more sophisticated thought processes. Thus, children are not only capable of making decisions, but they also gradually learn to navigate responsibility as their cognitive abilities develop. They often become more aware of which authority figures to approach for their desired response, carefully selecting the right person to ask for permission [80, 81]. In situations like parental separation, they may gravitate toward one parent over the other based on anticipated reactions. Alternatively, they may follow their instincts, drawing from past experiences and personal impulses when making decisions.

It is important to recognise that children, even as young as 2 years old, can make choices when guided appropriately by adults. For example, if the family is going on a picnic, a parent might ask the child to choose between two pairs of shoes. This provides a structured choice, allowing the child to feel responsible for their decision. Now, let us imagine that after selecting Slipper B, the child starts to complain. A parent anticipating such a situation can calmly remind the child that it was their choice, reinforcing the idea of responsibility. This assumes that the shoes fit properly and are not causing discomfort due to reasons like outgrowing them, something children may not always communicate clearly. In such cases, the parent's role is to observe and address any physical discomfort the child might not yet fully understand or express.

Choices given to children should be introduced gradually and thoughtfully, as this helps instil a sense of responsibility over time. When children are offered the opportunity to make decisions within reasonable and safe boundaries, they internalise that their choices carry positive and negative consequences [82, 83]. This sense of responsibility often starts to form at an unconscious level as children learn that when they choose something, they also bear the outcome of that choice. However, it is essential to remember that placing too much responsibility on a child is unfair. For instance, asking a four-year-old to care for a baby would be far beyond their capacity.

Appropriate responsibilities for young children might include tasks such as tidying up, adhering to a set bedtime, sleeping alone in their room, or deciding not to eat certain food because they dislike it unless an issue like an allergy is involved. These manageable choices help children learn to handle responsibility developmentally appropriately. By assigning small responsibilities and ensuring gentle consequences when they are not fulfilled, we foster two key traits in children: resilience and empathy [84, 85]. Children begin to bounce back from mistakes while also learning to consider how their actions affect others.

4.4 Principle 4: Resilience and empathy

Parents should not expect children to always be happy; there will be times when they are angry, frustrated, and disappointed. These challenging moments are inevitable and essential opportunities for parents to help their children develop resilience and empathy. While resilience can start being nurtured as early as 2 years old, empathy is more complex and typically develops later, often around six and beyond [86]. In these emotionally charged moments, guiding children through their feelings rather than dismissing them helps lay the foundation for emotional strength and understanding. Teaching them to navigate setbacks, frustrations, or disappointments builds resilience while gradually exposing them to others' perspectives as they mature and fosters empathic understanding. Developing these qualities requires patience, consistency, and mindful parenting [87] as children progress at their own pace in learning to manage their emotions and relate to the feelings of others.

Resilience can be built young because children learn how to navigate setbacks and frustrations through conditioning and modelling [88]. These processes involve children observing and imitating the behaviour of adults and caregivers and experiencing direct consequences for their actions. When children experience these moments of challenge early on, they begin to understand that not everything will go their way and that they can recover from disappointment or failure. For example, toddlers might not immediately get what they want and may feel frustrated. Still, they learn to manage this emotion and adapt over time, a foundational aspect of resilience [88]. In their early years, children often respond to situations based on imitation or through a fear of consequences, which begins to foster a sense of responsibility and guilt (Erikson's Psychosocial Development Stages, particularly the stage of "Autonomy vs. Shame and Doubt") [89]. This early form of understanding teaches them that actions have outcomes, and they begin to bounce back when things do not go as planned or when they are not immediately gratified.

By the time children reach the age of 6–7, they start to develop better problem-solving skills through logical thinking (Piaget's Concrete Operational Stage). At this stage, they can reason through situations, anticipate outcomes, and understand consequences more clearly. They begin to avoid specific actions not merely because they fear the immediate consequences but because they understand that these actions might lead to delayed or reduced gratification. This is also when empathic understanding starts to develop more deeply. Children at this age can recognise that others have emotions, perspectives, and experiences, allowing them to move beyond simple self-interest and react to others with empathy. By fostering resilience and compassion in tandem, starting with basic emotional regulation in early childhood and progressing to more sophisticated reasoning in later years, parents and caregivers help build the foundation for a well-rounded, emotionally intelligent individual.

Empathic understanding plays a crucial role in developing resilience, as it helps children move beyond egocentrism and realise that life involves different perspectives and challenges [86, 90]. As they mature, children begin to understand that there are "two sides to the coin" and that adversity is a normal part of life. This shift in perspective allows them to grasp that they would not always get what they want and that setbacks or negative consequences are inevitable. The early conditioning of accepting delayed gratification and understanding that mistakes or failures have consequences lays the groundwork for this more complex understanding. By the time they reach the age of 6 or older, children, especially with the guidance of adults, can begin to reason through these experiences. They start to understand that things sometimes go wrong, and rather than internalising these failures as personal shortcomings, they learn to process and reflect on what happened [91]. This reasoning helps them see that achieving life satisfaction often requires sacrifice and balance and that setbacks are part of the learning process.

When children are taught to view challenges as opportunities for growth, they begin to see that life, while not always easy, is manageable. With support, they understand that resilience is not about avoiding difficulties but learning to cope and bounce back [87]. This is where empathy reinforces resilience: children who recognise that others also experience challenges develop a broader sense of compassion and a more realistic view of life [92]. They realise that everyone faces difficulties and that strength lies in navigating through the "thorns" rather than expecting a life without obstacles. This dual understanding of empathy and resilience empowers children to face adversity with a stronger mindset, knowing that setbacks are not only expected but surmountable.

A solid foundation of resilience, built through learning how to bounce back from challenges, needs to be instilled early in childhood to achieve proper empathic understanding. Resilience is essential because it teaches children how to handle adversity and regulate their emotions in difficult situations, crucial skills for developing empathy [87]. Without resilience, children may struggle to see beyond their frustrations or disappointments, making connecting with others' emotions harder. If, by the age of 10–11, children have yet to develop this foundation of resilience or basic empathy, it becomes significantly more challenging to cultivate these traits. This stage of development, often referred to as the "latency period" in psychological theory (Freud), or the final phase of Piaget's Concrete Operational Stage [93], is a critical window where children transition from self-centred thinking to understanding the broader social world [89]. During this time, they refine their ability to relate to others and develop the social skills necessary for adolescence.

Once this window is missed and children enter adolescence without these critical skills, building resilience and empathy becomes more difficult. While it is still possible to foster these traits, it requires much more effort. Post-adolescence, individuals may need targeted interventions, such as reflective practices, mentorship, or therapy, to develop the emotional intelligence that ideally would have been built earlier in life [92]. The work becomes more challenging because the brain undergoes significant changes during adolescence; social dynamics intensify, identity formation becomes more complex, and self-awareness deepens. If resilience and empathy have not been established by this stage, navigating the challenges of the teenage years can be more overwhelming, as the individual may lack the tools to process both their emotions and those of others. However, it is important to emphasise that while building these skills later is harder, it is not impossible. With dedication, self-awareness, and external support, resilience and empathy can be developed in adolescence and even adulthood.

The key is to recognise that it will take conscious effort, emotional learning, and a strong desire to grow emotionally and socially.

Adolescence is a pivotal time in a young person's life, characterised by the search for identity and the struggle to understand their place in the world. However, this journey often comes with confusion and uncertainty, making it difficult for adolescents to make clear decisions. Suppose they have not been given opportunities to make choices, take responsibility for their actions, or learn to navigate adversity and bounce back. In that case, they may find themselves overwhelmed during this critical phase. When children have not had the chance to practice making decisions or experience the natural consequences of their actions in earlier years, they enter adolescence with a weaker foundation for understanding how their choices impact their future. The lack of early responsibility can leave them ill-equipped to deal with the heightened complexities of adolescence, where decisions carry more weight and emotional stakes are higher [91]. Instead of learning from past mistakes and setbacks, they may feel paralysed or impulsive, unable to anticipate the consequences of their actions because they have not developed the cognitive and emotional tools to do so.

Additionally, with resilience, adolescents may be able to cope with their inevitable challenges, leading to frustration, avoidance, or poor decision-making. Suppose they have not learnt how to turn adversity into a learning opportunity. In that case, they may be more likely to withdraw or act out when faced with difficulties, seeing obstacles as failures rather than growth opportunities. This lack of resilience can make the identity-searching process even more fraught, as they may lack the confidence to explore, fail, and try again.

Finally, the absence of empathic understanding compounds the issue. Empathy allows individuals to see beyond their perspective and understand the impact of their actions on others. Without this, adolescents may have difficulty forming socially and emotionally healthy relationships, which are crucial during this stage of development [86]. The result can be an adolescent who feels isolated, misunderstood, or unable to connect meaningfully with others, hindering their overall development and self-discovery. Through the inevitable 'trials and tribulations' of life, some adults may recognise the importance of resilience and empathy, working hard to cultivate these traits to lead healthier, more balanced lives. For many, this journey involves overcoming past mistakes and learning to manage the anxiety that often accompanies such self-awareness. With dedication and sometimes the support of therapists, mentors, or loved ones, individuals can grow from their experiences, learning to make better choices and adapt more effectively to life's challenges [92].

Nonetheless, not everyone has the same access to support systems or the internal strength to navigate these difficulties independently. Despite their best efforts, some individuals may find it incredibly difficult to overcome the weight of poor decisions, unresolved emotional pain, or entrenched patterns of behaviour. This is often where mental health challenges arise. For those unable to develop the resilience or empathy needed to bounce back from adversity, feelings of hopelessness, anxiety, and depression can take hold [92]. Without the right tools or support, they may feel overwhelmed by their circumstances, believing that change is beyond their reach. In these cases, it is essential to recognise that mental health struggles are not a reflection of personal failure but often the result of a complex interplay of factors, social, emotional, and biological that make resilience and emotional growth harder to achieve. Providing access to resources, supportive networks, and compassionate care can make all the difference for those who cannot independently overcome life's challenges.

DOI: http://dx.doi.org/10.5772/intechopen.1008384

5. Framework mindset for the application of the four parenting principles

The four parenting principles cannot be applied in isolation or out of context. Their successful implementation assumes at least four critical considerations that parents must keep in mind, namely, (i) parenting styles, (ii) horizontal, vertical and 360 degrees, (iii) understanding of child development, and (iv) contextualisation of the parenting approach.

5.1 Parenting styles: Parental adaptation

The four parenting principles cannot be applied in isolation or out of context. Their successful implementation assumes at least three critical considerations we will explore. Not all parents find it easy to apply abstract concepts, as principles are not tangible. Research suggests [94] that many people are kinaesthetic learners; they learn best through hands-on experiences and direct, tangible feedback. Several factors influence an individual's ability to think abstractly, including culture, education, genetic predispositions, profession, and developmental experiences [95, 96].

For various reasons, some adults may struggle to move beyond concrete thinking, relying instead on what is immediately observable and tangible when interpreting events or making decisions. Even those who have developed abstract thinking skills can sometimes revert to more concrete understandings, especially when stressed or overwhelmed [97]. This tendency reflects the complexity of human cognition, where abstract principles may sometimes feel less reliable or more challenging to apply than immediate, sensory-based experiences. In parenting, this means that while some parents can readily apply abstract principles across different situations, others may need more support or practice to leap from tangible experiences to abstract reasoning [98]. The ability to adapt these principles in a meaningful way often depends on a parent's capacity for flexible thinking and self-reflection, skills that can be nurtured but may not come naturally to everyone [99]. Thus, when adopting this principled approach to parenting, we need to take into consideration that parents need to have at least three essential personality qualities:

a. *The ability to think abstractly:* A principled approach to parenting does not provide a one-size-fits-all or ready-made recipe for responding to specific situations. Instead, it requires abstract thinking—the capacity to generalise and apply principles across various scenarios [96, 97]. Parents must consider multiple dimensions of a problem, including what has worked in the past, what is happening in the present, and how decisions made now will impact the future. For example, suppose the principle in question encourages responsibility. In that case, a parent must reflect on how it was applied to an older child and how it might be adapted to a younger one. Contextual factors also need to be weighed, such as differences in temperament, age, and needs between siblings. This requires metacognitive ability, or the capacity to think about one's thinking [98]. Parents must be able to step outside the immediate moment, reflect on different possible outcomes, and foresee how their actions in one situation might influence future events or relationships within the family. They must constantly balance consistency with flexibility, ensuring the principles they apply remain aligned across various contexts while still being tailored to each child's needs. For example, while one child might thrive with more autonomy in completing tasks, another might need more structure and guidance to build the same sense of responsibility. The parent's role is to apply the principle of responsibility consistently but adapt the execution of that principle to fit the individual child's situation and stage of development. Abstract thinking allows parents to take a broader view, considering past experiences, current circumstances, and future implications while remaining flexible and adaptive.

b. *The ability to think critically*: Besides abstract thinking, parents need to develop strong critical thinking skills when applying a principled approach to parenting. Critical thinking enables parents to approach decision-making more thoughtfully and analytically. This involves using hypothetical questioning to evaluate situations by reflecting on past experiences, considering current circumstances, and predicting how a decision made now will impact future outcomes [94, 99]. Essentially, critical thinking helps parents assess how the application of a principle will play out in real time and beyond. For example, when deciding how to address a child's refusal to follow instructions, a parent might ask themselves, "How did my past response to this situation impact the child?" "What consequences did it have for our relationship or their behaviour?" "If I respond the same way now, will it yield the same result?" "How might a different approach affect the short- and long-term outcome?" By critically evaluating their options, the parent can choose the most effective course of action that aligns with the principles they aim to instil, such as responsibility or resilience.

c. *Circular questioning:* A fundamental technique that supports critical thinking is 'circular questioning', which comes from systemic therapy [95]. In this method, the parent considers how their decision will affect the child in question and other family members. For instance, if a parent decides to allow one child a later bedtime as a reward, they must consider how this decision will impact siblings. "How might the other children react to this decision?" "Will they feel left out or develop feelings of unfairness?" "How will these reactions affect family dynamics?"

Circular questioning allows the parent to understand how each decision reverberates through the family system and helps them anticipate unintended consequences. Additionally, critical thinking involves reviewing past choices and their outcomes [94, 97, 98]. A reflective parent asks, "Did my previous response achieve the desired result?" If yes, the parent may apply the same strategy again. However, if the approach does not work, critical thinking leads the parent to explore alternative methods, always ensuring that their decision-making is grounded in the four guiding principles of parenting. Critical thinking helps parents navigate complex situations by considering multiple perspectives, anticipating consequences, and drawing on past experiences to make more informed, balanced decisions. This kind of reflective, strategic thinking ensures that parenting decisions are not reactionary but are aligned with long-term goals and values.

5.2 Horizontal, vertical, and 360 degrees

Parenting is a complex and evolving journey that requires balancing various approaches to effectively guide children in today's fast-paced world. Parents need to cultivate a comprehensive mindset, one that incorporates vertical, horizontal, and even 360-degree perspectives to nurture, discipline, and guide their children through different stages of life. These approaches help parents stay attuned to the demands of modern parenting, continuously adapt their methods, and foster a principle-based family environment.

In this section, we explore the importance of adopting a vertical and 360-degree approach to parenting, the significance of allowing parents to make and learn from mistakes, and practical strategies for refusing a child's wants. By understanding these multifaceted aspects, parents can develop stronger relationships with their children, maintain consistency in their values, and navigate challenges to support their children's growth and emotional resilience.

a. *Vertical and 360-degree approach to parenting:* An essential quality for parents adopting a principled approach is maintaining an open disposition toward continuous learning. Parenting is a challenging and dynamic task, particularly in the complex world we live in today, where children are exposed to a constant influx of information and external influences [100]. Historically, parents were the primary source of guidance and influence. Still, today's children are bombarded with stimuli from peers, media, technology, and social environments that are often beyond a parent's immediate control [101]. This flood of information can align with or conflict with a family's values and the principles guiding their parenting decisions. For example, an eight-year-old child may come home from school and ask for a mobile phone because a classmate already has one. This situation puts parents in a difficult position to balance their principles and values with external pressures. Decision-making in such cases requires continuous learning; parents must stay informed about the evolving social and technological landscape while understanding how it impacts their child's development [74].

   Parents may explain their decisions, but this might make children feel misunderstood or as though they are being mistreated. Therefore, decisions must be consistent with the values parents try to instil in their children and aligned with core principles such as responsibility, empathy, and consideration for others. Regarding the mobile phone request, a parent might evaluate the decision by reflecting on whether their child is ready to handle the responsibility of owning a phone while balancing the desire to fit in with peers.

   Moreover, parents need to learn how to communicate their decisions in a way that aligns with their values and addresses the child's feelings of fairness and understanding. Suppose the parent decides not to give their child a phone. In that case, they must explain the decision consistent with the principles they are trying to instil, such as responsibility, balance, and empathy, so that the child feels heard, even if they do not get what they want. This is crucial because children today can quickly feel misunderstood or perceive that they are being maltreated compared to their peers [100].

   Parents must constantly adapt and evolve to stay effective in this modern parenting environment. This involves staying current with new trends, technologies, and societal shifts that affect their children. It also means being willing to learn from mistakes, seek advice, and adjust strategies as their children grow and encounter new challenges. By nurturing this continuous learning disposition, parents can navigate the pressures of modern parenting and make informed, thoughtful decisions consistent with their values and core principles. This mindset lets parents balance their role as guides and role models with the ever-changing influences in their children's lives, allowing them to maintain healthy, principle-based relationships.

b. *Allowance to make mistakes:* Parents must recognise that they, too, are human and capable of making mistakes. Parenting involves difficult decision-making, and sometimes even well-intentioned decisions can negatively affect children [102]. Awareness is a key skill that parents need to nurture, acknowledging when a decision is wrong and being open to adjusting their approach. While consistency is vital, changing course after recognising a mistake is a sign of growth, not failure [101].

Parents should not feel ashamed or guilty when they realise they have made a poor decision, as guilt can be counterproductive if it prevents corrective action. Acting out of guilt or failing to admit mistakes can have long-term repercussions. Children may hold parents accountable for decisions that negatively impact them, mainly if the issue is not addressed or acknowledged [101]. Conversely, parents who openly admit their mistakes and change course create a healthier family dynamic, which children will appreciate, even if they do not immediately understand the reasons behind the change.

When parents explain their decision to reverse course, it offers children a valuable life lesson: that mistakes are a natural part of life, and how we respond to them matters. Children might not always grasp the situation's complexity now, but they will usually understand and forgive their parents for the mistake later. This teaches empathy and the importance of taking responsibility for one's actions, reinforcing the principles parents try to instil in them [74].

Ultimately, parents should take pride in recognising and correcting their mistakes. It shows they are reflective, open to learning, and committed to their children's well-being. What matters most is how the correction is handled: honesty, empathy, and a willingness to engage in meaningful conversation with their child. This kind of transparency fosters trust and resilience in the parent-child relationship and the child's emotional development [100].

c. *How to refuse a child's want:* Children, like adults, have desires and wants, but they often lack the cognitive and emotional maturity to understand why some of these wants must be refused entirely. Preparing and explaining decisions to children, especially when it involves refusal, is essential to healthy development. While adults may grasp explanations through verbal reasoning, children primarily process the world through nonverbal cues and sensory experiences. They are especially attuned to their parents' tone of voice, body language, eye contact, proximity, and openness to listening [102].

Refusing a child's wants is a necessary part of teaching delayed gratification and emotional resilience, skills that will serve them well throughout life. If parents give in to every request, children may grow up with unrealistic expectations, believing their desires will always be met without delay or compromise. This mindset can prevent them from learning how to cope with disappointment and frustration or working toward long-term goals [102]. Therefore, the act of refusal is a critical part of the parenting repertoire, but how, when, and why it is done makes all the difference. Parents often make the mistake of assuming their children comprehend the world as adults do. While older children can understand more complex explanations, younger children, especially those under seven, have a different perception of time, causality, and the logic behind adult decisions. To overcome this, parents need to adapt their communication to the child's level of understanding.

When refusing a request, such as a toy or treat, it is important to acknowledge their feelings. "I know you want that toy" and then provide a reason they can grasp: "We'll think about it for your birthday, but today, we are not buying anything extra." Additionally, parents need to prepare children ahead of time for the possibility of refusal, setting clear expectations to minimise disappointment. The timing of a refusal can significantly impact how a child responds. It is often more practical to prepare children ahead of time for the possibility of disappointment. If a refusal is necessary when a child is tired, hungry, or upset, parents should be exceptionally patient, empathetic, and calm in their delivery.

Refusing a child's wants is not just about saying "no" for the sake of it. It is about teaching essential life lessons. When denying a request, it is helpful for parents to explain the reason behind their decision in terms the child can understand. Let us bring another example. A child wants candy before dinner; a parent might explain, "If you eat candy now, you will not be hungry for dinner, and your body needs healthy food to grow strong." This helps the child connect the refusal with a broader principle about health or well-being rather than simply seeing it as arbitrary.

Children are incredibly sensitive to nonverbal communication. Even if a parent is saying the right words, children will pick up on tone, body language, and emotional energy. To avoid misunderstandings, parents need to ensure that their nonverbal cues align with their message. A calm tone of voice, gentle eye contact, and an open, empathetic posture can help soften the blow of a refusal [100].

5.3 Understanding of child development

Parents often choose to have children driven by a natural love for them and an unconscious desire to extend their legacy and meaning to the next generation [103]. When individuals become parents, they typically rely on their upbringing as a model, consciously or not, for how to parent their children [104]. While this can serve as a helpful guide, it is becoming increasingly clear that parenting today requires more than instinct; it demands intentionality and awareness. In the past, life was more straightforward, and parenting often followed the patterns of tradition, shaped by fewer choices and less societal complexity. However, today's world presents unique challenges, and children must develop broader skills and resilience to navigate them. As our understanding of human development and psychology has deepened [105], the approach to raising children must evolve. Parenting can no longer be a passive inheritance of old methods; it must be adapted to the sophisticated demands of modern life.

A century ago, little focus was on parenting education, mental health, or work-life balance. These concepts were largely irrelevant to a society where roles and expectations were more uniform and the pressures of life were more superficial. But today, children grow into adults with many choices, opportunities, and emotional complexities. With the expansion of human knowledge and creativity comes the need for parents to be equipped with new tools and insights, capable of guiding their children through a world far more intricate than previous generations [106].

While the beauty and greatness of human potential are evident in the world we have built, parents today must be more conscious of how their actions shape the future of society, a society that, unlike in the past, is no longer assumed to remain static [107]. As parenting becomes increasingly complex and sophisticated, parents must equip themselves with the knowledge and skills necessary to make thoughtful, informed decisions.

Psychology is pivotal, offering insights into how children perceive the world, what influences their emotional well-being, and how their minds develop over time. The groundbreaking work of twentieth-century psychologists such as Jean Piaget, Erik Erikson, Sigmund Freud, and Lev Vygotsky has given us a deeper understanding of child development, from how newborns process stimuli to how older children construct their knowledge of reality. A principled approach to parenting requires that parents have a deeper awareness of how children engage with the world around them and how their emotional and psychological development is shaped by their environment and experiences [108]. By understanding these stages of growth and perception, parents can foster healthier emotional development and make decisions that contribute positively to their children's well-being and, ultimately, to the society these children will 1 day inherit.

5.4 Contextualisation of the parenting approach

As Marshall McLuhan predicted in the 1950s, the world has become a global village [109]. This interconnectedness means that parenting must now be contextualised, considering a wide array of influences from an ever-evolving society. As a result, parenting has become more challenging and prone to missteps. Parents can no longer rely on a one-size-fits-all approach; the increasingly diverse and dynamic nature of society demands that they make decisions based on context rather than tradition [50]. In this rapidly changing world, children are constantly exposed to new ideas, trends, and cultural forces that shape their development. The strategies that worked when a child was five may need to be more effective or even counterproductive by the time that same child is six. The days of recipe-type parenting, where a fixed set of rules applied across a child's development, are long gone [110]. Instead, modern parents must remain flexible and adaptable, tailoring their approach as their children grow and change in response to external influences.

Understanding that parenting is an ongoing, evolving process will help parents navigate the complexities of raising children in a globalised world, where their choices and methods must reflect the unique circumstances they face at each stage of their child's life [111]. The diverse cultural societies we live in today demand a case-by-case approach to parenting. Parents must adapt to their child's unique environment while ensuring that core principles, such as empathy, communication, and consistency, are consistently applied. One of the critical skills parents' needs is the ability to recognise patterns in their child's behaviour. Children quickly pick up on patterns, and parents must be even quicker in identifying these cues. By combining these principles with a keen awareness of behavioural patterns, parents can better understand how their children are evolving and set clear goals for their growth.

A child's social behaviour, including how they respond to peer influences, can be observed even in their early years. Likewise, children are naturally inquisitive, and if a parent notices that their child lacks curiosity or is unusually passive in response to a situation, it is vital to question why. Inquisitiveness is crucial to healthy development, and a lack of reaction may signal that something is amiss [50]. Child development is like constructing a house, built layer by layer as the child grows. Personality, rather than being a fixed trait like "character" (a term that can imply something unchangeable and out of the parent's control), forms and evolves over time. This distinction is important because it empowers parents to actively shape their child's personality through conscious, intentional parenting choices [110]. As children develop, their personalities continue to build, much like adding bricks to a house. To support this development, parents must continuously learn about how children grow and change. This knowledge will enable them to implement the best parenting practices tailored to their child's unique needs and stage of development [112].

6. Conclusion

While various parenting methods have advantages and challenges, the four-principled approach stands out for its flexibility, adaptability, and focus on each child's unique needs and development. While various parenting methods have advantages and challenges, the four-principled approach stands out for its flexibility, adaptability, and focus on each child's unique needs and development. While various parenting methods each come with advantages and challenges, the four-principled approach stands out for its flexibility, adaptability, and focus on each child's unique needs and development. This approach recognises that even siblings growing up in the same family can have vastly different rent needs, not because one child necessarily has a condition or issue but simply because every child is inherently different. As Adler suggests, factors such as birth order, parental maturity, and individual experiences during childhood all contribute to shaping how each child responds to their environment. One potential of this approach is requiring parents to be continuously conscious in their decision-making. This necessitates a high level of awareness, introspection, and abstract thinking, which can be mentally and emotionally taxing.

The need to pause and reflect on every decision may initially feel overwhelming, as parents must navigate their thoughts, emotions, and behaviours in alignment with the four principles. This can also mean that parents may need to work through their psychological challenges to suspend judgement appropriately and make timely, thoughtful choices. However, as with any system, regular practice leads to familiarity. Over time, the continuous application of the four-principled approach can become second nature. As parents consistently engage with this method, it gradually becomes less stressful and more instinctive, allowing them to make decisions more fluidly as their children grow. The early effort invested in conscious parenting will pay off, as the approach will feel more natural with time.

A conclusive critical aspect supporting the four-principled approach is parents' values. These values, shaped by their upbringing, play a significant role in how parents interact with their partners and children. For this approach to be most effective, both parents must share a clear understanding of their core values and maintain alignment in their parenting. Consistent, value-driven decisions will ensure the successful implementation of this approach, creating a solid foundation for the family's growth and cohesion.

Author details

Jesmond Friggieri[1*] and Duncan Borg Ellul[2]

1 Malta Leadership Institute, School of Business and Management, Systemic Therapy, Birkirkara, Malta

2 Education Studies School, Malta Leadership Institute, Country in Southern Europe

*Address all correspondence to: jesmond.friggieri@maltaleadershipinstitute.com

References

[1] Balantekin KN, Anzman-Frasca S, Francis LA, Ventura AK, Fisher JO, Johnson SL. Positive parenting approaches and their association with child eating and weight: A narrative review from infancy to adolescence. Pediatric Obesity. 2020;**15**(10). DOI: 10.1111/ijpo.12722

[2] Surtees N, Bremner P. Gay and Lesbian Collaborative co-Parenting in New Zealand and the United Kingdom: "The Law doesn't Protect the Third Parent". Thousand Oaks, California, U.S.: Social & Legal Studies; 2020

[3] Schlink A, Williams J, Pizzano M, Gulsrud A, Kasari C. Parenting Stress in Caregiver-Mediated Interventions for Toddlers with Autism: An Application of Quantile Regression Mixed Models. Hoboken, New Jersey, U.S.: Autism Research; 2021

[4] Greene CA, Haisley L, Wallace C, Ford JD. Intergenerational effects of childhood maltreatment: A systematic review of the parenting practices of adult survivors of childhood abuse, neglect, and violence. Clinical Psychology Review. 2020;**80**(1):101891. DOI: 10.1016/j.cpr.2020.101891

[5] Faulhaber ME, Zarling A, Lee J. Acceptance commitment therapy intervention for custodial grandfamilies. Innovation in Aging. 2020;**4**(Supplement_1):928-928. DOI: 10.1093/geroni/igaa057.3403. Available from: https://academic.oup.com/innovateage/article/4/Supplement_1/928/6036128

[6] Gartrell N, Rothblum E, Koh AS, van Beusekom G, Bos H. "We were among the first non-traditional families": Thematic perceptions of lesbian parenting after 25 years. Frontiers in Psychology. 2019;**10**. DOI: 10.3389/fpsyg.2019.02414/full

[7] Ye FT, Gao X. Simulating family conversations using LLMs: Demonstration of parenting styles. ArXiv-CS.CY. 2024

[8] Young B, Seedall RB. Power dynamics in couple relationships: A review and applications for systemic family therapists. Family Process. 2024. DOI: 10.1111/famp.13008

[9] Lorås L, Whittaker K, Stokkebekk J, Tilden T. Researching what we practice-the paradigm of systemic family research: Part 1. Family Process. 2023

[10] Tseliou E, Burck C, Forbat L, Strong T, O'Reilly M. The discursive performance of change process in systemic and constructionist therapies: A systematic meta-synthesis review of in-session therapy discourse. Family Process. 2021;**60**(1):42-63

[11] Bowen M. Family Therapy in Clinical Practice. Lanham, Maryland, U.S.: Jason Aronson; 1978

[12] Józefik B. On the issues of power in the family and family therapy. Psychiatria Polska. 2020;**54**(4):777-789. DOI: 10.12740/PP/115438. Epub 2020 Aug 31

[13] Ugazio V, Pennacchio R, Fellin L, Guarnieri S, Anselmi P. Explaining symptoms in systemic therapy. Does triadic thinking come into play? Frontiers in Psychology. 2020;**11**:597

[14] Amorin-Woods D, Salvini M. The influence of the Milan approach: Five decades of intergenerational change.

A conversation with Matteo Selvini. Australian and New Zealand Journal of Family Therapy. 2023;**44**(1):108-121

[15] Mattsson M, Fernee CR, Pärnänen K, Lyytinen P. Restoring connectedness in and to nature: Three Nordic examples of recontextualising family therapy to the outdoors. Frontiers in Psychology. 2022;**13**. DOI: 10.3389/fpsyg.2022.768614. Available from: https://www.frontiersin.org/journals/psychology/articles/10.3389/fpsyg.2022.768614/full

[16] Van der Watt AS, Roos A, Du Plessis S, Bui E, Lesch E, Seedat S. An attachment theory approach to reframing romantic relationship breakups in university students: A narrative review of attachment, neural circuitry, and posttraumatic stress symptoms. Journal of Couple & Relationship Therapy. 2022;**21**(2):129-150

[17] Bitencourt N, Kramer J, Bermas BL, Solow EB, Wright T, Makris UE. Clinical team perspectives on the psychosocial aspects of the transition to adult care for patients with childhood-onset systemic lupus erythematosus. Arthritis Care & Research. 2020;**73**(1):39-47. DOI: 10.1002/acr.24463. Available from: https://pubmed.ncbi.nlm.nih.gov/32976698/

[18] Amorin-Woods D, Fraenkel P, Mosconi A, Nisse M, Munoz S. Family therapy and COVID-19: International reflections during the pandemic from systemic therapists across the globe. Australian and New Zealand Journal of Family Therapy. 2020;**41**(2):114-132. DOI: 10.1002/anzf.1416

[19] Bhattacharyya GS, Doval DC, Desai CJ, Chaturvedi H, Sharma S, Somashekhar SP. Overview of breast cancer and implications of overtreatment of early-stage breast cancer: An Indian perspective. JCO Global Oncology. 2020;**6**(6):789-798. DOI: 10.1200/GO.20.00033

[20] Cavagnis ME. An ethno-eco-systemic perspective: The coming into being of a family therapy institution in Argentina - politics, practices, and experiences. Australian and New Zealand Journal of Family Therapy. 2021;**42**(3):261-275. DOI: 10.1002/anzf.1463

[21] Münch U, Müller H, Deffner T, von Schmude A, Kern M, Kiepke-Ziemes S, et al. Recommendations for the support of suffering, severely ill, dying or grieving persons in the corona pandemic from a palliative care perspective : Recommendations of the German Society for Palliative Medicine (DGP), the German Interdisciplinary Association for Intensive and Emergency Medicine (DIVI), the Federal Association for Grief Counseling (BVT), the Working Group for Psycho-oncology in the German Cancer Society, the German Association for Social Work in the Healthcare System (DVSG) and the German Association for Systemic Therapy, Counseling and Family Therapy (DGSF). Schmerz (Berlin, Germany). 2020;**34**(4):303-313. DOI: 10.1007/s00482-020-00483-9. Available from: https://pubmed.ncbi.nlm.nih.gov/32488422/

[22] Sidis AE, Moore AR, Pickard JA, Deane FP. Each person's experience, each person's needs: How therapists open space for multiple perspectives during reflecting team family therapy supervision. Journal of Marital and Family Therapy. 2024. DOI: 10.1111/jmft.12740

[23] Medina Centeno R. Third-order critical family therapy: Rethinking psychopathology and psychotherapy. Interacciones. 2022;**e290**. DOI: 10.24016/2022.v8.290. Available from: https://ojs.revistainteracciones.com/index.php/rin/article/view/290

[24] Pinsof W, Zinbarg R, He Y, Goldsmith J, Latta T, Lebow J. Does the STIC measurement and feedback system improve multisystemic outcomes in individual, couple and family therapy? A randomised clinical trial. Psychotherapy Research. 2024:1-14

[25] He Y, Hardy NR, Russell WP. Integrative systemic supervision: Promoting supervisees' theoretical integration in systemic therapy. Family Process. 2022;**61**(1):58-75

[26] Becvar RJ, Becvar DS, Reif LV. Systems Theory and Family Therapy: A Primer. Lanham, Maryland, U.S.: Rowman & Littlefield; 2023

[27] Hayes AM, Andrews LA. A complex systems approach to the study of change in psychotherapy. BMC Medicine. 2020;**18**:1-13

[28] Reynolds M, Holwell S. Introducing systems approaches. In: Systems Approaches to Making Change: A Practical Guide. 2020. pp. 1-24

[29] Irvine TJ, Peluso PR, Benson K, Cole C, Cole D, Gottman JM, et al. A pilot study examining the effectiveness of Gottman method couples therapy over treatment-as-usual approaches for treating couples dealing with infidelity. The Family Journal. 2024;**32**(1):81-94

[30] Nastasic P. The development of the family system-therapeutic approach in the addictions treatment in Serbia. Interdisciplinary Description of Complex Systems. 2020;**18**(1):1-14

[31] Banerjee A, Singh J. Remodeling adipose tissue inflammasome for type 2 diabetes mellitus treatment: Current perspective and translational strategies. Bioengineering & Translational Medicine. 2019;**5**(2). DOI: 10.1002/btm2.10150

[32] Zhan X, Dowell S, Shen Y, Lee DL. Chloroquine to fight COVID-19: A consideration of mechanisms and adverse effects? Heliyon. 2020;**6**(9). DOI: 10.1016/j.heliyon.2020.e04900. Available from: https://www.cell.com/heliyon/fulltext/S2405-8440(20)31743-6

[33] Liu S, Xu W, Zheng J, Ngocho K, Chen H, Wang K, et al. G-quadruplex-based artificial transmembrane channels induce cancer cell apoptosis by perturbing potassium ion homeostasis. Advanced Healthcare Materials. 2024. DOI: 10.1002/adhm.202402023

[34] Zhang Y, Zhu X, Yu X, Novák P, Gui Q, Yin K. Enhancing intestinal barrier efficiency: A novel metabolic diseases therapy. Frontiers in Nutrition. 2023;**10**. DOI: 10.3389/fnut.2023.1120168

[35] Wang H, Li X, Lok GKI, Meng C, Tan Y, Lee UM, et al. Family-based therapy for internet addiction among adolescents and young adults: A meta-analysis. Journal of Behavioral Addictions. 2024;**13**(2):295-312. DOI: 10.1556/2006.2024.00015

[36] Parker ML, Diamond RM, Auwood LH. Exploring exceptions and discovering solutions: A case presentation of autism and the family. Family Process. 2019;**59**(4):1891-1902. DOI: 10.1111/famp.12500

[37] Chepin E. Robotics: From first-order cybernetics to third-order cybernetics. Procedia Computer Science. 2021;**190**:130-136

[38] Tilak S, Glassman M, Kuznetcova I, Pelfrey GL. Applications of cybernetics to psychological theory: Historical and conceptual explorations. Theory & Psychology. 2022;**32**(2):298-325

[39] Tzafestas SG. Systems, Cybernetics, Control, and Automation. Denmark: River Publishers; 2022

[40] Kjaer PF. Systems in Context: On the Outcome of the Habermas/Luhmann-Debate. Oxfordshire, England, UK: Luhmann and Law; 2021

[41] Songer RW, Yamamoto T. Towards educational recommender systems for self-directed learning: Profiling student achievement goals and identity formation to inform recommendation evaluation metrics. In: Fifth International Conference on Education. 2021

[42] Tze VMC, Li JC-H, Parker PC. A mediation analysis of emotions based on the control-value theory. Current Psychology. 2021. DOI: 10.1007/s12144-021-01840-2

[43] Hermanu AI, Sari D, Sondari MC, Dimyati M. Higher education research performance parameters classified by systems theory: Antecedents for the development of assessment models. Journal of Science and Technology Policy Management. 2024;**15**(4):818-838. DOI: 10.1108/JSTPM-05-2022-0089

[44] Lubis SK, Retnowati T, Syawalina S. Predictive power of intellectual ability test score on students' fine art learning outcomes. 2020:45-60. DOI: 10.2991/assehr.k.200703.009. Available from: https://www.atlantis-press.com/proceedings/icaae-19/125941661

[45] Agarwal PK, Nunes LD, Blunt JR. Retrieval practice consistently benefits student learning: A systematic review of applied research in schools and classrooms. Educational Psychology Review. 2021;**33**(4):1409-1453. DOI: 10.1007/s10648-021-09595-9

[46] Piekarczyk A. Organisation culture from systems theory of organisation perspective. In: Nedelko Z, Brzozowski M, editors. Exploring the Influence of Personal Values and Cultures in the Workplace. IGI Global: Hershey; 2017. pp. 39-52

[47] Hosseini SH, et al. Investigating the role of moderating the quality of working life on the relationship between psychological capital and organisational citizenship behaviour. International Journal of Services and Operations Management. 2020;**36**(4):425-439

[48] Heiden B, Tonino-Heiden B, Hartlieb E, Alieksieiev V. Digitisation model innovation system. In: Tenth International Conference on Industrial Technology. 2021

[49] Rosas FE, Mediano PAM, Jensen HJ, Seth AK, Barrett AB, Carhart-Harris R, et al. Reconciling emergences: An information-theoretic approach to identify causal emergence in multivariate data. PLoS Computational Biology. 2020;**16**(12):e1008289. DOI: 10.1371/journal.pcbi.1008289

[50] Lee E, Bristow J, Faircloth C, Macvarish J. Parenting culture studies. Hampshire: Palgrave Macmillan; 2024

[51] Ward FR, Belardinelli F, Toni F, Everitt T. Honesty is the best policy: Defining and mitigating AI deception. ArXiv-CS.AI. 2023

[52] Aguilera M, Millidge B, Tschantz A, Buckley CL. How particular is the physics of the free energy principle? Physics of Life Reviews. 2021. DOI: 10.48550/arXiv.2105.11203. Available from: https://www.sciencedirect.com/science/article/pii/S1571064521000749

[53] Weeland J, Helmerhorst KOW, Lucassen N. Understanding differential effectiveness of Behavioral parent training from a family systems perspective: Families are greater than "some of their parts". Journal of Family Theory & Review. 2021;**13**:34-57. DOI: 10.1111/jftr.12408

[54] Weeland J, Keijsers L, Branje S. Introduction to the special issue: Parenting and family dynamics in times of the COVID-19 pandemic. Developmental Psychology. 2021;**57**(10):1559-1562. DOI: 10.1037/dev0001252

[55] Keyzers A, Weiler L, Haddock S, Doty J. Family problem-solving and attachment quality: Associations with adolescent risk-taking behavior. Journal of Youth Development. 2019;**14**(1):70-92. DOI: 10.5195/jyd.2019.637

[56] Alqurashi FO, Awary BH, Khan BF, AlARhain SA, Alkhaleel AI, Albahrani BA, et al. Assessing knowledge of Saudi mothers about parenting and child developmental milestones. Journal of Family & Community Medicine. 2021;**28**(3):202-209. DOI: 10.4103/jfcm.jfcm_186_21. Available from: https://www.ncbi.nlm.nih.gov/pmc/articles/PMC8496704/ [Accessed: October 2, 2022]

[57] Ayoub M, Zhang B, Göllner R, Atherton OE, Trautwein U, Roberts BW. Longitudinal associations between parenting and child big five personality traits. Collabra: Psychology. 2021;**7**(1):29766. DOI: 10.1525/collabra.29766. Available from: https://online.ucpress.edu/collabra/article/7/1/29766/118998/Longitudinal-Associations-Between-Parenting-and

[58] Bell AV. "Bubble wrapping vs. helping him learn his way": Gender and definitions of parenting through the case of infertility. Journal of Family Studies. 2020;**26**(1):16-31. DOI: 10.1080/13229400.2017.1292943

[59] Dosman C, Gallagher S. Parenting principles primer. Paediatrics & Child Health. 2022;**27**(6):327-332. DOI: 10.1093/pch/pxac033. Available from: https://academic.oup.com/pch/article-abstract/27/6/327/6573843?redirectedFrom=fulltext

[60] Egeland T, Ruud TK, Hanevik HI, Magelssen M. A study of the experience of Norwegian IVF physicians in evaluating the parenting capacity of patients. Reproductive Biomedicine Online. 2023;**47**(6):103368

[61] Kyriazos TA, Stalikas A. Nicomachus-positive parenting (NPP): Development and initial validation of a parenting questionnaire within the positive psychology framework. Psychology. 2019;**10**:2115-2165. DOI: 10.4236/psych.2019.1015136

[62] Peleg N. Lydia bracken, same-sex parenting and the best interests principle. The International Journal of Children's Rights. 2021;**29**(1):249-254. DOI: 10.1163/15718182-29010003. Available from: https://brill.com/view/journals/chil/29/1/article-p249_249.xml

[63] Ren H, Hart CH, Cheah CSL, Porter CL, Nelson DA, Yavuz-Müren HM, et al. Parenting measurement, normativeness, and associations with child outcomes: Comparing evidence from four non-Western cultures. Developmental Science. 2023. DOI: 10.1111/desc.13388

[64] Stenason L, Moorman J, Romano E. The experiences of parents and facilitators in a positive parenting program. The Qualitative Report. 2020;**25**(1):1-13. DOI: 10.46743/2160-3715/2020.373. Available from: https://nsuworks.nova.edu/tqr/vol25/iss1/1/?utm_source

[65] Zortea TC, Gray CM, O'Connor RC. Perceptions of past parenting and adult attachment as vulnerability factors for suicidal ideation in the context of the integrated motivational-volitional model of suicidal behavior.

Suicide & Life-Threatening Behavior. 2019;**50**(2):515-533. DOI: 10.1111/sltb.12606

[66] Wileczek A. Applications supporting polish language acquisition by children: An outline of current issues. InScriptum: A Journal of Language and Literary Studies. 2020;**1**(1):s.49-s.66

[67] Quevedo-Sacoto DA, Erazo-Álvarez JC, Robalino-Peña EM, Narváez-Zurita CI. Problemática de tenencia compartida a partir del interés superior de los niños, niñas y adolescentes. IUSTITIA Socialis. 2020;**5**(1):678-678. DOI: 10.35381/racji.v5i1.636. Available from: https://fundacionkoinonia.com.ve/ojs/index.php/Iustitia_Socialis/article/view/636 [Accessed: March 26, 2025]

[68] Ignjatovic T. Assessments of the Social Welfare Centres on the Consequences, Security Risks and Recovery Needs of Children Witnesses of Violence in Parental Relationships. Washington, DC: TEMIDA; 2020

[69] Becker SJ, Helseth SA, Janssen T, Kelly LM, Escobar K, Spirito A. Parent smart: Effects of a technology-assisted intervention for parents of adolescents in residential substance use treatment on parental monitoring and communication. Evidence-Based Practice in Child and Adolescent Mental Health. 2021;**6**(4):459-472. DOI: 10.1080/23794925.2021.1961644

[70] Saunders R, Brack M, Renz B, et al. An evaluation of parent training interventions in Scotland: The psychology of parenting project (PoPP). Journal of Child and Family Studies. 2020;**29**:3369-3380. DOI: 10.1007/s10826-020-01817-y

[71] Pancieri L, Silva RMM, Wernet M, Fonseca LMM, Hameed S, Mello DF. Safe care for premature babies at home: Parenting and stimulating development. Journal of Child Health Care. 2022:136749352210894-136749352210894. DOI: 10.1177/13674935221089450

[72] Becker SJ, Helseth SA, Janssen T, Kelly LM, Escobar K, Spirito A. Parent smart: Effects of a technology-assisted intervention for parents of adolescents in residential substance use treatment on parental monitoring and communication. Evidence-Based Practice. Child and Adolescent Mental Health. 2021

[73] Huang L, Wang X, Liu G, et al. Parenting sense of competence among Chinese parents of premature infants: A cross-sectional study. BMC Pregnancy and Childbirth. 2023;**23**:399. DOI: 10.1186/s12884-023-05703-5

[74] Brooks RB. The power of parenting. In: Handbook of Resilience in Children. Cham: Springer International Publishing; 2023. pp. 377-395

[75] Kambouri M, Wilson T, Pieridou M, Quinn SF, Liu J. Making partnerships work: Proposing a model to support parent-practitioner partnerships in the early years. Early Childhood Education Journal. 2022:1-23

[76] Lévesque S, Bisson V, Charton L, Fernet M. Parenting and relational well-being during the transition to parenthood: Challenges for first-time parents. Journal of Child and Family Studies. 2020;**29**:1938-1956

[77] Dolan P, Žegarac N, Arsić J. Family support as a right of the child. Social Work and Social Sciences Review. 2020;**21**(2):8-26

[78] Johnston JR, Sullivan MJ. Parental alienation: In search of common ground for a more differentiated theory. Family Court Review. 2020;**58**(2):270-292

[79] Faherty AN, Mitra D. Emerging adulthoods: A microcultural approach to viewing the parent-child relationship. In: Ashdown BK, Faherty AN, editors. Parents and Caregivers across Cultures: Positive Development from Infancy through Adulthood. Cham, Switzerland: Springer Nature Switzerland AG; 2020. pp. 205-216

[80] Athamneh S, Benjamin O. Mothers' responsibility as transmitters of gendered moral rationalities: Working-class Palestinian mothers living in Israel. British Journal of Sociology of Education. 2021;**42**(4):571-587. DOI: 10.1080/01425692.2021.1902276

[81] Brito JN, Matsumoto M, Bonilla Z, Loth KA, Geppert J, McCoy MB, et al. Identification of positive parenting practices among parents of young children living in low-income and racially, ethnically, and culturally diverse households. Appetite. 2022

[82] Clavien C, Hurst S. The Undeserving Sick? An evaluation of patients' responsibility for their health condition. Cambridge Quarterly of Healthcare Ethics. 2020

[83] Kugelberg E. Responsibility for Reality: Social Norms and the Value of Constrained Choice. Philosophy & Economics: Politics; 2021

[84] Gemayel MEL. Food quality in the European Union: Does the consumer have free choice? European Journal of Risk Regulation. 2021:1-18. DOI: 10.1017/err.2021.39

[85] Lewis ACF, Molina SJ, Appelbaum PS, Dauda B, Fuentes A, Fullerton SM, et al. An ethical framework for research using genetic ancestry. Perspectives in Biology and Medicine. 2023;**66**(2):225-248. DOI: 10.1353/pbm.2023.0021. Available from: https://muse.jhu.edu/pub/1/article/894253/summary [Accessed: August 8, 2023]

[86] Decety J, Holvoet C. The emergence of empathy: A developmental neuroscience perspective. Developmental Review. 2021;**62**:100999

[87] Masten AS. Resilience in developmental systems. In: Multisystemic Resilience. 2021. pp. 113-134

[88] Saracho ON. Theories of child development and their impact on early childhood education and care. Early Childhood Education Journal. 2023;**51**(1):15-30

[89] Kumbar S, Pursnani VK, Patil AT, Paranna S, Bhurke RR, Prakash A. Evaluate the perspective of the concrete operational stage of Piaget's theory and its correlation with tell–show–do: A comparative study. Journal of Scientific Dentistry. 2023;**13**(2):41-44

[90] Ziv I, Golbez N, Shapira N. Parental sense of competence, resilience, and empathy in relation to fathers' responses to children's negative emotions in the context of everyday paternal childrearing decisions. Cogent Psychology. 2020;**7**(1):1794681

[91] Cline F, Fay J. Parenting with Love and Logic. Colorado Springs, CO: NavPress; 2020

[92] Bauer A, Stevens M, Purtscheller D, Knapp M, Fonagy P, Evans-Lacko S, et al. Mobilising social support to improve mental health for children and adolescents: A systematic review using principles of realist synthesis. PLoS One. 2021;**16**(5):e0251750

[93] Friedman SL, Scholnick EK. Theories of human development. In: Developmental-Behavioral Pediatrics. Wuhan, China: E-Book; 2022. p. 19

[94] Harpaz G, Grinshtain Y, Yaffe Y. Parental self-efficacy predicted by parents' subjective well-being and parenting styles with a possible role of help-seeking orientation from teachers. The Journal of Psychology. 2021;**155**(6):571-587. DOI: 10.1080/00223980.2021.1926896

[95] Morita M, Saito A, Nozaki M, Ihara Y. Childcare support and child social development in Japan: Investigating the mediating role of parental psychological condition and parenting style. Philosophical Transactions of the Royal Society B: Biological Sciences. 2021;**376**(1827). DOI: 10.1098/rstb.2020.0025

[96] Wang Y. Effects of parenting style on normal and dysfunctional emotional behaviors in small children. Psychiatria Danubina. 2022;**34**(1):34-40. DOI: 10.24869/psyd.2022.34

[97] Masud S, Mufarrih S, Qureshi NQ, Khan F, Khan S, Khan MN. Academic performance in adolescent students: The role of parenting styles and socio-demographic factors – A cross-sectional study from Peshawar, Pakistan. Frontiers in Psychology. 2019;**10**. DOI: 10.3389/fpsyg.2019.02497. Available from: https://www.ncbi.nlm.nih.gov/pmc/articles/PMC6856224/

[98] Xia X, Hackett RK, Webster LL. Chinese parental involvement and children's school readiness: The moderating role of parenting style. Early Education and Development. 2020:1-19. DOI: 10.1080/10409289.2019.1643439

[99] Lan L, Wang X. Parental rejection and adolescents' learning ability: A multiple mediating effects of values and self-esteem. Behavioral Sciences. 2023;**13**(2):143. DOI: 10.3390/bs13020143. Available from: https://www.mdpi.com/2076-328X/13/2/143

[100] Slemp GR, Field JG, Ryan RM, Forner VW, Van den Broeck A, Lewis KJ. Interpersonal supports for basic psychological needs and their relations with motivation, well-being, and performance: A meta-analysis. Journal of Personality and Social Psychology. 2024. DOI: 10.1037/pspi0000459. Available from: https://pubmed.ncbi.nlm.nih.gov/38635183/

[101] Clements L, Aiello AL. Institutionalising Parent Carer Blame: The Experiences of Families with Disabled Children in their Interactions with English Local Authority children's Services Departments. Cerebra: University of Leeds; 2021

[102] Peck S. Corrective emotional experiences: History, functions, and applications [Doctoral dissertation]. The Chicago School of Professional Psychology. 2021

[103] Kim W, Lee S, Kim S, Jo S, Yoo C, Hwang I, et al. Dyadic mirror. In: Proceedings of the ACM on Interactive, Mobile, Wearable. 2020

[104] Godleski SA, Ostrov JM. Parental influences on child report of relational attribution biases during early childhood. Journal of Experimental Child Psychology. 2020;**192**:104775. DOI: 10.1016/j.jecp.2019.104775. Available from: https://www.sciencedirect.com/science/article/abs/pii/S0022096519301365?via%3Dihub

[105] Gupta I, Rai C, Devegowda D, Sondergeld CH. Fracture hits in unconventional reservoirs: A critical review. SPE Journal. 2020;**40**(9):669-678. DOI: 10.1097/DBP.0000000000000736. Available from: https://journals.lww.com/jrnldbp/abstract/2019/12000/parents__consumer_preferences_for_early_childhood.2.aspx

[106] Riley AR, Walker BL, Hall TA. Development and initial validation of a measure of parents' preferences for behavioural counselling in primary care. Families, Systems & Health: The Journal of Collaborative. 2020

[107] Padilla-Walker LM, Coyne SM, Booth MA, Domoff SE, Summers K, Schvaneveldt E, et al. Parent-child joint media engagement in infancy. Infancy: The Official Journal of the International Society. 2020

[108] Braune-Krickau K, Schneebeli L, Pehlke-Milde J, Gemperle M, Koch R, von Wyl A. Smartphones in the nursery: Parental smartphone use and parental sensitivity and responsiveness within parent-child interaction in early childhood (0-5 years): A scoping review. Infant Mental Health Journal. 2021;**42**(2). DOI: 10.1002/imhj.21908. Available from: https://www.researchgate.net/publication/348544881_Smartphones_in_the_nursery_Parental_smartphone_use_and_parental_sensitivity_and_responsiveness_within_parent-child_interaction_in_early_childhood_0-5_years_A_scoping_review

[109] Tryphonopoulos PT. "Any technology creates its own environment": Progressive education in Marshall McLuhan's electronic age [Doctoral dissertation]. Queen's University. 2023

[110] Hong S. A Cord of Three Strands: A New Approach to Parent Engagement in Schools. Cambridge, Massachusetts, U.S.: Harvard Education Press; 2021

[111] Babore A, Trumello C, Lombardi L, Candelori C, Chirumbolo A, Cattelino E, et al. Mothers' and children's mental health during the COVID-19 pandemic lockdown: The mediating role of parenting stress. Child Psychiatry & Human Development. 2023;**54**(1):134-146

[112] Birhan W, Shiferaw G, Amsalu A, Tamiru M, Tiruye H. Exploring the context of teaching character education to children in preprimary and primary schools. Social Sciences & Humanities Open. 2021;**4**(1):100171

Chapter 2

Parenting Styles and Practices: Facing the Parenting Storm

Israel Kibirige and Israel Masiko Kafeero

Abstract

Families face a parenting storm. The ideal family comprises a father and mother, yet a father or mother may do parenting single-handedly. Parenting prepares children for holistic lives: mental, social, physical, and spiritual. The storm arises from globalisation, the COVID-19 pandemic, the Fourth Industrial Revolution (4IR), and socio-economic and political changes. The changes result in homeless, refugee, and ghettos living children. Parents work away from home, and thus, nannies and teachers take over parenting roles. Although there are various parenting mechanisms: parent to parent, online reading materials, government, and public support, these mechanisms do not meet individual parental contexts. Therefore, parenting styles and practices should lead to a holistic life. This chapter discusses parenting styles and practices for the twenty-first century. Hence, the authors concur with Dobson's view that parenting is for the brave to manage diverse contextual opportunities and challenges.

Keywords: parenting styles, holistic, parenting practices, parenting storm, twenty-first century

1. Introduction

Parenting is rearing, caring, loving, and guiding the growth and development of a child [1]. Parenting determines the moral foundation of society and transmits cultural values from one generation to the next through socialisation [2]. The socialisation process is the source of both social good and social evil in society [3]. Parents are the primary agents of socialisation, which occurs while they perform their parenting practices in different contexts. Parenting does not happen in a vacuum but is influenced by context [4]. For example, globalisation, the fourth industrial revolution (4IR), the COVID-19 pandemic, and changes in the socioeconomic [5] and political domains all have a direct bearing on families, parental roles [6], and parenting philosophies [7]. Parenting philosophies *influence parenting styles and vice versa* [8]. The choice of parenting style is influenced by the parent's perceptions of the pertinent skills that are necessary for decent living and success in life [9]. Ballantine [10] opine that parenting styles offer the emotional conditions for the parent-child relationship, which greatly impact the child's choices and quality of life. Thus, different styles and practices can be employed to rear children.

Parenting includes rearing a child from birth through education to adulthood. In this process, fathers and mothers play vital roles. As you can imagine, parenting is a big responsibility placed on parents and can be a stressful venture. Parents must deal with helpless babies, take care of those children that run up and down with little common sense, deal with the mad ages of adolescents and finally deal with adult children, who may sometimes be married [11–13]. Although the infant levels are interesting at first, they can be a parenting storm. Dobson [11] contends that small kids from months to 3 years are extremely inquisitive, crotchety-tempered, over-demanding, naïve, and threatening at the same time. The purpose of this chapter is to explore theoretical and conceptual issues regarding parenting. It uses parents as a unit of discourse to elucidate the less-known concept of parenting as a storm. What does parenting mean? How many parenting styles should a parent use, and when? What theoretical frameworks guide parenting children at various levels of development? These questions are of academic interest and pragmatic concern because many parents are frustrated with their parenting processes, especially when their children turn in different directions. This chapter delves into the child's power of choice, which is so powerful that it overrides the styles of parenting used, and yet it has been ignored in parenting literature. This chapter contributes to the existing knowledge by highlighting the need to consider children's choices, which can minimise the stress that heightens the parenting storm. The chapter deals with the following sections: dimensions of parenting styles, parenting practices, merits and demerits of different parenting styles, parenting challenges during the Fourth Industrial Revolution (4IR), challenging social, economic, and political aspects [14], and the digital age [15]. The chapter discusses three conceptual frameworks to be used when interpreting the parenting styles for (1) infants or kids, (2) adolescents, and (3) mature children. The chapter concludes with a model for raising a holistic twenty-first -century child.

2. Dimensions of parenting styles

Dimensions of parenting styles are crucial in the parenting of children at different levels of development. Research has focussed on parenting practices, which refer to visible actions that parents take to socialise their children [16]. Parenting styles have gained popularity in research. There are two broad categories of parenting styles: acceptance or responsiveness and demandingness or control [17] These two categories are further divided into four parenting styles. According to Williams et al. [18], three main parenting styles are reported in the literature. Later, uninvolved, the fourth parenting style was added [4, 7, 8]. Thus, the framework for parenting styles includes four unique parenting styles: (1) authoritative parents exhibit warmth and communication and exercise applicable control; (2) authoritarian exercise control but not warmth; (3) permissive exhibits warmth but lacks control; and (4) uninvolved, where there is no warmth, no control and no direction, and neglects children. At best, uninvolved allows a child to be free to do whatever with no limitations. In fact, the patterns and the extent to which parents exert demandingness and responsiveness indicate the dominant parenting style [19]. These parenting styles are distinguished from each other through practices parents employ to rear children. Parental practices create precise parental behaviours induced by parent-to-child relationships [19]. Thus, different parenting practices differ through levels of autonomy, explanations, and justification of guidelines, emotional support, and control [12].

3. Parenting practices

Parenting practices, according to Ballantine [20], are guided by the four frameworks stated below. For example, (1) authoritarian parents will exhibit these characteristics during the parenting process: excessive demands and controls, rendezvous from adult perspectives only, and do not communicate with their children because they fear losing control; (2) authoritative parents are modest in their demands and control; they allow dialogue with their children and grant some autonomy to their children; (3) permissive parents exhibit high acceptance and responsiveness and are not remindful; (4) uninvolved parents are not responsive and demanding they let their children live without control. In fact, these parents fail to guide their children's behaviour. The different types of parenting styles have a profound impact on children at different stages of their development. For example, children raised by permissive parents did exhibit maturity. They act disobediently and stubbornly when asked to do something that goes against their behaviours, which is associated with permissive parenting, especially when boys are the role players [11].

Globally, as children grow older, they spend more time at school and with friends, and the community, the dynamics between parents and children shift. They were too needy and reliant on adults in preschool, and they lacked resilience and were poor achievers in school. As children grow older and spend more time at school with teachers, friends, and other members of the community, the crescendos among parents and children change. Such changes are those in families where there is an increase in divorce rates among working mothers. Similarly, as children grow and become more independent, as in middle school, they rely more on the internet and friends and not parents whom they feel are not compliant with the technological developments of their times. Nevertheless, research shows that the authoritative parenting style is the best for raising children because of its modesty and the democratic values it holds for both the parent and the child [13, 14].

Parenting practices are the ways in which parents enact their parenting styles. These practices in each culture shape the mind of that child. It agrees with Hofstede's interpersonal model generation advocating the best mix for computer companies, which employed men from different cultures. He intended to explain the cross-cultural variations in the working environment. Consequently, the model was expanded to include national cultures. According to Ref. [15, 16], socialisation shapes the 'software of the mind' and the culture in which a person develops impacts behaviour. Thus, the goal of cultural dimensions is to offer a foundation for examining variations between cultures. Hofstede [21] initially suggested just four dimensions. Later, two other dimensions were added to the model by Minkov to make six Hofstede et al. [22], and it is now called the Minkov-Hofstede model [18]. The dimensions include individualism versus collectivism, power distance, uncertainty avoidance, masculinity versus femininity, long-term versus short-term orientation, and indulgence. The Minkov-Hofstede Model for parents can be understood in terms of tangible and intangible components of culture that differ among locations. In fact, travelling exposes people to drastically unfamiliar scenarios that also differ from one location to another. Hence, interacting with people from different cultures makes people more conscious of their context-specific values, while the practices prepare children for holistic lives in diverse contexts.

The theory of cultural values can be represented as a sphere, with the core components being the symbol, hero, ritual, and value. The symbol encompasses foods, logos, colours, or testimonials. A hero represents individuals in public life, such as politicians, sports persons, musicians, and traditional herbalists. Ritual components are represented by what people believe and do or take as their cultural understandings, like leisure use and societal meetings. Finally, the value component encompasses local, provincial, and national issues where one resides. These values are learned and mastered by parents who guide their children to survive in those environments. The values include evil-bad, good-dirty-clean, dangerous-safe, forbidden-permitted, decent-indecent, moral-immoral, ugly-beautiful, unnatural-natural, abnormal-normal, paradoxical-logical, and irrational-rational [22]. Parenting practices traverse these value components, and it is a challenge because not all parents may be able to know all levels. However, understanding and imparting these values is a crucial responsibility of parents, as it can significantly influence the behaviour of the raised children and ultimately contribute to the parenting journey.

4. Merits and demerits of different parenting styles

Parents must assist their children to grow responsively and be useful in the communities they domicile. Hence, parents need to understand the long-term effects of parenting styles and practices on children's personalities. Other factors are gender, personal background, financial status, personality traits, clans' demands, and cultural values. From Baumrind's study in 1967, we can draw the following main conclusions. In summary, the authoritarian parenting style makes children obedient and clever and yet less happy and not social due to the restrictive orders placed on their shoulders as they grow up [23].

On the other hand, the authoritative parenting style is the best because children are happy and exhibit low destructive behaviours. They are in harmony with their parents and are most likely to have good achievements in school [20]. Children from permissive and uninvolved parents are most likely to develop disruptive behaviours and exhibit low achievements in school. While these patterns of behaviour may not always be true to all parenting styles, the authors acknowledge that where there are rules and trends, there are also exceptions. So, there could be a few but not the norm that may not conform to the outcomes of the parenting style, and these can be attributed to other factors beyond the scope of this chapter and may need further study.

5. Parenting challenges

Delivering babies is good, but rearing babies to adulthood is not a bed of roses. These babies are maddeningly complex [24], and no formula works for every child because what works for Child A may be detrimental to Child B or C. It is no wonder parenting is not for the cowards but for the brave [24]. Parenting children is a challenging responsibility for fathers and mothers and, at times, other members of the community [25]. It implies that whoever bears and raises a child must experience stress at different levels. Studies on parenting of normal children (ND) and disabled children (DC) show that both parents experience parenting stress [20–22, 26]. The challenges emanate from birth to maturity [23, 25]. Parenting challenges are higher with parents of DC compared to parents of NC.

Parents with DC babies are stressed more when their babies do not pick up skills as fast as they are expected [27]. Hastings [28] contends that children's behaviour is positively correlated to parenting stress and is linked to chronological age. The stress does not end with the fathers and mothers, but it extends to other family and community members [29]. Furthermore, many parents with DC feel lonely and neglected because of the anxieties of not being understood by the communities in their domicile [20, 30]. The challenge of parenting a DC is well illustrated by Sadiki [31], who expresses it as excruciating. She adds on emotional and physical stress as well as being alone in the parenting process. Indeed, parents in general sacrifice much of their time rearing children, but those with DC spend more time than those with NC. The challenges can be even worse with single parents and other caregivers in the community [32, 33]. Here, the challenge is balancing their time and the time devoted to caring for their children [34]. To make matters worse, some children grow up, move to cities or anywhere they find a job, and forget about those who raised them.

In addition, the greatest parenting challenges lie with adolescents in relation to globalisation versus glocalisation. Globalisation has many descriptions such as widespread networks of economic, cultural, social, and political interconnectedness and practices that are across borders [35]. This intensification and increased flow of values, knowledge, and social interaction, a hallmark of globalisation [36–38], has created a shifting context in family relations and parenting. The flow of knowledge, values, and cultures has influenced the conventional methods of raising children. Parents in Africa practised authoritarian parenting, which is defined by low warmth and great control [18], and children were expected to obey without question. This situation is changing because of global influences and changes in gender role expectations. Currently, parents need to be made aware of what their children may become and where they will live, which makes parenting a storm of its kind. Glatzer and Rueschemeyer [39] describe globalisation as an aftermath of capitalist advancement. It is the reduction of state powers in favour of global integrated activities [40]. For example, the parent may be challenged by the enormous knowledge the children receive as well as the many powers that the child must interact with.

Another issue that challenged parenting in the recent past was the COVID-19 pandemic, which negatively impacted many facets of life. In addition to being a health issue, the sickness had an impact on family life and parenting because of social stigma and economic lockdown in various areas. COVID-19 had some direct and indirect economic expenses, which made many families financially vulnerable [41]. These expenses included lost wages and medical expenses. Parenting stress was exacerbated by a variety of constraints and financial pressure [42]. According to Chung et al. [42], COVID-19 worsened family connections by raising parental stress, which occasionally resulted in harsh parenting. Numerous people lost their lives to COVID-19, depriving many children of one or both parents, thus leaving parenting gaps.

5.1 Fourth industrial revolution (4IR)

The Industrial Revolution also influenced parenting. The globe has witnessed changes in industrialisation, which was termed an industrial revolution (IR) and has affected how people live. The First Industrial Revolution (1IR) 1760–1840 altered societies from an agricultural economy to an industrial one with machinery production, which led to increased production and efficiency, lower prices, more goods, improved wages, and rural-urban migration. The second IR (2IR) 1863–1947 was characterised by more scientific discovery and calibration, which enhanced bulk production.

The third IR (3IR) 1960–2011 was hailed for the initial automation of using computers. The fourth IR (4IR) is known for its information communication technology (ICT) through digitalisation. ICT use has also made a significant impact on parenting, especially for millennials who are tech-savvy and have the financial resources to purchase gadgets. ICT use has had a direct impact on parenting since many contemporary parents now engage their kids more through technology than through face-to-face interactions. Information-seeking children may become more astute in their negotiations with parents, occasionally countering the authoritarian parenting approach. Youngsters can learn a lot from the media, but if their access is unrestricted, they could also access inappropriate content, such as pornography, violence, and felonies. Thus, the parents' influence may be superseded by what the child picks from the internet. Many young people believe their parents with low digital competencies are backward. It is no wonder there are many unruly children, and juvenile delinquency is on the rise globally [43]. Parenting children in a digital era calls for a close, open parent-child communication channel so that the child can get support in time.

5.2 Social, economic, and political factors

Moreover, parenting styles are influenced by parents' characteristics and the parenting environment [44]. Parents' low socioeconomic capital can compromise the parenting role. Poor parents who cannot provide necessities to their children may not have the moral authority to instruct their children. Children from low-income families engage in child labour to contribute to the family's survival, and others end up in ghettos and on the streets, where they access much external influence. The reality of socioeconomic factors, particularly in developing countries, disrupting family structures is evident as family members seek employment outside their home countries. In sub-Saharan Africa, there has been a brain drain as individuals with high human capital leave the continent for greener pastures in the developed countries [45, 46]. Recently, due to push factors in different countries, many families are transnational. This disruption has a huge impact on parenting as, on the one hand, the migrated family must adjust to fit into the new environment with new cultures and values. Most African parents are authoritarian, and when they immigrate to more developed countries, parents are at a crossroads to figure out how to implement their role as parents in an environment where verbal hostility and corporal punishment are not permissible.

Due to socioeconomic and political changes, some families and children are forced to move to other parts of the world, often becoming homeless refugees and sometimes living in ghettos. When both parents work away from home, especially in urban areas, they often leave their children with nannies, who then take over the parenting roles. In other situations, families are split, with either the children remaining with one parent or being left with another relative. In all these cases, the unique roles of fathers and mothers in parenting are disrupted. Balanced parenting, ideally done by both parents, becomes a challenge with single parenting. Fathers and mothers carry out parenting roles differently, and grannies, other relatives, and nannies cannot adequately take the place of parents. All the scenarios painted above point to parents reduced social control over the children, which limits the parental influence on the children's character formation. The situation is likely to worsen, depicting a parenting storm. The negative consequences of this reduced social control over children due to socioeconomic factors are severe, highlighting the urgent need for further research and policy interventions to address these challenges.

5.3 Parenting challenges in the digital age

Globally, the increase in technological innovations undermines parental expertise, and this, in turn, weakens children's willingness to depend on parental guidance [47]. Regardless of the country, high, middle, and even low income, internet access using digital devices and cell phones has increased. Many children have access to technology and can access all sorts of information, good and bad. In the case of bad and damaging information, parents are challenged on how to manage and guide their children. It is a thorn in the parents' ribs. How do they rear children with cultural and societal values in the event of internet access? Children can learn more information about a particular phenomenon and even watch the simulations through Zoom and TikTok. Often, video clips of all sorts of information just pop up, and before you realise it, you have already seen what you either wanted to see or not. In the latter, the information can be detrimental to the person.

Parents from different societies are worried because they seem to lose their grip on parenting their children. It is as though digital technology is taking over the parenting role. Parents use all means at their disposal, such as resources and socioeconomic and cultural-value paradigms, to enhance positive parenting. Positive parenting embraces processes of stimulation, affection, and appraisals. Hence, enhanced autonomy should lead to children accepting set goals, established controls and the consequences of going against those controls [48]. For example, in developed countries, the trend is to ease children's restrictions regarding parental mediation, while the reverse is true for developing countries [49]. It is no wonder parents are stressed about which approach to take to minimise the influence of digital technology. It is easier said than done because adolescents from the age of 10 show parent-child relationships in favour of child-other relationships [50]. Adolescents change their allegiance from parents to others, which is another challenging phenomenon that stresses parents because they worry about the information their children may espouse and to what extent it will ruin their lives.

6. Parenting support

Despite the critical role parenting plays in character development, parents rarely get any training. Most parents start the parenting role by trial and error and realise too late that they made mistakes. New parents sometimes receive support from other family members and other parents. Parenting was a collective role in most African societies, where it took an entire village to raise a child. Some societies organise parenting seminars and workshops to equip parents with parenting skills. Today, digital parents can also access parenting materials on the Internet. In any case, it is important to recognise that each child is different, and each case needs to be handled as such. Thus, parenting practices differ according to the age of the child, as illustrated below.

6.1 Infants or kids

For children 0–12 years, parents need to initiate play games that they play with their kids. The kids, by endowment and instincts, know how to initiate games. For example, a kid will hide behind a corner of the building and bring the head in and out for the adult to see. It shows that the kid is seeking attention by initiating the seek and hide game. Hence, when dealing with kids, parents need to blend child-initiated games and parent-initiated games. Hence, they need to be guided by the theory of play as a spiral of learning [51]. In the theory of play as a spiral of learning, parents and children interact through play, starting at the centre of the smallest centre of the spiral with adult-led play, child-initiated play, mastery practice revision, restructuring accommodation, and accretion as the largest part of the spiral [51].

6.2 Adolescents

Adolescents 12–18 years old are the most traumatic group to parent. It is the age of maddening [24]. Knowing why this group is mad will ease the parents' stress in the storm and will help the parents deal with them as normal children. They are in this stage due to both chemical and biological developments that take them by surprise. For adolescent girls, the body smoothens and becomes very attractive, and they become aware of their beauty. Hence, she develops a sense of maintaining that beauty. She gets hormones that set her off the earlier balance with monthly periods initiated, and motherhood issues seem imminent. It is at such a time that a supportive parenting style would be applied to make her go through the phase. Thanks to the Almighty because the adolescent phase does not last forever. The body gets used to the chemicals initiated, and the adolescent soon learns how to manage the situation. The adolescents' behaviours can be explained by the Theory of Planned Behaviour (TPB) [51].

The Theory of Planned Behaviour (TPB) [52] depicts three tenets that influence human behaviours: (1) attitudes (favourable or unfavourable to enact the specific behaviour), (2) subjective norm (alleged to be a social pressure regarding persons who support or condemn the exhibited behaviour), and (3) perceived behavioural control beliefs (the ease or difficulty for one to behave in a particular manner). Thus, the Theory of Planned Behaviour (TPB) is worth espousing as a parent (mother or father) because it deals with attitudes, intentions, and behaviour which are made and enacted. Thus, when parenting adolescents one needs to have sympathy and be supportive to overcome the steep and traumatic phase in their lives. The parents need to take heed; after all, parenting is not for the cowards but for the brave [24]. The literature in the last 5 years shows that parenting is indeed stressful (**Table 1**).

6.3 Mature children

At this stage, parents are ready to let their daughters or sons leave their homes to be independent. More often, young adults are either forgotten, or the parents continue imposing their parenting styles [58, 59]. The Theory of Parenting Occupations and Purposes (POP) [60] as a framework explores parenting with a parent-centric emphasis. The POP framework has the occupation and the purposes sections. It advocates parenting practice as noble and places positive esteem on the parents [61]. Having surveyed POP, it suffices to say that POP is more to adult children and centres on three activities: protecting, nurturing, and educating children [62, 63].

The concepts for parenting a desired twenty-first-century child show that parenting styles can be considered a continuum ranging from authoritative to uninvolved. Permissive and authoritarian styles are also along the continuum. This implies that a parent can use all four parenting styles at some point in time (**Figure 1**).

Figure 1 shows that parenting styles can be considered as a continuum authoritative-uninvolved. Thus, one parenting style can work now but not two years from now on for the same child. Also, a parenting style that worked for Jane cannot work for Olga. It suggests that a parent must keep shifting the parenting styles along the continuum as the need arises to produce the desired twenty-first -century child.

Author	Challenges	Country	Approach	Type of study
Zuurmond et al. [33]	Single parents and other caregivers in the community	Ghana	Qualitative	Empirical
Hendriati and Okvitawanli [53]	Work away from home	Indonesia	Qualitative	Conceptual
Anjaswarni et al. [43]	Digital age	Indonesia	Qualitative	Desktop
Brunissen et al. [54]	Social and academic	Unites States of America	Qualitative	Empirical
Muzingili and Muntang [55]	Destructive children	Zimbabwe	Qualitative	Empirical
Zuurmond et al. [33]	Parental stress	Ghana	Qualitative	Empirical
Hassan et al. [27]	Parental burden	Egypt	Quantitative	Empirical
Chung et al. [42]	COVID-19 Parental stress, fear of infection, shortage or lack of money, and negative emotional states	Singapore	Quantitative	Empirical
Benesova and Sikorova [56]	Parental stress	Czech Republic	Quantitative	Empirical
Picardi et al. [57]	Parental stress work/life imbalance, and the lack of emotional bonding	Italy	Quantitative	Empirical
Johnson and Rogers [15]	Digital age	Australia	Qualitative	Empirical

Table 1.
Publication on parenting challenges and stresses in the last 5 years.

The need for the shift is not surprising because Dobson [11] reported that what works for infants 2–6 years may not work for adolescents and cannot work for those over 18 years [64]. All these shifts are to enhance the good life of the child in the twenty-first century, though parents cannot guarantee that the use of different parenting styles will yield the desired children because children are free moral agents. Thus, parents, take heart if your children do not turn out the way you thought. It is the choice children make for their lives and has little to do with you, the parent, failing to do this and that. Some parents take solace in prayer to the Almighty God to bless their parenting practices. Parenting practices in many developing countries conform to the Biblical admonition to teach at home, sitting, walking, working in the garden, or all places as they interact with their children (Deuteronomy 6:6–8) (English Standard Version—ESV, 2016). This text emphasises parents teaching their children organically at home and in different settings. Hence, parents need to take ample time with their children: infants, adolescents, and grown-ups.

Furthermore, single parenting may need such a model to determine which concept favours single mothers or single fathers [64, 65]. Parenting support to single parents is very important because globally, 6.8% of children are raised by single parents, 23% in the United States of America (USA) and 21% the United Kingdom (UK) [66, 67]. Globally, single mothers constitute 84% of single parents [65, 68, 69], and these mothers have several children, minimal education, and low economic status [65]. Single parenting research shows that adolescents are affected most compared to other age groups and do not easily embrace changes [66, 67]. It is because such single parents

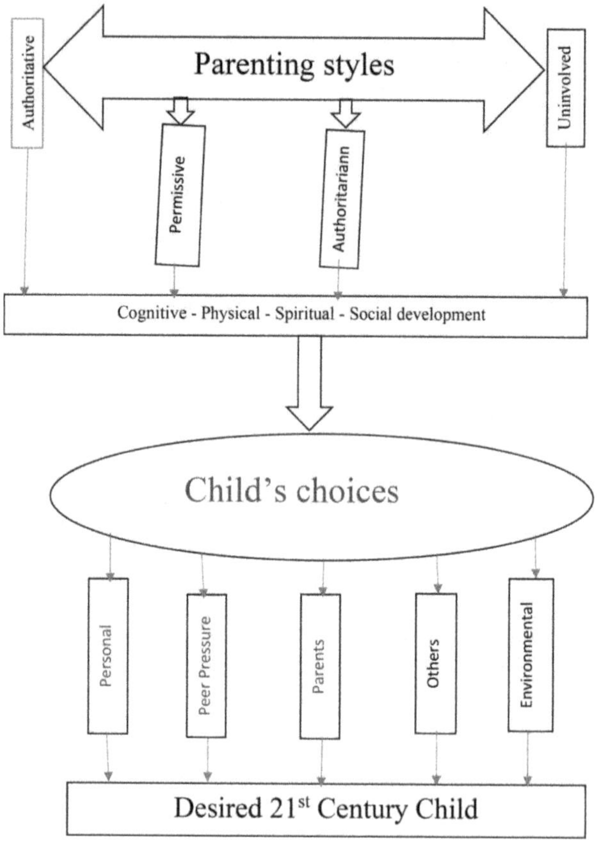

Figure 1.
The model for parenting a holistic twenty-first century child.

face economic hardships to meet the needs of their adolescents [70, 71] and work in different contexts [53]. At a disturbing stage, some adolescents prefer allegiance to external voices other than their parents [72], which adds stress to parents. Hence, it is not uncommon for adolescents to abandon their homes because they cannot express their emotions to their parents but to their peers. In addition, single parents have tendencies to overprotect children, which hinders the children's social skills progress [73].

7. Conclusion

The chapter highlighted parenting as a storm experienced by parents as their children go through the different stages of development, from infants 0–12 to adolescents (13–18) and finally to adulthood (above 18) years. Throughout these stages, parents go through a sweet and bitter experience. During the infant stage, several unexpected issues may overwhelm parents, and sometimes unplanned. Moving into the adolescent stage, children start claiming some autonomy that may be misused, and that can be contrary to the parent's wishes. Also, parents are not willing to let go of the grip they have on their children. Parenting can be a big storm to navigate through. In the adult stage, parents may face a full brown storm because the children have now turned adults, are looking for full independence in most of the decisions they make.

However, in the parent's mind, they are still children. However, the extent of the storm at this stage may depend on the culture where the family is located. In Western cultures, children are expected to be independent at the age of 18. In most African cultures, children at 18 are still under the care of parents. It, however, does not mean that children in the adult stage do not make decisions that may be painful to parents. Even those children who are culturally expected to be independent may still require parental care, which also causes a storm for the parents. It is important for parents to be educated about the four styles of parenting and to know how or when to use them. The challenge is balancing two extremes of parenting styles: authoritative and uninvolved. It is because parenting styles yield different characteristics among children, good and bad, desired and undesired. In addition, even with the best use of parenting style or blended styles, children can choose what they want to be in life. This, too, can cause a storm in families. The children's choices are key to a holistic lifestyle.

Parenting prepares children for holistic lives exhibited by enhancing mental, social, physical, and spiritual domains. When properly cultivated, they become vital in a children's choice-making process. This chapter endeavoured to introduce a parenting model for a holistic twenty-first-century child. The chapter depicts authoritative-uninvolved as a continuum, whereas the permissive and authoritarian styles lie along the continuum (**Figure 1**). Whereas there are several issues, this chapter discusses that an ideal family comprises a father and mother, but mothers or fathers may do parenting single-handedly. It is because of factors like globalisation, the COVID-19 pandemic, the Fourth Industrial Revolution (4IR), and socioeconomic and political changes that seem to have exacerbated the parenting storm. Although there are various parenting mechanisms in place, such as online reading materials, government control and support, and public support (in some cultures), all of which may enhance holistic parenting, not all mechanisms mentioned above may meet individual parental contexts, and the children's choices that may matter most in the parenting arena for a holistic life. That is why parenting can be a storm. It requires much effort and patience to raise a twenty-first -century holistic child. It is no wonder Dobson views parenting as an activity for the brave to manage diverse contextual opportunities and challenges. The discourse regarding parenting storm is a conceptual study. There is a need for empirical studies on how to raise holistic children. To what extent do parents accept their children's choices? What are the models to use for the holistic development of children? What can parents do to make their views more acceptable than the views of their children's peers?

Acknowledgements

We acknowledge the support from our dear wives during the writing process.

Conflict of interest

The authors declare no conflict of interest.

Author details

Israel Kibirige[1] and Israel Masiko Kafeero[2]*

1 University of Limpopo, Limpopo, South Africa

2 Bugema University, Kampala, Uganda

*Address all correspondence to: ikafeerom@gmail.com

References

[1] Virasiri S, Yunibhand J, Chaiyawat W. Parenting: What are the critical attributes? Journal of the Medical Association of Thailand. 2011;**94**(9):1109

[2] Atout M, Alrimawi I, Daibes MA, Abusalameh E. The lived experience of family members who care for children with cancer: An interpretative phenomenological approach. European Journal of Oncology Nursing. 2021;**52**:101978. DOI: 10.1016/j.ejon.2021.101978

[3] Paul D et al. Parenting behaviorally inhibited and socially withdrawn children. In: Bornstein MH, editor. Handbook of Parenting: Volume I Children and Parenting. New York: Routledge; 2019. pp. 484-513. DOI:10.4324/169780429440847

[4] Lavey-Khan S, Reddick D. Painting together: A parent-child dyadic art therapy group. The Arts in Psychotherapy. 2020;**70**:101687. Available from: https://www.sciencedirect.com/science/article/abs/pii/S0197455620300605

[5] Lantsoght EOL, Tse Crepaldi Y, Tavares SG, Leemans K, Paig-Tran EWM. Challenges and opportunities for academic parents during COVID-19. Frontiers in Psychology. 2021;**12**:645734. DOI: 10.3389/fpsyg.2021.645734

[6] Swit CS, Breen R. Parenting during a pandemic: Predictors of parental burnout. Journal of Family Issues. 2023;**44**(7):1817-1837

[7] Zhao Y. The influence of parenting patterns on children's behavior. Journal of Education, Humanities and Social Sciences. 2023;**24**:56-61

[8] Kamran M, Iqbal K, Zahra SB, Javaid ZK. Influence of parenting style on children's behavior in southern Punjab, Pakistan. IUB Journal of Social Sciences. 2023;**5**(2):292-305

[9] Mokwelu OB, Etele AV, Akunne LI. Perceived parent's social status as determinants of students' career choice in secondary schools in Anambra state. Journal of Advanced Education and Sciences. 2023;**3**(1):115-120

[10] Ballantine J. Raising competent kids: The authoritative parenting style. Childhood Education. 2001;**78**:46-47

[11] Dobson JC. Parenting Isn't for Cowards: The 'you Can Do It' Guide for Hassled Parents from America's Best-Loved Family Advocate. Illinois: Tyndale House Publishers, Inc; 2010

[12] Yaffe Y. Development and validation of a new parental authority instrument (PAI). North American Journal of Psychology. 2017;**19**(1):169-194

[13] Brooks RB. The power of parenting. In: Handbook of Resilience in Children. Cham: Springer International Publishing; 2023. pp. 377-395

[14] Macvarish J. The politics of parenting. In: Parenting Culture Studies. Cham: Springer International Publishing; 2023. pp. 99-130

[15] Johnson A, Rogers M. Strengthening and supporting parent–child relationships through digital technology: Benefits and challenges. Family Relations. 2024;**73**(3):1550-1567

[16] Darling N, Steinberg L. Parenting style as context: An integrative

model. Psychological Bulletin. 1993;**113**(3):487-496

[17] Sigelman CK. Lifespan Human Development. 3rd ed. Boston: Brooks/Cole Publishing Company; 1999

[18] Baumrind D. Current patterns of parental authority. Developmental Psychology Monograph. 1971;**4**:1-103

[19] Maccoby EE, Martin JA. Socialization in the context of the family: Parent-child interaction. In: Mussen PH, Hetheringtono EM, editors. Handbook of Child Psychology: Vol. IV. Socialization, Personality and Social Development. 4th ed. New York: Wiley; 1983. pp. 1-101

[20] Williams LR, Degnan KA, Perez-Edgar KE, Henderson HA, Rubin KH, Pine DS, et al. Impact of behavioral inhibition and parenting style on internalizing and externalizing problems from early childhood through adolescence. Journal of Abnormal Child Psychology. 2009;**37**:1063-1075

[21] Hofstede G. Culture's Consequences: International Differences in Work-Related Values. Beverly Hills, London: Sage; 1980

[22] Hofstede G, Hofstede J, Minkov M. Cultures and Organizations. Software of the Mind. Intercultural Cooperation and its Importance for Survival. The McGraw Hill Companies; 2010

[23] Cole M, Cole SR, Lightfoot C. The Development of Children. New York: Macmillan; 2005

[24] Martinez-Escudero JA, Villarejo S, Garcia OF, Garcia F. Parental socialization and its impact across the lifespan. Behavioral Sciences. 2020;**10**(6):101

[25] Nithya S, Farseena KP, Thomas S. Parental stress among parents across their parenting role. International Journal of Indian Psychology. 2021;**9**(1):611-615. DOI: 10.25215/0901.061. DIP: 18.01.061/20210901

[26] Minkov M, Kaasa A. Do dimensions of culture exist objectively? A validation of the revised MinkovHofstede model of culture with world values survey items and scores for 102 countries. Journal of International Management. 2022;**28**(4):100971. DOI: 10.1016/j.intman.2022.100971

[27] Hassan AA, Hamid AM, Eltayeb NH. Burden on parenting of children with special needs. EAS Journal of Nursing and Midwifery. 2021;**3**(2):63-67

[28] Hastings RP. Parental stress and behaviour problems of children with developmental disability. Journal of Intellectual and Developmental Disability. 2002;**27**(3):149-160

[29] Finardi G, Paleari FG, Fincham FD. Parenting a child with learning disabilities: Mothers' self-forgiveness, well-being, and parental behaviors. Journal of Child and Family Studies. 2022;**31**:2454-2471

[30] Park GA, Lee ON. The moderating effect of social support on parental stress and depression in mothers of children with disabilities. Occupational Therapy International. 2022;**2022**:5162954

[31] Sadiki MC. Parenting a child with disability: A mother's reflection on the significance of social support. African Journal of Disability. 2023;**12**:1157

[32] Zuurmond M, O'Banion D, Gladstone M, Carsamar S, Kerac M, Baltussen M, et al. Evaluating the impact of a community-based parent training programme for children with cerebral palsy in Ghana. PLoS One.

2018;**13**(9):1-17. DOI: 10.1371/journal.pone.0202096

[33] Zuurmond M, Nyante G, Baltussen M, Seeley J, Abanga J, Shakespeare T, et al. A support programme for caregivers of children with disabilities in Ghana: Understanding the impact on the wellbeing of caregivers. Child: Care, Health and Development. 2019;**45**(1):45-53. DOI: 10.1111/cch.12618

[34] Ljubicic M, Delin S, Kolcic I. Family and individual quality of life in parents of children with developmental disorders and diabetes type 1. Journal of Clinical Medicine. 2022;**11**(10):2861

[35] Yeates N. Globalization and Social Policy. 2007: 628-653

[36] Held D, McGrew A. Globalisation/Anti-Globalisation. Malden, MA: Polity Press; 2002

[37] International Institute of Rural Reconstruction (IIRR). Review of the Impacts of COVID-19 on Rural Population, Responses, and Policy Recommendations. 2020

[38] Giddens A. Runaway World: How Globalisation is Reshaping our Lives. New York: Routledge, Profile Books; 2002

[39] Glatzer M, Rueschemeyer D. An introduction to the problem. In: Globalization and the Future of the Welfare State. 2005. pp. 1-22

[40] Subasat T. What is globalisation and what is not? A historical perspective. Florya Chronicles of Political Economy. 2015;**1**(1):1-38. Available from: chrome-extension://efaidnbmnnnibpca mkaj/https://dergipark.org.tr/tr/download/article-file/#:~:text=definitions%20 Of%20 Globalisation&textThe%20 initia %20approach20 perceived %20globalisation%201996%3A%20 1).#509060]-620222.pdf

[41] Alkire S, Dirksen J, Nogales R, Oldiges C. Multidimensional Poverty and COVID-19 Risk Factors: A Rapid Overview of Interlinked Deprivations across 5.7 Billion People, OPHI Briefing 53. Oxford, UK: Oxford Poverty and Human Development Initiative, University of Oxford; 2020

[42] Chung G, Lanier P, Wong PYJ. Mediating effects of parental stress on harsh parenting and parent-child relationship during coronavirus (COVID-19) pandemic in Singapore. Journal of Family Violence. 2022;**37**(5):801-812

[43] Anjaswarni T, Nursalam N, Widati S, Yusuf A. Analysis of the risk factors related to the occurrence of juvenile delinquency behavior. Jurnal Ners. 2019;**14**(2):129-136. DOI: 10.20473/jn.v14i1.12465

[44] Van Ham M, Hedman L, Manley D, Coulter R, Osth J. Intergenerational transmission of neighbourhood poverty: An analysis of neighbourhood histories of individuals. Transactions of the Institute of British Geographers. 2014;**39**(3):402-417

[45] UNECA. Brain drain and capacity building in Africa. In: Proceedings of the Regional Conference on Brain Drain and Capacity Building in Africa, Aide Memoir, Addis Ababa: UN. ECA, Ethiopia, 22-24 February 2000

[46] Usman MA, Ozdeser H, Çavuşoğlu B, Aliyu US. On the sustainable economic growth in sub-Saharan Africa: Do remittances, human capital flight, and brain drain matter? Sustainability. 2022;**14**(4):2117

[47] Livingstone S, Byrne J. Parenting in the digital age. The challenges of

parental responsibility in comparative perspective. In: Mascheroni G, Ponte C, Jorge A, editors. Digital Parenting. The Challenges for Families in the Digital Age. Göteborg: Nordicom; 2018. pp. 19-30

[48] de Mooij B, Fekkes M, van den Akker AL, Vliek L, Scholte RH, Overbeek G. Does affirming children's autonomy and prosocial intentions help? A microtrial into intervention component effects to improve psychosocial behavior. Journal of School Psychology. 2022;**90**:60-81. DOI: 10.1016/j.jsp.2021.11.003

[49] De Stone S, Meinck F, Sherr L, Cluver L, Doubt J, Orkin FM, et al. Factors Associated with Good and Harsh Parenting of Pre-Adolescents and Adolescents in Southern Africa [Innocenti Working Paper No. 2016-20]. Florence: UNICEF Office of Research; 2016

[50] Patton GC, Sawyer SM, Santelli JS, Ross DA, Afifi R, Allen NB, et al. Our future: A lancet commission on adolescent health and wellbeing. The Lancet. 2016;**387**(10036):2423-2478

[51] Moyles J. Just Playing? The Role and Status of Play in Early Childhood Education. Milton Keynes: Open University Press; 1989

[52] Ajzen I. The theory of planned behavior. Organizational Behavior and Human Decision Processes. 1991;**50**(2):179-211. DOI: 10.1016/0749-5978(91)90020-T

[53] Hendriati A, Okvitawanli A. Challenges of parenting in an urban setting. Psychological Research on Urban Society. 2019;**2**(1):36-43. Article 12. DOI: 10.7454/proust.v2i1.43. Available from: https://scholarhub.ui.ac.id/proust/vol2/iss1/12

[54] Brunissen L, Rapoport E, Fruitman K, Adesman A. Parenting challenges of grandparents raising grandchildren: Discipline, child education, technology use, and outdated health beliefs. GrandFamilies: The Contemporary Journal of Research, Practice and Policy. 2020;**6**(1):16-33. Available from: https://scholarworks.wmich.edu/grandfamilies

[55] Muzingili T, Muntanga W. Opportunities and challenges associated with use of indigenous parenting practices on child discipline. African Journal of Social Work. 2020;**10**(2):61-69

[56] Benešová P, Sikorová L. Evaluation of stress of parents of children with disability and without disability–pilot study. Pielegniarstwo XXI wieku/Nursing in the 21st Century. 2022;**21**(2):102-105. Available from: http://creativecommons.org/licenses/by/4.0/

[57] Picardi A, Fagnani C, Gigantesco A, Toccaceli V, Stazi MA, Medda E. Stability and change in genetic and environmental influences on depressive symptoms in response to COVID-19 pandemic. Frontiers in Psychiatry. 2023;**14**:954737. DOI: 10.3389/fpsyt.2023.95473

[58] Hackett E, Cook S. Occupational therapists' perceptions of how they support the parenting role of mental health service users who have children. Occupational Therapy in Mental Health. 2016;**32**(1):32-49. DOI: 10.1080/0164212X.2015.1091280

[59] Sethi C. Mothering as a relational role: Re-evaluating everyday parenting occupations. Journal of Occupational Science. 2020;**27**(2):158-169. DOI: 10.1080/14427591.2019.1666423

[60] Lim YZG, Honey A, McGrath M. The parenting occupations and purposes

conceptual framework: A scoping review of 'doing' parenting. Australian Occupational Therapy Journal. 2022;**69**(1):98-111. DOI: doi/pdf/10.1111/1440-1630.12778

[61] Poole JL, Haygood D, Mendelson C. "I'm still dad": The impact of scleroderma on being a father. Occupational Therapy in Health Care. 2018;**32**(1):1-13. DOI: 10.1080/07380577.2017.1422087

[62] Cohn ES, Henry AD. Caregiving and childrearing. In: Crepeau EB, Cohn ES, Schell BAB, editors. Willard and Spackman's Occupational Therapy. Philadelphia: Wolters Kluwer Health; 2009. pp. 579-591

[63] Ruddick S. Maternal thinking. Feminist Studies. 1980;**6**(2):342-367. DOI: 10.2307/3177749

[64] Price SJ, Mckenry PC. Divorce Beverly hills. In: Ricciuti B et al., editors. Child Development and Social Policy. Illinois: University of Chicago Press; 2001. pp. 141-232

[65] Pujihasvuty R, Subeqi AT, Murniati C. Single parents in Indonesia: How to carry out the practice of the eight family functions? Family Journal. 2021. DOI: 10.1177/1066480720986500

[66] Amato P, Keith B. Parental divorce and the wellbeing. Metanal Psychology Bulletin. 2000;**110**(1):24-46

[67] Emery RE. Divorce and separation—Synthesis. In: Tremblay RE, Boivin M, RDEV P, editors. Encyclopedia on Early Childhood Development. Centre of Excellence for Early Childhood Development and Strategic Knowledge Cluster on Early Childhood Development. Virginia: University of Virginia; 2011. pp. i-iii

[68] Chavda K, Nisarga V. Single parenting: Impact on child's development. Journal of Indian Association for Child and Adolescent Mental Health. 2023;**19**(1):14-20. DOI: 10.1177/09731342231179017

[69] Bhatt A. Expert's Take: By Undercounting Single Mothers, We Underserve Families. New York: UN Women; 2020

[70] Stack RJ, Meredith A. The impact of financial hardship on single parents: An exploration of the journey from social distress to seeking help. Journal Family Economic Issues. 2018;**39**(2):233-242. DOI: 10.1007/s10834-017-9551-6

[71] Van Gasse D, Mortelmans D. With or without you—Starting single-parent families: A qualitative study on how single parents by choice reorganize their lives to facilitate single parenthood from a life course perspective. Journal Family Issues. 2020;**41**(11):2223-2248. DOI: 10.1177/0192513X20911971

[72] Leung A, Tunkel A, Yurovsky D. Parents fine-tune their speech to children's vocabulary knowledge. Psychological Science. 2021;**32**(7):975-984

[73] Chapani B. Impact of single parenting on adolescents' social development—Findings from wise owl high school in Marondera-Zimbabwe. Psychology and Psychological Research International Journal. 2021;**6**(3):000290

Chapter 3

Reverent Parenting: The Veiled Ontology of Self-Awakening

Renée Rolle-Whatley and Ramona Rolle-Berg

Abstract

Parenting behaviors exemplify ubiquitous human activities that evolve humanity physically (to ensure species survival), emotionally (to provide species safety and connection) and, we propose, transcendentally (for species self-awareness maturation). Here we introduce Reverent Parenting (RP), an emergent ontology guiding this veiled maturation through the experiences of individual parents. We applied the process of consilience to synthesize the understanding that as a learned ontology, RP not only informs how we parent, but also who we are as parents. Grounded theory methodology led us to identify external and internal pathways for parental awareness growth—namely, parents' life cycle experiences and vibrational catalysts respectively. Our current and published research provided grounded data revealing these basic psychosocial processes of devotion, relational loyalty, and humility as iterative and cyclic holonic structures representative of the ontology. Reverent Parenting cultivates an expanding sense of unity consciousness that shepherds a deepening love of self as part of a connected whole. Consilience revealed attributes of the ontology that, by virtue of their universality, inform all parenting styles: self-responsibility, selflessness, self-acceptance, and connection. Reverent Parenting, therefore, embodies an evolving state of beingness that manifests evolving states of doing (e.g., authoritarian, permissive, neglective, authoritative).

Keywords: parenting style, ontology, consilience, self-growth, biofield, morphic field, devotion, loyalty, humility, grounded theory, caregiving

1. Introduction

In December of 2019, when baffling cases of pneumonia originated in Wuhan, China, our world was forever changed. Most did not know it yet, but a scant three months later, on March 11, 2020, when the World Health Organization formally named this global pathogen as SARS-CoV-2, every human being—whether they understood what was happening or not—was impacted. And for the billions of parents already struggling with caregiving responsibilities, post-traumatic stress syndrome reactivity ensued and has today become their daily reality. Volatile employment, exorbitant childcare costs, excessive healthcare premiums, not to mention persistent food insecurity, and increasingly overt globally-experienced racial and culture-focused tensions continue to produce extreme levels of stress reactivity that not only negatively impact children's emotional well-being [1], but also contribute to a quantifiable worsening of parents' mental health [2].

Is it any surprise then, that despite Covid-19 "bust and rebound" birth cycles through 2022 [3], post-pandemic fertility rates maintain alarming downward trends? Widespread armed conflicts in the Middle East (e.g., Iraq, Israel, Syria), Africa (e.g., Somalia, Sudan, Nigeria), Asia (e.g., Afghanistan, India, Myanmar), Europe (e.g., Ukraine, Georgia, Moldova), and Latin America (e.g., Mexico, Colombia) [4] continue to generate high levels of fear and food insecurity that strongly—both biologically and psychologically—discourage childbearing. Even data within the animal kingdom corroborate that stressed animals do not breed [5].

The obvious question becomes, can humanity overcome grim global fertility forecasts implicating insufficient population growth by 2100 [6]? How can we, as a species, survive our separatist, materialist, and reductionist inflexibility? What mindset must we adapt to engage an enlightened and pliable healing that seeks to restore, co-create, and regenerate?

We propose that solutions to these questions are already being investigated. Pioneers like Lipton, Sheldrake, Haramein, and Currivan, are testing innovative hypotheses in genetics, biology, physics, and cosmology respectively. Their findings are recalibrating our macroscopic understanding of our place in the expanding cosmos and our microscopic understanding of why babies will continue to be born and parents, despite a host of PTSD-generating globally interwoven and surging crises, will continue to parent.

What then drives this ubiquitous impulse to parent? Participants in our published [7, 8] and current research [9] indicated that upon becoming parents they sought to reexperience or improve upon their own childhoods. They sought to create precious moments, foster shared and personal life-cycle experience(s) (LCEs), and pass on treasured religious and cultural traditions. Rarely was the impulse based solely upon creation of a specific familial genetic legacy. Significantly absent was an intrinsic understanding of the role children play in a parent's self-growth.

Eighty years of research into parenting practices and styles have yet to uncover the nature of the mysterious impulse to parent. If the primary purpose remains "to raise fully functional adults who can take care of themselves and make a positive contribution to society," [10] then how can we fathom why the millions of Syrian, Afghani, Columbian, and Ukranian parents persist with their caregiving efforts despite drought, famine, poverty, and seemingly unending war within their countries? What is driving them to continue?

We argue that cumulative daily parenting LCEs, especially difficult, challenging, traumatic experiences *trigger chaotic growth spurts of self-awareness* in parents. Findings from our previously published work suggest that such growth in awareness manifests as changes in a parent's perception of devotion and loyalty. Our current research expands upon and extends previous findings to include parental awareness growth with attributes fundamental to deepening perceptions of humility.

We propose, therefore, the ontology of RP: a way of being that expresses as a way of doing. Additionally, RP, as a fluid and internalized perspective that develops as parents parent, exhibits the traits representative of an evolved consciousness; namely, devotion, loyalty, and humility.

2. Parenting as a journey of self-awakening: The lure of discovery

As social scientists using a grounded theory approach, we have learned that uncertainty is a gift of discovery. As other grounded theorists have done, we began this study by seeking to uncover the meaning—assigned by the parents in our various studies—to a common experience. Like Nathaniel [11] we asked, *what is going on with this group of parents in this situation?* But it wasn't until we engaged with the processes, procedures, and analysis that is classic grounded theory (CGT) established by Glaser and Strauss [12] that the omnipresent uncertainty resolved into a trio of grounded theories. Stepping back to view our theories as a collective, the lure of discovery suggested that linking the substantive grounded theories might yield a deeper understanding about the nature of parenting.

2.1 Classic grounded theory: What is it?

Five aspects of the methodology prompted our decision to choose CGT. First was CGT's methodological rigor including strict guidelines for participant selection, interview methods that capture participant perspective, and guidelines for the abstraction of data towards conceptualization and theory development that is independent of particular persons, locations, or points in time [13].

Second, our personal philosophical perspectives, that agree with the holism of Duhem-Quine [14, 15], resonate with a qualitative methodology like CGT that produces answers to the "why" questions presented by complex social interactions resistant to quantitative inquiry. Almost 60 years after its creation, Glaser's clearly defined methodology continues to generate theory capable of explanation and prediction of behavioral processes.

Third, participant perspective, rather than researcher preconception, provides the structure upon which CGT theory concepts are built. This makes CGT perspective oriented and the problems that emerged through analysis (**Table 1**) grounded in participant experience.

Source-study emergent problems and key learnings		
Source-study	**Emergent problem**	**Key learning**
Study 1: Strengthening Devotion	How were they learning to mitigate feelings of entrapment?	Learning to love nonjudgmentally and with unqualified faith produced improved self-responsibility.
Study 2: Transforming Loyalty	How were they balancing self-interest against familial needs?	Learning to release self-interest and validate individual family members' right to autonomy produced improved selflessness.
Study 3: Purifying Humility	How were they learning to resolve conflicted sensibilities triggered by residual feelings of selfishness and fear?	Learning to resolve resistance to being humble produced an improved relationship with self-rule, self-reliance, and self-truth.

Source: Authors' elaboration.

Table 1.
Overview of source-study emergent problems and key learnings.

Fourth, CGT methodology is *inductive and modifiable*; that is, the theory emerges over time yet is open to correction as new evidence emerges. Because the theory emerges from individual cases in which the broader context is often similar, generalization of behaviors to a larger class is grounded in true experience. Application of the method creates abstraction from the specific primary cases and reduces bias and error through constant comparison. Emerged patterns fit and remain modifiable to new data, supporting the theory's continuing relevance.

Fifth, a tenet of CGT is that "all is data," [11, 16] by which Glaser meant that data exists in many forms and all forms may contribute to the development of theory. The methodology of CGT also explicitly supports a researcher's efforts to use any materials relevant to the area under investigation to expand on and extend previous research, an attribute Glaser termed "the research strategy of secondary analysis [17]".

2.1.1 CGT is not a positivist approach

In conceptualizing the meaning of various experiences provided by participants in our three CGT studies, it was essential to capture the fluid nature of a parent's inner landscape; to understand a parent's changing state of being. The ontology of RP conceptualizes this changing nature of a parent's reality.

As a philosophical term, ontology takes its meaning from historical metaphysical discussions around the nature of being. In the past, Plato, through Parmenides, and Aristotle focused their thoughts on the nature of reality as initiated through perception of actual physical form [18]. Descartes with his mind-body dualism, then released perception from an act of viewing a physical object to the jurisdiction of the mind alone with his famous concept, "I think therefore I am [19]." By the twentieth century, philosophy and social science researchers recognized that how the world was viewed was dependent upon individually perceived notions of reality. Ontological approaches mirroring the political, scientific, and philosophical schools of thought of that time, embraced four broad categories of perceiving, interpreting, and thus knowing the world: realism, empiricism, positivism, and post-modernism.

As the first of four ontological approaches, realism was a quick mismatch with Glaser's desire to explain and predict an individual's sense of reality. Recall, Glaser's focus was explanation and prediction through qualitative data. He was interested in answering "why" not "what" and "how [20]." Realism assumed that reality, as a collection of facts and universal truths, exists both static, unchanging, and independent of the observer's context. The assumption that reality was fixed while the observer's sense of reality was constantly changing, removed realism as a viable ontological approach for Glaser's qualitative CGT methodology.

Empiricism, the second ontological approach, rejected that universal truths existed at all unless those truths were observable, notable, and independent of the observer; in other words, an observer's perception or interpretation of their reality could in no way affect what was real in the world. Again, a mismatch, especially considering mid-twentieth century interpretations of quantum mechanics which included the central role for an observer of quantum phenomena.

Positivism, the third ontological approach, dealt with participant observations and did not engage with interpretation of the observations affect on the participant. Though Glaser was influenced by the mid-twentieth century scientistic zeitgeist espousing positivism, his CGT rejected many of the positivist assumptions: for example, an individual's context has no affect on reality, reality is unchanging

DOI: http://dx.doi.org/10.5772/intechopen.1007110

and thus quantifiable, and behavioral theory applies everywhere reality is present, regardless of context.

Post-modernism, the fourth ontological approach, embraced how observable interpretations shifted an individual's sense of reality and how that shift assisted them with perception and interpretation of the world around them [18]. Interestingly, Glaser (and earlier during their partnership Glaser and Strauss) remained moot about the ontological, epistemological, and methodological roots of CGT, leaving future researchers with questions about the foundational approach [21].

2.1.2 CGT process and procedure

In our effort to better understand the impact of parenting on parents, we choose CGT for the five reasons enumerated in 2.1. According to Glaser [22] existing theories, which provide data already grounded in the lived experiences of parents, should be utilized to support the generation of new theories and proposals like RP. To this end, source data for this paper derived from three CGT studies, namely, *Strengthening Devotion* [7], *Transforming Loyalty* [8], and *Purifying Humility* [9]. Each CGT source-study—SS1, SS2, and SS3, respectively—was approved by an official IRB governing body and an Informed Consent document was provided to all participants. Each CGT source-study incorporated data capturing personal perspective (**Table 2**) such as interviews, first-person recollections from books, blogs, web pages, audio and video recordings. Each CGT source-study used a grand tour question, an open-ended query deliberately designed to focus participant introspection and elicit participant perspective. For Strengthening Devotion, the grand tour question was "Tell me about your experiences as a caregiver [7]." For Transforming Loyalty, the grand-tour question was "Tell me about your experiences as a parent [8]." For Purifying Humility, the grand tour question was "Tell me about your experiences of doing good [9]."

In our three source-studies, we utilized purposive sampling [23] to direct participant selection. This sampling choice is not probabilistic; instead, allowed us to engage with participants one-at-a-time so that chosen participants enabled us to deepen our understanding of the experience of parenting we were looking to explicate through the respective grand tour questions. Interviews, which generally lasted 90 minutes, were transcribed and coded for incidences in an iterative process designed to allow participant data to inform the recruitment of subsequent contributors who could then be engaged to expand on concept-driven personal experiences of interest to

Source-study data and grand tour questions

Source-study	Primary data sources	Direct interviews	Grand-tour question
Study 1: Strengthening Devotion	33	5	"Tell me about your experiences as a caregiver."
Study 2: Transforming Loyalty	30	8	"Tell me about your experiences as a parent."
Study 3: Purifying Humility	30	23	Tell me about your experiences of doing good."

Source: Authors' elaboration.

Table 2.
Overview of source-study data and grand tour questions.

our evolving understanding. With the organizational support afforded by QSR International's Nvivo 10 [24] software, gathering participant data afforded us unimpeded development in the density of codes and concepts, management of participant data, and, of critical importance, the opportunity to visually represent developing patterns within the data which informed the direction of future data collection.

In each of our three source-studies, participants were 21 years of age or older. The 90 minute interviews were unstructured and conducted informally either in person or via video conference software. There were no group interview questions and no interview guides as the latter suggest preconceptions which do not align with CGT tenets. Interviews all began with an initial grand tour question (**Table 2**) to jump-start the journey of discovery. Subsequent researcher questions were unique to the information volunteered by each participant. Because we utilized purposive sampling, our focus was on clarification to maximize data acquisition and theoretically saturate specific aspects of the emerging theory. As each of the three source-studies advanced, interview questions narrowed until theoretical saturation was achieved.

In SS1, participants were parents and primary caregivers for a child(ren) with autism. They were single or married and provided caregiving in situations that included neurotypical children and multiple children. Their years of caregiving ranged from a minimum of eight to a maximum of four decades.

In SS2, participants were parents with custody of at least one child who was actively parented by the participant. They were also single, married, and divorced, and provided parenting in situations that included neurotypical children and children with autism. Their years of caregiving ranged from a minimum of three years to a maximum of four decades.

In SS3, participants were adults and primary caregivers of a minor child or young adult under 18 years of age; and/or active in the care and guidance of an organization or effort to which he/she committed at least four hours/month. They were also single, married, and divorced. Their years of caregiving ranged from a minimum of three years to a maximum of four decades.

2.2 Source-study findings

As researchers, our experience took the form of expertise with conceptualization supported by actions of deep listening, intuitive recognition of participants' triggered psychosocial behavior-patterns as well as curated cross-disciplinary research from the natural, humanistic, physical, and spiritual sciences. Our participants provided the descriptive evidence of their daily reality, (i.e., the grounded data), that then functioned as the stalwart foundation to our intuited abstractions and conceptualizations of their experiences dealing with their collective problem.

As parenting is ubiquitous and, of necessity, required for the survival of the human species, our research interest aimed to uncover the effects of parenting on parents themselves. In two studies, we gathered the lived experience of active parents with the caveat for the first source-study that parents were raising child(ren) on the autism spectrum. In a third source-study, we curated participants that also had long-term or professional experiences of caregiving for a group.

In SS1 caregivers were chosen to provide insight into the impact of a potentially life-time commitment of active parenting. How were they learning to mitigate feelings of entrapment? Recognizing that one in 36 children in the US (one in 100, globally) exhibits behaviors that fall onto the autism spectrum [25], millions of parents are finding themselves falling victim to post-traumatic-stress syndrome as an outgrowth of their parenting journey. We found the parenting experience of those caregivers in SS1 outlined a roadmap of strengthening devotion: their devotion as a parent; their devotion to the family unit, and lastly, their devotion to their own consciousness growth. In learning to love nonjudgmentally and with unqualified faith in the resilience of both their child(ren) and themselves, these active caregivers found their state of beingness changing to express more responsibility and accountability for self, and for a small fraction, a reclaimed re-engagement with their own life's unlimited potential [7].

In SS2 caregivers were chosen to provide insight into the impact of self-interest on active parenting. The parenting experience for those caregivers revealed a transformation of relational loyalty; that is, how their loyalty to themselves, their loyalty to their family unit, and lastly, their loyalty to all of Life transformed as a function of the influence of parenting experiences on themselves. In learning to release self-interest, to seek emotional balance through regulation, and to validate the autonomy of each individual, these caregivers found their state of beingness changing to express selflessness and for a small fraction, a self-acceptance that allowed for an awakening to unlimited possibility [8].

In SS3 caregivers were chosen to provide insight into how a sense of self as distinct and separate from others impacted personal acts of community volunteerism. The experiences of doing good for those caregivers in SS3 revealed the existence of independent yet related stages of becoming whole within which personal levels of humility were evaluated and weighed. Instances of conflicted sensibilities, occurring while volunteering, triggered a deepening awareness of a sacred dimension to consciousness; a continuing selfishness, attachment and fear needing integration; and a personal purpose of service to others. In resolving incidences of doing good calling for a greater expression of personal humility, these caregivers found their state of beingness changed to express a personal freedom that called for ever greater self-rule, self-reliance, and self-truth. **Table 1** presents these key components [9].

3. Beyond the veil: The emergence of reverent parenting

The patterns that express how parents approach parenting have been researched extensively since the mid 1960s. By the early 1990s, the typology of parenting styles grew to include authoritarian, authoritative, permissive and neglectful [26, 27] with dimensions that encompass aspects of parental support and parental behavioral control [28]. As modern society engages with ever more complex and diverse family structures and lifestyles, parents have also begun to engage with mindfulness techniques to moderate their own, and through familiar, daily association, their children's behavior [29, 30]. As researchers interested in developing theory grounded in experience, we categorize these patterns of parenting practices as *examples of doing*.

When parents in our studies were asked about their experiences of parenting, their responses delved deeply into how parenting affected them; in other words, *examples of changing beingness*. Grounded theory research offers up insight into a parents' state of being as they live their way of doing using parenting styles.

Ontologies are ways of being that correlate broadly with perspective and mindset; our internal state of awareness. Perspectives, created by the thoughts and emotions that link with feelings experienced during life lived daily in activity and expressed through body and language choices developed over time, represent the way we show up in the world; our state of being.

Our research into the lived experiences of parents reveals their state of beingness and their process of change or evolution of self-awareness. Thus, parenting changes both the next generation, i.e., children, and the current generation, i.e., the parents themselves. Reverent Parenting, as an ontology, therefore reflects this journey of consciousness change into a greater personal awareness through the development of attributes (Section 3.4) of consciousness that themselves reflect parents becoming more integrated and whole.

3.1 Consilience: What is it?

Einstein was a master at consilience. The term consilience, originally coined by William Whewell in his 1840 synthesis, *The Philosophy of the Inductive Sciences,* meant a "jumping together" of knowledge enabling the emergence not only of deeper understanding, but also of—and this was part of what excited us—a grand unification of the sciences. "It is a wonderful feeling to recognize the unity of a complex of phenomena that to direct observation appear to be quite separate things, [31]" Einstein wrote to his friend Marcel Grossmann.

Consilience is a convergence on an outcome from problems and their solutions proposed from within disparate though interconnected and entangled fields of knowledge. In our case, consilience manifested as a synthesis of mind/memory/feelings that converged from findings (of the three source-data CGT studies) and concepts from diverse fields of study focused on the parenting experience (i.e., within science, philosophy, spiritualism, and the humanities). As a testament to the depth of his understanding of the nature of the mind, Glaser himself coined the term theoretical sensitivity [32], to describe a hyper-affinity to patterns within the data, that would produce, within the researcher, unexpected higher order conceptualizations. The natural development of our theoretical sensitivity from years of exposure to the data supported and indeed helped combine disparate findings and knowledge into a consilience around a higher order concept: in our case, reverent parenting.

3.2 Life cycle experiences as catalysts

In this section we explore the catalysts at the heart of the proposed RP ontology, i.e., the actions precipitating the state-of-being. Using a common qualitative strategy designed to shed a broad light on the course of an action or idea, we identified the unifying problem and its impact for each of our studied sub-populations (**Table 1**). The goal was to determine if, from within the unified data, a catalyst common to all source-studies would emerge that would be suggestive of parents' continued adherence to the challenges presented by the often-times monumental responsibilities and activities of parenting. In SS1, parents dealt with how to mitigate feelings of entrapment engendered through the potential life-time commitment of parenting a child on the autism spectrum. In SS2, parents dealt with how to release the protective instincts of self-interest (i.e. ego) to redefine self as self-in-relationship. And in SS3, parents dealt with how to resolve conflicted sensibilities (i.e. consciousness) that resisted deepening involvement with community volunteerism.

We titled the first catalyst common to all source-studies as Life Cycle Experience(s) (LCEs) and propose that LCEs guide parents over time—possibly a lifetime—to adopt a mindset of RP. Further examination lead us to a consilience-derived identification of specific attributes parents gain as they experience LCEs and journey towards evolved self-awareness culminating with an adoption of a new outlook, i.e. the ontology of RP. We present these attributes in Section 3.4.

Life Cycle Experience(s) provided opportunities for the parents in our studies to exhume subconscious behavior patterns playing out in their personal and familial lives. We noted that an adherence to rigid belief systems, reoccurring thoughts about past incidences and unexpected destructive emotions led to a repeated cycling of damaging situations within family units. Our data illustrate that such outcomes are common. Failure to seek the deeper meaning and patterns behind these belief systems, thoughts, and emotions is what Buddhists refer to as lives lived in unskillful action [33] because parents inevitably cause themselves and others suffering via, for example, lying, malicious words, and harsh language. Skillful actions, on the other hand, are positive, thoughtful, and intention-filled. Skillful actions developed in a small number of participants—again, over time. These parents acquired proficiency through mindful adherence to intentions to resolve personal trials.

Reverent Parenting becomes a state of being that a parent naturally adopts as LCEs provide opportunities to re-evaluate deeply personal and fundamental questions. In source-study 1 (SS1), we called the parents' journey Strengthening Devotion, a basic psychosocial process that guided parents through LCEs that tested their ability to release past imaginings about themselves, accept the need to develop a new image, and adapt that image to not only "be okay" with an uncertain future in which they were the primary caregiver for a child on the autism spectrum, but to thrive within the challenge. Using CGT terminology, the core variable Strengthening Devotion explained how LCEs catalyzed parental learning using a cyclical/reiterative yet holonic approach that allowed each phase (e.g., accepting in SS1) to be self-assertive yet integrated into the entirety of the effort. In other words, learning to be devoted meant evolving relationally towards deepened expressions of fidelity and love by accepting, adapting, and ultimately expanding self-awareness via a reframing of self-responsibility (**Figure 1**).

In the stage of accepting, a parent's resistance to the autism diagnosis produced a profound sense of grief, overwhelm, and loss. During our interview, one source-study

Figure 1.
Impact of LCEs in source-study 1.

participant bluntly warned, "I'm pretty sure I will never forgive myself. I gave my son autism. I did it. Me. And no one can ever take that away [34]." In stage 2, the stage of adapting, post-trauma self-discovery improved self-esteem and emotion regulation as evidenced by this comment from another parent who resignedly remarked about her autistic son, "Even when he was quiet our minds were always on him: What is he doing? What will he do next? How will we manage him when he does it? [35]" In stage 3, the stage of reclaiming life, a reawakening to opportunities beyond the often-times decades long role of caregiver prompted a parent's striving towards self-fulfillment and a developing sense of nonattachment. A representative comment was uttered by this parent of two autistic children, the eldest now an adult: "He learned a lot. He's on his own. He's grocery shopping. He's learning to be independent and that's what we all strive for [36]".

In source-study 2 (SS2), we called the parents' journey Transforming Loyalty. This basic psychosocial process guided parents through LCEs that revealed the intensity of their self-centeredness, tested their willingness to release it in favor of a more metered parental control dynamic that could, in its most advanced expression, reveal a surprising freedom of self-expression for all parties within the familial hierarchy. Using CGT terminology, the core variable Transforming Loyalty explained how LCEs catalyzed parental learning in a cyclical/reiterative yet holonic approach that allowed each stage (e.g., redefining self-interest in SS2) to be self-assertive yet integrated into the entirety of the effort. In other words, in SS2, learning about loyalty meant evolving relationally to express familial allegiance and trust by releasing self-interest, embracing detachment, and ultimately accepting Self via a reframing of selflessness and self-acceptance (**Figure 2**).

In the stage of releasing self-interest, habituated approaches to a parent's self-centered and emotion driven thinking produced a broad spectrum of LCEs that manifested initially, for example, as outright self-righteous opposition to parenting responsibilities. As revealed by a parent of teenagers, "Both of 'em say they're never gonna leave home. And it just makes my blood run cold." In stage 2, embracing detachment, parents learn the importance of detachment as they refine an evolving altruism and empathy via LCEs that prompt them to question their need to respect

Figure 2.
Impact of LCEs in source-study 2.

the autonomy of family members. One mother recalled, "My kids are the center of my universe. But I don't show it; Now I realize that I'm in the center with them." In stage 3, living nonattached, a developing perspective of compassionate self-acceptance prompted an awakening of the consciousness of presence and an intuited spirit-driven guidance. A parent described an intuitive event as, "It's a sense, it's a feeling, is something very deep that you know is true but you cannot quite put your finger on it [37]".

In source-study 3 (SS3), we called the parents' journey Purifying Humility. This basic psychosocial process provided insight into how a sense of self as distinct and separate from others impacted personal acts of community volunteerism through LCEs that created a conscious awareness of conflicted sensibilities. Using CGT terminology, the core variable, Purifying Humility, explained how LCEs catalyzed parental learning using the same cyclical/reiterative holonic approach used in SS1 and SS2. A holonic representation better supported the equality of the phases of purification we identified while simultaneously allowing for phase integration opportunities (via LCEs) to impact a parent's evolving understanding about humility as an overall concept. Via a reframing of connection in all facets of familial interaction, parents evolved to over time personify individual freedom through holonic phases of encountering spirit, fostering awareness, embodying service, and breaking free (**Figure 3**).

In the phase of encountering spirit, parents evolve their concept of humility beyond that gleaned from birth via LCEs presented through culture, tradition, and family. The goal in this phase is metanoia, namely, LCEs that produce a profound change of heart perceived and actuated by the parent as a willing and voluntary engagement with aspects of gnosis. A participant remarked, "We know that there are dimensions of human existence that is tangible. It's there. And we know that that is part of the engine that makes us run, is the spiritual element [38]." In phase 2, the phase of fostering awareness, parents experience LCEs that foster an intra-personal consciousness of humility. The goal in this phase is building awareness of the need to release personal dependency on external manifestations that provide safety, security and ego identity. An American pastor, jailed in Turkey for two years commented:

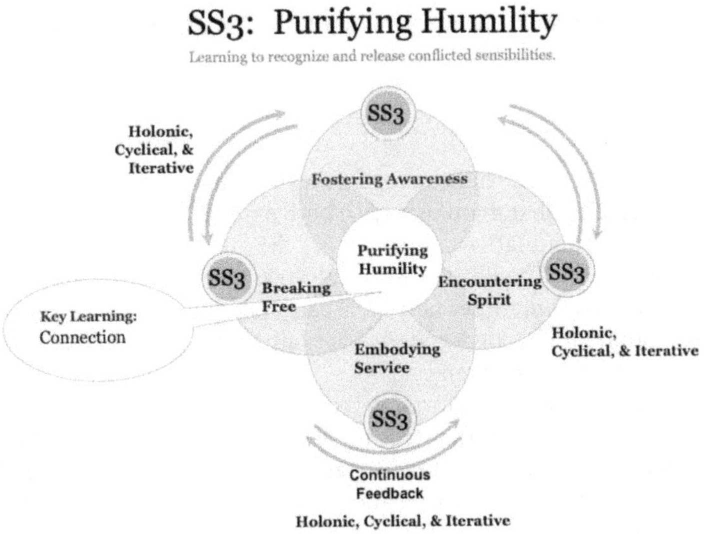

Figure 3.
Impact of LCEs in source-study 3.

> *"As I look back on my prison time...I see a pattern. I would get hit with a test, break and go low, and then work slowly towards a point of surrender to God, only to face a harder blow and go even lower. But each time I started to climb again and eventually made it back to surrender—a deeper surrender, because now I was more aware of the price. There were many ups and downs, but there was a gradual upward trajectory. This was a choice [39]."*

In phase 3, the phase of embodying service, parents learn through LCEs that humility must be an attribute to which service, whether towards the self, animals, humanity, or the environment, flows. A parent commented, "Have a big heart and connect with people...if we make everybody stronger, all the boats rise [40]." In phase 4, the phase of breaking free, parents experience how LCEs viewed from the lens of presence transform humility into a gateway to unity consciousness. A SS3 source remarked, "Being set apart was the only way I could learn how much I longed to be with everyone else. Being in charge was the only way I could learn how much I wanted to be in community [41]".

Key observations about LCEs:

- The (re)actions of family trigger LCEs for parents' self-growth about "why" full commitment to devotion, loyalty, and humility remains elusive and "how" to release identified blocks.
- Significant LCEs "gift" parents opportunities to broaden rigid perspectives about self-responsibility, selflessness, self-acceptance, and connection.
- Few parents experience advanced LCEs that awakened RP in its deepest expression, i.e. a life lived in Presence.

Beyond LCEs, we propose three additional catalysts that may influence the uptake of a parental mindset of RP, catalysts that provide a possible explanation for the observable drop in the numbers of parents, independent of source-study, experiencing LCEs representing advanced awakened consciousness. We discuss these information-based stimuli below.

3.3 Vibrational catalysts

The findings of our three studies suggest the existence of an impulse towards consciousness evolution that manifests with both external and internal indicators. We propose that parents' cumulative daily LCEs are the outward, sense-based, external aspects of its expression. The vibrational catalysts presented below represent the internal, non-physical, sometimes non-local aspects of its expression. Together, LCEs supported, surrounded, interpenetrated by certain vibrational catalysts, trigger and guide growth spurts of self-awareness.

Parental LCEs, supported by vibrational catalysts, become pathways of disruption for inflexible behavior; they set the stage to reboot the physical, emotional, mental, and spiritual integrated circuity of the human body so that parents remember their essential nature (as represented within ancient wisdom traditions) as beings of unconditional love. For us, that translates into helping parents to recognize, reconnect with, and adopt an ontology of RP that assists them to strive towards a daily execution of the higher ideals of parenthood: for example, empathy, compassion, altruism, and the right to autonomy, to name just a few. The vibrational catalysts presented below are broad reaching in their affects on the integrated human experience of daily life indicating short-range, long-range and, interestingly, coherent energy fields around the body: i.e., electromagnetic fields, biofields, and morphic fields.

In brief, we define each:

- *Bio-electromagnetic fields (Bio-EMFs)*: Fields of electric and electromagnetic energy that surround, permeate, and some scientists suggest regulate biological organisms. Produced by dynamic electrically charged particles exhibiting coordination, regulation, and coherent potentials, Bio-EMFs as electric fields are physically measurable, exist around living cells, and produce oscillating, variably coherent EM fields in both visible light and microwave (and lower) frequency range. They are considered a subset of the broader category of the biofield [42].

- *Biofields*: Fields of energy or information that include electric fields, EM fields, and more subtle fields that incorporate holistic possibly quantum vacuum engagement that together regulate the biological tasks of living systems' seeking organismic equilibrium. It has been hypothesized that biofields interact with and influence living systems in three ways: through pathways scientifically labeled as veritable, putative, and subtle. Veritable pathways are generally biochemical, neurological, cellular, and bioenergetic in nature. Putative pathways are considered to express as non-local, dynamic and massless interactions with e.g., the quantum field, consciousness, energetic and geometric representations of life (i.e., sacred geometry). Subtle pathways include meridians, chakras, the aura and representations of life force such as prana (India)/chi or qi (China)/ki (Japan)/ manna (Australia)/pneuma (Greeks)/holy spirit (Bible)/ka (Egypt) [43].

- *Morphic fields (MFs)*: These are putative fields that interact to guide the biological form, development, regulation, and regeneration of living organisms through the transfer of information. They are hypothesized to operate within physical space and over time, are specific to each species, and evolve through non-local resonance with like forms (morphic resonance) to influence the organizing fields of future generations via collective memory of cumulative patterns of psychological, social, and cultural activity [44].

All three of these vibration-based catalysts are dynamic, evolving, and transfer information in a manner that parents may not ever recognize until the aftermath of a LCE invites introspection. Given that, we suggest that the psychosocial processes of strengthening devotion (SS1), transforming loyalty (SS2) and purifying humility (SS3) produce—through the impulse of an information-based vibrational catalyst—an evolving self-awareness within parents and act as organizing fields, holonic in nature, together informing and evolving behavior and ultimately, consciousness.

3.3.1 The case for bio-electromagnetic fields

Though times are changing, conventional biology continues to apply a materialist (e.g., measurable) and often reductionist approach to understanding biochemical interactions within living systems. From that vantage then, the most intense EMF within the human body has long been identified as originating from "somewhere" within the human heart, an organ that, independent of the brain, has its own sensory neurons, physiological processes, emotional sensitivity, and capacity to learn and to remember [45]. Self-regulation techniques like deep breathing calm the heart's rhythmic beating, eventually producing a state of physiological coherence (a trainable energetic state of heart-mind-emotion alignment), which creates verifiable alpha brain-wave activity supportive of a plethora of positive outcomes such as stress relief, clarity, improved creativity and memory.

The heart's EMF is by far the strongest of any organ in the body. Its electrical field is 60 times greater and its electromagnetic field is 5000 times greater than that of the brain. The heart's EMF not only influences a biological system at the cellular level but also projects beyond the physical skin border of the body out to a minimum of three feet, enough to influence the heart fields of other living systems nearby. This minimum field distance is of particular relevance to our argument that a Bio-EMF, as a vibrational catalyst, can influence and entrain nearby Bio-EMFs and therefore, the mindsets of parents and their children.

Three studies in which caregivers of individuals with broad-based intellectual disabilities including autism spectrum disorder engaged in mindfulness-based training reported improved caregiver quality of life with their children/clients and showed significantly greater improvement in happiness and learning objectives with a complimentary reduction in behavioral and aggressive episodes [46–48]. Mindfulness-based training aims to calm the body/mind and create heart coherence. The effects of mindfulness training in these studies were significant enough that a study's author remarked, "parents may be able to accomplish all the objectives of a comprehensive intervention for changing their children's behaviors by changing their own behaviors [47]." Clearly, these practical empirical studies and the growing body of published research in biophotonics [42], biofield science [43] and heart coherence from the Institute of HeartMath [49] support our proposal that Bio-EMFs, particularly those generated by a heart emitting a harmonious pattern of coherence, are a form of vibrational catalyst that may influence collective behavior.

Mystics, ancient and modern, have long written and spoken about the mysteries hidden within the human heart. Breath is the medium through which field effects are focused to influence the psychoneuroendophysiology of not only spiritual aspirants but everyday people seeking to experience positive growth after stressful life events, i.e., LCEs. The physical, mental, emotional, and spiritual impact of inflexible behaviors, difficult relationships, and traumatic events and their memories, may be downregulated, as research has shown with genes in the epigenetic literature [50] to allow Bio-EMF entrainment the opportunity to establish new behaviors of cooperation and improved self-regulation. Coherent Bio-EMFs pave the way for a re-imagined pathway to well-being allowing parents to continuously evolve their understanding of themselves.

3.3.2 The case for biofields

How can a field influence perspective? Scientists, researchers, alternative health systems practitioners, and parents in our studies who have adopted the RP ontology ask a slightly different question—how can a field *not* influence perspective? Fields transmit information, and as heart EMFs in a state of coherence demonstrate, field effects alter behavior. One definition of the biofield suggests that "Biofield interactions can organize spatiotemporal biological processes across hierarchical levels: from the subatomic, atomic, molecular, cellular, organismic, to the interpersonal and cosmic levels [43]." Such a broad and deep scale suggests that a definitive understanding of all that a biofield is, how it works, what it affects, and what it can do, remains to be uncovered. Just what roles quantum phenomena like nonlocality, superposition, and complementarity play in the evolving understanding of the biofield and its interactions with living systems remains a topic of scientific inquiry and research [51].

Within healthcare, therapies incorporating biofields that impact well-being abound. The National Center for Complementary and Integrative Health currently separates biofield therapies into veritable and putative energy fields. Veritable fields are scientifically measurable and include, for example, electric fields displaying as the brain/heart potentials recorded on an electroencephalogram and electrocardiogram respectively; sound and vibration fields like Infrasound (effective for increasing vitality and accelerating healing) and Transcranial Ultrasound (a noninvasive technique for pain, mood, and depression); and mechanical/physical interactions made measurable via Traditional Chinese Medicine processes and medicinals. Putative energy fields are not overtly quantified with accepted scientific technology. Nevertheless, putative field studies utilize blinded study processes, the gold-standard of evidence-based research to record changes in physically measurable outcomes [51]. Examples of putative energy fields include Chi (accessed by Acupuncture and Emotional Field Therapies), Prana (accessed by Ayurvedic practices), Intention (accessed via prayer, meditation, sacred geometry, bioenergetics); and Vital Force (accessed by chiropractic, naturopathic medicine, Healing Touch, Reike, and qi gong).

Biofield therapies continue to receive global acceptance as viable healing alternatives especially for chronic conditions. As an aggregate, their popularity endures worldwide and drives scientific investigators to define studies that reveal biofield verity via measurable means. For parents, on a daily basis, biofields function simply in the background as an intrinsic aspect of their psychoneuroimmunological nature, impacting LCEs and, by extension, collective relations, and evolving RP ways of being.

3.3.3 The case for morphic fields

Once again, how can a field influence perspective? Developmental biologist Rupert Sheldrake suggests that MFs transfer mechanics is all about species inheritance processes and a special type of resonance. Morphic fields impose ordered pattern on random or indeterminate patterns of energetic (think rhythmic or vibratory) activity [52]. They are species specific, operate locally (in physical space over time), so affect the systems they organize from within and around them. The MFs operate as fields of probability (think quantum fields) by organizing energetic activity into embryonic shapes and by stabilizing the forms of the adults. Sheldrake proposes that MFs are actually transmitted to future members of a species through a type of non-local resonance, a morphic resonance, that does not transfer energy but transfers information based on species similarity. Each new member of a species is both in-formed by the field and contributes to the collective memory of the field through self-resonance with it. Thus MFs are not static, they evolve. Of interest to us is that MF theory includes the organizing fields of other animals as well as organizing fields informing human mind/body activity including psychological, social, and cultural activity [11]. Suggestions for how morphic resonance actually transfers information include zero-point field/quantum vacuum connections, David Bohm's implicate order connections [53], possibilities for transferring information via extra dimensions of space-time, and theories of physics not yet discovered.

Biology tells us that humans, animals and other organisms evolve, some full-spectrum; that is physically as well as mentally, emotionally, and spiritually. Though genes play a crucial role in molecular biology, for example they express according to the information in cellular fields of organization around them, they cannot explain the organized patterns themselves nor determine original form and shape [52]. Morphic field theory suggests that over time, characteristics of a self-organizing species (e.g., humans, animals) encode through morphic resonance to become habits of nature [54]; that is habits of shape, behavior, mindset, and activity that support and sustain life.

How do these mechanics connect to our proposal that a vibrational catalyst invites parents to adopt a RP ontological approach? The answer focuses on habits. Habits of nature have become our goals while the pathways towards the goals have become guides towards states of being that stabilize our mind/body/spirit against change or disorder. Waddington, in his work with complexity theory, identified these goals as attractors and the pathways leading to them as chreodes [55]. We call these goals attributes and the pathways leading to them LCEs.

There is a small but growing body of empirical evidence in support of the theory of morphic fields. Examples include inter-personal and group communication over distance; increased behavioral and mental learning speeds for tasks already learned but new to unrelated groups over time, the sense of being stared at (scopesthesia), telepathy, and the ability of animals to navigate home [52].

We propose that, in essence, these attractors perform as progressive developmental objectives for species. For animals, the successful attractors develop into instincts. For humans, successful attractors—as those that emerged from SS1, SS2, and SS3–become goals for continuing full-spectrum growth. With respect to the ontology of RP, our work using consilience has disclosed four main attractors to which parents are guided via LCEs and vibrational catalysts while parenting: self-responsibility, selflessness, self-acceptance, and connection.

Key observations about vibrational catalysts:

- Bio-electromagnetic fields: The heart's EMF expresses a coherence that can entrain coherent behavior in others within its vicinity. Breath is the medium through which field effects become focused, LCEs are managed, and a parent's self-awareness journey towards RP occurs.

- Biofields: Vibrational catalysts transfer energy or information, are often unnoticed and unrecognized, yet influence how parents parent and what they think of themselves as parents. Daily LCEs constantly reshape parental self-perceptions about self-responsibility, selflessness, self-acceptance, and connection, with the goal being the parent's adoption of an ontology of RP.

- Morphic fields: Species specific fields that are transmitted to future species-members via a dynamic non-local morphic resonance and daily LCEs that, in the case of human parents, groove pathways to attain goals that evolve reverent behaviors that strengthen, transform, and purify personal ways of being.

3.4 Attributes of reverent parenting

Parental perspective, gathered from members of relevant source-study communities and thus grounded, anchored the conceptual development of the three basic psychosocial processes of devotion (**Figure 1**), loyalty (**Figure 2**) and humility (**Figure 3**). Consilience then provided a pathway for a synthesis of concepts utilizing

DOI: http://dx.doi.org/10.5772/intechopen.1007110

the grounded data and the resultant researcher theoretical sensitivity combined with available scientific studies on parenting aspects. Taken together, these data support the relevance of RP as a distinguishable human ontology that evolves from the parenting process. **Figure 4** presents the ontology of RP.

The attributes of RP that define the ontology include self-responsibility, selflessness, self-acceptance, connection and supra to them as in a holarchy, unconditional love. Together they move parents towards a relationship with children that asks these parents to express the highest ideals of love. Resonance with these attributes represents a level of relational communication and self-awareness that extends a parent's way of being beyond the boundaries of the family and out into the world.

As producing and raising children remains a ubiquitous human behavior, being triggered by children is likely to remain a key way to affect awareness growth in their parents. Whatever parenting style is chosen, the level of parental resonance with the attributes of RP represents their way of being, not their way of doing. The mystical objective of parenting is the growth of reverence; that is, reverence for the growth of consciousness in children and reverence for the growth of consciousness in parents. In fact, we believe that the attributes of RP can lead the entire human species into a future of evolved self-awareness. The attributes defined below are, therefore, ways of being to which we can all aspire.

- *Self-responsibility*: A state of being encompassing accountability for personal behaviors and actions that impact others and the world with a willingness to be accountable for those decisions and actions, while allowing others the right to do the same.

- *Selflessness*: A state of being that prioritizes the welfare and needs of others before one's own.

- *Self-acceptance*: A state of being that embraces all personal attributes, positive and negative, without qualification, restriction or judgment.

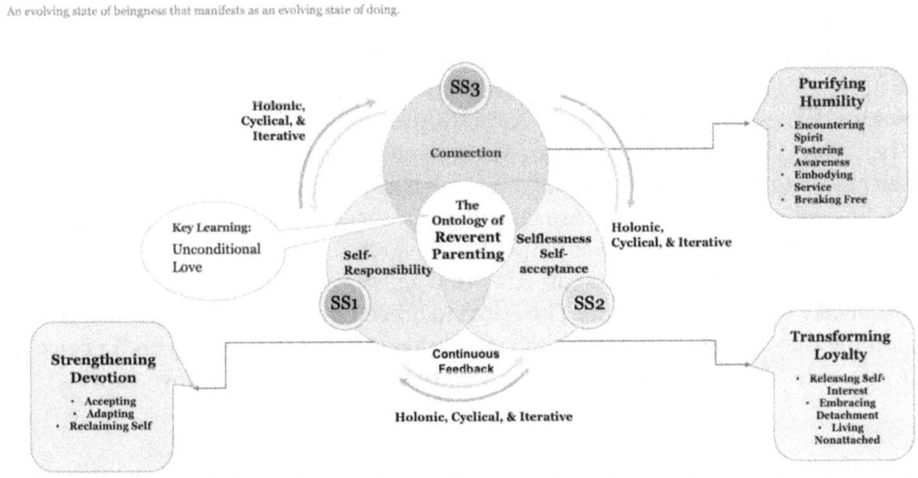

Figure 4.
The ontology of reverent parenting.

- *Connection*: A state of being that creates shared meaning and attachment through verbal and non-verbal means in which all experience feelings of being recognized, heard, and understood.
- *Unconditional love*: A state of being that offers love freely with full acceptance, and without condition or expectation of return.

3.5 Incidences of resistance

No matter when parents buy their tickets on the roller-coaster ride that is parenting, physical, psychological, and psychosocial changes will occur that influence how they ultimately strengthen personal devotion, transform their individual sense of loyalty to include others, and purify their personal level of humility by reconciling conflicts that challenge them to adjust their attachment to self as separate from others.

Nevertheless, during the CGT process with each source-study, we noted parents who were struggling to redefine themselves experienced more resistance and deeper resentment than those that initially welcomed the redefinition into what they perceived as an expanded self. Our study with parents of children on the autism spectrum provided similar evidence of a discernable parental resistance to the need to redefine themselves and their lifepaths to engage with the potentially life-time caregiving commitment presented by the diagnosis of autism. And then, as we engaged with the data from our doing-good study, and the impact on parental perspective for prioritizing the needs of others over self, we again encountered evidence of resistance to internal conflicts that arose when prompted to engage with doing good.

Leaning into our theoretical sensitivity with the source data and the consilience building out of broad cross-discipline exposure, we asked ourselves what could be motivating the discernable drop off in the numbers of parents experiencing advanced LCEs? Why were fewer parents experiencing the attributes of reclaiming (SS1), living non-detached (SS2), and breaking free (SS3)? Why were they not reaching towards awakened RP in its deepest expression, i.e. a life lived in Presence?

We propose one possibility: The chreodes of complexity theory. Chreodes can be understood as life paths that nature seeks preferentially as they are the most stable and minimize energy usage while maximizing efficiency [56]. They function like defensive channels that move individuals towards goals they wish to achieve. But channels can be both protective and imprisoning. For example, the human brain, being neuroplastic, allows for change, but the effort to re-form the grooves developed over time from reactive behavior is high. Discipline towards achieving the goal becomes really important. When parents grow resistant to change due to physical and environmental as well as psychological/social/cultural/spiritual challenges, the walls of the channel (think daily LCEs!) keep them trapped. Movement out of the groove generally requires a significant upheaval such that nature is forced to find a new, more stable path. Such upheavals often take the form of trauma. The effort to breech the walls and move towards reclaiming the self, living non-attached, and breaking free appears too high a price for many parents. Thus the journey towards adoption of a RP ontology slows down.

4. Conclusion

We have argued that self-awareness must evolve if we are to survive the increasingly formidable crises impacting our lives and the health of our planet. Reverent

DOI: http://dx.doi.org/10.5772/intechopen.1007110

Parenting—as a way of being that expresses as a way of doing—points out how important parental perspective is to the achievement of global healing that restores, co-creates, and regenerates family, arguably a foundational building block of a united society.

The three studies forming the basis for the RP proposal offered us an opportunity to pull back to view the bigger picture and at the same time, to more deeply investigate how parents' LCEs with devotion (SS1), loyalty (SS2), and humility (SS3) impacted their ability to accept self-responsibility; to behave selflessly and with self-acceptance; and to connect in service to others. Analysis identified two stimuli guiding parental adaptation and adoption of these attributes; namely, externally-motivated LCEs and internally-experienced vibrational catalysts of which we discussed three—bio-EMFs, biofields, and morphic fields—and how such fields might act to impact parental growth in self-awareness.

Additionally, we identified an observable drop in the numbers of parents experiencing LCEs representing advanced awakened consciousness. We proffered one possible explanation: the cost of compliance was just too high. Noticeably fewer parents were willing to engage the level of commitment and discipline necessary to achieve prodigious strides in self-awareness growth post LCE. Possibly because resistance to change is easier (despite our neuroplastic brains) than voluntary engagement with a trauma-filled struggle of self-growth. Data indicated that what it takes to live a life of deep devotion, loyalty, and humility extorted too great a sacrifice from parents distracted by the crises of family life. The ideals of reclaiming self (SS1), living non-detached (SS2), and breaking free (SS3) were not goals to be realized, rather far off horizons for future achievement. Given that most parents remained unaware of the existence of vibratory catalysts and their subtle yet ever-present guidance adds weight to this conclusion.

Nevertheless, we are aware that the three holonic basic psychosocial processes used as source-studies for this research about RP contribute to, and are supported by, an as yet scientifically uncharacterized frequency of universal love that many avatars (e.g., Buddha, Jesus), modern mystics (e.g., Fox, Harvey), regular parent-experiencers (e.g., our participants), and an increasing number of scientists (e.g., Sheldrake, Haramein), all agree exists.

One portal of entry to this unity-level of consciousness is through the universal love emitted by a coherent human heart committed to self-growth. Just as parents' self-awareness grows via LCEs to find balance and freedom in living life in the present moment, the processes of strengthening devotion and transforming relational loyalty find equilibrium and harmony in expressions of unconditional love through the purifying activity of a growth in humility. The reverence is in the journey towards wholeness.

Conflict of interest

The authors declare no conflict of interest.

Author details

Renée Rolle-Whatley* and Ramona Rolle-Berg
Rolle-Integrative Healing Solutions, LLC, TX, United States of America

*Address all correspondence to: drrenee@rolleihs.com

References

[1] Mat Hassan N, Salim HS, Amaran S, Yunus NI, Yusof NA, Daud N, et al. Prevalence of mental health problems among children with long COVID: A systematic review and meta-analysis. PLoS One. 2023;**18**(5):e0282538. [cited 2024 Jun 10]. Available from: https://www.ncbi.nlm.nih.gov/pmc/articles/PMC10191312/

[2] Whaley GL, Pfefferbaum B. Parental challenges during the COVID-19 pandemic: Psychological outcomes and risk and protective factors. Current Psychiatry Reports. 2023;**25**(4):165-174. [cited 2024 Jun 12]. Available from: https://www.ncbi.nlm.nih.gov/pmc/articles/PMC10031194/

[3] Kearney MS, Levine P. US Births Are Down Again, after the COVID Baby Bust and Rebound. Brookings; 2023. [cited 2024 Jun 12]. Available from: https://www.brookings.edu/articles/us-births-are-down-again-after-the-covid-baby-bust-and-rebound/

[4] Today's Armed Conflicts. Geneva Academy. [cited 2024 Jun 12]. Available from: https://geneva-academy.ch/galleries/today-s-armed-conflicts

[5] Ubuka T, Bu G, Tobari Y. Stress and reproduction in animal models. Frontiers in Endocrinology. 2023;**14**:1202275. [cited 2024 Jun 12]. Available from:. DOI: 10.3389/fendo.2023.1202275

[6] The lancet: Dramatic declines in global fertility rates set to transform global population patterns by 2100. Institute for Health Metrics and Evaluation 2024. [cited 2024 Jun 12]. Available from: https://www.healthdata.org/news-events/newsroom/news-releases/lancet-dramatic-declines-global-fertility-rates-set-transform

[7] Rolle-Berg R, Vander LK. Strengthening devotion: A classic grounded theory on acceptance, adaptability, and reclaiming self, by parents of children with autism spectrum disorders. Grounded Theory Review. 2020;**19**(1):6-29. [cited 2024 Jun 12]. Available from: https://groundedtheoryreview.com/pdf-archives/

[8] Rolle-Whatley R, Vander Linden K. Transforming loyalty: A classic grounded theory on growth of self-acceptance through active parenting. Grounded Theory Review. 2022;**20**(1):88-104. [cited 2024 Jun 12]. Available from: https://groundedtheoryreview.com/pdf-archives/

[9] Rolle-Whatley R, Rolle-Berg R. Purifying Humility: A Classic Grounded Theory of "Doing Good" in 21st Century America

[10] Hammond C. The primary purpose of parenting. Psych Central. 2016. [cited 2024 Jun 12]. Available from: https://psychcentral.com/pro/exhausted-woman/2016/08/the-primary-purpose-of-parenting

[11] Nathaniel A. When and how to use extant literature in classic grounded theory. American Journal of Qualitative Research. 2022;**6**(3):45-59

[12] Glaser BG, Strauss AL. The Discovery of Grounded Theory: Strategies for Qualitative Research. New Brunswick, NJ: Aldine Transaction; 1967. 271 p

[13] Glaser BG, Holton JA. Remodeling grounded theory. Forum, Qualitative Social Research / Forum, Qualitative Sozialforschung. 2004;**5**(2):1-18. [cited 2013 Jan 8]. Available from: http://www.

qualitative-research.net/index.php/fqs/article/view/607/1315

[14] Duhem P. The Aim and Structure of Physical Theory. Princeton, NJ: Princeton University Press; 1991. (original work published in 1954). [cited 2024 Jun 15]. 344 p. Available from: https://press.princeton.edu/books/paperback/9780691025247/the-aim-and-structure-of-physical-theory

[15] Quine WVO. Main trends in recent philosophy: The two dogmas of empiricism. Philosophical Review. 1951;**60**(1):20-43. DOI: 10.2307/2181906

[16] Glaser BG. All is data. Grounded Theory Review. 2007;**6**(2):1-22. [cited 2024 Jun 18]. Available from: https://groundedtheoryreview.com/2007/03/30/1194/

[17] Oh AKL. Theory of flowing: Going with the flow of the ups-and-downs of recovering from an ordeal. Grounded Theory Review. 2022;**21**(2):69-84. [cited 2024 Jun 13]. Available from: https://groundedtheoryreview.com/2022/12/31/theory-of-flowing-going-with-the-flow-of-the-ups-and-downs-of-recovering-from-an-ordeal/

[18] Vaid BS. Ontology and the nature of being. In: EDUC 867. [cited 2024 Jun 13]. Available from: https://www.sfu.ca/educ867/htm/ontology.htm

[19] Watson RA. Rene Descartes French Mathematician and Philosopher. 2024. [cited 2024 Jun 14]. Available from: https://www.britannica.com/biography/Rene-Descartes

[20] Birks M, Hoare K, Mills J. Grounded theory: The FAQs. International Journal of Qualitative Methods. 2019;**18**:160940691988253. [cited 2020 Dec 15]. DOI: 10.1177/1609406919882535

[21] Nathaniel A. Classic grounded theory: What it is and what it is not. Grounded Theory Review. 2022;**20**(1):1-7. [cited 2024 Jun 12]. Available from: https://groundedtheoryreview.com/pdf-archives/

[22] Glaser BG. Generating formal theory. In: Martin VB, Gynnild A, editors. Grounded Theory: The Philosophy, Method, and Work of Barney Glaser. Illustrated edition. Boca Raton: Brown Walker Press; 2011. pp. 257-276

[23] Butler CR, O'Hare AM, Kestenbaum BR, Sayre GG, SPY W. An introduction to qualitative inquiry. Journal of the American Society of Nephrology JASN. 2021;**32**(6):1275-1278. [cited 2024 Jun 13]. Available from:. DOI: 10.1681/ASN.2021040473

[24] About NVivo. In: NVIVO. [cited 2024 Jul 11]. Available from: https://help-nv.qsrinternational.com/14/win/Content/about-nvivo/about-nvivo.htm

[25] Elias M. 51 autism statistics: How many people have autism? In: Discovery ABA Therapy. 2023. [cited 2024 Jul 10]. Available from: https://www.discoveryaba.com/statistics/how-many-people-have-autism

[26] Baumrind D. Rearing competent children. In: Damon W, editor. Child Development Today and Tomorrow. 1st ed. San Francisco: Jossey-Bass; 1988. pp. 349-378

[27] Maccoby EE, Martin JA. Socialization in the context of the family: Parent-child interaction. In: Mussen PH, Hetherington EM, editors. Handbook of Child Psychology: Vol 4. 4th ed. New York: Wiley; 1983. pp. 1-101

[28] Kuppens S, Ceulemans E. Parenting styles: A closer look at a well-known concept. Journal of Child and

Family Studies. 2019;**28**(1):168-181. [cited 2024 May 10]. DOI: 10.1007/s10826-018-1242-x

[29] Kil H, Antonacci R, Shukla S, De Luca A. Correction to: Mindfulness and parenting: A meta-analysis and an exploratory meta-mediation. Mindfulness. 2021;**12**(11):2839-2839. [cited 2024 Jun 12]. DOI: 10.1007/s12671-021-01755-w

[30] Singh N, Lancioni G, Medvedev O, Hwang YS, Myers R, Townshend K. Using mindfulness to improve quality of life in caregivers of individuals with intellectual disabilities and autism spectrum disorder. International Journal of Developmental Disabilities. 2020;**66**(5):370-380. Available from:. DOI: 10.1080/20473869.2020.1827211

[31] Wilson EO. Consilience: The Unity of Knowledge. Reprint edition. New York: Vintage; 1999. 384 p

[32] Glaser BG. Theoretical Sensitivity: Advances in the Methodology of Grounded Theory. 1st ed. Mill Valley, CA: The Sociology Press; 1978. 164 p

[33] Gunaratana BH. Eight Mindful Steps to Happiness: Walking the Buddha's Path. Somerville, MA: Wisdom Publications; 2001. 290 p

[34] Mountain M. How I gave my son autism. In: The Thinking Moms' Revolution. 2014. [cited 2024 Jul 11]. Available from: https://thinkingmomsrevolution.com/how-i-gave-my-son-autism/

[35] Hughes R. Running with Walker: A Memoir. 2nd ed. London, England: Jessica Kingsley; 2003. 236 p

[36] Rolle-Berg R. Strengthening devotion: A classic grounded theory on acceptance, adaptability, and reclaiming self, for parents of children with autism spectrum disorders (thesis). [Available from ProQuest Dissertations and Theses database. (UMI No. 3628300)]. Saybrook University; 2014

[37] Rolle-Whatley R. Transforming loyalty: A classic grounded theory in growth in self-awareness, detachment, and presence through parenting. (thesis). [Available from ProQuest Dissertations and Theses database. (UMI No. 3628300)]. Saybrook University; 2014

[38] Participant 72020. Interview: Doing Good in 21st century America. 2020

[39] Brunson A, Borlase C. God's Hostage: A True Story of Persecution, Imprisonment, and Perseverance. Grand Rapids, Michigan: Baker Books; 2019. 256 p

[40] Participant 012020. Doing Good in 21st century America. 2020

[41] Taylor BB. Leaving Church: A Memoir of Faith. New York, NY: HarperOne; 2009. 277 p

[42] Jerman I, Leskovar R, Krašovec R. Evidence for biofield. In: Žerovnik E, Markič O, Ule A, editors. Philosophical Insights about Modern Science. Ljubljana, Slovenia: Nova Science Publishers, Inc.; 2009. pp. 197-214. Available from: https://www.researchgate.net/publication/305469096_EVIDENCES_FOR_BIOFIELD

[43] Kafatos MC, Chevalier G, Chopra D, Hubacher J, Kak S, Theise ND. Biofield science: Current physics perspectives. Global Advances in Integrative Medicine and Health. 2015;**4**(suppl):25-34. [cited 2015 Nov 22]. DOI: 10.7453/gahmj.2015.011.suppl

[44] Sheldrake R. The Presence of the Past: Morphic Resonance and the

Memory of Nature. 4th ed. Rochester, Vermont: Park Street Press; 2012. 479 p

[45] McCraty R. Science of the Heart: Exploring the Role of the Heart in Human Performance. Vol. 2. Boulder Creek, CA: HeartMath Institute; 2015. 118 p

[46] Singh NN, Lancioni GE, Winton ASW, Wahler RG, Singh J, Sage M. Mindful caregiving increases happiness among individuals with profound multiple disabilities. Research in Developmental Disabilities. 2004;**25**(2):207-218. [cited 2014 May 12]. DOI: 10.1016/j.ridd.2003.05.001

[47] Singh N, Lancioni GE, Winton ASW, Fisher BC, Wahler RG, Mcaleavey K, et al. Mindful parenting decreases aggression, noncompliance, and self-injury in children with autism. Journal of Emotional and Behavioral Disorders. 2006;**14**(3):169-177. [cited 2012 Aug 25]. Available from: http://ebx.sagepub.com/content/14/3/169.short

[48] Singh NN, Lancioni GE, Hwang YS, Myers RE, Townshend K, Medvedev ON. Using mindfulness to improve quality of life in caregivers of individuals with intellectual disabilities and autism spectrum disorder: Agency outcomes for caregivers and clients. Advances in Neurodevelopmental Disorders. 2023;**7**(4):604-615. [cited 2024 Jun 12]. Available from:. DOI: 10.1007/s41252-023-00353-2

[49] McCraty R. Cardiac coherence, self-regulation, autonomic stability and psychosocial well-being. CHI. 2020. [cited 2020 Aug 28]. Available from: https://www.chi.is/resource/cardiac-coherence-self-regulation-autonomic-stability-psychosocial-well/

[50] Alegría-Torres JA, Baccarelli A, Bollati V. Epigenetics and lifestyle. Epigenomics. 2011;**3**(3):267-277. [cited 2024 Aug 2]. DOI: 10.2217/epi.11.22

[51] Jain S, Kelly A. Healing Ourselves: Biofield Science and the Future of Health. Boulder, CO: Sounds True; 2021. p. 320

[52] Sheldrake R. Morphic resonance and Morphic fields—An introduction. In: Rupert Sheldrake—Author and Biologist. [cited 2024 May 12]. Available from: https://www.sheldrake.org/research/morphic-resonance/introduction

[53] Sheldrake R. Morphic Resonance: The Nature of Formative Causation. 4th ed. Rochester, Vermont: Park Street Press; 2009. 423 p

[54] Sheldrake R. Can morphic fields help explain telepathy and the sense of being stared at? Mind. 2010;**II**(1):26-33. Available from: www.parapsych.org

[55] Gare A. Chreods, homeorhesis and biofields: Finding the right path for science through Daoism. Progress in Biophysics and Molecular Biology. 2017;**131**:61-91. [cited 2024 Jul 17]. Available from:. DOI: 10.1016/j.pbiomolbio.2017.08.010

[56] Buchheit C. Chreodes, Entelechy and Human Potentiality. nlpmarin. [cited 2024 Jun 7]. Available from: https://nlpmarin.com/chreodes-entelechy-and-human-potentiality/

Chapter 4

Parenting Styles and Competencies: Their Influence on Children's Development

Jael Vargas-Rubilar, María Cristina Richaud and Viviana Noemí Lemos

Abstract

This chapter will describe parental styles and competencies and introduce those designed or adapted tests in Argentina to evaluate these constructs. It will include theoretical development and empirical results on how parental styles and competencies influence children's socio-emotional and cognitive development, specifically in prosociality, empathy, coping, aggression, depression, executive functions, etc. It will also examine how parental skills act as moderators or protective factors in crises, such as the COVID-19 pandemic. In addition, it will include findings on how parenting styles and competencies are affected depending on socioeconomic status. Finally, general guidelines will be introduced to design intervention programs promoting higher positive parenting, eventually enabling better children's development.

Keywords: parenting, development, children, adolescent, parents

1. Introduction

Parenting refers to the attitudes, styles, practices, and knowledge parents assume concerning the care, health, and chances to stimulate their children's learning [1]. Parenting is a construct that may enclose a wide range of parental attitudes and behaviors regarding their children's socialization.

Baumrind [2] performed the first studies on parenting styles and developed a typology based on the control parents exercised over their children or parental demandingness and the degree to which parents respond to their children's needs or responsiveness. By combining these two dimensions, Baumrind [2] classified parenting styles into authoritarian (high demandingness and low responsiveness), permissive (low demandingness and high responsiveness), and authoritative (moderate demandingness and moderate responsiveness). This first classification later included a fourth style named uninvolved or neglectful parenting, characterized by a lack of responsiveness and demandingness [3].

Darling and Steinberg [4, 5] assert that the variability in the effects of parenting style depends on the child's cultural background, the processes through which parenting style influences the child's development, and the operationalization of parenting style. They also claim that parenting style better appears as a context that mediates the influence of specific parenting practices on the child.

Given the importance of analyzing parenting styles as children perceive them, it is essential to have precise, valid, and reliable assessment instruments. From a cognitive perspective, it implies that children's perception of their parents' behavior will be more related to their behavior adaptation than to the 'real' behavior of the parents [6].

The first instruments to study children's perception of their relationship with their parents [6–8] involved boys and girls over 12 years of age and from a specific culture. Since it seems that interactional patterns develop significantly early in childhood [9, 10], it is required to have tests to establish the relationship styles perceived by children at younger ages and in other cultural contexts.

In this sense, in Argentina, we have developed or adapted questionnaires about children's perception of the relationship with their parents for 4–6-year-olds, 8–12-year-olds, and adolescents.

We took the model proposed by Schaefer [6] on this topic as a basis, but we formulated a simplified version since we worked with young children. The children's perception of their relationships with their parents—4–6 years old version [10] comprised 26 items that no longer included all the subdimensions proposed by Schaefer but the most relevant dimensions, namely Acceptance versus Rejection, Psychological Autonomy versus Psychological Control, and Lax Discipline versus Firm Discipline. The resulting versions for mother and father showed acceptable reliability, considering the number of items and for dealing with children whose responses were more variable than those of adults. When studying the validity of the test, in general, the factorial structure of both versions was clear, establishing dimensions with a theoretical psychological meaning and with differences for fathers and mothers, which provides the inventory construct validity [11]. The questionnaire mainly estimated the topics: acceptance, control, and rejection of the mother and father. Results showed that control and possessiveness became characteristics of the mother while coercion and disinterest of the father.

The Argentine Scale of Perception of Relationships with Parents for Children Aged 8–12 [12] consists of 32 items. As a result of the analysis of the structure underlying the parents' behaviors as perceived by their children, it came across that there are three main types of relationships: acceptance vs. strict control, pathological control, and Extreme Autonomy or permissiveness. Cronbach's alphas also showed acceptable values. We understand that this inventory provides information about types of relationships. When examined together, it allows us to define parental behavior styles that family socialization theories propose as partly descriptive when imparting social patterns, the development of secure attachment, and coping with conflict.

Children Report of Parental Behavior (CRPBI) [6] was adapted to Argentine adolescents [13], resulting in a scale of 72 items distributed concerning the mother in five factors: Acceptance, Autonomy vs. Control, Possessiveness and Intrusiveness, Control vs. Extreme Autonomy, and Reinforcement. Concerning the father, four factors resulted: Acceptance, Possessiveness, Extreme Autonomy, and Intrusiveness. Based on this latest version, a new inventory of 32 items was constructed [14], which is more adaptable to collective administrations in school requirements. Both the forms for the mother and the father provided information about three factors: Acceptance, Pathological Control, and Extreme Autonomy.

This new abbreviated version has revealed adequate criterion validity when used to assess the relationship between perceived parenting styles and coping in adolescents. Likewise, despite considering fewer items, reliability and internal consistency were satisfactory.

Furthermore, the study of parental skills has become more relevant in the last two decades [15, 16]. Parenting competencies refer to those parental skills regarding their children's education, care, and socialization [17]. In turn, Bronfenbrenner and Evans [18] described parenting capacity as the proven acquisition and subsequent development of knowledge and abilities to drive parental behavior through different parenting circumstances in various areas of development (i.e., socioemotional, physical, and cognitive).

Although being considered from various theoretical approaches, most converge on four main aspects: (a) the importance of sensitivity and affection toward the basic needs of children depending on the different stages of development [15, 19], (b) coercive, rejecting and inconsistent parenting has harmful effects on the socio-emotional and cognitive development of children [15, 20], (c) although involvement is relevant for parenting, it is not sufficient in itself to guarantee positive parenting [17, 21], and (d) the relevance of respectful parenting as a basis for ensuring the rights and best interests of children [22, 23].

Regarding its assessment, some instruments have been developed or adapted for the Spanish-speaking population. For instance, in Chile, Gómez et al. [15] developed the positive parenting scale (E2P) to measure four parenting competencies from the perspective of parents or caregivers of infants, children, and adolescents. These authors proposed four areas to assess parenting abilities: (a) bonding parental competencies, namely, the ability to provide a secure attachment, understand and respond appropriately to their children's emotional needs, and get involved in their children's daily lives, (b) formative competencies, which refer to the ability to stimulate learning, progressive autonomy, and children's self-regulation, through children's socialization, (c) protective parental competencies, aimed at safeguarding children's multidimensional development, guaranteeing their rights and organizing their daily routine and, finally, and (d) reflective competencies that encourage the anticipation and monitoring of conflicts in parenting and allow reflection on the influence of parents own parenting history in their current practices. Vargas Rubilar et al. [23] validated this instrument for Argentina and suggested a brief version for parents or caregivers of school going children. Likewise, Azar et al. [24] adapted and validated the Perceived Parental Competence Scale (ECPP-p) [25] for Argentine parents of children aged 9–12 years. Both adapted instruments showed good psychometric performance in the Argentine population.

Furthermore, two brief instruments to measure parenting skills from the children's perspective were recently adapted and validated in the Argentine population. Waigel et al. [26] adapted a scale to assess the perception of parental skills in Argentine adolescents. This scale assesses three dimensions in the mother version: bonding, formative, and protective skills, and two dimensions in the father one: bonding and formative-protective skills. Likewise, Vargas Rubilar et al. [27] adapted a scale to analyze the perception of parental skills in children aged 9–12 years. This instrument assesses three dimensions: bonding skills, formative-protective skills, and parental rejection. Both scales allow for the evaluation of the perception of parental skills of both parents. This aspect is significant given that fathers and mothers exercise differentiated parenting through different roles, styles, practices, and abilities [28, 29]. Hence, the importance of separately evaluating the perception of maternal and paternal parenting [12, 26, 29] and analyzing its effect on the psychosocial development of children differentially.

In summary, the development and validation of self-report scales for parents and children has favored improvements in the study of this important construct.

The validation of these instruments will also promote the study of the effect of parental styles and skills on children's socio-emotional and cognitive development.

2. Influence of parental styles and parental competencies in children's socioemotional and cognitive development

2.1 Relationship between parental styles and attachment related to with loneliness and depression in children

In a study about the relationship between loneliness and depression in middle and late childhood with attachment and parental styles [30], the interpersonal relationship styles with parents came to explain significantly the development of the attachment style. However, the unexplained variance allows us to presume that constructs attachment and parenting styles, as perceived by their children, are nearly related but even different. As already noticed in a previous study [31], a relationship based on acceptance appeared to facilitate adjustment, while a bad relationship, mainly if characterized by distancing, is connected to non-adjusted behavior, such as inhibition. This study leads us to assume that acceptance by mother and father is positively related to the development of a secure attachment. It is worth noting that although all researchers emphasize the mother's influence on the shape of the attachment system, it would seem that in middle and late childhood, the father gains more relevance in the system, mainly and negatively, through carelessness and negligence [30]. It is worth noting the importance of the kind of relationship established with the father in the development of feelings of depression among children. According to Harter and Nowakowsky [32], those feelings become the counterpart of feelings of security constituent of positive attachment. In the former case, the children's perception of indifference on the father's part is the most influential factor.

At the same time, children who perceive that their parents accept them, respect their opinions, and feel proud of them would not feel depressed. According to parental styles, parents' acceptance and commitment, especially the father, are essential for children's scholarly achievement [30].

A relevant difference is that in the study of the influence of attachment on competence, there is no counterpart connected to the negative weight of the father's style of relationship Extreme Autonomy [30]. From the attachment style, it would probably correspond to a lack of father availability. However, it seems that availability is more connected to a feeling of being able to depend emotionally on an attachment figure. In turn, Extreme Autonomy would relate to perceiving a behavior of negligence or lack of interest. As to perceived social acceptance (social self-competence), mother availability becomes most important, with no perception of father's influence as it occurs in the analysis of relationship styles. In the case of the latter, the father's pathological control becomes quite relevant, as it seems to inhibit the child's perception of social acceptance, for threats of punishment and expressions of concern about the children's inadequate performance make them feel rejected by others. As far as loneliness is concerned, lack of a secure attachment accounts for feelings of loneliness in children more than the style of relationship with parents. The model that explains the development of social competence among children may be the same in connection to loneliness [30].

The feeling of loneliness referring to parents depends on children's perception of parents' acceptance and trust in their love. In general, it seems that the use of coercive discipline to control children and turn them submissive would favor social isolation [33]. However, full autonomy with poor parental monitoring of children's activities was associated with antisocial behavior [34]. Indulgently raised children who may enjoy benefits in the domain of psychosocial development demonstrate higher rates of deviance [35].

Concerning gender, we may remark that within a general, familiar pattern, like the influence of the system of attachment and parent/child parenting styles, girls tend to perceive positive characteristics in the father and negative ones in the mother, while being the opposite for boys. This aspect coincides with the patterns of Latin culture, where the father is more permissive, understanding, and protective toward girls and more demanding and harsher with boys. The mother is more considerate and permissive with boys and more challenging and controlling with girls [33].

2.2 Parental styles, practices, and empathy

The study examining the role of parental styles, practices, and empathy in shaping specific prosocial behaviors in children [36] highlights that these factors influence and motivate prosocial behavior in distinct ways. Regarding altruism—characterized as the sole intrinsically motivated prosocial behavior—an inverse relationship was observed with parental practices specifically designed to promote it. As anticipated, children's altruism appears to arise without requiring external motivation and attempts to stimulate it externally may undermine its development. Maternal acceptance emerged as the sole predictive parental style, while children's perception of paternal empathic concern was identified as the only significant predictive dimension of perceived parental empathy [36].

The second key finding was the association between maternal pathological control and children's public prosocial behavior, with parental styles outperforming parental practices in accounting for variance in this behavior. Parental empathy contributed to the explained variance but to a lesser extent compared to parental styles and practices [36].

Regarding anonymous prosocial behavior, the only significant predictors were parental practices, particularly the mother's use of learning experiences and material rewards. This type of prosocial behavior, characterized as the least clear and least explained by parental styles, practices, and empathy, differs from altruism. Although they may appear similar, anonymous prosocial behavior is extrinsically motivated, driven by the expectation of receiving a material reward [36].

In summary, prosocial behavior encompasses various motivations that are influenced by distinct parental factors, including parenting style, parental practices, and parental empathy. Altruism stands out as the only intrinsically motivated prosocial behavior, negatively impacted by parental practices while positively associated with parental acceptance and empathic concern. In contrast, all other forms of prosocial behavior are extrinsically motivated, with their development shaped to varying degrees by these parental variables [36].

2.3 Types of parents modeling and children prosocial behavior

Bandura [37] argues that when children experience models of some behavior, such as prosocial behavior, they will probably imitate those actions (especially if children admire the model or feel closely identified with it). Therefore, one would expect that parents who model and encourage prosocial behaviors might promote the latter in their children.

There are two different kinds of modeling. One is based on intentional behaviors to encourage prosocial behaviors in children. This parental practice is called observational learning. The other one is the continuous and unintentional behavior that occurs every day incidentally; the latter is named direct modeling [38, 39].

Previous research has revealed that the relations between parenting practices and prosocial behaviors varied as a function of the specific parenting practice and the specific prosocial behavior [36, 40].

Furthermore, Richaud and Mesurado [39] underlined the significant role of parents explicitly modeling prosocial behaviors. It becomes relevant that altruistic behavior was not significantly related to any parenting practice, but in all cases, it depended on the perception of children of parenting altruistic prosocial behavior. As in the case of altruism, the direct modeling of public prosocial behavior by parents is crucial for children to develop public prosocial behavior. Indeed, this study offered evidence of the vital importance of direct modeling for prosocial behavior; this would suggest that this behavior is principally rooted in the children's perception of the kind of relationships that parents develop with them and others. Finally, it would suggest the existence of different kinds of prosocial behaviors and how concrete parental actions influence them.

2.4 Parental styles and skills related to preschoolers, children, and adolescents coping and cognitive and socioemotional development

Richaud [41, 42] found that authoritative families promote adaptive coping with threats and defend children from depression and loneliness. In contrast, rejecting families promotes maladaptive coping, loneliness in front of peers, and depression. On the other hand, authoritarian families imply searching for support from people other than themselves, which leads to apparent insecurity when facing threats since those children do not take action on the problems. Regarding the feelings associated with maladaptive coping, depression and affinity for solitude in children appear mainly associated with rejection and lack of interest from parents. In turn, aversion to solitude is primarily related to normal and pathological control [41].

During adolescence, threat perception, centered around events that characterize this developmental stage, becomes uncontrolled, though with some concern connected to the immediate environment. This aspect would emphasize the hypothesis of stress as a transactional process but also as a period when styles of attribution develop based on traits related to temperament, personality, and stage of maturation, as well as the development of resources through interpersonal experiences. Although receptive to events in the environment, this style of attribution provides a definite and distinct mark [41].

Regarding coping styles in typical adolescents, adaptive strategies seem to lead, including cognitive restructuring, acting on the actual problem, and looking for emotional support [41]. The most remarkable characteristic seen in this study was coping with anxiety or concern for the major concerns of the human race or its future as a way of gradually solving the challenges imposed by adolescence.

Processes guiding to maturity run parallel to an increase in problem-focusing and, as a gender-related characteristic, females go in for emotions-centered coping, while males evade them through action [41].

Finally, the interpersonal relationships with significant others, parents, and peers demonstrated a relevant influence on the development of coping strategies in adolescents, adopting their characteristics when considering the sex and age of the adolescents and their father's gender. However, generally, although the father's acceptance has more influence on older adolescents and males, and the mother's has it on younger adolescents and females, the perception of being loved and valued, both by parents and peers, favors the development of functional coping strategies [41]. The latter does not occur in the case already discussed, in which peer acceptance has a negative connotation in the sense of unconditional and disproportionate acceptance. Furthermore, pathological control by significant figures is related to maladaptive or dysfunctional strategies for dealing with conflict, especially emotional dependence, self-blame, and paralysis. Finally, the perception of negligence on the part of both parents leads mainly to strategies of evasion of problems and lack of responsibility [41].

Parenting skills enable raising, protecting, accompanying, and stimulating positive results in children's development [16]. Thus, they become essential to ensure the psychosocial well-being of children and adolescents [43].

Although there are some recent studies on the influence of parental skills on children's development, this aspect is still emerging in Argentina; for instance, Azar et al. [44] found that parenting abilities significantly influence executive functions and reading and dangerousness. Results mainly showed a substantial difference in executive functions between children with a higher degree of parenting skills (i.e., shared leisure time and the adequate assumption of the role of parents) and those with a lower one. We regarded that shared leisure time and the adequate assumption of the role of parents positively influence children's executive functions. These findings suggested that the perception of parental competence favors effectiveness in children's cognitive performance. Likewise, there is evidence that executive functions mediated the relationship between parental competencies and children's reading and mathematics skills [44].

Regarding the effect of parental skills on socio-emotional development, an Argentine study [45] analyzed the influence of parental bonding skills on calmness and social skills in preschoolers. The results showed that the relevant differences in the latter skills were higher in the children who reported more bonding parenting skills [45].

Furthermore, Waigel et al. [26] found that perceived parenting skills were positively associated with all dimensions of adolescent development. In particular, there was a high association between bonding skills, both maternal and paternal, and the pillars of positive relationships and emotions and achievement. These results confirmed that bonding skills favor socio-emotional connection with children, in line with what the positive parenting approach indicates [46]. Similarly, parental formative-protective competencies were associated with positive relationships and engagement of adolescents. These findings prove that positive parenting is associated with adolescents' well-being, flourishing, and psychosocial adjustment, as suggested by previous international studies [26, 47].

3. Parental competencies in the context of COVID-19 pandemic

Crises, such as the global pandemic due to the COVID-19 outbreak, certainly impact the general family dynamic and their members in a particular way. Specifically, in Argentina, the measures taken by the government to prevent infections and mitigate the spread of the virus involved mandatory social isolation from the end of March to December 2020. The consequences of these measures involved many challenges related to parenting, such as difficulties in accessing health services and prenatal care for pregnant women [48], home education, given the closure of schools [49, 50], the loss of social support from close family and friends [48, 49, 51, 52], the lack of external help with household chores due to the impossibility of having housekeepers, as well as changes in work routines [53]. Thus, many parents felt anxious, overloaded, and stressed [50, 54–56].

According to a report by UNICEF [57], the pandemic appears to have had a more negative impact, especially on maternal upbringing, because mothers bore a higher burden of unpaid work and the demands of multitasking concerning their jobs, housework, and childcare, especially in Latin American cultures [54]. In this context, in a study that we carried out in Argentina, we evaluated 646 mothers with school-age children. We examined the perception that they had about three dimensions of parenting (positive parenting, parental stress, and school support) in times of pandemic, the perception of behavioral changes (e.g., in sleep, appetite, mood, obedience, fighting with siblings, participation and attitude toward online classes, etc.) that they perceived in their children since the pandemic, analyzing How the different dimensions of parenting influenced the perception of their children's behavioral changes [53].

Based on the results obtained, we observed that the dimensions of parenting influenced the perceived behavior of children. Mothers with a low level of positive parenting perceived that their children shouted, fought more with their siblings, were more anxious and disobedient, and displayed more defiant and dependent behaviors. Mothers with higher parenting stress perceived more negative changes in almost all behaviors evaluated. Additionally, they also observed more internalizing behaviors in their children, such as higher sadness and regressive behaviors, compared to less stressed mothers. Mothers who reported providing more school support to their children perceived that their children adapted better to online classes, consistently completed their homework, enjoyed their classes, and were less frustrated when doing schoolwork at home.

The results strengthen the idea suggested in the literature about how positive parenting can function as a protective factor against stressful events [58] and as a facilitator of family resilience [59]. Parents' beliefs, thoughts, and expectations about their children and their role in parenting are critical in family interactions, directly affecting children's behavior [60]. The reciprocal nature of these interactions means that parents may also feel influenced by their children's attitudes and behaviors [61]. For instance, children who are more irritable or have sleep or behavior difficulties tend to get more negative responses from their parents [62]. Considering the reciprocal effect of child behavior on parental stress perceptions, we also examined this aspect among mothers who reported changes in their children's behaviors during the pandemic and those who did not. In 10 of the 12 behaviors assessed (e.g., sleep problems, sibling conflicts, challenging behavior, and dependent behavior), significant differences in parental stress were found, being higher in mothers who perceived changes in their children's behavior [53]. Thus, the development of stressors negatively impacts parental behavior, eventually increasing irritability and behavioral problems in children, yielding more negative responses from parents [62].

Some studies, consistent with the already mentioned report by UNICEF [57], indicated that, during the pandemic, mothers reported assuming greater responsibility for childcare and household chores [54], experiencing more symptoms of anxiety and burnout, along with higher worries and fears related to parenting compared to fathers [63]. Thus, in the context of the previous study [28], we compared a sample of 70 mothers and 50 fathers to evaluate possible differences in the perception of behavioral changes in their children and the different aspects of their parenting during the COVID-19 pandemic. The results indicated that, in all the behaviors evaluated, mothers perceived more prevalent changes in their children than fathers, mainly differences in behaviors: higher anxiety/nervousness, screams, and nightmares.

Furthermore, regarding possible differences in the perception of their parenting, mothers reported a more positive one. However, they experienced higher parental stress and felt they should offer more school support than fathers [28].

In summary, crises, such as the global pandemic due to COVID-19, negatively impact children at a behavioral and emotional level and on the upbringing and parents' experiences. However, this impact became positively modulated by protective factors such as positive parenting and school support. Similarly, the differences between parents demonstrate characteristics in families' ordinary conditions, which are determined by preexisting social patterns, especially gender differences observed in various cultures, according to the studies reviewed.

These findings reveal the challenges families, especially mothers, faced during the critical period of compulsory social isolation and emphasize the importance of addressing gender differences in the family environment that imply a reorganization of parental burdens and responsibilities.

4. Parental styles and competencies and social status

Studies on parenting styles in the context of social vulnerability emphasize the importance of considering economic, cultural, and social factors [64, 65]. Some studies [64–67] suggest that parents from different social strata adopt distinct parenting styles influenced by environmental conditions, culture, the parents' personal characteristics, and the interaction styles of each social and family group. Differences in education, occupation, and financial status collectively contribute to these socioeconomic status (SES)-related variations, with education playing the most significant role in shaping the parents' characteristics and circumstances [66].

Parents in conditions of social vulnerability face difficulties that can affect their parenting styles and skills in addition to disadvantaged economic conditions, such as insecurity or limited access to services. The latter can lead to a weakening of essential parenting functions. A study in Argentina [68] found that parents at higher psychosocial risk used punitive and neglectful practices, justifying strict control due to the dangerousness of their environment. However, children perceived this style as inconsistent and careless despite the parents' intention to protect them.

A study conducted in Argentina [69] found significant differences in the perception of parental skills based on the families' social status. Parents or caregivers from middle social status described themselves as more involved in the educational process of their children and dedicated more time to guiding and caring for their children. They also reported sharing more recreational moments with their children and assuming a more active parental role in raising them. In contrast, parents or caregivers from lower social status perceived themselves as less competent regarding school participation, dedication, shared games, and assuming their parental role [67].

5. Intervention proposal and implications

In the past, parenting was considered an autonomous and private practice that parents learned through intergenerational processes of culture and society. Due to social changes that have impacted family realities, parenting nowadays is a complex task that requires professional training and support [70].

In this sense, parenting support and strengthening programs promote positive and nurturing bonds between parents and children [71]. These initiatives provide unique social support to foster positive parenting in different relevant areas of child development. These programs offer a context that increases the chances of parents or caregivers improving their parenting skills of sensitivity, self-regulation, self-efficacy, and personal agency, among other skills that favor problem-solving and more responsive and respectful parenting [71, 72]. Such interventions aimed at parents or caregivers are carried out, especially in low- and middle-income countries, to support parents in caregiving roles [73].

To date, interventions based on social learning theory, the cognitive-behavioral approach, and positive parenting principles have shown greater effectiveness [65, 70, 71]. These evidence-based programs are usually structured in sessions and propose homework tasks to strengthen parental and family resources [71].

The advances in Argentine research presented here suggest the relevance of positive parenting (i.e., parenting styles and competencies) for the adequate emotional, social, and cognitive development of children and adolescents. Consequently, the importance of designing, implementing, and evaluating parenting-strengthening programs is highlighted, especially in socially vulnerable contexts [65]. These approaches should rely on evidence and sound theoretical approaches to ensure effectiveness [16]. Likewise, the findings of studies carried out in the pandemic context [28, 53] highlight the need to develop family intervention programs to mitigate the adverse psychosocial effects of the COVID-19 pandemic and other similar crises.

6. Conclusions

This chapter emphasizes the fundamental importance of parenting styles and competencies for the optimal holistic development of children and adolescents. As discussed, effective parenting practices characterized by acceptance, positive regulation, and empathy foster socioemotional and cognitive development, whereas negative styles, such as pathological control or neglect, are associated with adverse effects on psychosocial adjustment.

The chapter also explores various parenting typologies and competencies, highlighting their role in promoting prosocial and adaptive behaviors in children. Additionally, the validation of instruments to assess these aspects in Argentina provides empirical support that enriches the study of parenting within specific cultural contexts.

In the context of the COVID-19 pandemic, positive parenting and school support emerged as key factors in mitigating the negative impacts on children's behavior and mental health, underscoring the importance of fostering sensitive and adaptive parenting practices, particularly during crises.

The practical implications of these findings highlight the need to develop and implement parenting-strengthening programs that not only address basic competencies but also include specific approaches for stress management and adaptation to adverse situations. In socially vulnerable contexts, where positive parenting may be compromised by economic and social conditions, such programs should incorporate resource and training support, taking into account the contextual barriers faced by these families.

It is particularly important that these programs adopt a gender-inclusive perspective, promoting equitable distribution of parenting responsibilities between mothers and fathers. This approach can address tensions arising from traditional gender roles, which, as demonstrated during the pandemic, often disproportionately burden mothers with caregiving and school support responsibilities.

For future research, it is recommended to delve deeper into the relationship between specific parenting competencies and their impact on children's psychosocial adaptation across different cultural contexts. Further exploration of the dynamics between parenting styles and the development of resilience in children, particularly during crises, is suggested. Additionally, evaluating how positive parenting-based interventions can strengthen resilience in children presents a promising avenue.

Another area of interest involves studying gendered perceptions of parenting in Latin American contexts, where traditional roles for mothers and fathers often persist. Moreover, investigating the long-term effects of parenting competencies on the development of executive functions and academic achievement in childhood and adolescence would enable a longitudinal analysis of how parenting quality influences children's holistic development throughout their lives.

Finally, the evaluation and optimization of interventions that integrate self-regulation methods, cognitive-behavioral approaches, and positive parenting principles represent a significant avenue for future research. These efforts aim to foster more effective parenting practices adapted to the needs of families across diverse social contexts.

Acknowledgements

The authors wish to thank the National Council for Scientific and Technical Research of Argentina (CONICET) and the Adventist University of the Plata.

Author details

Jael Vargas-Rubilar*, María Cristina Richaud and Viviana Noemí Lemos
National Scientific and Technical Research Council (CONICET), Interdisciplinary Center for Health and Behavior Sciences Research (CIICSAC), Adventist University of the Plata, Libertador San Martín, Argentina

*Address all correspondence to: psicojael@gmail.com

References

[1] Eraso J, Bravo DM. Creencias, actitudes y prácticas sobre crianza enmadres cabeza de familia en Popayán: un estudio cualitativo. Pediatria. 2006;**41**(3):23-40

[2] Baumrind D. Effects of authoritative parental control on child behavior. Child Development. 1966;**37**:887-907

[3] Maccoby EE, Martin J. Socialization in the context of the family parent-child interactions. In: Herherington EM, Mussen PH, editors. Handbook of Child Psychology. New York: Wiley; 1983. pp. 1-101

[4] Darling N, Steinberg L. Parenting style as context: An integrative model. Psychological Bulletin. 1993;**113**:487-496

[5] Darling N. Steimberg, parenting style as context: An integrative model. In: Zukauskiene R, editor. Interpersonal Development. London: Routledge; 2007

[6] Schaefer ES. Children's reports of parental behavior: An inventory. Child Development. 1965;**36**:413-424

[7] Parker G, Tupling H, Brown LB. A parental bonding instrument. The British Journal of Medical Psychology. 1979;**52**:1-10

[8] Roe A, Siegelman M. A parent-child relations questionnaire. Child Development. 1963;**34**:355-369

[9] Richaud, De Minzi MC, Sacchi C. Relationship with significant others and loneliness feelings during adolescence. In: VII European Congress of Psychology July 7-12; Roma, Italia. 1999

[10] Richaud de Minzi MC. Inventario acerca de la percepción que tienen los niños y las niñas de las relaciones con sus padres y madres. Versión para 4 a 6 años [Children's perception of their relationships with their parents. 4 to 6 years' version]. Revista Interamericana de Psicología. 2002;**36**(1 y 2):149-165

[11] Cronbach LJ, Meehl PE. Construct validity in psychological tests. Psychological Bulletin. 1955;**52**:281-302

[12] Richaud de Minzi MC. Inventario de Percepción de estilos parentales en niños de 8 a 12 años. Revista Iberoamericana de Diagnostico y Evaluacion Psicologica. 2007;**23**(1):63-81 Available from: http://hdl.handle.net/11336/102478

[13] Klimkiewicz A. Percepción del comportamiento parental en adolescentes: Adaptación argentina del CRPBI [Adolescent perception of parental behavior: Argentine version of CRPBI]. Interdisciplinarity. 1996;**13**(1):67-77

[14] Richaud, de Minzi MC. Versión abreviada del Inventario de la Percepción de los Hijos acerca de las Relaciones con sus Padres para adolescentes. Psicodiagnostico. 2005a;**15**:99-106

[15] Gómez Muzzio E, Yévenes L, Sandoval J. Positive parenting scale: Evidence of validity and reliability in a Chilean sample. Journal of Child and Family Studies. 2022;**31**(12):3372-3384. DOI: 10.1007/s10826-022-02410-1

[16] Richaud MC, Vargas-Rubilar J, Lemos V. Advances in the study of parenting in Argentina. En: Selin H, editor. Parenting across Cultures. Science across Cultures: The History of Non-Western Science, Vol. 12. Springer, Cham; 2022. DOI: 10.1007/978-3-031-15359-4_7.

[17] Barudy J, Dantagnan M. Los desafíos invisibles de ser madre o padre. Gedisa: Manual de evaluación de competencias y resiliencia parental; 2010

[18] Bronfenbrenner U, Evans G. Developmental science in the 21st century: Emerging questions, theoretical models, research designs and empirical findings. Social Development. 2000;**9**(1):115-125. DOI: 0.1111/1467-9507.00114

[19] Liu D, Chen D, Brown BB. Do parenting practices and child disclosure predict parental knowledge? A meta-analysis. Journal of Youth and Adolescence. 2020;**49**(1):1-16. DOI: 10.1007/s10964-019-01154-4

[20] Scharf M, Goldner L. "If you really love me, you will do/be...": Parental psychological control and its implications for children's adjustment. Developmental Review. 2018;**49**:16-30. DOI: 10.1016/j.dr.2018.07.002

[21] Teti DM, Candelaria MA. Parenting competence. In: Bornstein MH, editor. Handbook of Parenting: Social Conditions and Applied Parenting. 2nd ed. New Jersey: Lawrence Erlbaum Associates Publishers; 2002. pp. 149-180

[22] Rodrigo MJ, Máiquez ML, Martín JC, Rodríguez B. La parentalidad positiva desde la prevención y la promoción. Manual práctico de parentalidad positiva. 2015;**2**:25-43. DOI: 10.55414/ap.v34i2-3.601

[23] Vargas-Rubilar J, Lemos VN, Richaud MC. Adaptación y validación argentina de una versión breve de la Escala de Parentalidad Positiva (E2p). Liberabit. 2020;**26**(2):1-17. DOI: 10.24265/liberabit. 2020.v26n2.08

[24] Azar E, Vargas-Rubilar J, Arán-Filippetti V. Adaptación de la escala de competencia parental percibida a una población de padres argentinos. Anuario de Investigaciones. 2019;**25**:393-401

[25] Bayot Mestre B, Hernández Viadel J. Evaluación de la Competencia Parental. Madrid: CEPE; 2008

[26] Waigel N, Vargas Rubilar J, Lemos V. Assessment of perceived parental competencies in argentine adolescents: Two brief scales for its measurement. Revista de Psicología Clínica con Niños y Adolescentes. 2025;**12**:58-67. DOI: 10.21134/rpcna.2025.12.1.3

[27] Vargas Rubilar J, Richaud MC, Figueroa J, Lemos V. Estudio preliminar de una escala de competencias parentales percibidas para niños argentinos. En: XIX Reunión Nacional y VIII Encuentro Internacional de la Asociación Argentina de Ciencias del Comportamiento; 2023; Buenos Aires, Argentina. 2023.

[28] Vargas-Rubilar J, Richaud MC, Balabanian C, Lemos V. Parenting, gender, and perception of changes in Children's behavior during the COVID-19 pandemic. International Journal of Environmental Research and Public Health. 2023;**20**:6452. DOI: 10.3390/ijerph20156452

[29] Yaffe Y. Systematic review of the differences between mothers and fathers in parenting styles and practices. Current Psychology. 2023;**42**(19):16011-16024. DOI: 10.1007/s12144-020-01014-6

[30] Richaud de Minzi MC. Loneliness and depression in middle and late childhood: The relationship to attachment and parental styles. The Journal of Genetic Psychology. 2006a;**167**(2):189-210

[31] Richaud, de Minzi MC, Sacchi C. Relationships in the infancy and coping

resources [summary]. In: Proceedings of XXVI Interamerican Congress of Psychology; July 6-11; San Pablo, Brasil. 1997

[32] Harter S, Nowakowski M. Dimensions of Depression Profile for Children and Adolescents. Denver: University of Denver; 1987

[33] Richaud de Minzi MC. Relationship with significant others and loneliness feelings during adolescence. In: VII European Congress of Psychology. Roma: Italia; 1999

[34] Dishion TJ. The ecology of boys' peer relations in middle school. Child Development. 1990;**61**:874-892

[35] Lamborn SD, Mounts NS, Steinberg L, Dornbusch SM. Patterns of competence and adjustment among adolescents from authoritative, authoritarian, indulgent, and neglectful families. Child Development. 1991;**62**:1049-1065

[36] Richaud de Minzi MC, Mesurado B, Lemos V. Links between perception of parental actions and prosocial behavior in early adolescence. Journal of Child and Family Studies. 2013;**22**(5):637-646. DOI: 10.1007/s10826-012-9617-x

[37] Bandura A. Social Foundations of Thought and Action: A Social Cognitive Theory. Englewood Cliffs, NJ: Prentice Hall; 1986

[38] Richaud MC, Mesurado B, Lemos V. Prosociality: Types, targets, and related and contextual variables in childhood and adolescence. In: Cadena CHG, editor. Research on Hispanic Psychology. New York: Nova Science Publishers; 2018. pp. 211-239

[39] Richaud MC, Mesurado B. Influence of parental practices expectations and modeling in youth prosocial behavior. In: International Congress of Applied Psychology. Melbourne Australia; 11-16 July 2010

[40] Richaud MC, Carlo G, Mesurado B, Fernández C. Links between perception of parental behaviour, social cognitions and prosocial behaviour in early adolescence. In: Biennial Meeting of the Society for Research on Adolescence. Filadelfia, USA; 11-13 March 2010

[41] Richaud de Minzi MC. Estilos parentales y afrontamiento en niños. Revista Latinoamericana de Psicología. 2005b;**37**(1):47-58

[42] Richaud de Minzi MC. Evaluación del afrontamiento en niños de 8 a 12 años. Revista Mexicana de Psicología. 2006b;**23**(2):196-201

[43] Vargas, Rubilar J, Richaud MC. Childhood parenting: Main approaches and aspects analyzed from psychology. In: García C, editor. Research on Hispanic Psychology. Vol. 1. New York: Nova Science Publishers Inc.; 2018. pp. 241-276

[44] Azar E, Vargas Rubilar J, Arán FV. Parental competences and academic competences in school children: The mediator role of executive functions. Revista Colombiana de Psicología. 2023;**32**(1):11-27. DOI: 10.15446/rcp.v32n1.94808

[45] Callaey T, Oros LB. Competencias parentales vinculares: Su incidencia en las habilidades sociales y la serenidad de niños preescolares. Universidad Católica Argentina: Manuscrito no publicado; 2024

[46] Muzzio EG, Yévenes LC, Sandoval JP. Positive parenting scale (E2P): Evidence of validity and reliability in a Chilean sample. Journal of Child and Family Studies. 2022;**31**(12):3372-3384

[47] Chen Y, Haines J, Charlton B, VanderWeele T. Positive parenting improves multiple aspects of health and well-being in young adulthood. Nature Human Behaviour. 2019;**3**(7):684-691. DOI: 10.1038/s41562-019-0602-x

[48] Lebel C, MacKinnon A, Bagshawe M, Tomfohr-Madsen L, Giesbrecht G. Elevated depression and anxiety symptoms among pregnant individuals during the COVID-19 pandemic. Journal of Affective Disorders. 2020;**277**:5-13. DOI: 10.1016/j.jad.2020.07.126

[49] Brom C, Lukavský J, Greger D, Hannemann T, Straková J, Švaříček R. Mandatory home education during the COVID-19 lockdown in the Czech Republic: A rapid survey of 1st-9th grader's parents. Frontiers in Education. 2020;**5**:103. DOI: 10.3389/feduc.2020.00103

[50] RoosLE, SalisburyM, Penner-GoekeL, Cameron EE, Protudjer JLP, Giuliano R, et al. Supporting families to protect child health: Parenting quality and household needs during the COVID-19 pandemic. PLoS One. 2021;**16**:e0251720. DOI: 10.1371/journal.pone.0251720

[51] Asbury K, Fox L, Deniz E, Code A, Toseeb U. How is COVID-19 affecting the mental health of children with special educational needs and disabilities and their families? Journal of Autism and Developmental Disorders. 2021;**51**(5):1772-1780

[52] Wu Y, Zhang C, Liu H, Duan C, Li C, Jianxia Fan J, et al. Perinatal depressive and anxiety symptoms of pregnant women during the coronavirus disease 2019 outbreak in China. American Journal of Obstetrics and Gynecology. 2020;**223**(2):240.e1-240.e9. Available from: https://www.ncbi.nlm.nih.gov/pmc/articles/PMC7211756/pdf/main.pdf

[53] Vargas Rubilar J, Richaud MC, Lemos VN, Balabanian C. Crianza y comportamiento de los niños durante la pandemia de COVID 19: la perspectiva de la madre. Frontiers in Psychology. 2022;**13**:801614

[54] Almeida M, Shrestha A, Stojanac D, Miller L. The impact of the COVID-19 pandemic on women's mental health. Archives of Women's Mental Health. 2020;**23**:741-748. DOI: 10.1007/s00737-020-01092-2

[55] Brown SM, Doom JR, Lechuga-Peña S, Watamura SE, Koppels T. Stress and parenting during the global COVID-19 pandemic. Child Abuse and Neglect. 2020;**110**:104699. DOI: 10.1016/j.chiabu.2020.104699

[56] Olhaberry M, Escobar J, Oyarce D, Sieverson C, Aldoney D, Pérez C. Criar y Crecer en Tiempos de COVID: Cómo la Pandemia ha Deteriorado el Bienestar de Madres, Padre's y Niñas/Os [Raising and Growin Up in Times of COVID: How the Pandemic Has Deteriorated the Wellbeing of Mothers, Fathers and Children]. Santiago: Ciper Académico; 2021. Available from: https://www.ciperchile.cl/2021/04/05/criar-y-crecer-en-tiempos-de-covid-comola-pandemia-ha-deteriorado-el-bienestar-de-madres-padres-y-ninas-os/ [Accessed: July 20, 2021]

[57] UNICEF. Encuesta de Percepción y Actitudes de la Población. Impacto de la Pandemia COVID-19 y Las Medidas Adoptadas Por el Gobierno Sobre la Vida Cotidiana [Survey on Perception and Attitudes of Population. Impact of the COVID-19 Pandemic and the Measures Adopted by the Government on Daily Life]. 1st ed. 2020. Available from: https://www.unicef.org/argentina/sites/unicef.org.argentina/files/2020-06/EncuestaCOVID_GENERAL.pdf [Accessed: 15 March, 2023]

[58] Sanders MR, Turner KM. The importance of parenting in influencing the lives of children. In: Sanders MR, Morawska A, editors. Handbook of Parenting and Child Development across the Lifespan. Berlin/Heidelberg: Springer; 2018. pp. 3-26

[59] Miller-Graff LE, Scheid CR, Guzmán DB, Grein K. Caregiver and family factors promoting child resilience in at-risk families living in Lima, Peru. Child Abuse and Neglect. 2020;**108**:104639

[60] Johnston C, Park JL, Miller NV. Parental cognitions: Relations to parenting and child behavior. In: Sanders MR, Morawska A, editors. Handbook of Parenting and Child Development across the Lifespan. Berlin: Springer; 2018. pp. 3-26

[61] Biglan A. The Nurture Effect: How the Science of Human Behavior Can Improve our Lives and our World. Oakland, CA: New Harbinger Publications; 2015

[62] McQuillan ME, Bates JE. Parental stress and child temperament. In: Deater-Deckard K, Panneton R, editors. Parental Stress and Early Child Development. New York, NY: Springer; 2017. pp. 75-106. DOI: 10.1007/978-3-319-55376

[63] Kerr ML, Rasmussen HF, Fanning KA, Braaten SM. Parenting during COVID-19: A study of parents' experiences across gender and income levels. Family Relations. 2021;**70**:1327-1342

[64] Bornstein L, Bornstein MH. Estilos parentales y el desarrollo social del niño [Parental styles and child's social development]. In: Tremblay RE, Barr RG, DeV, Peters DeV, Boivin M, editors. Enciclopedia Sobre el Desarrollo de la Primera Infancia [Encyclopedia about Early Childhood Development]. Montreal, Quebec: Centre of excellence for early childhood development; 2010. Available from: http://www.enciclopediainfantes.com/documents/BornsteinESPxp.pdf

[65] Vargas Rubilar J, Richaud MC, Oros L. Programa de promoción de la parentalidad positiva en la escuela: un estudio preliminar en un contexto de vulnerabilidad social. Pensando Psicología. 2018;**14**(23):1-15. DOI: 10.16925/pe. v14i23.2265

[66] Hoff E, Laursen B. Socioeconomic status and parenting. In: Handbook of Parenting. New Jersey: Lawrence Erlbaum Associates Publishers; 2019. pp. 421-447

[67] Kalil A, Ryan R. Parenting practices and socioeconomic gaps in childhood outcomes. The Future of Children. 2020;**30**(1):29-54

[68] Vargas-Rubilar J. Un estudio de Parentalidad en Contextos de Vulnerabilidad Social. Tesis doctoral. Buenos Aires: Pontificia Universidad Católica "Santa María de los Buenos Aires"; 2014

[69] Azar E. Competencias parentales, funciones ejecutivas, estrategias de aprendizaje y competencias académicas en la niñez intermedia, según el estrato socioeconómico. Tesis doctoral no publicada. Buenos Aires: Pontificia Universidad Católica "Santa María de los Buenos Aires"; 2021

[70] Byrne S, López-Larrosa S, Martín JC, Callejas E, Máiquez ML, Rodrigo MJ. Context, process, and participant response in the implementation of family support programmes in Spain. Psicología Educativa. 2023;**29**:20-33. DOI: 10.5093/psed2022a

[71] Sanders MR, Turner KMT, Metzler CW. Applying self-regulation principles in the delivery of parenting interventions. Clinical Child and Family Psychology Review. 2019;**22**:24-42

[72] Sanders MR. The triple P system of evidence-based parenting support: Past, present, and future directions. Clinical Child and Family Psychology Review. 2023;**26**(4):880-903

[73] Bornstein MH, Cluver L, Deater-Deckard K, Hill NE, Jager J, Krutikova S, et al. The future of parenting programs: I design. Parenting. 2022;**22**(3):201-234

Chapter 5

Supporting Children's Communication Development through Parental Education

Nuzhat Sultana and Suzanne C. Purdy

Abstract

This chapter explores the pivotal role of parental education in addressing the complexities of modern-day parenting, particularly in supporting children's communication development. Communication is a key aspect of early development which underpins children's social–emotional and cognitive development. This chapter reports the impact of parents' communication styles on child speech, language and communication development and aims to equip parents with the skills to use communication strategies and successfully engage with parent education teaching methodologies. Through evidence-based strategies and collaboration, parents can be empowered to create an environment that is conducive to holistic growth and learning for their children. When challenges arise – whether they stem from communication or learning difficulties, social conflicts, academic or other setbacks – parents equipped with effective strategies and understanding can support and advocate for their children. By fostering an environment that supports children's holistic development including communication and learning, parents can effectively support their children's overall growth.

Keywords: parental education and learning, child speech/language/communication development, communication strategies, collaborative engagement, responsiveness

1. Introduction

Communication is a critical factor in children's development, serving as a fundamental building block for social, emotional, and cognitive growth. Effective communication skills enable children to express their thoughts, feelings, and needs, fostering meaningful connections with caregivers, peers, and the wider community [1]. Moreover, research underscores the profound impact of parent–child communication on various domains of development, including language acquisition, literacy skills, and socio-emotional competence [2, 3]. By engaging in responsive and supportive communication interactions, parents can create nurturing environments that promote language development, cognitive stimulation, and socio-emotional well-being in their children [3, 4].

Parents, as social partners, play a crucial role in language acquisition by shaping the parent-child interactive environment that promotes language development [5, 6].

Hart and Risley's research established that early exposure to adult language input is linked to cognitive development, including intelligence, in young children [6]. However, the quantity of words spoken by children and their engagement in conversational turns with adults significantly impact their receptive and expressive language skills [7].

The relationship between parenting and socialization is bidirectional. For example, a parent can use their language to ensure the child acts in a certain way, and a child is able to behave in a way that encourages the parent to say something to modify that behavior [8]. Therefore, coaching and educating the parents regarding their use of language and interaction strategies during communication with their children can have a significant impact [9, 10]. A parent's behavior and language both towards the child as well as around their child can support the development of socialization skills, by teaching the child the language and behavior that can help them to flourish in other contexts.

Parental education plays a pivotal role in modern parenting, equipping caregivers with the knowledge, skills, and resources necessary to navigate the complexities of raising children in today's rapidly changing world. Research consistently highlights the positive impact of parental education programs on various aspects of child development, including academic achievement, socio-emotional competence, and behavioral outcomes [11]. By providing caregivers with evidence-based parenting strategies, such programs empower parents to establish nurturing and supportive environments that foster optimal growth and well-being in their children. Parental education initiatives can promote positive parent–child relationships, enhance communication skills, and strengthen parental confidence, thereby contributing to more positive parenting practices and improved family dynamics [12].

In summary, parental education to support effective communication is an integral component of modern parenting, offering essential support for caregivers as they navigate the intricacies of raising children in today's dynamic society. By investing in parental education initiatives and prioritizing positive communication practices, caregivers can foster optimal development and well-being in their children, laying the foundation for a brighter future.

2. Communication development

Recently, scholars have started paying more attention to how children develop language. Social context supports and shapes language learning skills [8]. Factors contributing to language development encompass the inherent capabilities of the child which are influenced by biological factors (nature) as well as environmental influences (social context or nurture) [13–15]. Parents play a significant role in the early development of child language as they provide the primary source of linguistic input and serve as models for language acquisition [8].

Language acquisition begins very early in development and is influenced by both the quality and quantity of language exposure [6, 16]. Effective communicative interactions between parents (or other primary caregivers) and children, along with rich language input, are crucial during the early years in particular [16]. Interactions that occur naturally throughout daily routines and activities provide numerous opportunities to enhance a child's language and communication skills [17, 18]. Given their understanding of their children and daily routines, parents can create language-rich environments by integrating language and communication opportunities into everyday activities [18].

A significant focus in the literature is on the simplification of speech by caregivers when interacting with young children. This simplification involves strategies like slowing down speech, exaggerating intonation, and using simpler sentence structures and shorter utterances. Caregivers also employ verbal and nonverbal cues to understand the child's communicative intentions, such as attending to the child's actions, gaze direction, and behavior [19–21]. Furthermore, caregivers often seek clarification by repeating or paraphrasing the child's utterances with a questioning intonation [22]. They also can facilitate communication by co-expressing propositions with the child, typically through asking questions that prompt the child to provide missing information already known to the caregiver [22].

Previous research underscores the extensive accommodations caregivers make to support children's language development, highlighting their ability to adopt the child's perspective during conversational interactions [23]. This interactional approach has been supported by studies on caregiver-child interaction, emphasizing the importance of reciprocal engagement in language development [8, 22, 24–28].

2.1 Language developmental theories

There are several prominent theories of language development, each proposing different mechanisms and factors that contribute to how children acquire language.

2.1.1 Nativist theory of language development

Chomsky introduced the Principles and Parameters theory, asserting that all languages share fundamental principles, with variations occurring in their parameters [14, 29]. According to this theory and the concept of Universal Grammar, all languages possess common basic grammatical structures. These universal features are so abstract that they cannot be learned through imitation or communication with adults. Consequently, Chomsky argues that these universal grammatical principles are innate, part of a child's genetic endowment. This theory suggests that children are born with an inherent understanding of these universal principles, which simplifies the process of first language acquisition. Children do not need to learn the common principles of language; instead, they must acquire the specific parameters unique to their native language. As outlined by Radford [30], these parameters are limited and binary, meaning a particular feature either exists or does not. For example, in English, a "head-first" language, the subject of a sentence typically appears at the beginning. In contrast, Persian is a "head-last" language, where the subject can be omitted. Through rich exposure to a language, a typically developing child readily learns the language as head-first or head-last [31].

2.1.2 Constructivist theory of language development

Language is a manifestation of an individual's cognitive and emotional abilities to talk about the world, talk about others, and talk about the self. Vygotsky's theory emphasizes the dynamic interaction between language and thought, positing that their development is not parallel. According to Vygotsky [32], language and thought have distinct genetic origins and initially operate independently. During early childhood, these two domains intersect and integrate, leading to significant developmental changes. In the early stages of development, thought is nonverbal, relying on mental images, while language is pre-rational and not yet connected to thought. In the first year, a child's language serves primarily a social function, showing no evidence of intellectual development. However, around the age of two, the trajectories of language and thought intersect, resulting in a new behavioral form. At this point, children begin to use language as a tool for thinking, and their speech starts to reflect their thoughts. This integration marks a crucial period where language transitions from a social tool to a cognitive one, enabling children to articulate their thoughts and engage in more complex intellectual processes. Vygotsky's theory underscores the importance of this intersection of language development and the development of higher cognitive functions in children.

2.1.3 Environmental theory of language development

Language, despite its complexities, is fundamentally a simple behavior [33]. Behaviorists, in general, focus on observable linguistic behaviors and aim to identify the relationships between environmental stimuli and responses. From a behaviorist perspective, effective linguistic behavior is viewed as the correct response to a given stimulus. When a specific response is reinforced, it becomes a habit or conditioned behavior, leading children to repeat those reinforced linguistic responses, see **Figure 1.**

3. Role of natural language environment

The natural language environment plays a crucial role in developing verbal language skills in young children [6, 34]. Research indicates that children's language acquisition is significantly influenced by the language input they receive, with parents serving as the primary source during early childhood [6, 35–38]. The extent of parental language input varies in terms of the quantity of conversation directed at and shared with children [6, 30], as well as the quality and style of these verbal interactions [35, 39–41].

3.1 Impact of parental interaction strategies on language development

The quantity of parent–child language interactions during the first few years profoundly shapes a child's linguistic and overall developmental trajectory [42]. Hart and Risley examined conversations within 42 households of children aged under two, and found significant differences in linguistic exposure across families with different socioeconomic status (SES). Across a week, children from high SES backgrounds were immersed in approximately 215,000 words, while those from middle SES families encountered around 125,000 words, and children from lower SES households were exposed to merely 62,000 words. In this study SES was strongly linked with the number of words children were exposed to. SES-related differentials in vocabulary acquisition emerged early in speech development and expanded over time. By age three, high SES children typically possessed vocabularies exceeding 1000 words, compared to around 500 words for their low SES counterparts [6]. Many factors could contribute to SES effects, including parents' education levels and available time to spend with their child. Other recent studies have shown that mothers with higher levels of education (postgraduate) and high SES used more adult words and engaged in more conversational interactions with their typically developing children under five years old [18, 43]. These mothers' communication strategies were advanced and significantly associated with better receptive and expressive language skills in their children.

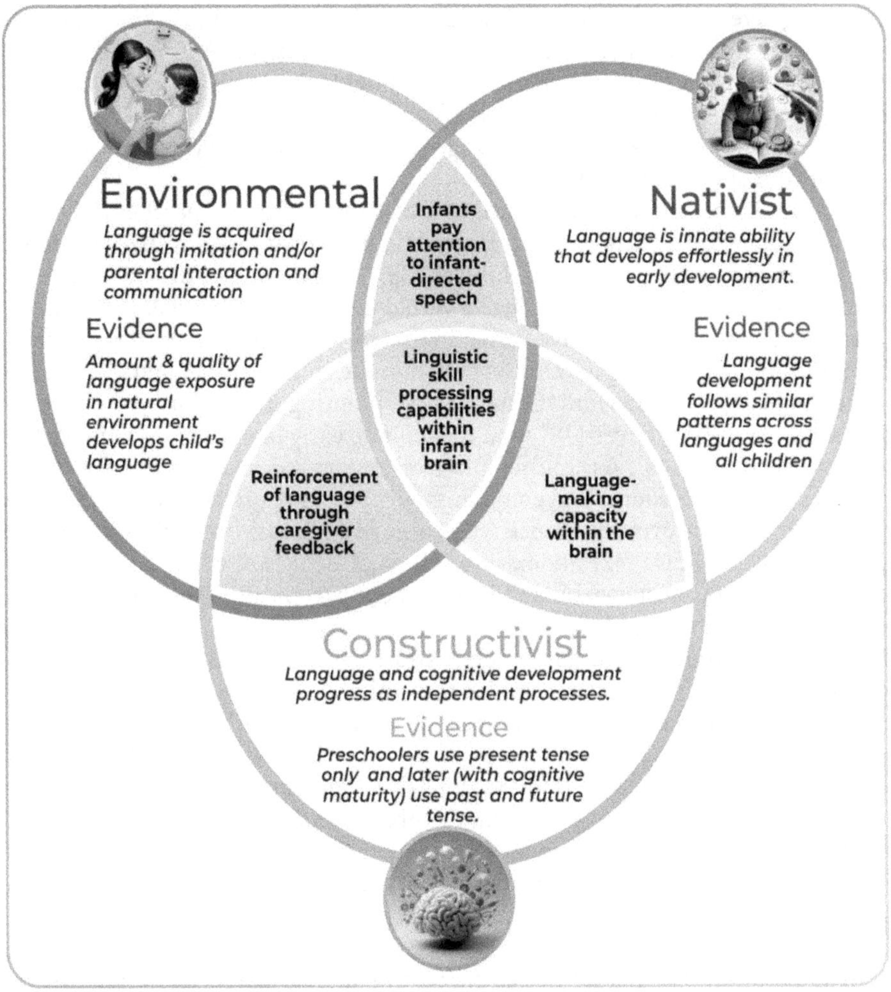

Figure 1.
Theories of language development.

Consistent with Hart and Risley, a recent study [44] has also shown a strong correlation between the amount of adult talk children are exposed to and their subsequent speech production rates, with this effect becoming more pronounced as children develop. This was based on an analysis of data extracted from a dataset comprising over 2500 day-long recordings of parent–child conversation. These recordings captured the interactions of 1001 children aged between 2 and 48 months, representing a diverse range of language backgrounds spanning 33 different languages and cultures. Languages included Arabic, American Sign Language (ASL), Berber, Cantonese, Croatian, Danish, Farsi, Frisian, German, Greek, Hindi, Hungarian, Indonesian, Italian, Japanese, Khmer, Korean, Macedonian, Malay, Malayalam, Mandarin, Norwegian, Papiamento, Polish, Portuguese, Romanian, Russian, Sahaptin, Slovenian, Solomon-Islands Pidgin, Thai, Turkish, and Yoruba, representing various language families and linguistic typologies such as Afro-Asiatic, Austroasiatic, Austronesian, Deaf Sign Languages, Dravidian, Japonic, Koreanic, Sahaptin, Sino-Tibetan, Tai-Kadai, Turkic, Atlantic-Congo, Indo-European, and Uralic. These results support the significance of parents' language input on children's language development across diverse linguistic and cultural contexts. This extensive dataset, encompassing recordings of children from many different language backgrounds, highlights the universality of this phenomenon, which is not limited to specific languages or cultures. The findings also underscore the crucial role of adult language input in shaping children's language acquisition and development [44].

The quality of parent–child interactions is also important. Researchers have examined caregiver interaction strategies and their correlation with language acquisition in young typically developing children [35, 45]. These investigations have consistently shown that highly responsive verbal interactions positively influence language development. Responsive verbal interactions involve promptly responding to child initiations and using questions to sustain the child's engagement [12, 46, 47]. Interactive strategies such as imitation, labeling, pointing, commenting on the child's actions, and issuing directives [48] tend to facilitate early language development stages (0–2 years) [35, 48]. As children progress to ages 2–6 years, open-ended or "wh-" questions, expansions, and comments become more effective in promoting the use of grammatically correct sentence structures and phrases [48, 49]. A longitudinal study conducted by Rowe [42] underscored the significance of expansions and narrations in fostering robust vocabulary development in typically developing children aged 12–48 months, see **Table 1.**

Parental communication and interactive strategies are pivotal factors in children's language development, impacting children's cognitive and socio-emotional development profoundly. Hence, understanding the critical role of early natural language exposure and responsive verbal interactions is paramount for parents. Caregiver interaction strategies, adjusted to suit various developmental stages, significantly influence language acquisition from infancy through early childhood. Parent–child interaction is bidirectional and depends on the communication environment and the child's communication level. Parents can optimize language development if they have a strong understanding of these interactions [52].

3.2 Multifaceted challenges related to parenting natural language behaviors

The child's language environment can be challenging and complex due to the influence of numerous factors, such as the inherent talkativeness, or lack of talkativeness, of parents or primary caregivers, their family practices, living conditions, and their knowledge and awareness, and parents' attentiveness towards enhancing their children's language development [3]. It is important to understand and manage the effects of these factors, as they contribute to the variation in parents' natural language behaviors in different home environments [3]. One of the most important factors is sensitive responsiveness in parents. This is defined by parent's capacity to accurately perceive, interpret, and promptly respond to their children's cues in an appropriate manner [53, 54]. This requires that parents' responses to be contingent on and promote coordinated communicative interactions with their child [53, 54]. Warmth in caregiving, characterized by physical affection and positive emotional interactions with the child, plays a significant role in shaping these exchanges. Both sensitive responsiveness and warmth are crucial aspects of parental language behaviors that interact with environmental factors, such as SES [6, 55, 56], and parental education [18] to influence children's language development and the overall language-richness of the home environment [53].

DOI: http://dx.doi.org/10.5772/intechopen.1006856

Parent interactive strategies	Description	Impact on language development
High Level		
Wh question	"Wh" question is used in a phrase or sentence to get a response from the child in a simple justification using more than two words. There are two types of Wh questions: 1. Questions that prompt children to express opinions, provide explanations, or evaluate situations encourage the use of inferential language skills (e.g., What do you think will happen to the ice cube during snack time? Why?). 2. Questions offer chances for children to explore beyond the surface and expand their learning, fostering critical thinking skills in the process [48].	These interactional strategies are helpful in developing grammatical sentence structure, syntax, and pragmatic skills for using language comprehension and expression in routine communication.
Expansion	An expansion is a technique used to repeat a child's statement with additional information to make the child's sentence more informative and complete in a more grammatical language model.	
Recast	A recast is a technique used to repeat a child's statement, adding more information, and rephrasing it as a question.	
Narration	The parent provides the child with a detailed explanation about the situation, like a story to make connections in language expression.	
Low level		
Linguistic mapping	Linguistic mapping is a technique used to respond to the child's unrecognizable or unclear vocalization/utterance to make it meaningful. This teaches the child about conversational exchange and provides a language model.	These interactional strategies are helpful in exposing children to a variety of different words, improving semantics and vocabulary, structure simple sentences, and building foundational communication skills.
Imitation	The parent imitates the child's vocalization or words without adding new extra words.	
Comments	Comments is a technique that a parent uses to make a statement or comment in response to the child's utterance as a signal that the message has been received or to keep their conversation going.	
Labeling	The parent indicates the name of the animal, building, road, fruit, object, etc.	
Directive	The parent gives a direct command to the child to guide them to do something.	
Close-ended question	The parent makes a statement to which the child can only answer with one word.	

Note: definitions adapted from studies [40, 50, 51].

Table 1.
Parent interactive strategies.

Research has shown that one way to increase children's language input and expose them to a rich language environment is through parental education [57]. For example, intervention programs that increase the main caregiver's verbal language input during interactions with their young children have a positive influence on children's language learning skills [52, 58].

4. Parental education to support children's communication

Parental education involves coaching parents on interactional strategies to enhance a child's language and communication abilities through verbal (e.g., spoken words) and nonverbal (e.g., gestures, signs) interactions with adults (e.g., parents, teachers). These strategies allow parents to foster their child's language development through genuine learning experiences [57]. Research has demonstrated that parent-implemented interaction strategies are effective in improving children's language and communication skills [59]. However, the application of direct and incidental teaching procedures in everyday settings, as well as responsive interaction strategies such as expansions, building turn-taking, and following the child's lead, can vary from parent to parent in natural situations [60].

Teaching parents to use effective language interventions is a key element in supporting the child's language skills [57]. Research has shown that coaching parents enhances their knowledge about communication strategies and promotes their competence and confidence to implement effective communication strategies [16]. Language skills that improve as a result of parent coaching include, but are not limited, to speech production, word utterances, vocalizations, intentional communication, and spontaneous use of targeted words [60]. The most consistent changes in child and parent behavior occur when parents receive individualized instructions that include clearly defined training techniques, such as coaching, feedback, and precise focus on the child's language developmental goals [57].

Early interventionists also highlight the importance of coaching parents to actively participate in their child's communication skills. Since parents spend significant time interacting with their children, this can lead to improved language and communication outcomes [49]. This was evident in a randomized control trial which compared language outcomes for children with language delay aged 24–41 months for a group of parents who received coaching compared to a control group. Coaching on how to enrich language learning skills in their children focused on strategies like match turns, interactional responsiveness, expansion, time delay, and prompts. Children whose parents received coaching had significantly better receptive language outcomes compared to a control group [59]. Further analysis showed that children whose parents did not receive coaching had a 1.4 times greater risk of language delay than those whose parents' received coaching/intervention [59]. Another meta-analysis of 25 studies found that parent coaching programs were effective in promoting language development in children under 5 years of age. The analysis showed that coaching/assistance programs led to significant improvements in expressive and receptive language skills and parent–child interactions [61]. In a smaller intervention study involving four parents of young children with hearing loss aged 16–26 months, parents were taught naturalistic interaction strategies such as matched turns, expansion, and prompting to support their child's language development [62]. There were improvements in the parents' use of natural interactional strategies as language input as well as in the language outcomes of the children with hearing loss.

Parent education programmes investigated in the literature are summarized in **Table 2**. Overall, research shows that parent educational coaching, support, and facilitating programs can be an effective way to promote language development in children and improve natural parent–child interactions in typical daily routines.

S.No	Parent education programme	Description
1	Community-based parent education program [63]	Interventions that provide family-focused services within the family's primary residence, which aim to address health, social service and educational needs [64].
2	Participatory Adult Learning Strategy (PALS) [65]	Four essential components make up the PALS model: Introduction, Application, Informed Understanding, and Repeat Learning Process. These components involve a range of actions such as observing trainees and providing feedback, guiding self-assessment, offering suggestions, and collaborating in joint planning [66].
3	More Than Words (The Hanen Centre) [67]	This program is a parent-mediated intervention model developed by the Hanen Centre in Canada. It focuses on empowering parents to support their child's language development through everyday interactions [68, 69].
4	It Takes Two to Talk (The Hanen Centre) [67]	
5	Naturalistic Language Paradigm (NLP) [70, 71]	NLP aims to enhance the quality of parental language input. It promotes spontaneous language use in children with autism spectrum disorder. This intervention approach combines behavioral language techniques with naturalistic strategies and utilizes Pivotal Response Treatment (PRT) to achieve these goals [70–72].
6	Milieu Teaching (MT) and Enhanced Milieu Teaching (EMT) [73]	MT and EMT employ several empirically validated and theoretically based strategies for caregiver language facilitation: (a) structuring the child's environment to promote communication, (b) intentionally responding to all communicative efforts, (c) demonstrating language at the child's current production level, (d) enriching the child's communication by introducing more complex forms, (e) using time delays to prompt spontaneous communication, and (f) implementing prompting techniques to support the child's use of language targets [73].
7	Teach-Model-Coach-Review Model [74]	Teach-Model-Coach-Review Model introduced a systematic approach for training parents to implement interactional strategies. The teach component consists of an hour-long workshop in which parents learn about interactional target strategies to enhance language acquisition skills in children. The model component is based on the expert's modeling of strategy use with the child and highlighting the use for parents. The coach component involves parent practice of the target strategy with the child with the expert's feedback. Finally, the review component gives the parent and expert the opportunity to discuss and reflect on strategy use during natural parent–child interactions [74].
8	The KidTalk-TaCTICS Project (KTTP) [75]	KTTP is a combination of EMT and routines-based strategies, designed as a caregiver-led language intervention [75].

S.No	Parent education programme	Description
9	The Parent-Implemented Communication Strategies (PiCS) [76]	Visual support is a fundamental aspect of the PiCS project, which utilizes evidence-based coaching methods to teach routine language strategies. The project underscores the significance of coaching over traditional training in enhancing parents' skills to provide more effective language input to their children [76].
10	Language and Play Everyday (LAPE) [77]	The LAPE program combines group training and individual coaching sessions, using evidence-based strategies to teach parents how to identify and respond to their child's communication. It is also focused on creating opportunities for communication and adjusting parental language to match their child's developmental level [77].
11	The Muenster Parental Programme (MPP) [78]	MPP is a parent training intervention that aims to build parental confidence and empower parents to communicate with their child. The program consists of 11 sessions, integrating group training for parents and individual sessions with parents and children. It employs video feedback, video demonstrations, and role-playing activities. MPP aims to help parents develop skills in establishing joint attention, imitating and mirroring their child's utterances, engaging in communicative turn-taking, and enhancing their child's verbal and non-verbal communication behaviors [78].
12	Parent–child interaction therapy (PCIT) [79]	The PCIT model consists of two primary components. The first focuses on child-directed interaction, which resembles play therapy, while the second emphasizes parent-directed interaction, adopting a more structured format like clinical behavior therapy [79–81].
13	Parent–Child Early Approaches to Raising Language Skills (PEARLS) [82]	PEARLS is a structured 10-week program aimed at parents and their children specifically for children with hearing loss who are working on spoken language skills. Each session is divided into three 20-minute parts: free play with sensitivity modeling, training in advanced facilitative language techniques (FLTs), and auditory training techniques. The program includes handouts, homework, and real-time coaching to enhance maternal sensitivity and the use of advanced FLTs [82].
14	Teaching Caregivers to Implement the Caregivers Optimizing Achievement of Children With Hearing Loss (COACH) Intervention [62].	The COACH intervention trains caregivers based on EMT language techniques tailored for children with hearing loss. It addresses their unique needs, such as reliance on visual input, challenges with acoustic conditions, and inconsistent access to linguistic details, to support their spoken language development [62].

Table 2.
Overview of parent education programmes to enhance parent–child communication.

5. Complexities of modern-day parenting

Parenting in the modern era is exciting, yet increasingly complex due to various factors. The rapid advancement of technology introduces challenges in managing screen time and online safety [83]. Parents must also navigate the pressures of balancing work and family life, often in an environment where both parents work full-time [84]. Additionally, there is a heightened awareness of mental health and the need to foster emotional intelligence in children, which requires parents to be more attuned and responsive to their children's emotional needs [85]. The influence of social media further complicates parenting, as it can create unrealistic expectations and increase the pressure to meet certain parenting standards [86]. Moreover, modern parents face diverse educational choices and extracurricular demands, requiring careful planning and support [77]. All these factors contribute to the intricate nature of parenting today.

In navigating the complexities of modern parenting, collaborative engagement, adaptability, and responsiveness are key to fostering better language skills in children.

5.1 Collaborative engagement, adaptability and responsiveness

Collaborative engagement involves involvement with educators and support groups, as well as interactive learning activities [87]. Adaptability entails flexible approaches to language learning, balanced screen time [88], and responsiveness to the child's interests [89]. Responsiveness includes active listening, emotional support, and modeling language use [89]. By integrating these strategies, parents can create a supportive environment conducive to language development despite the challenges of modern parenting. A solid foundation in language skills is linked to positive long-term outcomes in academic performance, career success, and social interactions. Individual differences in language development emerge early, with about 16% of children experiencing delays during the initial stages. Of these children, around half face persistent challenges which could be mitigated by appropriate support for the development of communication skills [90].

6. Conclusion

In conclusion, parental education plays a crucial role in supporting children's communication development. By providing caregivers with knowledge and skills related to language stimulation, responsive interaction, and the creation of language-rich environments, parental education empowers parents to become effective language models and facilitators for their children. Through collaborative engagement, adaptability to individual needs, and responsiveness to children's cues, parents can create supportive environments that foster language growth and communication skills from an early age. Investing in parental education not only benefits children's linguistic development but also strengthens parent–child bonds and promotes positive socio-emotional outcomes. As we continue to explore innovative approaches and evidence-based practices in parental education, we pave the way for nurturing environments where every child can thrive linguistically and communicatively.

Conflict of interest

No potential conflicts of interest are reported by the authors.

Author details

Nuzhat Sultana[1*] and Suzanne C. Purdy[1,2]

1 School of Psychology, University of Auckland, Auckland, New Zealand

2 Eisdell Moore Centre for Hearing and Balance Research, Auckland, New Zealand

*Address all correspondence to: nuzhat.sultana@auckland.ac.nz

References

[1] Kolucki B, Lemish D. Communicating with children: Principles and practices to nurture, inspire, excite, educate and heal. United Nations Children's Fund (UNICEF). 2011. Available from: Communicating With Children.pdf (triatmamulya.ac.id)

[2] Rocha NACF, dos Santos Silva FP, Dos Santos MM, Dusing SC. Impact of mother–infant interaction on development during the first year of life: A systematic review. Journal of Child Health Care. 2020;**24**(3):365-385. DOI: 10.1177/13674935198647

[3] Topping K, Dekhinet R, Zeedyk S. Parent–infant interaction and children's language development. Educational Psychology. 2013;**33**(4):391-426. DOI: 10.1080/01443410.2012.744159

[4] Tamis-LeMonda CS, Baumwell L, Cristofaro T. Parent–child conversations during play. First Language. 2012;**32**(4):413-438. DOI: 10.1177/0142723711419321

[5] Vygotsky LS. Mind in Society: The Development of Higher Psychological Processes. Cambridge, MA: Harvard University Press; 1978

[6] Hart B, Risley T. Meaningful Differences in the Everyday Experience of Young American Children. Baltimore, MD: Paul H. Brooks Publishing Co; 1995

[7] Gilkerson J, Richards JA, Warren SF, Oller DK, Russo R, Vohr B. Language experience in the second year of life and language outcomes in late childhood. Pediatrics. 2018;**142**(4):1-11. DOI: 10.1542/peds.2017-4276

[8] Hoff E. How social contexts support and shape language development. Developmental Review. 2006;**26**(1):55-88. DOI: 10.1016/j.dr.2005.11.002

[9] Hanft BE, Rush DD, Shelden ML. Coaching Families and Colleagues in Early Childhood. Baltimore, MD: Paul H. Brookes; 2004

[10] Moore HW, Barton EE, Chironis M. A program for improving toddler communication through parent coaching. Topics in Early Childhood Special Education. 2014;**33**:212-224. DOI: 10.1177/0271121413497520

[11] Chen M, Chan KL. Effects of parenting programs on child maltreatment prevention: A meta-analysis. Trauma, Violence, and Abuse. 2016;**17**(1):88-104. DOI: 10.1177/1524838014566718

[12] Landry SH, Smith KE, Swank PR. Responsive parenting: Establishing early foundations for social, communication, and independent problem-solving skills. Developmental Psychology. 2006;**42**(4):627. DOI: 10.1037/0012-1649.42.4.627

[13] Skinner BF. Verbal Behavior. New York: Appleton-Century-Crofts; 1957

[14] Chomsky N. Review of verbal behavior by B. F. Skinner. In: Munger MP, editor. The History of Psychology: Fundamental Questions. Oxford, England: Oxford University Press; 2003. pp. 408-429

[15] Piattelli-Palmarini M. Language and Learning: The Debate between Jean Piaget and Noam Chomsky. Cambridge: Mass. Harvard University Press; 1980

[16] McWilliam RA. Implementing and preparing for home visits.

Topics in Early Childhood Special Education. 2012;**31**:224-231. DOI: 10.1177/0271121411426488

[17] Woods J, Kashinath S, Goldstein H. Children's communication outcomes. Journal of Early Intervention. 2004;**26**:175-193. DOI: 10.1177/105381510402600302

[18] Sultana N, Wong LL, Purdy SC. Natural language input: Maternal education, socioeconomic deprivation, and language outcomes in typically developing children. Language, Speech, and Hearing Services in Schools. 2020;**51**(4):1049-1070. DOI: 10.1044/2020_LSHSS-19-00095

[19] Golinkoff R. The Transition from Prelinguistic to Linguistic Communication. Hillsdale: N.J. Erlbaum; 1983

[20] Keenan E, Ochs E, Schieffelin BB. Topic as a discourse notion: A study of topic in the conversations of children and adults. In: Li C, editor. Subject and Topic. New York: Academic Press; 1976

[21] Bloom L. One Word at a Time. The Hague: Mouton; 1973

[22] Bruner JS. Early social interaction and language acquisition. In: Schaffer HR, editor. Studies in Mother-Infant Interaction. London: Academic Press; 1977. pp. 271-289

[23] Bullowa M. Introduction: Prelinguistic communication: A field for scientific research. In: Bullowa M, editor. Before Speech: The Beginnings of Interpersonal Communication. Cambridge: Cambridge University Press; 1979

[24] Lock A. Action, Gesture and Symbol. London: Academic Press; 1978

[25] Nelson K. Concept, word and sentence: Interrelations in acquisition and development. Psychological Review. 1974;**81**:267-285. DOI: 10.1037/h0036592

[26] Schaffer HR. Studies in Mother Infant Interaction. London: Academic Press; 1977

[27] Shotter J. The cultural context of communication studies: Theoretical and methodological issues. In: Lock A, editor. Action, Gesture and Symbol. London: Academic Press; 1978

[28] Law J, Garrett Z, Nye C. Speech and Language Therapy Interventions for Children with Primary Speech and Language Delay or Disorder. Oxford: The Cochrane Library; 2003. Available from: http://www.cochrane.co.uk/en/index.html

[29] Chomsky N. Reflections on Language. New York: Pantheon; 1975

[30] Radford A. Syntactic Theory and the Acquisition of English Syntax: The Nature of Early Child Grammars of English. Oxford: Blackwell; 1990

[31] Valian V. Innateness and learnability. In: Bavin EL, editor. The Cambridge Handbook of Child Language. Cambridge: Cambridge University Press; 2009

[32] Vygotsky L. Thought and Language. Cambridge, Mass: MIT Press; 1962

[33] Watson JB. Psychology as the behaviorist views it. Psychological Review. 1913;**20**(2):158-177. DOI: 10.1037/h0074428

[34] Zimmerman FJ, Gilkerson J, Richards JA, Christakis DA, Xu D, Gray S, et al. Teaching by listening: The importance of adult-child conversations to language development (clinical report). Pediatrics. 2009;**124**(1):342-349. DOI: 10.1542/peds.2008-2267

[35] Girolametto L, Weitzman E. Responsiveness of child care providers in interactions with toddlers and preschoolers. Language, Speech, and Hearing Services in Schools. 2002;**33**(4):268. DOI: 10.1044/0161-1461(2002/022)

[36] Cox Eriksson C. Children's vocabulary development: The role of parental input, vocabulary composition and early communicative skills [Doctoral dissertation]. Department of Special Education, Stockholm University. 2014

[37] Mishina-Mori S. A longitudinal analysis of language choice in bilingual children: The role of parental input and interaction. Journal of Pragmatics. 2011;**43**(13):3122-3138. DOI: 10.1016/j.pragma.2011.03.016

[38] Vernon-Feagans L, Pancsofar N, Willoughby M, Odom E, Quade A, Cox M. Predictors of maternal language to infants during a picture book task in the home: Family SES, child characteristics and the parenting environment. Journal of Applied Developmental Psychology. 2008;**29**(3):213-226. DOI: 10.1016/j.appdev.2008.02.007

[39] Gilkerson J, Richards JA. The Power of Talk: Impact of Adult Talk, Conversational Turns, and TV during the Critical 0-4 Years of Child Development. Boulder, CO: LENA Foundation; 2009. Available from: The-Power-of-Talk-1.pdf (larandelek.se)

[40] Cruz I, Quittner AL, Marker C, DesJardin JL. Identification of effective strategies to promote language in deaf children with cochlear implants. Child Development. 2013;**84**(2):543-559. DOI: 10.1111/j.1467-8624.2012.01863.x

[41] Huttenlocher J, Waterfall H, Vasilyeva M, Vevea J, Hedges LV. Sources of variability in children's language growth. Cognitive Psychology. 2010;**61**(4):343-365. DOI: 10.1016/j.cogpsych.2010.08.002

[42] Rowe ML. A longitudinal investigation of the role of quantity and quality of child-directed speech in vocabulary development. Child Development. 2012;**83**(5):1762-1774. DOI: 10.1111/j.1467-8624.2012.01805.x

[43] Kaiser AP, Hancock TB, Trent A. Teaching parents communication strategies. Early Childhood Services. 2007;**1**(2):107-136

[44] Bergelson E, Soderstrom M, Schwarz C, Rowland C, Ramfrez-Esparza N, Hamrick LR, et al. Everyday language input and production in 1,001 children from six continents. Proceedings of the National Academy of Sciences. 2023;**120**(52):e2300671120. DOI: 10.1073/pnas.2300671120

[45] Baumwell L, Tamis-LeMonda CS, Bornstein MH. Maternal verbal sensitivity and child language comprehension. Infant Behavior and Development. 1997;**20**(2):247-258. DOI: 10.1016/S0163-6383(97)90026-6

[46] Hampson J, Nelson K. The relation of maternal language to variation in rate and style of language acquisition. Journal of Child Language. 1993;**1993**(20):313-342. DOI: 10.1017/S0305000900008308

[47] Walker D, Bigelow K, Harjusola-Webb S, Small C, Kirk S. Strategies for Promoting Communication and Language of Infants and Toddlers. Kansas City, KS: Juniper Gardens Children's Project; 2004

[48] Robertson L, Dow GA, Hainzinger SL. Story retelling patterns among children with and without hearing loss: Effects of repeated practice

and parent-child attunement. The Volta Review. 2006;**106**(2):147-170

[49] Friedman M, Woods J, Salisbury C. Caregiver coaching strategies for early intervention providers: Moving toward operational definitions. Infants and Young Children. 2012;**25**(1):62-82. DOI: 10.1097/IYC.0b013e31823d8f12

[50] Eyberg SM, Nelson MM, Duke M, Boggs SR. Manual for the Dyadic Parent-Child Interaction Coding System. 3rd ed. 2005. Gainesville, FL: The University of Florida; 2005. Available from: www.PCIT.org

[51] DesJardin JL, Eisenberg LS. Maternal contributions: Supporting language development in young children with cochlear implants. Ear and Hearing. 2007;**28**(4):456-469. DOI: 10.1097/AUD.0b013e31806dc1ab

[52] Nittrouer S, Lowenstein JH, Antonelli J. Parental language input to children with hearing loss: Does it matter in the end? Journal of Speech, Language, and Hearing Research. 2020;**63**(1):234-258. DOI: 10.1044/2019_JSLHR-19-00123

[53] Madigan S, Prime H, Graham SA, Rodrigues M, Anderson N, Khoury J, et al. Parenting behavior and child language: A meta-analysis. Pediatrics. 2019;**144**(4):1-12. DOI: 10.1542/peds.2018-3556

[54] Feldman HM. The importance of language-learning environments to child language outcomes. Pediatrics. 2019;**144**(4):e20192157. DOI: 10.1542/peds.2019-2157

[55] Hoff E. The specificity of environmental influence: Socioeconomic status affects early vocabulary development via maternal speech. Child Development. 2003;**74**(5):1368-1378. DOI: 10.1111/1467-8624.00612

[56] Hoff E, Tian C. Socioeconomic status and cultural influences on language. Journal of Communication Disorders. 2005;**38**(4):271-278. DOI: 10.1016/j.jcomdis.2005.02.003

[57] Kaiser AP, Hancock TB, Nietfeld JP. The effects of parent implemented enhanced milieu teaching on the social communication of children who have autism. Early Education and Development. 2010;**11**:423-446. DOI: 10.1207/s15566935eed1104_4

[58] Moeller MP, Carr G, Seaver L, Stredler-Brown A, Holzinger D. Best practices in family-centered early intervention for children who are deaf or hard of hearing: An international consensus statement. Journal of Deaf Studies and Deaf Education. 2013;**18**(4):429-445. DOI: 10.1093/deafed/ent034

[59] Roberts MY, Kaiser AP. Early intervention for toddlers with language delays: A randomized controlled trial. Pediatrics. 2015;**135**(4):686-693. DOI: 10.1542/peds.2014-2134

[60] Roberts MY, Kaiser AP. The effectiveness of parent-implemented language interventions: A meta-analysis. American Journal of Speech Language Pathology. 2011;**20**:180-199. DOI: 10.1044/1058-0360(2011/10-0055)

[61] Heidlage JK, Cunningham JE, Kaiser AP, Trivette CM, Barton EE, Frey JR, et al. The effects of parent-implemented language interventions on child linguistic outcomes: A meta-analysis. Early Childhood Research Quarterly. 2020;**50**:6-23. DOI: 10.1016/j.ecresq.2018.12.006

[62] Ambrose SE, Appenzeller M, Kaiser AP. Teaching caregivers to implement the caregivers optimizing achievement of children with

hearing loss (COACH) intervention. American Journal of Speech-Language Pathology. 2023;**32**(3):1131-1153. DOI: 10.1044/2022_AJSLP-22-00223

[63] Henwood T, Channon S, Penny H, Robling M, Waters CS. Do home visiting programmes improve children's language development? A systematic review. International Journal of Nursing Studies. 2020;**109**:103610. DOI: 10.1016/j.ijnurstu.2020.103610

[64] Iván A, Perry J, Johnson V. Benefits of increased home-visitation services: Exploring a case management model. Family and Community Health. 2009;**32**(1):58-75. DOI: 10.1097/01.FCH.0000342817.95390.7e

[65] Dunst CJ, Trivette CM. Let's be PALS: An evidence-based approach to professional development. Infants and Young Children. 2009;**22**(3):164-176. DOI: 10.1097/IYC.0b013e3181abe169

[66] Rush DD, Shelden ML. Evidence-based definition of coaching practices. CASEinPoint. 2005;**1**(6):1-6

[67] Girolametto L, Weitzman E. It takes two to talk—The Hanen program for parents: Early language intervention through caregiver training. Treatment of Language Disorders in Children. 2006;**1**:77-103

[68] Girolametto L, Pearce PS, Weitzman E. Interactive focused stimulation for toddlers with expressive vocabulary delays. Journal of Speech, Language, and Hearing Research. 1996;**39**(6):1274-1283. DOI: 10.1044/jshr.3906.1274

[69] Girolametto L, Pearce PS, Weitzman E. The effects of focused stimulation for promoting vocabulary. Journal of Children's Communication Development. 1996;**17**(2):39-49

[70] Koegel RL, O'Dell MC, Koegel LK. A natural language teaching paradigm for nonverbal autistic children. Journal of Autism and Developmental Disorders. 1987;**17**(2):187-200. DOI: 10.1007/BF01495055

[71] Gillett JN, LeBlanc LA. Parent-implemented natural language paradigm to increase language and play in children with autism. Research in Autism Spectrum Disorders. 2007;**1**(3):247-255. DOI: 10.1016/j.rasd.2006.09.003

[72] Coolican J, Smith IM, Bryson SE. Brief parent training in pivotal response treatment for preschoolers with autism. Journal of Child Psychology and Psychiatry and Allied Disciplines. 2010;**51**(12):1321-1330. DOI: 10.1111/j.1469-7610.2010.02326.x

[73] Kaiser AP, Hampton LH. Enhanced milieu teaching. In: McCauley R, Fey M, Gilliam R, editors. Treatment of Language Disorders in Children. 2nd ed. Baltimore MD: Brookes Publishing Co; 2017. pp. 87-120

[74] Kaiser AP, Roberts MY. Parent-implemented enhanced milieu teaching with preschool children who have intellectual disabilities. Journal of Speech, Language, and Hearing Research. 2013;**56**:295-309. DOI: 10.1044/1092-4388(2012/11-0231)

[75] Brown JA, Woods JJ. Effects of a triadic parent-implemented home-based communication intervention for toddlers. Journal of Early Intervention. 2015;**37**(1):44-68. DOI: 10.1177/1053815115589350

[76] Stoner J, Meadan H, Angell M. A model for coaching parents to implement teaching strategies with their young children with language delay or developmental disabilities. Perspectives

on Language Learning and Education. 2013;**20**(3):112-113. DOI: 10.1044/lle20.3.112

[77] Moore HW, Barton EE, Chironis M. A program for improving toddler communication through parent coaching. Topics in Early Childhood Special Education. 2013;**33**(4):212-224. DOI: 10.1177/0271121413497520

[78] Glanemann R, Reichmuth K, Matulat P, Zehnhoff-Dinnesen A. Muenster parental programme empowers parents in communicating with their infant with hearing loss. International Journal of Pediatric Otorhinolaryngology. 2013;**77**(12):2023-2029. DOI: 10.1016/j.ijporl.2013.10.001

[79] Eyberg SM, Nelson MM, Boggs SR. Evidence-based psychosocial treatments for children and adolescents with disruptive behavior. Journal of Clinical Child and Adolescent Psychology. 2008;**37**(1):215-237. DOI: 10.1080/15374410701820117

[80] Bagner DM, Garcia D, Hill R. Direct and indirect effects of behavioral parent training on infant language production. Behavior Therapy. 2016;**47**(2):184-197. DOI: 10.1016/j.beth.2015.11.001

[81] Falkus G, Tilley C, Thomas C, Hockey H, Kennedy A, Arnold T, et al. Assessing the effectiveness of parent-child interaction therapy with language delayed children: A clinical investigation. Child Language Teaching and Therapy. 2016;**32**(1):7-17. DOI: 10.1177/0265659015574918

[82] Cejas I, Quittner AL. Pearls: An intervention to improve parent-child interactions and communication. The Volta Review. 2019;**119**(2):96-109

[83] Hill D, Ameenuddin N, Reid Chassiakos YL, Cross C, Hutchinson J, Levine A, et al. Media and young minds. Pediatrics. 2016;**138**(5):e20162591. DOI: 10.1542/peds.2016-2591

[84] Galinsky E, Aumann K, Bond JT. Times are Changing: Gender and Generation at Work and at Home in the USA. Expanding the Boundaries of Work-Family Research. London: Palgrave Macmillan; 2013. pp. 279-296

[85] Denham SA. Emotional Development in Young Children. New York: Guilford Press; 1998

[86] Reid Chassiakos YL, Radesky J, Christakis D, Moreno MA, Cross C, Hill D, et al. Children and adolescents and digital media. Pediatrics. 2016;**138**(5):e20162593. DOI: 10.1542/peds.2016-2593

[87] Feiler A. Engaging 'hard to reach' Parents: Teacher-Parent Collaboration to Promote children's Learning. Chichester, UK: John Wiley and Sons; 2009

[88] Zimmerman FJ, Christakis DA, Meltzoff AN. Television and DVD/video viewing in children younger than 2 years. Archives of Pediatrics and Adolescent Medicine. 2007;**161**(5):473-479. DOI: 10.1001/archpedi.161.5.473

[89] Galasyuk IN, Mitina OV. The interaction of the parent with the young child: Structure and dynamics of parental responsiveness. Cultural-Historical Psychology. 2020;**16**(4):72-86. DOI: 10.17759/chp.2020160408

[90] Simon P, Rosenbaum S. Speech and Language Disorders in Children: Implications for the Social Security Administration's Supplemental Security Income Program. Washington, D.C.: National Academies Press; 2016. pp. 62-67

Chapter 6

Self-Help Among Foster Parents in Italy: Analysis of the Phenomenon and Implications for Social Services and Researchers

Marco Giordano, Marilena Di Lollo and Carmela Carotenuto

Abstract

The experiences of group self-help represent an important entity of mutual support in various fields of social life. Within the context of family fostering, there are over a hundred mutual-help groups in Italy that offer participants support, sharing, and awareness. Only to some extent is this extensive and diverse presence known and appreciated by the competent social services in charge of child protection. This study proposes an analysis of the main characteristics of Italian self-help groups among foster families, based on the study of 60 entities. The aim is to foster a greater understanding of the phenomenon, in order to provide guidance for the actions of social service operators and avenues of study for researchers. In particular, the origin and nature of the groups, their geographical presence, the characteristics of participants and beneficiaries, internal organisation, areas of activity, networking, economic resources, difficulties, and opportunities faced by such groups are explored.

Keywords: self-help among Foster parents, social services and self-help, child protection, Foster care, self-help groups

1. Introduction

Mutual aid has always characterised community life. Self-help groups, as we know them today, emerged from the experience of *Alcoholics Anonymous*, founded in 1935 and widespread worldwide [1]. At the heart of these realities is the principle that when people share their difficulties and reflect together, significant mutual help arises [2]. Developed in varied forms [3], self-help in Italy involves hundreds of thousands of people, generating enormous social benefits with negligible economic burdens on public finances. In a time of crisis in social bonds, expanding social vulnerability, and a shortage of public economic resources, social services can find in the varied reality of self-help groups a valid and dynamic ally capable of bringing about comprehensive changes in individuals beyond immediate problems [4].

An area of particular relevance in which to explore the development of Italian self-help and its interaction with social services is that of foster care. Governed by Law 184/83 and subsequent amendments, foster care aims to ensure care, education, instruction, and emotional relationships for minors temporarily lacking a suitable family environment. Currently practised by approximately 7.7 thousand individuals/ families [5], foster care represents a particular intersection between the community and institutional dimensions. National regulations assign social services the task of promoting public opinion formation on foster care and preparing willing families and individuals by collaborating with non-profit organisations active in the field.

Despite clear regulatory indications, recent ministerial data indicate a slow decline in foster care in Italy. Among the main reasons for this crisis is the insufficient number of people available for fostering compared to the need for foster care of minors residing in residential facilities [6]. One way to contribute to the revival of foster care in Italy is to ensure foster parents receive the support they need. The forty-year experience of implementing foster care in Italy has shown that among the main forms of support, the participation of foster parents in spaces for sharing, comparison, and mutual support with other foster parents stands out [7–9].

International scientific literature includes various studies on the importance of this aspect. For example, a cluster analysis on *peer support* among foster parents in Canada highlighted the presence of 5 areas of support considered important by respondents: self-care, effective self-use, knowledge of procedures, information search, and coping with common challenges [10]. A study conducted in the United States, after emphasising how foster parents experience a myriad of stress factors exposing them to high turnover rates, highlighted the need for services active in the field to reinforce foster parents' self-help capacity and to strengthen various dimensions such as emotional self-awareness and better management of interpersonal boundaries. In this regard, among the main sources of help are support groups, offering friendly support. The study urges services to activate support before rather than after the emergence of critical issues to maintain adequate levels of well-being and satisfaction [11]. A study on self-help groups among foster parents conducted in Lithuania highlighted that these groups can become, through shared needs and commonality, places of real help among foster parents, promoting growth and fostering positive changes in relationships [12]. As early as the 1980s, the usefulness of mutual support groups among foster parents had been highlighted by studies on the pain associated with the separation that occurs at the end of foster placements. These studies particularly highlighted how group empathy facilitates coping with and processing experiences of loss [13] and experiences of "anticipated grief" towards an impending conclusion [14], especially in cases where initially there was the prospect that the placement could be extended over time and become permanent. A group with shared experiences—especially if led by expert guidance—can provide a safe place for foster parents to express these feelings, which can be accompanied by intense anger towards services and, in general, the child protection system. In some situations, it will be necessary to revisit the entire area of unresolved grief among foster parents [15]. According to Maclay and other authors of a study in Great Britain, support networks among foster parents constitute a true "survival mechanism" as they develop a high level of support [16]. It has also been observed that mutual mentoring between foster parents is the method that most easily consolidates foster parents' experience. A real power of mutual support for caregivers emerges, particularly in transmitting practical wisdom, safely releasing emotional burdens, solving practical problems, and supporting each other in organising breaks during placements [17]. The importance of initiating group self-help among foster parents is already evident from the initial training phase of foster parents themselves. The study above by Brown et al. indicates that programs providing foster parents with peer support pathways have great potential to positively impact the long-term resilience of foster parents themselves. In particular, the study emphasises the circularity of the benefits arising from participation in mutual support pathways among foster parents because foster parents who provide peer support also receive training and support in return. Individual mentoring is also important, usually provided to a novice by an experienced foster parent. It would be supported by specific training opportunities for the mentor foster parents, expense reimbursements, mentor coordination activities, etc. [18].

In the Italian context, it is estimated that there are over a hundred local groups of foster families. Although some mutual support pathways have emerged at the social services initiative, the majority have arisen from the voluntary initiative of foster parents, who have joined together in groups and networks, often evolving into formally established associations. This represents a very important pool of mutual aid with which only a minority of social services interact continuously. A sample survey by the Ministry of Labor and Social Policies highlighted the frequency with which social services interact with informal networks of foster families (12.9% always; 46.2% often; 22.7% rarely; 18.2% never) and associations of foster families (21.3% always; 36.8% often; 16.2% rarely; 25.7% never) [19]. The partial development of coordination between services and foster parent mutual aid realities encourages the improvement of mutual knowledge between them. This research aims to contribute in this regard, particularly by offering local Italian social services an analysis of the main characteristics of self-help groups among foster parents. To this end, it attempts to answer the following questions: Where are these groups located? How long have they been established? How big are they? Are they legally constituted? What is their internal organisation? What actions and dynamics do they pursue? Who are the main beneficiaries of the activities? Are they connected to national networks? How do they financially support their activities? What difficulties do they face and what support do they receive?

2. Sample, method, and research tools

2.1 Sample

The studied sample consists of all Italian self-help groups among foster parents that were identified, contacted, and made available for analysis. In total, 112 entities were identified. The starting point was the list provided by the Tavolo Nazionale Affido (a national network of foster parents associations) supplemented by the analysis of associations listed by the Istituto degli Innocenti in Florence and published on the website www.bancadatiaffido.minori.it. The lists of local groups belonging to the main Italian national networks/associations were also checked. Public Foster Care Services adhering to the CNSA (National Coordination of Foster Care Services) were also consulted. Additional entities identified through major web search engines were included. Additional entities reported by local groups interviewed were gradually added using the "avalanche sampling" technique: once a subject belonging to the target population was identified, they were asked to indicate other subjects with the characteristics under investigation. "The subjects reported will in turn become, in addition to part of the sample, informants for identifying further contacts and so on, according to the metaphor of the avalanche which, although with a very limited origin, quickly assumes ever wider proportions" [20].

Of the identified entities, 60 groups participated in the research. The others were found to be no longer active (16 entities) or did not respond to invitations, so it is unknown whether they are active or not (27 entities). Other groups (8 entities) were not available for the survey. It is reasonable to assume that additional active local entities were not reached because they were not identified. However, it is believed that this number may be small.

2.2 Research method and tool

Information regarding participating groups was collected, between spring and summer 2020, through self-administered online questionnaires [21], a survey technique utilising the computer assisted web interviewing (CAWI) methodology [22]. In most cases (37 out of 60 questionnaires, 62%), the group's manager/representative completed the questionnaires. In smaller quotas, they were completed by individuals delegated by them, that is, a participating foster parent (6 questionnaires), an operator (7 questionnaires), or individuals who are both operators and foster parents (10 questionnaires). The compilation took place through a dedicated online form and was preceded by an individual presentation of the research, conducted via phone or video call by the research group. Specifically, the "Google Forms" program was used to prepare the questionnaire, generate the link to be sent to respondents, record the responses in the data matrix, and export them in compatible formats for subsequent analysis. The draft questionnaire design was developed with the contribution of thematic experts (associations and networks of foster families adhering to the Tavolo Nazionale Affido), to whom a first version developed by the research group was submitted. The final structure of the questionnaire comprises various sections: genesis, nature, and contacts; geographical presence; participants; beneficiaries; internal organisation; areas of activity; network; economic resources; difficulties and opportunities.

3. Description and data analysis

3.1 General characteristics of the groups

3.1.1 Reference associations of the groups

Slightly more than half of the surveyed groups, 33 out of 60 groups (55%), belong to a larger associative or federative entity. These include associations such as Famiglie per l'Accoglienza, Comunità Papa Giovanni XXIII, Cometa, Federazione Progetto Famiglia, and La Carovana.

3.1.2 Year of establishment of the groups

Regarding the year of establishment, the oldest group dates back to 1983, while the most recent was established in 2018. Dividing this timeframe into three equal periods, it emerges that: in the first twelve-year period (between 1983 and 1994), 14 groups were established; in the second twelve-year period (between 1995 and 2006),

27 groups were established; in the third twelve-year period (between 2007 and 2018), 19 groups were established. Nearly half of the groups were born between 1995 and 2006. Investigating the reasons for this period's greater "fertility" and why the trend subsequently decreased will be useful.

3.1.3 Origins of the groups

From the analysis of the questionnaires, it emerges that the establishment of the groups occurred in 35 cases (58% of the total) as a result of the stimulus from an existing entity. This was almost always a third-sector entity (30 groups). Additionally, there were three groups established from the stimulus of a public entity, one group established from a collaboration between a public entity and a third-sector entity, and one group whose establishment was promoted by a parish. The remaining 25 groups (42% of cases) were self-promoted by the members.

3.1.4 Stability of the groups

The reality of foster groups shows high levels of stability. All the groups studied (except one) declared themselves to be entities with "a stable existence due to the self-organisation of those who participate and/or the presence of permanent paths from the promoting entity". In only one case, the interviewed manager declared it to be an entity whose "existence depends on the presence of temporary projects managed by the promoting entity".

3.1.5 Formal constitution of the groups

50 out of 60 groups are formally constituted, meaning they have articles of association, statutes, tax codes, legal addresses, representative bodies, etc. The remaining 10 groups are informal entities. It should be noted that even the informal groups refer to an established association (in eight cases, it is a national association; in two cases, it is a local association).

3.1.6 Legal nature

Regarding the legal nature of the groups, the most common type is "volunteer organisation", present in 45% of cases (27 groups). There are also 20% of groups (12 entities) with the legal nature of "social promotion association". There are two social cooperatives, one foundation, one family solidarity association (a legal type regulated by a regional law of Lombardy not found in other regional systems), and seven non-profit associations. Completing the count are the 10 entities not formally constituted (17% of the analysed groups).

3.2 Geographic presence

3.2.1 Geographical distribution of the groups

The geographic distribution of the 60 surveyed groups is as follows:

- 32 groups are located in Northwestern Italy (19 in Lombardy, 10 in Piedmont, and 3 in Liguria).

- 12 groups are based in Northeastern regions (five in Veneto, four in Emilia Romagna, and three in Friuli Venezia Giulia).
- Eight groups are present in central Italy (three in Lazio, two in Tuscany, two in Abruzzo, one in Marche).
- Eight groups are located in Southern Italy and the Islands (four in Sicily, three in Campania, and one in Apulia).

3.2.2 Meeting place of the groups

27 groups (48% of the sample) meet on premises provided free of charge by third-party subjects: third-sector entities, public entities, parishes, and volunteer service centres. One group out of three (31.3% of the sample, 19 groups) meets on premises owned by the group itself or by the third-sector entity that promoted its establishment. 12 groups (19.7% of the sample) meet in premises rented by members. 11 groups (18%) meet at the members' homes. About one group out of two uses more than one type of venue.

3.3 Participants

3.3.1 Number of members

The size of the groups in 35% of cases consists of 21–30 members (21 groups), and in 33% of cases, it consists of 11–20 members (20 groups). Groups composed of 10 or fewer people are less frequent (five groups), as are those with 31 to 40 people (four groups) and those with 41 to 50 people (three groups). Finally, six entities report the presence of over 100 members and one with over 200 members. In these cases, they are broad and composite entities, often present in territories or even dispersed across distant areas. The latter are characterised by organisational and relational structures different from small local family groups, with a relational net with a low intensity. In the future, exploring small local groups and broad networks separately will be appropriate.

3.3.2 Type of members

The proposed questionnaire included the possibility of indicating one or more types of participants. Almost all groups (59 out of 60) indicated two or more types. Only one group indicated a single type: the presence of "individuals/couples with residential foster care".

It is interesting to note that in 19 groups (equal to 32% of the sample), there are both foster and adoptive parents, indicating an interesting tendency to involve different forms of family care together. Only three groups (equal to 5% of the sample) gather together foster families and families of origin of minors in foster care or individuals/families facing other forms of difficulties. This aspect highlights the general tendency to follow the usual (but not necessarily preferable) dichotomy between benefactors and beneficiaries. The three entities that are experimenting with coexistence are particularly interesting and deserve further exploration (they are the "Famiglia per Tutti" Association in Bari, a group from Piedmont of the "Comunità Papa Giovanni XXIII" Association, and a Sicilian group belonging to the "Famiglie per l'Accoglienza" Association). The questionnaire also asked to indicate the type of members most present. It emerged that the prevailing members in the 40 groups are "individuals/couples with any type of ongoing residential foster care", consistent with the target audience to which this research refers.

3.3.3 Age groups of members

68% of the surveyed groups (41 groups) mainly consist of members belonging to the same age group. Specifically, in 31 cases (52% of the sample), the age group is 41–50 years; in 8 cases (13% of the sample), it is 51–60 years; and in 2 cases (3.3% of the sample), it is 31–40 years. There are no groups with predominant members under the age of 31, and only one group with some members aged 60. 32% of the surveyed groups (the remaining 19) have members of two or more age groups. The range spans twenty years in 11 groups (mostly within the 41–60 age group), thirty years in 7 groups (within the 31–60 age group), and one group with a participation range of a remarkable 40 years (31–70 years).

3.4 Beneficiaries

3.4.1 Number of fostered minors

As of 31st of December 2019, among the foster parents of the 60 surveyed groups, 717 children and adolescents were received, approximately 10% of the total number of minors in foster care in Italy that year. This data highlights the study sample's significance and encourages further determination in the path towards the total census of foster parent groups in Italy. Furthermore, the significance of the studied realities emerges from the total number of minors fostered since their establishment until 2019, totalling 2319 children and adolescents. This represents a valuable wealth of experience and solidarity.

3.4.2 Age groups of fostered minors

The questionnaire investigated the age ranges of the received minors, asking to indicate the prevalent ones. The possibility to indicate more than one range led the 60 groups to provide a total of 157 responses, distributed as follows:

- 0–2 years: 14 responses (8.2%)
- 3–5 years: 22 responses (14%)
- 6–10 years: 47 responses (29.9%)
- 11–14 years: 48 responses (30.6%)
- 15–17 years: 20 responses (12.7%)
- Young adults: six responses (3.8%)

Thus, the most recurring age ranges are 6–10 and 11–14 years, covering almost two-thirds of the total responses.

3.4.3 Young adults and administrative continuation

As of 31st of December 2019, out of the 60 surveyed groups, 52 had at least one foster parent of a young adult among their members. Among these, in 31 groups, the process was based on an administrative continuation measure issued by the Juvenile Court. Conversely, 21 groups reported the presence of young adults among their members without continuation measures.

3.4.4 Daytime solidarity and family support

Of the 60 surveyed groups, 65% (39 groups) are also active in daytime solidarity towards children and adolescents from the neighbourhood not based on foster care measures. It would be interesting to investigate the nature of these activities, such as whether they serve as preventive measures against the causes of separation, or if there are also actions for permanent support after the conclusion of a period of residential foster care. 48% of the sample (29 groups) is engaged in family support paths to aid families in difficulty. These are paths of interfamily solidarity where support is directed towards minors and the entire family unit.

3.5 Organisation

3.5.1 Group managers and representatives

In response to the question "Does the group have managers/representatives?", almost all groups (58 out of 60) answered affirmatively. Most groups (40 groups, 67% of the sample) have one or two managers/representatives. 13 groups have three or five managers/representatives. Five groups have more than five. In the latter case, these are large groups, with 40 or more members.

Regarding the "type of manager/representative", the questionnaire asked to specify whether they were "foster parents", "professionals", or "foster parents and professionals". 56 groups responded to the question (of the other four, two groups lacked managers, and the other two did not respond). 30 groups indicated that the task of manager/representative is carried out by one or more of the foster parents within the group. In 22 groups, the responsibility is shared between foster parents and professionals. Finally, there are four groups of foster parents led solely by professionals.

3.5.2 Technical-specialist support

Out of the 60 foster parent groups, 45 (75% of the sample) have enlisted the support of one or more professionals. Among these, 32 groups are accompanied by one or two professionals, 5 groups by three or four professionals, and 8 groups by five or more professionals. Regarding their professional qualifications, 24 groups benefit from the support of social workers, 32 groups from psychologists, 20 groups from educators, and 12 groups from other professionals. Thus, psychologists are the most common category, present in over half of the total groups and two-thirds of the groups followed by professionals.

There are 23 groups followed by a single professional. Even in these cases, psychologists are more common (10 groups) compared to social workers (6 groups), educators (4 groups), and other professionals (3 groups). Seven groups benefit from simultaneous support from social workers, psychologists, educators, and other professionals. In six of these cases, the "other professionals" are psychotherapists.

Regarding the type of relationship between professionals and associations, in 17 groups, it is exclusively "volunteer personnel" (37.8% of the groups with professionals). In addition to these, there are six groups with both volunteer and paid professionals. Paid professionals are categorised as "consultants" in 17 groups, "collaborators" in 10 groups, and "employees" in 15 groups.

3.5.3 Sub-groups

Thirteen out of sixty groups (22%) are structured into smaller sub-units (sub-groups). The reasons indicated in the questionnaires are various. In seven cases, the dispersal of foster parents over an excessively large geographic area was highlighted, which made it appropriate to establish local sub-groups. Three groups have divided into smaller units dedicated to different types of members (for example, between foster families and adoptive families) while maintaining common meetings. Finally, three groups have organised into sub-groups due to the excessive number of members, which necessitated the activation of more intimate and less dispersing spaces.

3.6 Group meetings

3.6.1 Frequency of group meetings

More than three-quarters of the groups meet once a month or more (46 out of 60 groups, 77%). Among these, 36 groups (60%) meet monthly, and 10 groups (17%) meet multiple times a month. 14 groups indicate a frequency of multiple meetings per year (11 groups, 18%), and 3 groups indicate an irregular frequency. It is noteworthy that no group indicated a weekly or multi-weekly meeting frequency nor, at the other extreme, a frequency of once a year. It is worth mentioning that among the 10 entities that hold more meetings per month, seven are organised into sub-groups. The other three groups are of medium-small size.

3.6.2 Days, time slots, and duration of meetings

Regarding the day of the week on which meetings are held, 25 groups prefer weekdays, 19 groups meet on weekends, and 16 groups have a variable schedule that intertwines weekdays and holidays. 30 groups prefer evening hours. 12 groups prefer the afternoon time slot. 13 groups do not have a fixed time slot and choose the meeting time each time. Three groups meet in the morning, and three for the whole day.

It is useful to highlight that by crossing the data on time slots with those on days, it emerges that 75% of the groups (46 out of 60) meet at times usually free from work (weekday evenings and/or weekends). Furthermore, considering that of the remaining 14 groups, 12 have indicated "variable days and times" (which does not exclude them from meeting on weekday evenings and/or holidays), we conclude (also intuitively based on common sense) that the meetings of foster parents are hardly conceivable during working hours.

Regarding the duration of meetings, the majority (56 out of 60 groups) tend to have meetings lasting no more than four hours. More specifically, 12 groups have meetings lasting between one and two hours, 31 groups between two and three hours, and 12 groups between three and four hours. Only four groups hold meetings lasting five or more hours.

3.6.3 Parallel activities with children

One last piece of information about meetings concerns the number of groups that, parallel to their appointments, organise activities to entertain the children of the participating families, thus facilitating their participation. These parallel activities are implemented by 38 groups, 63% of the sample. Out of the 22 groups that do not provide this type of activity, 19 are characterised by members aged 41 years or older, probably with children old enough not to need entertainment spaces. Therefore, almost all groups with members aged 40 years or younger, often with young children, provide such activities. Among the 38 groups organising this activity, 25 do so using free resources: in 22 cases, these are volunteers (from the group or even from other local entities, such as, for example, the Scouts), and in three cases, they are the older children of the participants. In the remaining 13 cases, professional children's entertainers, educators, or paid babysitters are hired.

3.6.4 Experiences of telematic connection between foster parents

The questionnaire investigated the presence of any experiences of telematic connection between individuals from various regions and countries. This activity is practised by 18 out of 60 groups (29.5% of the sample), largely among foster parents from different regions of Italy. The frequency of these connections is monthly in almost 50% of cases. Experiences of connection with foster parents from other countries, numerically less common, involve Switzerland, Spain, and the USA.

3.7 Activities carried out by the group

The questionnaire surveyed the areas of activity in which the groups are engaged. Both activities carried out by individual groups and those implemented by the entities (association, network, etc.) to which the groups belong were indicated.

The questionnaire listed typical activities, offering the possibility to specify additional ones. Each group had the opportunity to report one or more areas of activity. Below are the frequencies:

a. sensitisation/recruitment of individuals/couples available for fostering: 53 groups (86.9%);

b. training of individuals/couples available for fostering: 48 groups (78.7%);

c. collaboration with social services in the planning of foster care: 47 groups (77%);

d. support to foster parents and minors by professionals: 38 groups (62.3%);

e. support to foster parents and minors by individuals/couples with fostering experience: 51 groups (83.6%);

f. support to foster parents and minors by individuals/couples without fostering experience: 9 groups (14.8%);

g. periodic socialisation and conviviality among participating individuals/couples: 55 groups (90.2%);

h. groups for foster parents' children and/or minors in care: 10 groups (16.4%);

i. management of blogs or social pages for discussion, sharing, and dialogue: 8 groups (13.1%).

Organising the data into percentage ranges, the following picture emerges:

- *90–100% range*: the main activity carried out by the groups, present in more than 90% of cases, is to promote socialisation and conviviality among their members. We can consider this as the type of activity that substantiates and "makes the group exist".

- *80–90% range*: following closely, with a presence of 86.9% and 83.6% of groups, are the sensitisation activities for recruiting new members and support for members during foster care.

- *70–80% range*: also highly practised are the activities of member training (78.7%) and collaboration with social services (77%).

- *60–70% range*: closing the "ranking" of the most practised activities is support for foster care by the group's professionals (62.3%).

The questionnaire responses also highlight the presence of three areas of activity practised only by a minority of groups, all falling within the *10–20% range*. These include the presence of groups for children (16.4%), support for foster care by non-foster volunteers (14.8%), and the use of blogs and social networks (13.1%).

3.8 Network

3.8.1 Collaboration with territorial social services

Out of 60 surveyed groups, 59 have collaboration agreements with territorial social services. For 76.7% of the groups (46 out of 60), collaboration is based on explicit recognition (sometimes formalised in a written document) by the entity managing social services (municipality, consortium or association of municipalities, local health authority, etc.). In 45% of cases (27 groups), collaboration occurs continuously, i.e., with a frequency of once or more times per month. The remaining 33 groups have occasional collaborations, with irregular frequency and, in any case, not monthly. It is important to note that in 65.5% of cases, social services encourage the participation of foster parents in groups. This important data point also prompts an inquiry into the remaining 34.5% of cases (20 groups), which experience a lack of willingness from social services to facilitate foster parent participation in group experiences. Investigating the causes of this disconnect between groups and services would be interesting.

3.8.2 Collaboration with other territorial entities

70.5% of the groups also collaborate with other territorial institutions: 23 groups collaborate with municipalities, districts, and social services from other territories; 14 groups collaborate with regions; 13 groups with juvenile courts; 9 groups with local health authorities and/or hospitals; 4 groups with parishes and/or dioceses. Experiences of collaboration with other third-sector entities in the territory (associations, cooperatives, foundations, etc.) are present in 77% of the groups.

3.8.3 Collaboration with regional/national associations/networks

48 groups (80.3% of the sample) belong to a regional or national association or network. Among these, 33 groups have a real "membership" in a larger associative or federative reality. The remaining 15 groups have other forms of collaboration with the regional and/or national entity that do not constitute membership.

3.9 Economic resources

3.9.1 Most frequent economic sources

To support their activities, groups rely on various economic sources. The questionnaire listed various types of sources, asking to indicate one or more options. The emerged frequencies are as follows:

a. Membership fees/self-taxation of participants: 41 groups (68.3%)

b. Funds from private donations: 37 groups (61.7%)

c. Funds from the 5xMille donation scheme: 27 groups (45%)

d. Funds from Volunteering Service Centres: 6 groups (10%)

e. Funds from banking foundations: 11 groups (18.3%)

f. Funds from the entity managing social services (municipality, consortium, local health authority, etc.): 29 groups (48.3%)

g. Funds from other public entities: 7 groups (11.7%)

The most frequent economic sources are membership fees/self-taxation and the collection of private donations. Funds from the 5xMille and support from the entities managing social services are present in almost half of the groups. Contributions from other public entities, Volunteering Service Centres, and banking foundations are less common.

3.9.2 Most relevant economic sources

The economic source most frequently indicated as predominant (by 23 groups, 38.3% of the sample) is that of membership fees/self-taxation. For 10 groups, the

DOI: http://dx.doi.org/10.5772/intechopen.1007407

predominant source is funds from private donations. Nine groups indicate that funds from the entities managing social services are the most prevalent.

3.10 Difficulties and opportunities

3.10.1 Obstacles to group progress

The survey identified obstacles encountered by the groups in carrying out their activities. A range of predefined types was proposed, with the possibility of selecting more than one and indicating any additional obstacles not included in the list:

a. Difficulty in finding premises: 9 groups (15%)

b. Difficulty in finding professionals: 7 groups (11.7%)

c. Lack of economic resources to carry out activities: 30 groups (50%)

d. Difficulty in finding individuals/couples interested in participating: 23 groups (38.3%)

e. Difficulty in ensuring continuity in the involvement of individuals/couples: 24 groups (40%)

f. Difficulty in interacting with social services: 27 groups (45%)

g. Difficulty in interacting with other institutions: 9 groups (15%)

The responses allow distinguishing three ranges of frequency:

- *41–50% range*: The most frequent obstacle is economic (50% of groups).

- *31–40% range*: This range includes the difficulty in ensuring continuity over time in the involvement of people (40% of cases) and in finding individuals and couples willing to engage in group activities (38.3% of cases).

- *11–20% range*: Obstacles related to premises (15%), the recruitment of professionals (11.7%), and various difficulties with institutions other than social services (15%) are less frequent.

The subsequent question posed by the questionnaire, regarding the most significant difficulty, highlights a similar ranking, with 15 groups indicating the relationship with social services as their main problem. Following are, with 11 groups each, the difficulties in recruiting and retaining people in the groups.

3.10.2 Facilitations to group progress

The subsequent questions explore the support and facilitations encountered by the groups in carrying out their activities. Again, the questionnaire proposed a predefined list, with the possibility of specifying additional types. The emerged frequencies are as follows:

a. Support from social services: 13 groups (21.7%)

b. Support from other institutions: 2 groups (3.3%)

c. Passion and interest of foster parents: 57 groups (95%)

d. Support from the association/network/entity to which they belong: 47 groups (78.3%)

e. Support from other third sector entities: 9 groups (15%)

f. Support from Volunteering Service Centres: 5 groups (8.3%)

As expected, the main strength the groups rely on is their members' passion and interest. The comparison between the support provided by associations/networks (78.3%) and that provided by social services (21.7%) is interesting. Support from Volunteering Service Centres (8.3%) and other institutions (3.3%) is almost non-existent.

4. Reflections and implications for social services and researchers

The variety of aspects and data the questionnaire investigated suggests possible implications for social services and a wide range of further research avenues. For the sake of brevity, let us focus on some of the most relevant insights.

4.1 Implications for social services: Self-help among foster families to be recognised, valued, and supported

Already in the introduction of this research, mention was made of the presence of worrying levels of "non-connection" between social services and self-help realities among foster families. We cited a sample survey conducted in 2019 by the Ministry of Labor and Social Policies, which highlighted that in over 40% of cases, there is little or no collaboration between social services and foster care networks. The analysis of what was revealed by the interviews with the 60 groups in our sample confirms and deepens this scenario. For example, in terms of support provided, 78.3% of the groups have benefited from significant assistance from networks and associations, while only 21.7% of them have been well-supported by social services. In practice, support from the public service has had an impact of less than one-third of the support offered to groups by associative realities. 15% of the groups even declare explicit difficulties in coordinating with social services. Also, on the front of the "paternity" of the groups, the reduced fertility of public action emerges. Only 7% of the self-help groups were born at the initiative of institutions. This data could be determined by several factors: reduced commitment of public entities in promoting foster care, reduced attention of public entities in accompanying foster families to meet in groups, and the failure to identify or detect existing groups promoted by the services. In this regard, some work paths, deducible from this research, on which to focus the action of social services could include providing economic support, since the lack of resources is indicated as the "main problem" by about half of the groups; offering training and support actions for foster families at non-working hours and days, since—as highlighted by the research—these are the spaces that foster families most choose for self-help activities; activating training and support interventions for group managers, since 52 out of 60 groups are led by foster parents and in 30 groups this leadership is not shared with professional operators; and activating parallel activities for the children of foster parents, if it is decided to involve couples under the age of 40.

4.2 The three seasons of self-help among foster families in Italy: A phenomenon to be studied

The prevalence of self-help groups born in the period 1995–2006 (almost double compared to periods of similar duration before and after) highlights three seasons: the first (1983–1994), of establishment; the second (1995–2006), of positive expansion; the third (2007–2019), of slowdown. This scenario could be attributed to the more intense and emphatic promotion of family foster care and the development of child welfare that precisely between the end of the 1990s and the beginning of the new millennium saw important steps forward, characterised—among many aspects—by the promulgation of three important national laws: Law 285/97 concerning provisions for the promotion of rights and opportunities for childhood and adolescence, Law 328/00 framework law for the implementation of the integrated system of social interventions and services, Law 149/01 reforming family foster care. Similarly, the lower fertility observed in recent years could be connected to various converging phenomena: the development of neoliberal policies that have promoted, also through radical cuts in financial resources, the disengagement of the state from welfare; the shift from the state to the regions of legislative competences in social matters introduced by the constitutional reform of 2001 and the unpreparedness of many regional administrative systems, especially in central-southern Italy, already burdened by the difficult activation of the territorial social areas provided for by framework Law 328/00; the increasingly frequent anti-social protection and anti-removal campaigns of minors that have gradually developed in Italy following certain illicit acts committed by reception facilities (cf. the case of Forteto) and by services (cf. the case of Bibbiano). It would also be necessary to investigate further elements: for example, whether the slowdown in recent years could have been due to a lesser "propulsive force" exerted by national associations/networks or, broadening the picture, how much the rampant "crisis of participation" and "sociality" counts, with the lesser willingness of new generations to gather in groups and associations and the tendency to connect through virtual platforms rather than physical spaces. The study and understanding of the causes of the lower creation of groups of foster families in the last period could be the basis for *ad hoc* research, also to understand whether self-help among foster families is a reality destined for marginality or, rather, if and under what conditions it can be promoted and supported.

4.3 Further insights for researchers

The study reveals further interesting insights that can be considered in the design of further research. For example:

- regarding the legal nature of self-help groups, it will be interesting to observe the evolutions that it has had as a result of the Third Sector Reform;

- regarding the geographical distribution, it will be useful to understand what determines the prevailing northern composition of the studied entities: the failure to identify the entities present in the absent or underrepresented regions? The lower presence of groups of foster families in these areas? This latter hypothesis could in turn be determined by a lesser development of family foster care in these territories or by a lesser tendency of central-southern foster families to gather in self-help groups. It will be useful to investigate the incidence, in this respect, of the lower presence of Third Sector Entities in the southern regions compared to other areas of the country: 48.5 TSEs per 10 thousand inhabitants, compared to 63.1 in the Northwest, 68.3 in the Centre, 70.5 in the Northeast [23].

- regarding the continuation of fostering of young adults, it is necessary to understand why there is a widespread, although not majority, presence of "de facto" placements of young adults, not supported by any type of acts or provisions. Are they unofficial modalities that respond to particular situations and needs of young adults? Are they indicative of a different practice by some services and juvenile judges? Other causes?

- regarding the size of self-help groups and the frequency of their meetings, it would be interesting to investigate any "effects" of these on maintaining the availability of foster families and the quality of the support provided to ongoing placements. Do small-sized groups manage to offer more consistent and effective self-help paths? What is the most suitable meeting frequency, which favours the best relationship between participation commitment and benefits received?

- considering the strong presence, among the difficulties reported by the groups, of problems with the continuity over time of people and recruitment of young members, it would be necessary to search for best practices that have been able to address such critical issues and spread their implementation.

Author details

Marco Giordano[1,2]*, Marilena Di Lollo[2] and Carmela Carotenuto[2]

1 "Aldo Moro" University of Bari, Italy

2 "Foster Care" Study Center, Italy

*Address all correspondence to: marcogiordano@centrostudiaffido.it

References

[1] Albanesi C. I gruppi di auto-aiuto. Roma: Carocci; 2004. p. 8

[2] Steinberg DM. L'auto/mutuo aiuto. Guida per i facilitatori di Gruppo. Trento: Erickson; 2002. p. 11

[3] Lavanco G, Novara C. Elementi di psicologia di comunità, Elementi di psicologia di comunità. Progettare, attuare e partecipare il cambiamento sociale. Milano: McGraw-Hill; 2012. pp. 84-88

[4] Tognetti BM. Promuovere i gruppi di self-help. Milano: Franco Angeli; 2002. p. 18

[5] Mlps – Ministero del Lavoro e delle Politiche Sociali. Bambini e ragazzi in affidamento familiare e nei servizi residenziali per minorenni. Quaderni della Ricerca sociale. 2021;**49**:5-20

[6] Giordano M. Promuovere l'Affidamento familiare. Buone prassi e indicazioni metodologiche per l'intervento dei servizi sociali. Milano: Franco Angeli; 2019. pp. 13-15

[7] Cnsa – Coordinamento Nazionale dei Servizi Affidi. Proposte di Linee Guida per l'Affidamento Familiare [Internet]2007. pp. 6-7. Available from: https://smart.comune.genova.it/sites/default/files/archivio/documenti/proposte_di_linee_guida_per_laffidamento_familiare.pdf

[8] Tavolo Nazionale Affido. Le associazioni e reti di famiglie affidatarie. [Internet]. 2013. Available from: https://www.tavolonazionaleaffido.it/a/ji/files/888946/content

[9] Mlps – Ministero del Lavoro e delle Politiche Sociali. Parole nuove per l'Affidamento Familiare. Sussidiario per operatori e famiglie. Potenza: Edizioni Le Penseur; 2014. pp. 83-85

[10] Brown J, Kapasi A, Eyre V, Weindels S. A cluster analysis of peer support training needs for Foster parents. Journal of Child and Family Studies. 2021;**30**:2756-2765

[11] Miller AE, Duren Green T, Lambros KM. Foster parent self-help. A conceptual model. Children and Youth Services Review. 2019;**99**:107-114

[12] Gvaldaite L. Promoting foster families' selfhelp groups in Lithuania. Relational Social work. 2018;**II**(2):34-49

[13] Edelstein S. When foster children leave: Helping foster parent to grieve. Child Welfare. 1981;**LX**(7):467-473

[14] Anderson GR, Gurdin P, Thomas A. Parenting children with AIDS. In: Doka K, editor. Disenfranchised Grief: Recognizing Hidden Sorrow. New York: Lexington Books; 1989. pp. 43-53

[15] Edelstein SB, Burge D, Waterman J. Helping foster parents cope with separation, loss, and grief. Child Welfare. 2001;**LXXX**(1):5-25

[16] Maclay F, Bunce M, Purves DG. Surviving the system as a foster carer. Adoption & Fostering. 2006;**30**(3):33

[17] Sellick C. Supporting Short-Term Foster Carers. Hants: Ashgate Publishing Ltd; 1992. p. 113

[18] McInerney A. Somebody to lean on: Peer mentoring as a support mechanism for Foster carers. Critical Social Thinking: Policy and Practice. 2009;**I**:249-263

[19] Mlps – Ministero del Lavoro e delle Politiche Sociali. Bambini e ragazzi in accoglienza in Italia. Esiti dell'indagine campionaria sull'affidamento familiare e i servizi residenziali. Questioni e documenti. 2019;**66**:92

[20] Caselli M. Indagare col questionario. Introduzione alla ricerca sociale di tipo standard. Milano: Vita e Pensiero; 2005

[21] Corbetta P. Metodologia e tecniche della ricerca sociale. Bologna: Il Mulino; 1999. p. 208

[22] Rogers R. Metodi digitali. Fare ricerca sociale con il web. Bologna: Il Mulino; 2016

[23] Istat. Struttura e profili del settore no profit – Anno 2020 [Internet]. 2022. p. 2. Available from: https://www.istat.it/wp-content/uploads/2022/10/REPORT-NON-PROFIT-2022.pdf

Chapter 7

Choosing Schools: The Trade-Offs Parents of Black Students Must Navigate

Joan M. Blakey, Labibah M. Buraik, Channel Lowery and Jessica M. Coleman

Abstract

Historically, education has been a way of achieving societal success for Black families. As schools became integrated, many Black parents sought the best educational opportunities for their children, often choosing predominantly White institutions. This study aims to understand the factors parents of Black children used when choosing high schools for their children. Through thematic analysis, the research revealed that Black parents equated the best academic experiences possible with high graduation rates, preparation for future success, comprehensive and well-rounded education, access to extracurricular activities and support services, a "one-stop-shop" for educational needs, living near the school, and diversity within the school. Despite these priorities, many children reported negative experiences rooted in racism, which impacted their overall educational experience. Even when parents became aware of these racial challenges, they often prioritized the perceived quality of education over the emotional and psychological toll on their children. These findings reveal the complex trade-offs that Black parents navigate between securing quality education and ensuring their children's overall health and well-being. The study underscores the need for supportive and inclusive educational environments where Black students can excel academically and personally.

Keywords: Black families, education, high school selection, academic experiences, racism and microaggressions, qualitative

1. Introduction

> *"For me, education is absolutely a civil right because that is the key to being able to fully realize the American dream, access a livable wage, and participate in civil society."*
>
> *~ Khadijah Williams ~*

During the more than 200-year period of slavery in the United States, many enslaved Black people were forced to educate themselves in secret, as it was illegal for them to learn to read and write. Reading or instructing others to read during slavery posed significant risks, with many enslaved people facing severe consequences, including mutilation and even death. Despite these dangers, Black people have persistently pursued knowledge and formal education, even in the face of severe oppression and adversity [1].

Even after the abolition of slavery, they continued to face significant barriers to education. Freedpeople's schools were established during the Reconstruction period following the Civil War. Nonetheless, these institutions struggled to access the resources necessary to educate students effectively [1]. Although anti-literacy laws were no longer enforceable, new challenges emerged. The doctrine of "separate but equal" led to the establishment of segregated schools, which were far from equal in practice. Black students faced unequal access to educational resources, poorly maintained facilities, limited funding, and constant threats of violence and intimidation. These factors severely restricted Black people's access to quality educational opportunities, perpetuating the inequalities that had existed during slavery.

Despite these profound obstacles, the determination of Black people to pursue education often surpassed the numerous obstacles they encountered. During an era when Black students were systematically excluded from historically white institutions due to segregation and discriminatory admissions policies, HBCUs were established to provide Black Americans with access to exemplary educational experiences and professional advancement. However, their creation was driven by more than just exclusion; HBCUs also served as essential institutions for nurturing Black intellectualism, leadership, and community development [2]. These institutions became vital spaces where Black students could receive a quality education, cultivate a sense of cultural pride, and gain the skills necessary for professional and civic leadership in a society that largely marginalized their contributions [3].

The educational landscape of the United States has changed with the passing of pivotal legislation like Brown v. Board of Education in 1954, which declared racial segregation in public schools unconstitutional, and the Civil Rights Act of 1964, which further enforced desegregation and prohibited discrimination based on race [4, 5]. Despite these landmark rulings, Black students still face significant challenges in obtaining a quality education. The promise of equal educational opportunities remains unfulfilled for many Black students as they continue to encounter systemic inequities, including segregation by socioeconomic status, underfunded schools, and racial bias in the classroom [6].

Black parents view their children's academic success through multiple lenses: as a pathway to financial independence, a form of protection in a racist society, and a means of providing their children with broader life opportunities [7–9]. Additionally, Black parents see education as expressing collective and individual dignity [10]. The significance of education within the Black community is rooted in the awareness that, historically, Black people's intellectual, social, and political contributions have been devalued and marginalized in the United States, contributing to the school-to-prison pipeline [7, 11]. Thus, the pursuit of education is seen as a crucial means to level the playing field and shield Black children from some of the limitations faced by previous generations.

These findings reveal the intricate and difficult trade-offs that Black parents must navigate as they balance the need for quality education with the necessity of ensuring their children's overall health and well-being. Black parents often find themselves making complex decisions about whether to send their children to underfunded schools that may offer a sense of community and identity or to better-resourced schools where diversity among students, teachers, staff, and administrators is lacking. This dilemma highlights the ongoing systemic inequities within the education system

DOI: http://dx.doi.org/10.5772/intechopen.1007500

that force Black parents to choose between academic excellence and a nurturing, culturally affirming environment. The study emphasizes the critical need for supportive and inclusive educational spaces where Black students can thrive academically and personally without sacrificing one for the other. Black parents' strategic and multifaceted decisions reflect their deep commitment to protecting and preparing their children for the future while navigating a system that often fails to support their needs fully [7, 12–14].

2. Literature review

Research reveals that when Black parents choose elementary and high schools for their children, they navigate a multifaceted landscape of considerations. These factors encompass not only academic quality [15, 16] family income [15, 16], and proximity [15], but also a deep awareness of racial dynamics [14] school diversity [14], and the broader environment in which their children will be immersed. While much of the existing research emphasizes academic quality—often measured by school ratings, resource availability, and academic performance—Black parents frequently adopt a broader perspective when envisioning the "best education possible." For them, education transcends academic achievement; it is about cultivating a nurturing environment where their children can thrive socially, emotionally, and culturally [17]. Black parents view education as a comprehensive experience that should address their children's social, emotional, and cultural needs alongside their academic development.

2.1 Diversity, relationships, and racial impacts

A study by XXX (in press) [18] found that Black students in predominantly white schools often struggle with a profound lack of belonging, experiencing feelings of being unwelcome, not mattering, encountering racial insensitivity, and not seeing themselves reflected in their environment. These challenges underscore the critical importance of diversity in the school environment, which influences Black parents' decisions in ways that extend beyond traditional academic metrics.

For Black parents, diversity is a multifaceted concept that includes not only the composition of the student body [14, 15, 19] but also the cultural capital of teachers and staff [14, 19] and the quality of relationships among students, staff, teachers, and parents. Diversity also encompasses exposure to various groups, knowledge, and cultures [14] the racial composition and demographics of the student body [15, 19] the alignment between the race of students and school staff [19], and the staff's awareness of how racism shapes the experiences of Black families and children [14].

Ultimately, Black parents recognize that a truly holistic education must account for their children's racial and cultural realities, ensuring that their intellectual growth is supported by their development as a whole, empowered individuals. This holistic view of diversity highlights the importance of having teachers and staff who reflect the students' identities and understand and are allies in their experiences. The presence of educators who are aware of the historical and ongoing impacts of racialized experiences is crucial, as it fosters an environment where Black children can see themselves represented and supported in their educational journey [20]. In light of these considerations, Black parents must carefully evaluate the impact of belonging on their children when making school choices, recognizing that their children's social and emotional well-being is as vital as academic success.

3. School environment and proximity

Some parents select their housing based on the schools they wish their children to attend. Others prioritize proximity, choosing schools close to home, while others still weigh the trade-off between proximity and quality [21]. Across the studies cited, factors influencing school choice often centered around predominantly white schools, magnet schools, public schools, and schools in various geographic locations. A key difference in school choice was highlighted in [16] which reported that while parents across different races and income levels consistently preferred academic quality, those with lower incomes were more likely to prioritize proximity over quality. Conversely, parents with lower levels of education tended to prioritize the quality of education over proximity [16].

While parents consider multiple factors when choosing schools for their children, their decisions are often "characterized by trade-offs," with academic quality frequently taking precedence over other crucial considerations such as diversity, proximity, and the impact of racism [21] Black parents, in particular, face these trade-offs across various school types (e.g., public, private), grade levels, and geographic locations, underscoring the difficult choices they must navigate. Although schools' racial makeup and diversity are acknowledged as necessary, academic achievement remains the primary priority for many parents. For those who weigh multiple factors and continually monitor their children's experiences, school choice evolves into a complex and ongoing process of risk assessment and balancing trade-offs, as illustrated in [21].

Black parents often see academic success as more than just an educational milestone—it is a vital pathway to financial independence, a protective measure against the challenges of a racially biased society, and a gateway to broader life opportunities for their children [7–9]. Education also embodies personal and collective pride, holding deep cultural significance within the Black community [10]. While academic achievement is understandably prioritized, it is essential to recognize that school choice for Black parents involves navigating a complex web of considerations. These include balancing academic quality with proximity, diversity, and the potential impacts of racism within the school environment. Parents must also weigh the trade-offs between these factors, acknowledging that decisions made in the best interest of their children's academic future may have broader implications on their social and emotional development. Ultimately, Black parents are tasked with making decisions that not only prioritize academic excellence but also consider the long-term well-being of their children in a society where racial dynamics significantly influence educational experiences.

4. Methods

Thematic analysis is a qualitative research method used to systematically identify, organize, and interpret patterns within data, offering a way to gain meaningful insights into the research question guiding this study [22]. This method is particularly effective when trying to uncover shared meanings and experiences among participants, thus providing a richer understanding of the factors parents of Black children use when deciding what the best possible education means for their children [22]. Thematic analysis is well-suited for an in-depth examination of specific phenomena, such as understanding the considerations of parents and students when selecting schools, enabling researchers to delve into the intricate factors influencing these decisions [22]. Furthermore, thematic analysis places significant emphasis on the voices and experiences of participants, ensuring that their perspectives are central to developing theories and interpretations, enabling us to capture the essence of their lived experiences [23].

4.1 Sample

The Crestview community (pseudonym) is a suburb north of a large midwestern city. The Crestview community characterizes itself as an urban-suburban village. Crest is known for its public schools, which provide a liberal arts education and is classified as one of the best school districts in the state. The school district serves around 2000 students annually, spread across two primary schools (Grades K-6), one junior high school (Grades 7 and 8 primary), and one high school (i.e., Grades 9–12). Almost 90% of high school students in this district go to colleges and universities nationally upon graduation.

Using a criterion sample, a type of purposive sample, participants had to meet the following criteria. They had to (1) be Black, (2) attend Crest Academy High School (i.e., Grades 9–12), (3) if under 18 years old, had to have parental consent, and (4) voluntarily agreed to participate in the study. Thirty-eight high school students participated in the study (**Table 1**).

The parents in the study had to have a Black child who participated in the focus groups. There were 14 parents of Black students in the study (**Table 2**).

Demographic characteristics	*N*	**Percent (%)**
Gender		
Female	23	61
Male	15	39
Age in years (mean)	15–18	
15 years old	10	26
16 years old	13	34
17 years old	12	32
18 years old	3	8
Race/ethnicity		
Black	26	68
Black & Hispanic ethnicity	4	11
Multi-racial (Black and White)	8	21
School attended		
Crest Academy Secondary School (i.e., Grades 9–12)	38	100
Family structure		
Lived with both parents	20	53
Lived with mother	17	45
Lived with father only or foster care	1	2

Table 1.
Student demographic characteristics (N = 38).

Parent's name	Race of parent	Number of children in school district	Grades	Living inside or outside the district
Aaliyah	Black	1	9th grade	In
Solomon	Black	2	10th grade and 7th grade	In
Sarah	White	1	9th grade	In
JT	Black	1	12th grade	In
Imani	Black	3	11th grade and two recent high school graduates	In
Isabel	Black	1	12th grade	In
Eliza	Black	2	8th grade and 6th grade	In
Annie & Franklin	Black	1	9th grade	Out
Amber & Bill	Black	3	2–11th grade and 8th grade	Out
Frank	Black	1	9th grade	Out
Afua	Black	1	11th grade	In
Yaa	Black	1	10th grade	In

Table 2.
Parent demographics characteristics (N = 14).

4.2 Recruitment

This study is a subset of a larger study in which we conducted five focus groups (three with high school students and two with junior high school) with 51 junior high and high school students regarding their experience as Black students in a predominantly White school district. In this book chapter, we only focused on high school students. Participants for the study were enlisted through a flier sent to the homes of all Black students enrolled at Crest Academy High School. The school staff collected completed consent forms. Focus group sessions were organized once at least five students had returned their consent forms. These sessions were conducted in a designated room or classroom, as identified by staff employed at the high school. All focus group meetings took place during the lunch break, which was deemed the least disruptive time by the superintendent.

We conducted focus groups with parents to share the study results, highlighting their children's experiences and getting their feedback, thoughts, and impressions of the findings. We contacted the parents of the students who participated in the study via email or phone call. We identified four dates, and parents chose the best date for them. We conducted two focus groups. Five parents attended the first focus group. Seven parents participated in the second focus group. Two parents who were scheduled to attend the focus group had a last-minute emergency and could not participate in the focus groups. We conducted individual interviews with those parents.

A research team conducted the focus groups. They were in person, at the school, in the evening. Dinner was provided to the parents. Each parent also received a $20 Walmart gift card. All focus group interviews were audiotaped using a digital recorder and professionally transcribed. The focus groups lasted 120–150 minutes. All study protocols were approved by the XXX's Institutional Review Board (IRB), which oversees research with human subjects. Study protocols consisted of a complete explanation of the study, consent forms, recruitment materials, and interview guides.

DOI: http://dx.doi.org/10.5772/intechopen.1007500

4.3 Data collection methods

Data for this study consisted of transcripts from two focus groups and two individual interviews. Focus groups were the primary data collection method because they are a great way to collect information regarding participants' perceptions, opinions, beliefs, and attitudes [24]. Focus groups allowed for group dialog and participants to hear differing or similar viewpoints related to their children's experiences. Focus groups often provide rich information and insights [24]. Finally, focus groups allowed the exploration of theories, devolving deeper into specific topics and clarifying questions and answers in real time.

4.4 Data analysis

Data analysis of the focus group and individual interviews involved several steps. The first step consisted of memo and note-taking, often during the focus groups, to capture early impressions and thoughts emerging from the interviews. Memos are a tool for documenting analytic reflections and impressions derived from the information shared [25]. The second step involved reviewing the transcripts to ensure accuracy and fixing mistakes and errors before coding data. The third step consisted of coding the data using a line-by-line approach. According to Charmaz [26] "Coding is the pivotal link between collecting data and developing an emergent theory to explain the data" (p. 113). The fourth step focused on refining codes, combining similar codes, and identifying a final list of codes [27]. The fifth step involved looking for linkages and relationships between codes, grouping similar codes, and identifying themes based on larger groupings of codes. The final step consisted of establishing connections between categories of codes used to create themes [26].

Data analysis was conducted collaboratively by the lead researcher who initially collected the data and the three authors. Together, we coded the data and reviewed our codes, engaging in discussions to resolve disagreements about how best to code specific data sections. This approach aligns with Braun and Clarke's [22] recommendations for thematic analysis, where reflexivity and dialog among team members play a crucial role in achieving reliable and meaningful themes. While we did not employ formal inter-rater reliability measures, we worked through our differences until we reached a consensus that all members felt comfortable with, a method supported by [28], who emphasized the importance of reflexivity and teamwork in qualitative research. Although the absence of formal inter-rater reliability may be considered a limitation of this work, as it introduces the potential for subjective bias in the coding process [29] our thorough discussions and consensus-building approach aimed to enhance the reliability of the findings. Guest et al. [30] further endorse this approach, noting that consensus-building can be an effective alternative to inter-rater reliability in qualitative research, ensuring that the derived themes are valid and reflect the data.

5. Findings

Black parents chose Crest Academy because they believed that this school would provide their children with the best academic experiences possible. They considered eight primary factors when deciding the best high school for their children.

5.1 Parental factors

5.1.1 Factor 1: Graduation rates

- "I researched area schools and settled on Crest Academy because of their graduation rates, and most of them go to college." *Labdhi, Black Parent*

5.1.2 Factor 2: Preparation for the future

- "When they graduate, they will be prepared to go to Stanford or Harvard. I have lived in this community all my life. Crest is a great school. They will be prepared to go to whatever college they want to attend." *Solomon, Black Parent*

5.1.3 Factor 3: Comprehensive, well-rounded education

- "We were looking for a school that provided a comprehensive education for the girls where programs weren't being cut a lot, like arts and music and languages. Those are things we wanted, and I knew that they were being cut in the city, so we wanted to be somewhere where that wasn't happening." *Eliza, Black Parent*

5.1.4 Factor 4: Extracurricular activities and support services that enrich their children

- "We want our children to be exposed to a wide range of experiences and perspectives, which will help them become well-rounded individuals ready to tackle any challenge." *Louis, Black Parent*

5.1.5 Factor 5: Exposure to different activities and experiences

- "My son said "If I never went to Crest Academy, I would have never gotten into soccer. Soccer is big in every place in the world except the United States. It's definitely growing, but do you know – in Africa that's all they play is soccer...He has gotten to where he is good at it...I went and got him soccer cleats the other day. He loves that game. After the camp, when he was a counselor there, he said, "Ma, I'm ready to go back into soccer." He said the Black kids were like teasing me, "How do you play soccer? That's gay." He was like, "I don't care what they say. I'm going to do what I'm good at." *Afua Kobi, Black Parent*

5.1.6 Factor 6: One stop shop

- We paid for all of her extra stuff. I had to pay for her to speak a foreign language. I had to pay for her to have music lessons. I had to pay for everything I wanted extra for her...But now they're all included. And now I can get it all in one place...I can see her skills have grown and become so defined. I'm thinking, "Man, if she would have gotten this so much sooner she would be so much more ahead than where she is now. *Labdhi, Black Parent*

5.1.7 Factor 7: Going to school in the district where they live

- I recommend they live in the district. I drove my child 20 minutes every day to school in the Puffin Bluff area. Sometimes not living in the community and being bussed in, they can't really participate because of transportation issues. I think that sometimes, your experience is a little bit different when living in the community...He will be able to participate in more things and get more out of his education, not to mention friends in the community. *Afua Kobi*

5.1.8 Factor 8: Diversity

- We moved here from the U.K. so she was born in England, she has an African dad and was raised in Britain which is very multicultural, very diverse...So, for me, the big thing was when we moved here, I wanted to keep her in a system that I think would resemble an area in terms of cultural diversity, not just racial diversity, to what she was accustomed to, and I think Crest Academy offered that in terms of other children who speak multiple languages like she does...When I really searched the different schools, it really came down to the diversity that Crest Academy offered that's how she ended up here. *Sarah is a parent who is a White British woman whose daughter is biracial.*

Black parents chose Crest Academy for its promise of delivering a top-tier academic experience, with the school's graduation rates and college preparedness being major deciding factors. They valued a comprehensive, well-rounded education that included access to extracurricular activities and support services, all within a diverse and culturally enriching environment. The convenience of having these offerings in a single location was also significant. Furthermore, parents appreciated the opportunity for their children to attend a school within their district, enhancing their ability to participate fully in school activities.

5.2 Black students' factors

From their children's perspective, the following factors were most valuable about their Crest Academy experience.

5.2.1 Factor 1: Preparation for the future

- In five years, I'll probably be finishing off my degree in Political Science at Wash U down where my grandparents live and everyone in my family has gone. I have already started going there to help plan people's campaigns and make future plans. *Kofi, Black High School Student*

5.2.2 Factor 2: Extracurricular activities

- "I would say their academics are really good. Our opportunities for the future and with sports and arts and all that different kinda stuff is really high." *Emeka, Black High School Student*

5.2.3 Factor 3: Freedom

- "I would say the freedoms that they let you do during the school day and let you have your phones and have the open campus lunches...During free periods, you get to leave campus. No one's watching you, you just—like, I guess people treat you like an adult and like they, they give the responsibility to you to keep yourself up to date with all your school work. And I think that's different from a lot of schools around here." *Ekon, Black High School Student*

5.2.4 Factor 4: Supportive and inclusive environment where they can thrive

- "There are teachers here that like make me feel comfortable here like cool like Mr. Hawkins, Mr. Saul, Mr. Thomas... They're gonna like give you advice, and they're also gonna get on you if you're not doing what you're supposed to do." *Femi, Black High School Student*

From the students' perspective, the most valued aspects of their experience at Crest Academy included preparation for future academic and career opportunities, the availability of extracurricular activities, and the sense of freedom and responsibility they enjoyed within the school. Additionally, a supportive and inclusive environment, fostered by teachers who both challenge and care for them, was crucial in making their high school experience positive and conducive to their overall growth.

Black students and their parents shared similar aspirations for the high school experience. Both prioritized a robust academic foundation to prepare the students for the future. The school's extracurricular activities were also highly valued. Additionally, students emphasized the importance of freedom to express themselves and the need for a supportive and inclusive school environment.

5.3 Underestimating racism: How racial dynamics compromise children's educational experience

The Black students and their parents underestimated the impact that being Black in a predominantly White school would have on their educational experience. Many parents considered the diversity of the administrators, teachers, and staff when choosing a school, but this did not necessarily translate into a better experience for their Black children. Their children had a lot of negative experiences rooted in racial bias and racism that adversely affected their educational experience. Black students described:

5.3.1 Constantly needing to prove themselves

- "I'll just say it's like you always have to kind of like prove yourself. Like if you're smart like me, I'm in like advanced classes, and my teachers like expect more of me, but then like it seems like I have to like prove myself." *Ifeoma, Black High School Student*

5.3.2 Lower expectations of Black students

- "I had an experience with a teacher where she gave me a reading test, and I read a lot higher than I was supposed to. She gave me a reading test that was a lot lower than even the grade that I was in. Like she assumed that I was gonna be dumber, and then I passed it, and she kept giving me higher ones, and she was surprised when she had to get the higher ones." *Binta, Black High School Student*

5.3.3 Lack of representation

- "I have not had a Black teacher or any teacher of color throughout all of my schooling in the Crestview district. I went to kindergarten here, and now I am in high school. You mean to tell me they can't find not one Black teacher. Heck, I will take a teacher of color; they don't have to be Black. It is important to see people like us in positions of power within the school district, and that is severely lacking." *Taraji, Black High School Student*

5.3.4 Feeling targeted and singled out

- "Last year, we had two teachers. There was a group of us standing in the hallway, and then there were just two teachers watching us. He was kind of walking through us and, like the teacher, was throwing out his elbows. He said, "I've dealt with bigger kids than you guys. I deal with juniors and seniors," and then he just kind of walked away...We got called to the office out of nowhere, and they threatened to suspend us for standing in the hallway talking to each other. *Davu, Black High School Student*

5.3.5 Mistreatment

- "I don't know. This one teacher was really mean to me for no reason. I never did anything to her. She would always touch me in my face, and like I mostly – I didn't say anything because I didn't wanna disrespect a teacher, but she was getting out of hand, and she would make me cry, and I never cry. She was just so mean to me for two years in a row. I didn't even have her as a teacher. I never even had her for P.E., which is her job, but she just went out of her way to be mean to me. She just like hated me. She tried to get in my face, and I was mad about it, but I didn't know what else to do." *Taraji, Black High School Student*

5.3.6 Unequal treatment

- "Yeah, math lab, we didn't have work that day, and we usually have work to do. When we don't, we're like usually quiet, and we aren't doing anything. A group of us were friends, and we kind of stayed to ourselves. We were just conversing, and a teacher kind of got on us about doing our work, but we were not doing anything. We're not causing a scene, but there are other kids who are White that are doing the same thing. Another kid sits on his phone every day. I mean, he's not doing anything, but she never gets on him, and it's like she's always pressing us to do our work, but she's never pressing them." *Amare, Black High School Student*

5.3.7 Constantly dealing with microaggressions and racism

- "I think the only issue I really have is like when race is brought up. I know personally for me, if I try to speak on it, White people will intervene as if they know about it." *Zuri, Black High School Student*

- "I think they should be focused on their approach... Like someone who voted for Donald Trump, but then they'll be treating me like I'm like a higher-up black person or something like that because, like, I do well in school. And I don't think that should be like that because doing well in school for a black person should not be rare like something that's not normal, and just because they don't see that in certain students here doesn't mean that that represents the whole race." *Ifeoma, Black High School Student*

- "Like, I know sometimes my hair gets a lot of attention, and sometimes it gets annoying because they always wanna touch it and like to mess it up, and sometimes that gets annoying, but other than that, it's—I'm fine." *Taraji, Black High School Student*

- "I know that students in the class, some who have graduated and just some who are in my class... have gone to this school all the way from kindergarten like I have. That also will say that microaggressions have always been a problem. Like they will say, 'You're smart, you know, for a black girl' and stuff like that." *Asha, Black High School Student*

Many of the Black students nor their parents anticipated the full extent of what it meant to be Black in a predominantly White environment. They revealed several key themes associated with being Black in such environments: the need to see people who look like them, the struggle for fair treatment and equal opportunities, the emotional toll of microaggressions and racism, and the pervasive sense of demoralization.

Despite the shock and dismay parents felt upon learning about specific racist incidents their children encountered at Crest Academy, many expressed that they would still choose the school even with the knowledge they have now. Their commitment to providing their children with the best possible education remained their top priority. While parents acknowledged the need to intervene if the treatment escalated to severe levels, they also believed that these experiences were, in some ways, preparing their children for the harsh realities of being Black in America. As Frank put it, "I can't shield my children from the real world; they need to understand what it is like to be Black in America." Afua Kobi shared a similar perspective: "Kofi did mention little racial things that happen. You always experience some kind of little stuff, but you just blow off certain things if they're not really direct. But if it's something real direct, you're going to address it." This pragmatic approach reflects a nuanced understanding of the balance between protecting their children and equipping them with the resilience needed to navigate a society where racial challenges are, unfortunately, a reality.

Parents considered various factors when choosing a school they believed would provide their children with the best education possible. Ultimately, they prioritized their children's education and future college prospects above all else. However, a couple of parents did question whether the education their children received outweighed what the process took from them. Eliza discussed how the process changed her daughter. She stated:

> *It's been really hard, And now she's discouraged. Every chance she gets to say, "I hate school," she will say it, and that hasn't been her. She has all this other stuff going but has not thrived here. I mean, I was up at the school. I don't even know how many times in the last two years. She didn't have the best teachers. I had to get her moved out of one class to the next. It hasn't been great for her.*

Another parent noticed something similar. Isabel said:

> *Hearing about these experiences is really validating. I didn't know what was happening to my daughter, but I saw how it took her confidence and how it changed the core of who my daughter was. She became depressed and withdrawn. You know a young Black boy committed suicide this year. I am thinking that could have been her. Yeah, I am questioning whether it was worth it.*

DOI: http://dx.doi.org/10.5772/intechopen.1007500

These reflections raise critical questions: If school leaves children feeling demoralized, inferior, or traumatized, can they genuinely perform their best?? If teachers expect less of them and fail to push them to excel, are they receiving the best education possible? If educational experiences are so damaging that children no longer want to attend school, is what they gain worth the cost? Some parents might argue that the academic benefits outweigh these costs. However, it is essential to recognize the profound impact racism has on children's psychological, emotional, social, and relational well-being. Racism diminishes their learning, self-esteem, and confidence and reduces the information they can absorb when they do not feel safe, valued, or celebrated for who they are [31].

Ensuring that Black children are placed in educational settings where they can thrive, be pushed to excel, and be nurtured for who they are must be a primary factor in school choice. Schools must provide quality education and cultivate environments where all students feel supported and empowered. Only then can Black students' full potential be realized and the harmful effects of systemic racism be mitigated.

6. Implications for practice

As you navigate the challenging decisions around choosing the right school for your child, it's essential to consider the academic offerings and the broader environment in which your child will grow and learn. This study, like many others focusing on the experiences of students of color, highlights the importance of understanding the profound impact that racialized experiences can have on your child's well-being.

Key considerations for school decision-making:

1. *Beyond academic quality*: while academic excellence is undoubtedly important, it is crucial to weigh whether focusing on academic achievements comes at the expense of your child's social and emotional well-being. Schools that prioritize test scores and college placements may not always provide the nurturing environment your child needs to thrive as a whole person.

2. *Understanding racialized experiences*: consider the potential for both positive and negative racialized experiences at the school. Ask yourself how the school's environment might affect your child's sense of identity, belonging, and self-worth. Schools that lack diversity or cultural awareness can inadvertently create spaces where your child may feel isolated or misunderstood.

3. *The role of culturally responsive education*: culturally responsive teachers and staff play a vital role in mitigating the adverse effects of racialized experiences. It's essential to seek out schools where educators are not only aware of the challenges that Black children face but are also equipped to support and empower them through culturally relevant teaching practices and policies.

4. *Redefining what makes a good school*: it may be necessary to shift your perspective on what defines a "good" school. A truly good school is one that offers more than just high academic standards—it is a place where your child feels safe, valued, and supported in all aspects of their development. Consider whether the school fosters an environment where diversity is celebrated, and your child can build

positive relationships with peers and teachers who understand and respect their cultural background.

5. *Long-term well-being over short-term gains*: finally, reflect on the long-term implications of your school choice. While a school's reputation for academic excellence may seem like the best choice initially, consider whether this environment will support your child's long-term well-being and success. A balanced approach that values both academic achievement and emotional resilience will better prepare your child for the future.

By keeping these considerations in mind, you can make a more informed decision that prioritizes not only your child's academic success but also their overall happiness, health, and development.

7. Conclusion

The study highlights the importance of understanding the experiences shared by Black students in predominantly White school districts, particularly for Black parents, school teachers, staff, and administrators. It also underscores the necessity for Black parents to actively engage in their children's academic life as an advocate and support persons when their children report negative racialized experiences. The study also highlights the urgent need for systemic changes to foster a more inclusive and equitable educational environment to improve educational and well-being outcomes for Black children. The study emphasizes the need to address issues of representation, ensure fair treatment and equal opportunities, and actively combat microaggressions and racism, which are crucial steps in supporting the academic and emotional well-being of Black students. Schools must actively prioritize these changes to create a supportive and nurturing environment where all students can thrive.

Conflict of interest

The authors declare no conflict of interest.

Author details

Joan M. Blakey*, Labibah M. Buraik, Channel Lowery and Jessica M. Coleman
University of Minnesota - Twin Cities, Saint Paul, MN, USA

*Address all correspondence to: blak0014@umn.edu

References

[1] Williams HA. Self-Taught: African American Education in Slavery and Freedom. Chapel Hill, NC: University of North Carolina Press; 2009

[2] Gasman M, Baez B, Turner CSV. Understanding Minority-Serving Institutions. Albany, NY: State University of New York Press; 2008

[3] Bracey EN. The significance of historically Black colleges and universities (HBCUs) in the 21st century: Will such institutions of higher learning survive? American Journal of Economics and Sociology. 2017;**76**(3):670-696

[4] Ladson-Billings G. From the achievement gap to the education debt: Understanding achievement in U.S. Schools. Educational Researcher. 2006;**35**(7):3-12

[5] Walker VS. Hello Professor: A Black Principal and Professional Leadership in the Segregated South. Chapel Hill, NC: University of North Carolina Press; 2009

[6] Allen Q. “I’m trying to get my A”: Black male achievers talk about race, school, and achievement. The Urban Review. 2015;**47**:209-231

[7] Cooper CW. School choice and the standpoint of African American mothers: Considering the power of positionality. The Journal of Negro Education. 2005;**74**(2):174-189

[8] Clergé O. A moving target: Black middle-class parents school strategies in a segregated city and suburb. Race Ethnicity and Education. 2023;**26**(3):352-367

[9] Pattillo M. Everyday politics of school choice in the Black community. Du Bois Review: Social Science Research on Race. 2015;**12**(1):41-71

[10] Anderson JD. The Education of Blacks in the South, 1860-1935. Chapel Hill, NC: University of North Carolina Press; 1988

[11] Annamma S, Morrison D, Jackson D. Disproportionality fills in the gaps: Connections between achievement, discipline, and special education in the school-to-prison pipeline. Berkeley Review of Education. 2014;**5**(1):53-87

[12] Cooper CW. School choice as ‘motherwork’: Valuing African-American women’s educational advocacy and resistance. International Journal of Qualitative Studies in Education. 2007;**20**(5):491-512

[13] Saporito S. School choice in black and white: Private school enrollment among racial groups, 1990-2000. Peabody Journal of Education. 2009;**84**(2):172-190

[14] Herrelle TI. To protect and to prepare: Black mothers’ school-selection decision-making. Race, Ethnicity and Education. 2022:1-19. Ahead-of-print. DOI: 10.1080/13613324.2022.2106474

[15] Rowley KJ, McNeill SM. Choosing predominantly black magnet schools: The importance of school racial composition in parental decision-making. Journal of School Choice. 2021;**15**(4):603-623. DOI: 10.1080/15582159.2020.1863136

[16] Teske P, Fitzpatrick J, Kaplan G. Opening Doors: How Low-Income Parents Search for the Right School. Seattle, WA: University of Washington Press; 2007

[17] Collins PH. Intersectionality as Critical Social Theory. Durham, NC: Duke University Press; 2019

[18] Blakey JM, Ngui E, Buraik B, Vang H, Williams G. In their words: Black students' perception of the achievement and discipline gap in a predominantly white secondary school. Advances in Social Work. 2024

[19] Ukanwa K, Jones AC, Turner BL. School choice increases racial segregation even when parents do not care about race. Proceedings of the National Academy of Sciences. 2022;**119**(35):e2117979119. DOI: 10.1073/pnas.2117979119

[20] White T, Woodward B, Graham D, Milner HR IV, Howard TC. Education policy and Black teachers: Perspectives on race, policy, and teacher diversity. Journal of Teacher Education. 2020;**71**(4):449-463

[21] Posey-Maddox L, de Royston MM, Holman AR, Rall RM, Johnson RA. No choice is the "right" choice: Black parents' educational decision-making in their search for a "good" school. Harvard Educational Review. 2021;**91**(1):38-61. DOI: 10.17763/1943-5045-91.1.38

[22] Braun V, Clarke V. Thematic analysis. In: Cooper H, Camic PM, Long DL, Panter AT, Rindskopf D, Sher KJ, editors. APA Handbook of Research Methods in Psychology, Research designs: Quantitative, qualitative, neuropsychological, and biological. Vol. 2. Washington, DC: American Psychological Association; 2012. pp. 57-71. DOI: 10.1037/13620-004

[23] Oktay JS. Grounded Theory. Oxford, UK: Oxford University Press; 2012. DOI: 10.1093/acprof:oso/9780199753697.001.0001

[24] Leung F-H, Savithiri R. Spotlight on focus groups. Canadian Family Physician. 2009;**55**(2):218-219

[25] Qureshi HA, Ünlü Z. Beyond the paradigm conflicts: A four-step coding instrument for grounded theory. International Journal of Qualitative Methods. 2020;**19**:160940692092818. DOI: 10.1177/1609406920928188

[26] Charmaz K. Constructing Grounded Theory. 2nd ed. London, UK: SAGE Publications; 2014. DOI: 10.1002/9781405165518.wbeosg070.pub2

[27] Birks M, Mills J. Grounded Theory: A Practical Guide. Los Angeles, CA: Sage; 2015

[28] Barry CA, Britten N, Barber N, Bradley C, Stevenson F. Using reflexivity to optimize teamwork in qualitative research. Qualitative Health Research. 1999;**9**(1):26-44. DOI: 10.1177/104973299129121677

[29] Armstrong D, Gosling A, Weinman J, Marteau T. The place of inter-rater reliability in qualitative research: An empirical study. Sociology. 1997;**31**(3):597-606. DOI: 10.1177/0038038597031003015

[30] Guest G, MacQueen KM, Namey EE. Applied Thematic Analysis. Los Angeles, CA: SAGE; 2012. DOI: 10.4135/9781483384436

[31] Hope EC, Brinkman M, Hoggard LS, Stokes MN, Hatton V, Volpe VV, et al. Black adolescents' anticipatory stress responses to multilevel racism: The role of racial identity. American Journal of Orthopsychiatry. 2021;**91**(4):487-499

www.ingramcontent.com/pod-product-compliance
Lightning Source LLC
LaVergne TN
LVHW081937200926
848484LV00009B/2448
* 9 7 8 1 8 3 7 6 9 4 2 5 9 *